Frommer's®

POSTCARDS

FROM

SAN DIEGO

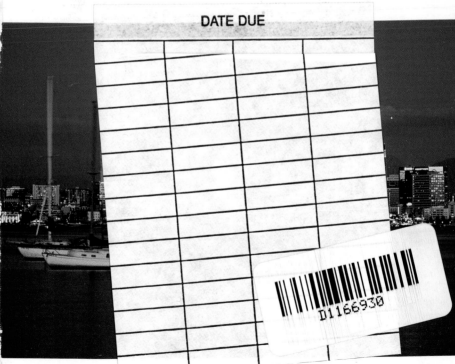

A dinner cruise on S_____ _____ is one of the best ways to see the city skyline at night. See chapter 7. © Michael J. Pettypool/Dave G. Houser Photography.

Sea lions and penguins are among the aquatic animals competing for attention (and stealing fish) at Sea World. See chapter 7. © James Lemass Photography; photo opposite, top © Kelly/Mooney Photography.

Children love the hippos, pandas, and other exotic creatures at the renowned San Diego Zoo. See chapter 7. © Zoological Society of San Diego.

Koalas are among the most famous residents of the San Diego Zoo. See chapter 7. © Kelly/Mooney Photography.

The Wild Animal Park's "Heart of Africa" offers the opportunity to see cheetahs, giraffes, and other exotic animals up close rather than behind bars. See chapter 7. © San Diego Wild Animal Park; photo opposite © Robert Holmes Photography.

The Giant Dipper in Belmont Park, built in 1925, is one of the last wooden roller coasters in the country. See chapter 7. © James C. Simmons/Dave G. Houser Photography.

The U.S. Open Sandcastle Competition is held at Imperial Beach Pier in late July or early August. See "When to Go" in chapter 2. © Kelly/ Mooney Photography.

The Hotel del Coronado, designated a National Landmark, has hosted movie stars from Mary Pickford to Jack Lemmon, as well as visiting royalty. It's still one of the finest hotels in the San Diego area. See chapter 5. © Lou Palmieri/New England Stock.

Torrey Pines State Reserve offers secluded beaches as well as hiking trails with gorgeous views. See chapter 7. Photos above and opposite © James Blank Photography.

The cliffs at Point Loma are a great place to watch the sunset. See chapter 7. © *Richard Cummins/The Viesti Collection.*

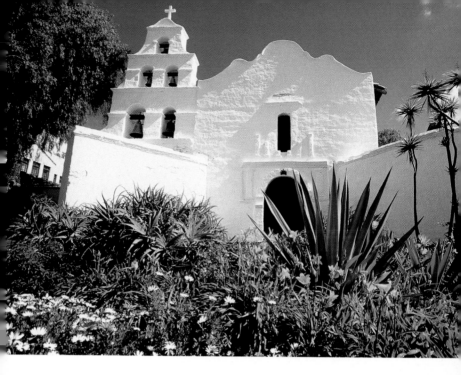

The 18th-century Mission Basilica San Diego de Alcala was the first in the chain of 21 missions established by Spanish missionary Junípero Serra. See chapter 7. Photo top © David Olsen/Tony Stone Images; photo bottom © Robert Landau Photography.

Seaport Village is a waterfront shopping and dining complex designed to look like a small Cape Cod community. See chapter 9. © James Lemass Photography.

The Old Town section of San Diego is a reminder of the 19th-century days when the city was an outpost of Mexico. See the walking tour in chapter 8. © Kelly/Mooney Photography.

Balboa Park is home to more than two dozen attractions, including several museums, botanical gardens, and an outdoor theater. See chapter 7. © John Elk III Photography.

Water, water everywhere . . . boating, beaches, and water sports make up a huge part of San Diego's appeal. © James Blank Photography.

The bullfights of Tijuana and the cantinas found in every town throughout Baja are two reasons to explore south of the border. Many appealing Mexican towns are within easy driving distance of San Diego. See chapter 11. © Nik Wheeler Photography.

After the spring rains, thousands of wildflowers burst into bloom in Anza-Borrego Desert State Park, 90 miles east of San Diego. See chapter 11. © Christopher Talbot Frank Photography.

Frommer's® 2000

San Diego

by Stephanie Avnet Yates

with Online Directory by Michael Shapiro

MACMILLAN • USA

ABOUT THE AUTHOR

A native of Los Angeles and an avid traveler, antique hound, and pop-history enthusiast, **Stephanie Avnet Yates** believes that California is best seen from behind the wheel of a little red convertible. Prior to becoming a travel writer, she worked in the music business, but now prefers to hit the road exploring the Golden State. Stephanie authors *Frommer's Los Angeles* and *Frommer's Wonderful Weekends from Los Angeles,* in addition to cowriting *Frommer's California* and *Frommer's California from $60 a Day.* She confesses to a special fondness for San Diego, having attended the University of California at San Diego (UCSD) in La Jolla.

MACMILLAN TRAVEL USA

Macmillan General Reference USA, Inc.
1633 Broadway
New York, NY 10019

Find us online at **www.frommers.com**

ISBN 0-02-863032-7
ISSN 1047-787X

Editor: Marie Morris
Production Editor: Carol Sheehan
Photo Editor: Richard Fox
Design by Michele Laseau
Digital Cartography by Robin D'Amato
Staff Cartographers: John Decamillis, Roberta Stockwell
Page Creation by: Natalie Hollifield, Terri Sheehan

SPECIAL SALES

Bulk purchases (10+ copies) of Frommer's and selected Macmillan travel guides are available to corporations, organizations, mail-order catalogs, institutions, and charities at special discounts, and can be customized to suit individual needs. For more information write to Special Sales, Macmillan General Reference, 1633 Broadway, New York, NY 10019.

Manufactured in the United States of America

5   4   3   2   1

F
869
.S22
Y38
2000

Contents

iii

List of Maps

An Invitation to the Reader

In researching this book, we discovered many wonderful places—hotels, restaurants, shops, and more. We're sure you'll find others. Please tell us about them, so we can share the information with your fellow travelers in upcoming editions. If you were disappointed with a recommendation, we'd love to know that, too. Please write to:

Frommer's San Diego 2000
Macmillan Travel USA
1633 Broadway
New York, NY 10019

An Additional Note

Please be advised that travel information is subject to change at any time—and this is especially true of prices. We therefore suggest that you write or call ahead for confirmation when making your travel plans. The authors, editors, and publisher cannot be held responsible for the experiences of readers while traveling. Your safety is important to us, however, so we encourage you to stay alert and be aware of your surroundings. Keep a close eye on cameras, purses, and wallets, all favorite targets of thieves and pickpockets.

What the Symbols Mean

✪ Frommer's Favorites

Our favorite places and experiences—outstanding for quality, value, or both.

The following abbreviations are used for credit cards:

AE	American Express	EURO	Eurocard
CB	Carte Blanche	JCB	Japan Credit Bank
DC	Diners Club	MC	MasterCard
DISC	Discover	V	Visa
ER	EnRoute		

Find Frommer's Online

Arthur Frommer's Budget Travel Online (**www.frommers.com**) offers more than 6,000 pages of up-to-the-minute travel information—including the latest bargains and candid, personal articles updated daily by Arthur Frommer himself. No other Web site offers such comprehensive and timely coverage of the world of travel.

The Best of San Diego

If you've never been to San Diego or your last visit was more than a few years ago, this relaxed and scenic city will hold some surprises for you. It's grown up. San Diego is no longer just a laid-back navy town—avant-garde architecture, sophisticated dining options, and a booming tourist industry all point to its coming-of-age.

You'll notice the architecture right away. If you're driving to San Diego from the north, you'll pass the eye-catching Hyatt Regency La Jolla alongside Interstate 5. Near this striking neoclassical structure, the snow-white, multiturreted Mormon temple seems an unlikely neighbor. If you're flying in, you'll notice some changes as you approach Lindbergh Field, including new high-rise office towers and hotels in the downtown area adjacent to San Diego Bay.

Approximately 1.2 million people live in San Diego, making it the sixth-largest city in the United States (after New York, Los Angeles, Chicago, Houston, Philadelphia, and Phoenix). Although the city's population keeps increasing, you'll find that San Diego hasn't lost its small-town ambiance, and it retains a strong connection with its Hispanic heritage and culture.

1 Frommer's Favorite San Diego Experiences

- **Strolling Through the Gaslamp Quarter.** Victorian commercial buildings that fill a 16½-block area will make you think you've stepped back in time. The beautifully restored buildings, in the heart of downtown, house some of the city's most popular shops, restaurants, and nightspots.
- **Shopping and Sipping Margaritas in Bazaar del Mundo.** Old Mexico is alive and well in this colorful retail destination. The lively strains of mariachi music add to the atmosphere.
- **Renting Bikes, Skates, or Kayaks in Mission Bay.** Landscaped shores, calm waters, paved paths, and friendly neighbors make Mission Bay an aquatic playground like no other. Explore on land or water, depending on your energy level, then grab a bite at funky Mission Cafe.
- **Listening to Free Sunday Organ Recitals in Balboa Park.** Even if you usually don't like organ music, you might enjoy these outdoor concerts and the crowds they draw—San Diegans with their

parents, their children, their dogs. The music, enhanced by the organist's commentary, runs the gamut from classical to contemporary. Concerts start at 2pm.

- **Relaxing with Afternoon Tea.** A genteel tradition in San Diego, the custom of afternoon tea is at its most elegant at the U.S. Grant Hotel and quite cozy at the Horton Grand. Take your pick.

- **Taking the Ferry to Coronado.** The 15-minute ride gets you out onto San Diego Harbor and provides some of the best views of the city. The ferry runs every hour from the Broadway Pier, so you can tour Coronado on foot, by bike, or by trolley and return whenever you please.

- **Driving Over the Bridge to Coronado.** The first time or the fiftieth, there's always an adrenaline rush as you follow this engineering marvel's dramatic curves and catch a glimpse of the panoramic view to either side. Driving west, you can easily pick out the distinctive Hotel Del in the distance long before you reach the "island."

- **Riding on the San Diego Trolley to Mexico.** The trip from downtown costs a mere $2 and takes only 40 minutes, and the clean, quick trolleys are fun in their own right. Once in Tijuana, load up on colorful souvenirs and authentic Mexican food.

- **Listening to Jazz at Croce's.** Ideally located in the center of downtown in a historic Gaslamp Quarter building, Croce's celebrates the life of musician Jim Croce and showcases the city's jazz musicians.

- **Watching the Sun Set Over the Ocean.** It's a free and memorable experience. Excellent sunset-watching spots include the Mission Beach and Pacific Beach boardwalks, as well as the beach in Coronado in front of the Hotel del Coronado. At La Jolla's Windansea Beach, wandering down to the water at dusk, wineglass in hand, is a nightly neighborhood event.

- **Drinking Coffee at a La Jolla Sidewalk Cafe.** San Diego offers a plethora of places to enjoy lattes, espressos, and cappuccinos, but the coffeehouses in La Jolla serve them up with special panache. For some favorites, see the "Java Joints in La Jolla" box in chapter 6.

- **Purchasing Just-Picked Produce at a Farmers' Market.** Markets throughout the area sell the bountiful harvest of San Diego County. For directions, see chapter 9.

- **Walking Along the Water.** The city offers walkers several great places to stroll. One of my favorites, along the waterfront from the Convention Center to the Maritime Museum, affords views of aircraft carriers, tuna seiners, and sailboats.

- **Going to the Movies Before the Mast.** Imagine sitting on the deck of the world's oldest merchant ship afloat, watching a film projected on the "screen-sail," or floating on a raft in a huge indoor pool while a movie is shown on the wall. Only in San Diego! See "Only in San Diego," in chapter 10.

- **Visiting the "Lobster Village" in Puerto Nuevo.** South of the border, they serve lobster with rice, beans, and tortillas, and it's delicious. See chapter 11.

- **Floating Up, Up, and Away Over North County.** Hot-air balloons carry passengers over the golf courses and luxury homes north of the city. These rides are especially enjoyable at sunset. For details, see chapter 11.

- **Watching the Grunion Run.** These tiny fish spawn on San Diego beaches between March and August, and the locals love to be there. To find the date of the next run, pick up a free tide chart at a surf shop or consult the daily newspaper.

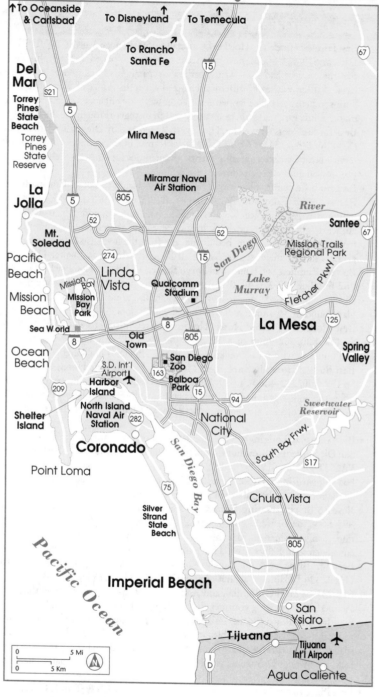

↑ To Oceanside & Carlsbad
↑ To Disneyland
↑ To Temecula

↗ To Rancho Santa Fe

Del Mar
S21
Torrey Pines State Beach
Torrey Pines State Reserve

Mira Mesa

15

67

Miramar Naval Air Station

River

Santee
67

La Jolla

52

52

15

San Diego

Mission Trails Regional Park

Mt. Soledad
274

Pacific Beach

Linda Vista

Mission Bay

Mission Bay Park

Qualcomm Stadium

Lake Murray

Fletcher Pkwy.

Mission Beach

Sea World

La Mesa
125

8

805

Ocean Beach
209

Old Town

8

San Diego Zoo

S.D. Int'l Airport
163

Balboa Park

Spring Valley

Harbor Island

North Island Naval Air Station
282

15

94

National City

Sweetwater Reservoir

Shelter Island

Coronado

San Diego Bay

Point Loma

75

South Bay Frwy.

S17

Chula Vista

Silver Strand State Beach

5

805

Pacific Ocean

Imperial Beach

San Ysidro

Tijuana

Tijuana Int'l Airport

Agua Caliente

I D

0   5 Mi
0   5 Km

3

2 Best Hotel Bets

- **Best Historic Hotel:** The **Hotel del Coronado,** 1500 Orange Ave. (☎ **800/HOTEL-DEL** or 619/435-8000), positively reeks of history. Opened in 1888, this Victorian masterpiece had some of the earliest electric lights in existence, and legend has it that the course of history was changed when the Prince of Wales met Wallis Simpson here at a ball. Planned restoration will only enhance this glorious landmark, whose early days are well chronicled in displays throughout the hotel.
- **Best for Business Travelers:** The **Hyatt Regency San Diego,** 1 Market Place (☎ **800/233-1234** or 619/232-1234), screams "business traveler," with a full-service business center offering plenty of amenities for suits on the go. Its location is prime for access to downtown.
- **Best for a Romantic Getaway:** The sense of seclusion at **Loews Coronado Bay Resort,** 4000 Coronado Bay Rd. (☎ **800/23-LOEWS** or 619/424-4000), makes it a good choice for a tryst. You can snuggle under blankets on an authentic gondola ride or drink in the view from the elegant restaurant; large marble bathrooms and fine bed linens help frost the lovin' cake. (For a romantic getaway farther afield, see the listing for Rancho Valencia in chapter 11.)
- **Best for Families:** The **Hilton San Diego Resort,** 1775 E. Mission Bay Dr. (☎ **800/962-6307** or 619/276-4010), offers enough activities to keep family members of all ages happy. In addition to a virtual Disneyland of on-site options, the aquatic playground of Mission Bay lies outside the back door.
- **Best Moderately Priced Hotel:** The **Sommerset Suites Hotel,** 606 Washington St. (☎ **800/962-9665** or 619/692-5200), feels like a home away from home and puts you within easy walking distance of Hillcrest's hot spots.
- **Best Budget Hotel:** In San Diego's Little Italy, **La Pensione Hotel,** 606 W. Date St. (☎ **800/232-4683** or 619/236-8000), feels like a small European hotel and offers tidy lodgings at bargain prices. There's an abundance of great dining in the surrounding blocks, and you'll be perfectly situated to explore the rest of town by car.
- **Best Unusual Lodgings:** Fulfill the fantasies of your inner yachtsman with the **San Diego Yacht & Breakfast Company,** 1880 Harbor Island Dr., G-Dock (☎ **800/YACHT-DO** or 619/297-9484). It provides powerboats, sailboats, and houseboats docked in a Harbor Island marina. You can sleep on board, lulled by the gentle rocking of the hull, then have breakfast nearby.
- **Best B&B:** The **Keating House,** 2331 Second Ave., at Juniper Street (☎ **800/995-8644** or 619/239-8585), has all the elements of the perfect B&B: An impeccably restored historic home, a lively and gracious host, and a location equally close to Balboa Park, Hillcrest, the Gaslamp Quarter, and the harbor.
- **Best for Bringing Your Pooch:** Check in with your dog at the **U.S. Grant Hotel,** 326 Broadway (☎ **800/237-5029** outside California, **800/334-6957** or 619/232-3121 in California), and your pet might just be treated better than you. Pampering starts with gourmet dinners, chewy bones, sleeping pillows, and a nightly "turn-down biscuit." Walking service and special dog-walk maps (guide to local hydrants?) are available, and you'll be welcomed in all the hotel's public spaces. There's a grassy square across the street where you may even run into Flapjack, the owner's Dalmatian, a full-time hotel resident. The best part? There's no extra charge.
- **Best Place to Stay on the Beach:** At **The La Jolla Beach & Tennis Club,** 2000 Spindrift Dr. (☎ **800/624-CLUB** or 858/454-7126), you can walk right onto

The City Today

San Diego has always had great weather and beaches, but now it has a lot more to offer than just surf and sun. This change has resulted in part from the influx of high-tech (especially biotech) industry. The new arrivals contribute to the growth of the performing arts and support sophisticated dining, nightlife, and shopping.

The 1990 completion of the Convention Center, which took nearly 3 years to build (and is currently being expanded further, with completion scheduled for 2001), has also made a tremendous difference. The center attracts several hundred meetings, conventions, exhibits, and trade shows each year. Its proximity to the Gaslamp Quarter initiated the Quarter's rebirth. Wandering among the chic restaurants and hot nightspots along Fourth and Fifth avenues, it's hard to remember how run-down this area used to be.

Some things about San Diego, however, haven't changed. The residents still love to get out and enjoy their beautiful surroundings. San Diegans are often busy in-line skating, cycling, sailing, and surfing; and it's no coincidence the most activity-oriented parts of town are the most desirable in which to live.

San Diegans' enthusiasm for active pursuits goes hand-in-hand with an interest in being healthy (and a very L.A.-style propensity toward vanity). It's not just a rumor that some embrace exotic herbs, holistic remedies, and non-traditional therapies at a rate unknown in other parts of the country. Large numbers also eschew red meat, and smokers are herded into smaller and smaller areas. It's not surprising that nationally renowned author Deepak Chopra makes his home here. Logically enough, San Diego County is also home to several health spas (see chapter 11).

Although San Diegans generally prefer to keep things the way they are—and eagerly vote to pass "no growth" measures—the city is pleased and proud of a recent (and sorely needed) airport expansion. After heated debate about moving the airport to recently decommissioned Miramar Naval Air Station (a measure that would certainly have reduced noise pollution and traffic downtown), the city decided instead to expand Lindbergh Field. Arriving visitors now find a state-of-the-art, architecturally modern expansion, with high-profile works of art throughout the facility.

Another recent hot topic was Super Bowl XXXII. First there was the controversial expansion of Jack Murphy Stadium, ultimately bankrolled by Qualcomm in time to lure the 1998 event to San Diego. Despite resentment about the facility's bearing the communications giant's name, and skepticism that the event might be the marketing dud Super Bowl XXII had been 10 years earlier, 1998 was a winner for city planners, hotels, and the media. The weeklong celebration was enjoyed throughout the city, state, and country—except by Green Bay Packer fans, that is!

Concern persists about water—and not the sparkling blue kind usually associated with this bay- and oceanside city. San Diego is still experiencing the fresh-water shortage that plagued most of California during the 1980s and early '90s. Many restaurants will serve water only on request, and lots of hotels—even upscale ones—discreetly let you know that, given your approval, they'll change towels and linens less than daily.

Thanks be to God, I have arrived at this Port of San Diego. It is beautiful to behold and does not belie its reputation.

—Father Junípero Serra, 1769

I thought San Diego must be a Heaven on Earth . . . . It seemed to me the best spot for building a city I ever saw.

—Alonzo Horton, who developed San Diego's first downtown

the wide beach and frolic in the great waves. Lifeguards and the lack of undertow make this a popular choice for families. Though the rooms are plain, the country-club staff will cater to your every whim.

- **Best for Disabled Travelers:** While many of San Diego's hotels make minimal concessions to wheelchair accessibility code, downtown's **Hyatt Regency,** 1 Market Place (☎ **800/233-1234** or 619/232-1234), goes the distance. There are 23 rooms with roll-in showers, and lowered closet racks and peepholes. Ramps are an integral part of all the public spaces, rather than an afterthought. The hotel's Braille labeling is also thorough.
- **Best Hotel Pool:** The genteel pool at **La Valencia,** 1132 Prospect St. (☎ **800/451-0772** or 858/454-0771), is oh-so-special, with its spectacular setting overlooking Scripps Park and the Pacific.

3 Best Dining Bets

- **Best Spot for a Business Lunch: Dakota Grill and Spirits,** 901 Fifth Ave., in the Gaslamp Quarter (☎ **619/234-5554**), has the three important ingredients of a business lunch locale: great location, appropriate atmosphere, and excellent food.
- **Best View:** Many restaurants overlook the ocean, but only from **Brockton Villa,** 1235 Coast Blvd., La Jolla (☎ **858/454-7393**), can you see the La Jolla Cove. Diners with a window seat will feel as if they're looking out on a gigantic picture postcard.
- **Best Value:** The word *huge* barely begins to describe the portions at **Filippi's Pizza Grotto,** 1747 India St. (☎ **619/232-5095**), where a salad for one is enough for three and an order of lasagne must weigh a pound. There's a kids' menu, and Filippi's has locations all over: in Pacific Beach, Mission Valley, and Escondido, among others.
- **Best for Kids:** At the **Old Spaghetti Factory,** 275 Fifth Ave., in the Gaslamp Quarter (☎ **619/233-4323**), family dining is the name of the game—so if your kids are noisy, nobody will notice.
- **Best Chinese Cuisine: Panda Inn,** Horton Plaza (☎ **619/233-7800**), on the top floor of the mega-mall, is full of surprises. You wouldn't expect culinary greatness from a shopping mall, but this sleeper serves up artfully flavored Mandarin and Szechuan dishes in an elegant setting far removed from the consumer throngs just outside.
- **Best Italian Cuisine: Fio's,** 801 Fifth Ave., in the Gaslamp Quarter (☎ **619/234-3467**), offers fine northern Italian food in chic surroundings.

- **Best Seafood:** Not only does **The Fish Market/Top of the Market,** 750 N. Harbor Dr. (☎ **619/232-FISH** or 619/234-4TOP), offer the city's best fish, it also offers a memorable view across San Diego Bay.
- **Best American Cuisine:** The menu at **Croce's,** 802 Fifth Ave., in the Gaslamp Quarter (☎ **619/233-4355**), cleverly fuses American and Southwestern with international touches. The results are delicious.
- **Best Mexican Cuisine:** Rather than the "combination #1" fare that's common on this side of the border, **Palenque,** 1653 Garnet Ave., Pacific Beach (☎ **619/ 272-7816**), offers a delightful combination of freshly prepared, generations-old recipes from Veracruz, Chapas, Puebla, and Mexico City.
- **Best Vegetarian:** The **Vegetarian Zone,** 2949 Fifth Ave., Hillcrest (☎ **619/ 298-7302**), offers tasty meat-free dishes influenced by a variety of ethnic cuisine.
- **Best Pizza:** For gourmet pizza from a wood-fired oven, head for **D'Lish,** 7514 Girard Ave., La Jolla (☎ **858/459-8118**). For the traditional Sicilian variety, you'll have to visit **Filippi's Pizza Grotto** (see above).
- **Best Desserts:** You'll forget your diet at **Extraordinary Desserts,** 2929 Fifth Ave., Hillcrest (☎ **619/294-7001**)—heck, it's so good you might forget your name! Proprietor Karen Krasne has a *Certificate de Patisserie* from Le Cordon Bleu in Paris, and she makes everything fresh on the premises daily.
- **Best Late-Night Dining:** Open later than anyplace else downtown, **Café Lulu,** 419 F St. (☎ **619/238-0114**), serves eclectic meat-free fare and inventive espresso drinks until 2am during the week, 4am on weekends.
- **Best Fast Food:** Fish tacos from **Rubio's,** 4504 E. Mission Bay Dr. (☎ **619/ 272-2801**), and other locations, are legendary in San Diego. Taste one and you'll know why.
- **Best Picnic Fare:** Pack a humongous sandwich from the **Cheese Shop,** 401 G St. (☎ **619/232-2303**), for a picnic lunch and you won't be hungry for dinner. In La Jolla, head to **Girard Gourmet,** 7837 Girard Ave. (☎ **858/454-3321**), for sandwiches, prepared salads, imported cheeses, and baked goods.

2 Planning a Trip to San Diego

This chapter contains all the practical information and logistical advise you need to make your travel arrangements a snap, from deciding when to go to finding the best airfare.

1 Visitor Information

You can do your homework by contacting the **International Visitor Information Center**, 11 Horton Plaza, San Diego, CA 92101 (☎ **619/ 236-1212**; fax 619/230-7084; www.sandiego.org; e-mail: sdinfo@ sandiego.org). Ask for the *San Diego Official Visitors Guide*, which includes information on accommodations, activities, and attractions, and has excellent maps. Also request the *Super Savings Coupon Book*, which is full of discount coupons. The staff at the center is multilingual, and brochures are available in English, French, German, Japanese, Portuguese, and Spanish. The center is open Monday through Saturday from 8:30am to 5pm year-round and Sunday from 11am to 5pm June through August.

Some of the same materials are available from the **Mission Bay Visitor Information Center**, 2688 Mission Bay Dr., San Diego, CA 92109 (☎ **619/276-8200**), which is also helpful with recreational activities in the bay and beyond.

The **Coronado Visitors Bureau**, 1047 B Ave., Coronado, CA 92118-3418 (☎ **800/622-8300** or 619/437-8788; fax 619/ 437-6006; www.coronado.ca.us; e-mail: corcvb@aol.com) is a must for anyone visiting the "island." The bureau staff has maps of the area, information-packed brochures and newsletters, and enthusiasm that just won't quit.

Information on La Jolla is distributed by the **La Jolla Town Council**, 7734 Herschel Ave., La Jolla, CA 92038 (☎ **619/454-1444**).

Additional visitor information is available from the **Balboa Park Visitors Center**, 1549 El Prado, San Diego, CA 92101 (☎ **619/239-0512**).

If you're thinking of attending the **theater** while you're in town, contact the San Diego Performing Arts League (☎ **619/238-0700**) for a copy of *What's Playing?*, which contains information on upcoming performances.

Another good source of information is the San Diego North County Convention and Visitors Bureau. Call ☎ **800/848-3336** to request its *Visitors Guide*.

SITE SEEING: SAN DIEGO ON THE WEB

You can find lots of information on San Diego at the following Web sites (and don't forget to check out the Frommer's Online Directory at the end of the book).

- **gocalif.ca.gov/guidebook/SD** has helpful information on San Diego County, including maps that can be downloaded.
- **www.infosandiego.com** is the Web site for the San Diego Visitor Center.
- **www.sandiego.org** is maintained by the San Diego Convention & Visitors Bureau and provides, among other things, up-to-date weather data.
- **www.sandiego-online.com,** the *San Diego* magazine Web site, features abbreviated stories from the current month's issue, plus dining and events listings.
- **www.sannet.gov** is San Diego's home page, maintained by the city.
- **www.sdreader.com,** the site of the free weekly *Reader,* is a great source for club and show listings, plus edgy topical journalism.
- **travel.to/san.diego** is "The Local Guy's Guide to San Diego." It gives lots of information on things to do and local history and facts, plus some good links to other regional sites.
- **www.gaslamp.com** is the online home of the Gaslamp Quarter Historical Foundation.
- **www.iaco.com/features/lajolla/homepage.htm** features information about what's happening in La Jolla.
- **www.coronado.ca.us/Visitor** is the Coronado Visitors' Bureau's site.
- **America Online** subscribers can access Digital City San Diego by using the keyword "digital city san diego."

2 Money

If you're visiting from outside the United States, you can find more information on American currency and money exchange in chapter 3, "For Foreign Visitors."

ATMs

One of California's most popular banks is Wells Fargo, part of the Star, Pulse, Cirrus, and GlobalAccess systems. It has hundreds of ATMs at branches and stores (including most Vons supermarkets) throughout San Diego County. To find the one nearest you, call ☎ 800/869-3557 or visit **www.wellsfargo.com/findus.** Other statewide banks include Bank of America (which accepts Plus, Star, and Interlink cards), and First Interstate Bank (Cirrus).

To locate other ATMs in the **Cirrus** system, call ☎ 800/424-7787 or search **www.mastercard.com;** to find a **Plus** ATM, call ☎ 800/843-7587 or visit **www.visa.com.** Be sure to check your bank's daily withdrawal limit before you depart.

TRAVELER'S CHECKS

Once the only safe method of guaranteeing ready cash, traveler's checks now seem anachronistic. Most cities (including San Diego) have plenty of 24-hour ATMs that allow you to withdraw small amounts of cash as needed.

But if you want to avoid the fees associated with ATM withdrawals, or feel more comfortable with checks that can be replaced if lost or stolen, you can get traveler's checks at almost any bank. **American Express** offers denominations of $10, $20, $50, $100, $500, and $1,000; you'll pay a service charge ranging from 1 to 4%. You can also get American Express traveler's checks over the phone by calling ☎ 800/221-7282;

What Things Cost in San Diego	U.S. $
Taxi from the airport to downtown	8.50
Bus from the airport to downtown	2.00
Local telephone call	.25–.35
Double at the Hotel del Coronado (very expensive)	200.00
Double at the Westgate Hotel (expensive)	184.00
Double at the Best Western Bayside Inn (moderate)	104.00
Double at La Pensione Hotel (inexpensive)	60.00
Two-course lunch for one at Bay Beach Cafe (moderate)	17.00
Two-course lunch for one at the Vegetarian Zone (inexpensive)	12.00
Three-course dinner for one at Fio's (expensive)	33.00
Three-course dinner for one at Mixx (moderate)	26.00
Three-course dinner for one at the Old Spaghetti Factory (inexpensive)	8.25
Bottle of beer	2.50
Coca-Cola	1.25
Cup of coffee	1.25
Roll of ASA 100 Kodacolor film, 36 exposures	5.20
San Diego Zoo adult admission	16.00
San Diego Zoo children's admission	7.00
Theater ticket at Old Globe	36.00

by using this number, Amex gold and platinum cardholders avoid the 1% fee. AAA members can obtain checks without a fee at most AAA offices.

Visa offers traveler's checks at Citibank locations nationwide, as well as several other banks. The service charge ranges from 1.5 to 2%; checks come in denominations of $20, $50, $100, $500, and $1,000. **MasterCard** also offers traveler's checks. Call ☎ **800/223-9920** for a location near you.

If you opt to carry traveler's checks, be sure to keep a record of their serial numbers, separate from the checks, so you're ensured a refund in an emergency.

CREDIT CARDS

San Diego's hotels, restaurants, and attractions accept most major credit cards; the most popular are Visa, MasterCard, American Express, and Discover. A handful of stores and restaurants accept only cash, however, so be sure to ask if you're unsure. The hotel and restaurant listings in chapters 5 and 6 list the credit cards each establishment accepts.

Almost every credit card company has an emergency 800 number that you can call if your wallet or purse is stolen. It may be able to wire you a cash advance against your credit card immediately; in many places, it can deliver an emergency credit card in a day or two. **Citicorp Visa's** U.S. emergency number is ☎ **800/336-8472. American Express** cardholders and traveler's check holders should call ☎ **800/221-7282** for all money emergencies. **MasterCard** holders should call ☎ **800/307-7309.**

3 When to Go

San Diego is blessed with a mild climate, low humidity, good air quality, and welcoming blue skies. In fact, *Pleasant Weather Rankings,* published by Consumer Travel, ranked San Diego's weather number two in the world (behind Las Palmas, in the Canary Islands). Oceanside, the northernmost town in San Diego County, was number five.

Although the temperature can change 20°F to 30°F between day and evening, it doesn't usually reach a point of extreme heat. San Diego receives very little precipitation (9½ inches of rainfall in an average year); what rain does fall comes primarily between late December and mid-April.

San Diego is most crowded between Memorial Day and Labor Day. The kids are out of school and *everyone* wants to be by the seashore; so if you visit in summer, you can expect fully booked hotels, crowded family attractions, and full parking lots at the beach. San Diego's popularity as a convention destination and its year-round pleasant weather keep the tourism business steady the rest of the year, too. The only "slow" season is from Thanksgiving through mid-February. Hotels are less full, and the beaches are peaceful and uncrowded; the big family attractions are still busy, though, with residents taking advantage of holiday breaks.

Average Monthly Temperature & Rainfall (inches)

	Jan	Feb	Mar	Apr	May	June	July	Aug	Sept	Oct	Nov	Dec
High(°F)	65	66	66	68	70	71	75	77	76	74	70	66
(°C)	18	19	19	20	21	21	24	25	25	23	21	19
Low(°F)	46	47	50	54	57	60	64	66	63	58	52	47
(°C)	7	9	10	12	14	15	17	19	17	15	10	8
Rainfall	1.88	1.48	1.55	0.81	0.15	0.05	0.01	0.07	0.13	0.34	1.25	1.73

San Diego Calendar of Events

You might want to plan your trip around one of these annual events in the San Diego area (including the destinations covered in chapter 11, "Side Trips from San Diego"). For even more up-to-date planning information, contact the **International Visitor Information Center** (☎ **619/236-1212; www.sandiego.org**).

January

○ **Whale Watching.** Mid-December to mid-March is the eagerly anticipated whale-watching season. Scores of graceful yet gargantuan California gray whales make their annual migration to warm breeding lagoons in Baja, then return with their calves to springtime feeding grounds in Alaska. For information on vantage points and excursions that bring you closer to the largest mammals, see "Whale Watching," in chapter 7.

• **San Diego Marathon.** The course begins at Plaza Camino Real in Carlsbad and stretches 26.2 miles, mainly along the coast. It's a gorgeous run, and spectators don't need tickets. For more information, call ☎ **858/792-2900.** For an entry application, send a self-addressed stamped envelope to In Motion, 511 S. Cedros, Suite B, Solana Beach, CA 92075. Third Sunday in January.

• **Nations of San Diego International Dance Festival.** Founded in 1993, this 10-day festival focuses on San Diego's numerous ethnic dance groups and companies.

Performances are at the Lyceum Theatre, and free shows take place in public areas. Call ☎ **619/239-9255.** Mid-January.

February

- **Wildflowers bloom in the desert,** usually February through April at Anza–Borrego Desert State Park. The timing varies from year to year, depending on the winter rainfall (see chapter 11). For details, call ☎ **760/767-4684** or 760/767-4205 (park information).

- ☼ **Buick Invitational,** Torrey Pines Golf Course, La Jolla. This PGA Tour men's tournament, an annual event since 1952, draws more than 100,000 spectators each year. It features 150 of the finest professionals in the world. For information, call ☎ **800/888-BUICK** or 619/281-4653, fax 619/281-7947, or write Buick Invitational, 3333 Camino Del Rio S., Suite 100, San Diego, CA 92108. Early to mid-February.

- **Old Town Temecula Rod Run.** It's a far cry from the clippity-clop of the Butterfield Overland Stagecoach when the Old Town Temecula Rod Run roars down the Old West streets of Temecula. More than 1,200 street rods are on display during the 2-day event, including many vintage muscle cars. Admission is free to spectators; you'll also find food vendors, beer booths, and a lively Casino Night. For more information, call the **Temecula Town Association** (☎ **909/676-4718**). See chapter 11 for information on Temecula. Middle of the month.

March

- **Ocean Beach Kite Festival.** The late-winter skies over the Ocean Beach Recreational Center get a brilliant shot of color. Not only can you learn to make and decorate a kite of your own, but there's an all-ages flying contest and lots of food and entertainment, culminating in a parade down to the beach. For more information, call ☎ **619/224-0189.** First weekend of March.

- **St. Patrick's Day Parade.** A tradition since 1980, the parade starts at Sixth and Juniper and ends at Sixth and Laurel. An **Irish Festival** follows. For details, call ☎ **619/299-7812.** Sunday before March 17.

- **Flower Fields in Bloom at Carlsbad Ranch.** One of the most spectacular sights in North County is the yearly blossoming of a gigantic sea of bright ranunculuses during March and April, creating a striped blanket that's visible from the freeway. Visitors are welcome to view and tour the fields, which are off Interstate 5 at the Palomar Airport Road exit. For more information, call ☎ **760/431-0352.**

April

- **Rosarito–Ensenada 50-Mile Fun Bicycle Ride,** Mexico. About 8,000 participants cycle from the Rosarito Beach Hotel along the two-lane free road to Ensenada and the Finish Line Fiesta. There's another ride in September. For information, call ☎ **619/583-3001** or visit **www.adventuresports.com/bike/ rosarito/welcome.htm.** Middle to end of the month.

- **San Diego Crew Classic,** Crown Point Shores, Mission Bay. Since 1973, it has drawn collegiate teams of more than 2,000 athletes from the United States and Canada. Call ☎ **619/488-0700.** First or second weekend in April.
- **Del Mar National Horse Show,** Del Mar Fairgrounds. The first event in the Del Mar racing season takes place from late April into early May at famous Del Mar Fairgrounds. The field at this show includes Olympic-caliber and national championship horse-and-rider teams; there are also Western fashion boutiques and artist displays and demonstrations. For more information, call ☎ **858/792-4288** or 619/755-1161.
- **Day at the Docks,** Harbor Drive and Scott Street, Point Loma. This sportfishing tournament and festival features food, entertainment, and free boat rides. It's usually the last weekend of April or the first weekend in May. Call ☎ **800/994-FISH.**
- **Newport–Ensenada Regatta,** Ensenada, Mexico. Sailing aficionados might want to visit Ensenada in late April, when some 400 participants in the annual Newport–Ensenada Regatta turn the town into a nautical party. They sail from Newport Beach, California, on Friday at noon, and trickle into port until Sunday afternoon's trophy presentation. The event celebrated its 52nd anniversary in 1999; for this year's schedule, contact the Newport Ocean Sailing Association (☎ **949/435-9553**).
- **Temecula Valley Balloon & Wine Festival.** Colorful hot-air balloons dominate the sky over Lake Skinner during the 3-day festival, which also features wine tastings, good food, jazz music, and other entertainment. General admission is $15 ($12 in advance), and reservations for balloon rides ($100 and up) should be made in advance. The lake is about 10 miles northeast of Temecula. To find out about this year's festival or purchase advance tickets, call the event organizers (☎ **909/676-6713**). See chapter 11 for information on Temecula. Late April.

May

- **Cinco de Mayo Celebration,** Old Town. Uniformed troops march and guns blast to mark the 1862 triumph of Mexican soldiers over the French. Festivities include a battle reenactment with costumed actors, mariachi music, and margaritas galore. Free admission. For further details, call ☎ **619/296-3161.** Weekend closest to May 5.

June

- **Indian Fair,** Museum of Man, Balboa Park. Native Americans from the southwestern United States gather to demonstrate tribal dances and sell arts and crafts. Call ☎ **619/239-2001.** Mid-June.
- **Twilight in the Park Concerts,** Spreckels Organ Pavilion, Balboa Park. These free concerts have been held since 1979 and run from late June through late August. For information, call ☎ **619/226-0819.**
- **Del Mar Fair.** This is the *other* event at the Del Mar Fairgrounds. All of San Diego County participates in this annual fair. Livestock competitions, thrill-a-minute rides, food and craft booths, carnival games, and home arts exhibits dominate the event, and concerts by top-name performers are free with admission. The fair usually lasts three weeks, from mid-June to early July. For details, call ☎ **858/793-5555.**

July

- ✪ **World Championship Over-the-Line Tournament,** Mission Bay. This tournament is a San Diego original; the beach softball event dates from 1953 and is renowned for boisterous, anything-goes behavior—it's a heap of fun for the

open-minded, but might be a bit much for small kids. It takes place on two consecutive weekends in July, on Fiesta Island in Mission Bay, and the public is
invited. Admission is free. For more details, call ☎ **619/688-0817.**

- **Festival of the Bells,** Mission San Diego de Alcala. This fiesta commemorates the
founding of California's first church. Music, dancing, food, and the blessing of the
animals are included. For details, call ☎ **619/281-8449.** Mid-July.

- **Annual San Diego Lesbian and Gay Pride Parade, Rally, and Festival.** This parade
is one of San Diego's biggest draws. It begins at noon on Saturday, followed by a massive festival into the night. The festival continues Sunday afternoon and evening. The
parade route is along University Avenue from Normal Street to Sixth Avenue. For
more information, call ☎ **619/297-7683.** Third or fourth weekend of the month.

- **Thoroughbred Racing Season.** The "turf meets the surf" in Del Mar from July
to September during the Thoroughbred racing season at the Del Mar Race Track.
Post time is 2pm (4pm on the first four Fridays only), and the track is dark on
Tuesday. Hollywood stars continue to flock here, in the grand tradition begun by
Bing Crosby, Betty Grable, and Jimmy Durante. For this year's schedule of
events, call ☎ **858/792-4242** or 858/755-1141.

August

- **Hillcrest Street Fair,** Fifth Avenue, between Ivy Lane and University Avenue.
Held since 1983, the street fair features arts and crafts, food booths, a beer
garden, and live entertainment. Call ☎ **619/299-3330.** The 1-day fair usually
takes place at the beginning of the month.

- **U.S. Open Sandcastle Competition,** Imperial Beach Pier. I consider this the
quintessential beach event. There's a parade and children's sandcastle contest on
Saturday, followed by the main competition Sunday. Past years have seen creations of astounding complexity, and (weather permitting) the castles remain on
view for a while after the event. For further details, call ☎ **619/424-6663.**

- **Sunset Cinema Film Festival.** If you're visiting in August, try to catch a flick
during the weeklong film festival, one of the city's more unusual events. The
audience sits on the beach (B.Y.O. chair or blanket) and views movies projected
onto offshore floating barges. Classic and current films are featured, as well as
cartoons. The free event takes place at various locations; for a schedule, call
☎ **619/454-7373.**

- **Harvest Festival,** Guadalupe Valley, Mexico. The fertile valleys of northern
Baja produce most of the nation's wine, and several vintners in the Guadalupe
Valley near Ensenada join for a weeklong festival celebrating the first crush.
Activities include the traditional blessing of the grapes, wine tastings, live
music and dancing, riding exhibitions, and fireworks. Plenty of earlier vintages
are for sale. For dates and locations, contact the **Baja California Information
Office** (☎ **800/522-1516** or 619/298-4105), or **Baja California Tours**
(☎ **619/454-7166**), which organizes a special day-long excursion from San
Diego. End of August.

- **Julian Weed Show,** Julian. This is one event that's better than its name. It displays and sells artwork and arrangements culled from the area's myriad wildflowers and indigenous plants (okay, weeds). The Julian Chamber of Commerce
(☎ **760/765-1857**) has further details. Second half of the month.

- **Surfing Competitions.** Oceanside's world-famous surfing spots attract
numerous competitions, including the **World Bodysurfing Championships**
and **Longboard Surf Club Competition.** For information on the Bodysurfing
Championships, held at the pier over a 3-day weekend in mid-August, call ☎ **760/
966-4535.** The Longboard Competition takes place the following weekend, also

at the pier, and includes a trade show and gala awards presentation with music and dancers. For further details, call ☎ **760/439-5334.**

September

- **Street Scene, Gaslamp Quarter.** This 3-day extravaganza fills the historic streets of downtown's Gaslamp Quarter with music, food, dance, and international character. Twelve separate stages are erected to showcase jazz, blues, reggae, rock, and soul music all weekend. Saturday is usually all-ages day—attendees must be 21 or over the other two days. For ticket and show information, call ☎ **619/ 557-8487.** Weekend after Labor Day.
- ✪ **La Jolla Rough-Water Swim,** La Jolla Cove. The country's largest rough-water swimming competition began in 1916 and features masters men's and women's swims, a junior swim, and an amateur swim. All are 1-mile events except the junior swim and gatorman 3-mile championship. Spectators don't need tickets. To register or receive more information, call ☎ **858/456-2100.** For an entry form, send a self-addressed stamped envelope to Entries Chairman, La Jolla Rough-Water Swim, P.O. Box 46, La Jolla, CA 92038. Sunday after Labor Day (September 10, 2000).
- **Art Festival in the Village of La Jolla,** along Prospect and Girard streets. This free festival includes prize-winning artwork, live entertainment, gourmet food, and children's activities. For information, call ☎ **888/ART-FEST** or 858/454-5718. Usually held the last weekend in September.
- **Julian's Arts and Crafts Show,** Julian. Coinciding with the phenomenally popular apple harvest season, the town's arts-and-crafts show is held every weekend from mid-September through the end of November. Local artisans display their wares; there's also plenty of cider and apple pie, plus entertainment and brilliant fall foliage. For more information, contact the Chamber of Commerce (☎ **760/765-1857**).
- **Rosarito–Ensenada 50-Mile Fun Bicycle Ride,** Mexico. This race is held in September and April. See the April entry, above.

October

- **Zoo Founders Day.** Admission to the San Diego Zoo is free for everyone on the first Monday of October, and children enter free all month. Call ☎ **619/234-3153.**
- **Concours d'Elegance,** Torrey Pines Golf Course, La Jolla. Classic car buffs won't want to pass this up. And we're not talking hot rods and jalopies here; the show features antique cars of the highest caliber, such as classic Jaguars, Rolls Royces, and Aston Martins. One year featured a salute to Ferrari, another to Alfa Romeo. For more information, call ☎ **619/283-4221.** Mid-October.
- **Underwater Pumpkin Carving Contest,** La Jolla. The event might never make it to the Olympics, but plenty of divers have turned out each year since 1981. The rules are relaxed, the panel of judges is serendipitous (one year it was the staff of a local dive shop, the next year five kids off the beach), and it's always a fun party. Spectators can hang out and wait for triumphant artists to break the surface with their creations. For details, call ☎ **858/565-6054.** Weekend before Halloween.

November

- **Carlsbad Village Faire.** Billed as the largest 1-day street fair in the United States, this festival features more than 800 vendors on 24 city blocks. Items for sale include ceramics, jewelry, clothing, glassware, and plants. Mexican, Italian, Japanese, Korean, Indonesian, and other edible fare is sold at booths along the way. Ground zero is the intersection of Grand Avenue and Jefferson Street. Call ☎ **760/ 931-8400** for dates.

- **New & Nouveau Wine & Food Tasting,** Temecula. This is your chance to sample the newest wines of the harvest, complemented by international foods. After you pick up the official map and souvenir wineglass, you're on your own to visit the dozen or so participating wineries over the 2-day period, meeting winemakers and learning to taste young wine. Tickets ($45) usually sell out in advance. Contact the **Temecula Valley Vintners Association** (☎ **800/801-WINE** or 909/699-3626). Third weekend of November.

December

- **Dr. Seuss Christmas Readings.** The late Theodor Geisel's adopted home honors the author by celebrating the holidays with his best-loved characters. Beginning the weekend after Thanksgiving, the lobby of **Loews Coronado Bay Resort** is transformed into "Who-ville," where the Cat in the Hat assembles an eager young (and not-so-young) audience for regular readings of *How the Grinch Stole Christmas.* Punch and cookies are served, and carolers perform following each reading. The free event runs through Christmas Eve, with readings Saturday afternoons and Sunday through Tuesday evenings. For more information, call ☎ **619/424-4000.**
- **Coronado Christmas Celebration and Parade.** Santa's arrival by ferry is followed by a small-town parade along Orange Avenue. Call ☎ **800/622-8300** or 619/437-8788. First Friday of December.
- **Christmas on the Prado,** Balboa Park. Lovely Balboa Park is decked out in holiday splendor for a magical weekend of evening events. A candlelight procession, traditional caroling, and baroque music ensembles are just part of the entertainment. There are craft displays, ethnic food, traditional hot cider, and a grand Christmas tree and nativity scene in Spreckels Pavilion. The event is free and lasts from 5 to 9pm both days; the park's museums are free during those hours. For more information, call ☎ **619/239-0512.** Early December.
- **Whale Watching.** The season starts in mid-December; see the January listing (above).
- **Fall Flower Tours** and the **Poinsettia Street Festival,** Encinitas. Like its close neighbor Carlsbad, Encinitas is a flower-growing center—90% of the world's poinsettia plants get their start here. These two events celebrate the quintessential holiday plant and other late-flowering blooms. For information, call the Encinitas Visitors Center (☎ **800/953-6041** or 760/753-6041).
- **Mission Bay Boat Parade of Lights,** from Quivira Basin in Mission Bay. Held on a Saturday, it concludes with the lighting of a 320-foot tower of Christmas lights at Sea World. Call ☎ **619/488-0501.** Mid-December.
- **San Diego Harbor Parade of Lights,** from Shelter Island to Harbor Island to Seaport Village. Decorated boats of all sizes and types participate, and spectators line the shore and cheer for their favorites. Held since 1971, it's on a Sunday in mid-December. Check the local newspapers for exact day and time.

4 Health & Insurance

WHAT TO DO IF YOU GET SICK AWAY FROM HOME

If you worry about getting sick away from home, you may want to consider **travel medical insurance** (see below). In most cases, however, your existing health plan will provide all the coverage you need. Be sure to carry your identification card in your wallet.

If you suffer from a chronic illness, consult your doctor before your departure. For conditions like epilepsy, diabetes, or heart problems, wear a **Medic Alert Identification Tag** (☎ **800/825-3785**; www.medicalert.org), which will immediately alert doctors to your condition and give them access to your records through Medic Alert's 24-hour hot line.

Pack prescription medications in your carry-on luggage. Carry written prescriptions in generic, not brand-name, form, and dispense all prescription medications from their original labeled vials. Also bring along copies of your prescriptions in case you lose your pills or run out.

INSURANCE

There are three kinds of travel insurance: trip cancellation, medical, and lost luggage coverage. **Trip-cancellation insurance** is a good idea if you have paid a large portion of your vacation expenses up front, say, by buying a package or cruise. The other two types of insurance, however, don't make sense for most travelers.

Travel medical insurance is usually unnecessary; your existing health insurance should cover you if you get sick while on vacation. If you belong to an HMO, you should check to see whether you are fully covered when away from home. It's the same with **lost luggage insurance;** your homeowner's insurance should cover stolen bags, and the airlines are responsible for $1,250 on domestic flights if they lose your luggage. If you plan to bring anything valuable, keep it in your carry-on bag.

Some credit and charge card companies may insure you against travel accidents if you buy plane, train, or bus tickets with their cards. Before buying additional insurance you might not really need, read your policies and agreements carefully. Call your insurers or credit card companies if you have questions.

If you do require additional insurance, try one of these reputable companies: **Access America,** 6600 W. Broad St., Richmond, VA 23230 (☎ 800/284-8300); **Travel Guard International,** 1145 Clark St., Stevens Point, WI 54481 (☎ 800/826-1300); **Travel Insured International, Inc.,** P.O. Box 280568, East Hartford, CT 06128 (☎ 800/243-3174); or **Travelex Insurance Services,** P.O. Box 9408, Garden City, NY 11530-9408 (☎ 800/228-9792).

For information on car renter's insurance, see "Getting Around: By Car" in chapter 4.

5 Tips for Travelers with Special Needs

FOR TRAVELERS WITH DISABILITIES

The Accessible San Diego hot line (☎ **619/279-0704;** fax 619/279-5118; www.accessandiego.com) helps travelers with disabilities find accessible hotels, tours, attractions, and transportation. If you call long distance and get the answering machine, leave a message and the staff will call you back collect. Ask for the annual *Access in San Diego* pamphlet, a city-wide guide with specifics on which establishments are accessible for those with visual, mobility, or hearing disabilities.

In the **San Diego Convention & Visitors Bureau's Dining and Accommodations** guide, a wheelchair symbol designates places that are accessible to persons with disabilities.

On buses and trolleys, riders with disabilities pay a fixed fare of 75¢. Many MTS buses and all trolleys are equipped with wheelchair lifts; priority seating is available on buses and trolleys. Stops served by accessible buses are marked with a wheelchair symbol. People with visual impairments benefit from the white reflecting ring that circles the bottom of the trolley door to increase its visibility.

Airport transportation for travelers with disabilities is available from **Cloud 9 Shuttle** (☎ **800/9-SHUTTLE** or 619/278-8877).

Other information sources to consider include the **Society for the Advancement of Travel for the Handicapped,** 347 Fifth Ave., Suite 610, New York, NY 10016 (☎ **212/447-7284;** fax 212-725-8253; www.sath.org). Membership costs $45 annually, $30 for seniors and students, and allows access to a vast network of connections in the travel industry. The society provides information sheets on travel destinations and referrals to tour operators that specialize in traveling with disabilities. The quarterly magazine, *Open World for Disability and Mature Travel,* is full of good information and resources. A year's subscription is $13 ($21 outside the United States).

Vision-impaired travelers should contact the **American Foundation for the Blind,** 11 Penn Plaza, Suite 300, New York, NY 10001 (☎ **800/232-5463**), for information on traveling with seeing-eye dogs.

Many of the major car-rental companies offer hand-controlled cars. **Avis** can provide a vehicle at any of its locations in the United States with 48-hour advance notice; **Hertz** requires 24 to 72 hours of advance reservation at most of its locations. **Wheelchair Getaways** (☎ **800/873-4973;** www.blvd.com/wg.htm) rents specialized vans with wheelchair lifts and other features for the disabled in more than 100 cities across the United States.

FOR GAY & LESBIAN TRAVELERS

Gay and lesbian visitors might already know about Hillcrest, the stylish part of town near Balboa Park that's the city's most prominent gay community. Many gay-owned restaurants, boutiques, and nightspots cater to a gay and straight clientele, and the scene is lively and colorful most nights of the week.

The **Lesbian and Gay Men's Community Center** is at 3916 Normal St. (☎ **619/ 692-2077**). It's open Monday through Friday from 9am to 10pm and Saturday from 9am to 7pm. Community outreach and counseling are offered.

The **Annual San Diego Lesbian and Gay Pride Parade, Rally, and Festival** is held the third or fourth weekend in July. The parade begins at noon on Saturday at University Avenue and Normal Street, and proceeds west on University to Sixth Avenue. A festival follows on Saturday from 2 to 10pm and Sunday from noon to 10pm. For more information, call ☎ **619/297-7683.**

The free *San Diego Gay and Lesbian Times,* published every Thursday, is often available at Obelisk bookstore, 1029 University Ave., Hillcrest (☎ **619/297-4171**).

The **International Gay & Lesbian Travel Association** (☎ **800/448-8550** or 954/776-2626; fax 954/776-3303; www.iglta.org), links travelers with the appropriate gay-friendly service organization or tour specialist. It has about 1,200 members, and offers quarterly newsletters, marketing mailings, and a membership directory that's updated quarterly.

Out and About, 8 W. 19th St. #401, New York, NY 10011 (☎ 800/929-2268 or 212/645-6922), offers guidebooks and a monthly newsletter packed with good information on the global gay and lesbian scene. A year's subscription to the newsletter costs $49. *Our World,* 1104 North Nova Rd., Suite 251, Daytona Beach, FL 32117 (☎ 904/441-5367) is a slicker monthly magazine promoting and highlighting travel bargains and opportunities. Annual subscription rates are $35 in the United States, $45 outside the United States.

FOR SENIORS

Nearly every attraction in San Diego offers a senior discount; age requirements vary, and prices are discussed in chapter 7. Public transportation and movie theaters also have reduced rates. Don't be shy about asking for discounts, but always carry identification, such as a driver's license, that shows your date of birth. Also, mention the fact that you're a senior citizen when you first make your travel reservations. For example, both **Amtrak** (☎ 800/USA-RAIL; www.amtrak.com) and **Greyhound** (☎ 800/752-4841; www.greyhound.com) offer discounts to persons over 62, as do many airlines.

A delightful way to meet older San Diegans, many of whom are retired, is to join a free Saturday-morning stroll with **Downtown Sam,** a footloose retiree and guide with **Walkabout International** (see "Organized Tours," in chapter 7).

San Diego's special senior citizens referral and information line is ☎ **619/560-2500.**

Members of the **American Association of Retired Persons,** 601 E St. NW, Washington, DC 20049 (☎ 800/424-3410 or 202/434-2277; www.aarp.org), get discounts not only on hotels but on airfares and car rentals, too. AARP offers members a wide range of special benefits, including *Modern Maturity* magazine and a monthly newsletter.

Mature Outlook, P.O. Box 9390, Des Moines, IA 50306 (☎ **800/336-6330),** began as a travel organization for people over 50, though it now caters to people of all ages. Annual membership is $19.95, which entitles members to discounts on hotels, a bimonthly magazine, and, often, coupons for discounted merchandise from Sears.

The Mature Traveler, a monthly 12-page newsletter on senior citizen travel, is a valuable resource. It is available by subscription ($30 a year) from GEM Publishing Group, Box 50400, Reno, NV 89513-0400. GEM also publishes *The Book of Deals,* a collection of more than 1,000 senior discounts on airlines, lodging, tours, and attractions around the country; it's available for $9.95 by calling ☎ **800/460-6676.** Another helpful publication is *101 Tips for the Mature Traveler,* available from Grand Circle Travel, 347 Congress St., Suite 3A, Boston, MA 02210 (☎ **800/221-2610** or 617/350-7500; fax 617/346-6700). Also check your newsstand for the quarterly magazine *Travel 50 & Beyond.*

If you want something more than the average vacation or guided tour, try **Elderhostel,** 75 Federal St., Boston, MA 02110-1941 (☎ **877/426-8056;** www.elderhostel.org). It organizes educational travel for people 55 and over (plus a spouse or companion of any age). On these escorted tours, the days are packed with seminars, lectures, and field trips, and academic experts lead the sightseeing. Most courses last about 3 weeks, and many include airfare, accommodations in student dormitories or modest inns, meals, and tuition. There is an Elderhostel educational program in the San Diego area, at the Point Loma Youth Hostel.

FOR FAMILIES

Several books offer tips on traveling with kids. *Family Travel* (Lanier Publishing International) and *How to Take Great Trips with Your Kids* (The Harvard Common Press) are full of good general advice. *The Unofficial Guide to California with Kids* (Macmillan) is an excellent resource that covers the entire state. It rates and ranks attractions for each age group, lists dozens of family-friendly accomodations and resturants, and suggests lots of beaches and activities that are fun for the whole clan.

Family Travel Times is published six times a year by Travel with Your Children, or TWYCH (☎ 888/822-4388 or 212/477-5524), and includes a weekly call-in service for subscribers. Subscriptions are $40 a year. A free publication list and a sample issue are available by calling or sending a request to the above address.

Families Welcome!, 92 N. Main, Ashland, OR 97520 (☎ **800/326-0724** or 541/ 482-6121), is a travel company specializing in worry-free vacations for families.

Be sure to check out the "Family-Friendly" boxes in the hotel and restaurant chapters, which will point you to the most accommodating and fun establishments. The "Especially for Kids" section in chapter 7 offers tips about which San Diego sights and attractions have the most appeal for the little ones.

6 Getting There

BY PLANE

Flights arrive at San Diego International Airport/Lindbergh Field (named after aviation hero Charles Lindbergh), served by many national and regional air carriers as well as Aeromexico and British Airways.

Terminal 1 airlines include: **Aeromexico** (☎ 800/237-6639), **Alaska Airlines** (☎ 800/426-0333; www.alaskaair.com), **Southwest Airlines** (☎ 800/435-9792; www.iflyswa.com), **Trans World Airlines** (☎ 800/221-2000; www.twa.com), **United Airlines** (☎ 800/241-6522; www.ual.com), and **US Airways** (☎ 800/428-4322; www.usair.com).

Terminal 2 airlines include: **American Airlines** (☎ 800/433-7300; www.aa.com), **British Airways** (☎ 800/247-9297; www.british-airways.com), **Canadian Airlines** (☎ 800/426-7000; www.cdnair.com), **Midwest Express** (☎ 800/452-2022), **Northwest Airlines** (☎ 800/225-2525; www.nwa.com), and **Reno Air** (☎ 800/RENO-AIR; www.renoair.com).

The airlines in the Terminal 2 expansion are **America West** (☎ 800/235-9292; www.americawest.com), **Continental Airlines** (☎ 800/525-0280; www.flycontinental.com), and **Delta Airlines** (☎ 800/221-1212; www.delta-air.com).

The following airlines arrive at the Commuter Terminal: Alaska Commuter, American Eagle, Continental Connection, Delta Connection, Northwest AirLink, Skywest Airlines, United Express, and US Airways Express. For contact information on these regional carriers, turn to the Appendix at the back of this book.

FLYING FOR LESS: TIPS FOR GETTING THE BEST AIRFARE

- Keep checking your newspaper for **sales.** You'll almost never see a sale during the peak summer vacation months of July and August, or during the Thanksgiving or Christmas holidays, but during slower times, airlines may slash their fares dramatically.
- If your schedule is flexible, ask if you can secure a cheaper fare by staying an extra day by staying over Saturday night, or by flying midweek. Many airlines won't volunteer this information, so ask them lots of questions.
- Formerly known as "bucket shops," **consolidators** (wholesalers who buy tickets in bulk at a discount) today are legitimate and offer some of the best deals around. You

Packing Tips

Bring a **sweater or light jacket,** even in summer. Because the ocean is close by, cold, damp breezes are common after the sun sets. But leave behind your heavy coats and cold-weather gear, no matter when you're coming. Pack **casual clothes.** Shorts, jeans, and T-shirts are common at all tourist attractions and many restaurants. Men who plan to try one of San Diego's nicer restaurants may want to bring a sports jacket, but this is really an informal town. Bring **good, comfortable walking shoes;** you can cover a lot of ground in this pleasant, outdoorsy city.

Don't forget **sunglasses,** an essential accessory (especially if you'll be on or near the water, which reflects and amplifies the sun's rays). If you have **binoculars,** bring them—they'll come in handy during whale-watching season. Regardless of the time of year, it's wise to pack a **bathing suit.** Most hotels have heated pools and whirlpools, and you might be surprised by a day warm enough for the beach.

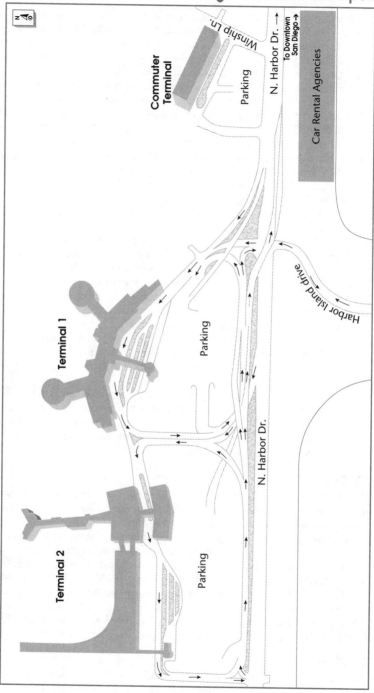

San Diego International Airport

Terminal 1

Terminal 2

Commuter Terminal

Parking

Parking

Parking

Winship Ln.

N. Harbor Dr.

To Downtown
San Diego →

Car Rental Agencies

Harbor Island drive

N. Harbor Dr.

21

can get virtually any flight, on any airline, from them; sometimes their fare is identical to the airline's, but often it's discounted 15 to 50%. The tickets carry the same restrictions the airline imposes on advance and discount fares. Their ads usually run in the Sunday travel section, and many have followed the lead of the major airlines and travel agencies by setting up online reservations systems.

There are lots of fly-by-night consolidators, though, and problems can range from disputing never-received tickets to finding you have no seat booked when you get to the airport. Play it safe by going with a reputable business. Here are some suggestions: **1-800-FLY-CHEAP** (www.1800flycheap.com); **Cheap Seats** (☎ 800/451-7200; www.cheapseatstravel.com); or my favorite, **Cheap Tickets** (☎ 800/377-1000; www.cheaptickets.com). **Council Travel** (☎ 800/226-8624; www.counciltravel.com) and **STA Travel** (☎ 800/781-4040; www.sta.travel.com) cater especially to young travelers, but their bargain-basement prices are available to people of all ages; **Travel Bargains** (☎ 800/AIR-FARE; www.1800airfare.com) was formerly owned by TWA, but now offers the deepest discounts on many other airlines, with a 4-day advance purchase.

• **Surf the Net** for bargains. Start out by consulting "Frommer's Online Directory" at the back of this book. Among the best sites for finding great deals are Arthur Frommer's Budget Travel (**www.frommers.com**), Microsoft Expedia (**www.expedia.com**) and Travelocity (**www.travelocity.com**). The Internet Travel Network (**www.itn.net**) provides one-stop shopping destination for air, car, and hotel bookings. Its "Fare Mail" keeps you informed of low-cost deals to any of six locations you request; you can eliminate unwanted messages by specifying, for example, that you only want to be notified when flights from New York to San Diego drop below $300. Smarter Living (www.smarterliving.com) also offers a customized e-mail summarizing the discount fares available from your departure city.

• Several major airlines offer a free e-mail service known as **E-Savers,** which allow them to send you their best bargain airfares on a regular basis. It's a service for the spontaneously inclined and travelers looking for a quick getaway. But the fares are cheap, so it's worth taking a look. Check directly with the individual airlines' Web sites (see above, or the Appendix at the end of the book).

BY CAR

Visitors driving to San Diego from Los Angeles and points north do so via coastal route I-5. From points northeast, take I-15 (link up with I-8 West and Highway 163 South or Highway 94 West); from the east, use I-8 (link up with Highway 163 South). Entering the downtown area, Highway 163 turns into 10th Avenue, and Highway 94 turns into F Street. Try to avoid arriving during weekday rush hours, between 7 and 9am and 3 and 6pm. If you are heading to Coronado, take the Coronado Bridge from I-5. If you have a passenger, stay in the far-right lanes to avoid paying the toll. Maximum speed in the San Diego area is 65 miles (105km) per hour, and many areas are limited to 55.

San Diego is 130 miles and 2 hours from **Los Angeles;** 149 miles from **Palm Springs,** a 2½-hour trip; and 532 miles, or 8 hours, from **San Francisco.**

BY TRAIN

Trains from all points in the United States and Canada will take you to Los Angeles, where you'll need to change trains for the 3-hour journey on to San Diego. You'll

---

Travel Tip

If you're planning a road trip, it's a good idea to be a member of the **American Automobile Association (AAA).** Members who carry their cards with them not only receive free roadside assistance, but also have access to a wealth of free travel information (detailed maps and guidebooks). Also, many hotels and attractions throughout California offer discounts to AAA members—always inquire. Call ☎ **800/ 922-8228** or your local branch for membership information.

---

arrive at the striking mission-style Santa Fe Station, built in 1914 and located downtown at Broadway and Kettner Boulevard. For price and schedule information, call **Amtrak** (☎ 800/USA-RAIL; www.amtrak.com).

7 Package Deals

For information on independent fly-drive packages (no escorted tour groups, just a bulk rate on your airfare, hotel, and possibly rental car), contact **American Airlines Fly AAway Vacations** (☎ 800/321-2121), **American Express Vacations** (☎ 800/ 241-1700; www.americanexpress.com/travel), **Continental Airlines Vacations** (☎ 800/634-5555), **Delta Vacations** (☎ 800/872-7786), **TWA Getaway Vacations** (☎ 800/438-2929), or **United Vacations** (☎ 800/328-6877). Availability varies widely based upon season and demand, but it always pays to investigate what the major air carriers are offering.

The packages are best suited to travelers who can be flexible in the following ways:

- Understand that not every hotel in the city will be an option. That's not to say packages force you to stay in dumps—quite the contrary, they often include the city's top choices—but you'll have a limited selection. Pinpoint roughly where you'd like to stay, and ask if there's a participating hotel there. (The biggest hotel chains and resorts also offer package deals. If you already know where you want to stay, call the resort and ask if it offers land-air packages.)
- If you can schedule your departure and arrival so you're not flying on the weekend, airfares will usually be at least $25 to $50 lower per person. And it goes without saying that the popular season (summer in San Diego) is the most restrictive season. Package deals will still save you some money over booking separately, though.
- Ask the reservationist lots of questions, and mention the activities you're considering for your visit. All the companies have access to various "goodies" they can hitch to your package for far less than you'd pay separately. Examples include tickets to Sea World, the San Diego Zoo, or the Wild Animal Park; passes for city tours, harbor cruises, and other excursions; tickets for theater events; rental-car upgrades; and other specials.

3 For Foreign Visitors

The pervasiveness of American culture around the world may make you feel that you know the United States pretty well, but leaving your own country still requires an additional degree of planning. This chapter will help prepare you for common issues and problems that visitors may encounter.

1 Preparing for Your Trip

ENTRY REQUIREMENTS

Immigration laws are a hot political issue in the United States, and the following requirements may have changed somewhat by the time you plan your trip. Check at any U.S. embassy or consulate for current information and requirements. You can also plug into the **U.S. State Department's** Internet site (**www.state.gov**).

VISAS

The U.S. State Department's **Visa Waiver Pilot Program** allows citizens of certain countries to enter the United States without a visa for stays of up to 90 days. At press time these included Andorra, Argentina, Australia, Austria, Belgium, Brunei, Denmark, Finland, France, Germany, Iceland, Ireland, Italy, Japan, Liechtenstein, Luxembourg, Monaco, the Netherlands, New Zealand, Norway, San Marino, Slovenia, Spain, Sweden, Switzerland, and the United Kingdom. Citizens of these countries need only a valid passport and a round-trip air or cruise ticket in their possession upon arrival. If they first enter the United States, they may also visit Mexico, Canada, Bermuda, and the Caribbean islands and return to the United States without a visa. Further information is available from any U.S. embassy or consulate. Canadian citizens may enter the United States without visas; they need only proof of residence.

Citizens of all other countries must have (1) a valid passport that expires at least 6 months later than the scheduled end of their visit to the United States, and (2) a tourist visa, which may be obtained without charge from any U.S. consulate.

OBTAINING A VISA To obtain a visa, the traveler must submit a completed application form (either in person or by mail) with a 1½-inch-square photo, and must demonstrate binding ties to a residence abroad. Usually you can obtain a visa at once or within 24 hours, but it may take longer during the summer rush from June through August.

Plan Ahead for the Unexpected

Before you leave home, make two sets of photocopies of every traveler's ID (including passports for international travelers), credit cards (front and back), and plane tickets or itinerary confirmation. Leave one at home with a trusted friend, and carry one with you separate from your wallet and purse (your cosmetic case or shaving kit is a safe bet). In case of unexpected loss, you'll have proof of your identity, everything necessary to cancel and replace your credit cards, and a receipt for your plane trip home.

If you cannot go in person, contact the nearest U.S. embassy or consulate for directions on applying by mail. Your travel agent or airline office may also be able to provide you with visa applications and instructions. The U.S. consulate or embassy that issues your visa will determine whether you will be issued a multiple- or single-entry visa and any restrictions regarding the length of your stay.

British subjects can obtain up-to-date passport and visa information by calling the **U.S. Embassy Visa Information Line** (☎ **0891/200-290**) or the **London Passport Office** (☎ **0990/210-410** for recorded information).

IMMIGRATION QUESTIONS

Telephone operators at the **Immigration and Naturalization Service's Customer Information Center** (☎ **800/375-5283**) will answer your inquiries regarding U.S. immigration policies or laws. Representatives are available from 9am to 3pm, Monday through Friday. The INS also answers commonly asked questions through a 24-hour automated information service (☎ **800/755-0777**).

MEDICAL REQUIREMENTS

Unless you're arriving from an area known to be suffering from an epidemic (particularly cholera or yellow fever), inoculations or vaccinations are not required for entry into the United States. If you have a disease that requires treatment with narcotics or syringe-administered medications, carry a valid signed prescription from your physician to allay any suspicions that you may be smuggling narcotics (a serious offense that carries severe penalties).

For HIV-positive visitors, requirements for entering the United States are somewhat vague and change frequently. According to the latest publication of *HIV and Immigrants: A Manual for AIDS Service Providers,* although the INS doesn't require a medical exam for every one trying to come into the United States, INS officials may keep out people who they suspect are HIV positive. INS may stop people because they look sick or because they are carrying AIDS/HIV medicine.

If an HIV-positive non-citizen applying for a non-immigrant visa knows that HIV is a communicable disease of public health significance but checks "no" on the question about communicable diseases, INS may deny the visa because it thinks the applicant committed fraud. If a non-immigrant visa applicant checks "yes," or if INS suspects the person is HIV positive, it will deny the visa unless the applicant asks for a special waiver for visitors. This waiver is for people visiting the United States for a short time, to attend a conference, for instance, to visit close relatives, or to receive medical treatment. It can be a confusing situation, so for up-to-the-minute information concerning HIV-positive travelers, contact the Centers for Disease Control's **National Center for HIV** (☎ **404/332-4559;** www.hivatis.org) or the **Gay Men's Health Crisis** (☎ **212/367-1000;** www.gmhc.org).

PASSPORT INFORMATION

Safeguard your passport in an inconspicuous, inaccessible place like a money belt. If you lose it, visit the nearest consulate of your native country as soon as possible for a replacement. Passport applications are downloadable from the Internet sites listed below.

FOR RESIDENTS OF CANADA   You can pick up a passport application at one of 28 regional passport offices or most travel agencies. The passport is valid for 5 years and costs CAN$60. Children under 16 may be included on a parent's passport, but need their own to travel unaccompanied by the parent. Applications, which must be accompanied by two identical passport-sized photographs and proof of Canadian citizenship, are also available from the central **Passport Office, Department of Foreign Affairs and International Trade,** Ottawa K1A 0G3 (☎ **800/567-6868;** www.dfait-maeci.gc.ca/passport). Processing takes 5 to 10 days if you apply in person, or about 3 weeks by mail.

FOR RESIDENTS OF THE UNITED KINGDOM   To pick up an application for a regular 10-year passport (the visitor's passport has been abolished), visit your nearest passport office, major post office, or travel agency. You can also contact the **London Passport Office** (☎ **0171/271-3000;** www.open.gov.uk/ukpass/ukpass. htm). Passports are £21 for adults and £11 for children under 16.

FOR RESIDENTS OF IRELAND   You can apply for a 10-year passport (IR£45) at the **Passport Office,** Setanta Centre, Molesworth Street, Dublin 2 (☎ **01/671-1633;** www.irlgov.ie/iveagh/foreignaffairs/services). Those under age 18 and over 65 must apply for an IR£10 3-year passport. You can also apply at 1A South Mall, Cork (☎ **021/272-525**), or over the counter at most main post offices.

FOR RESIDENTS OF AUSTRALIA   Apply at your local post office or passport office or search the government Web site at www.dfat.gov.au/passports/. Passports for adults are A$126; for those under 18, A$63.

FOR RESIDENTS OF NEW ZEALAND   You can pick up a passport application at any travel agency or Link Centre. For more information, contact the **Passport Office,** P.O. Box 805, Wellington (☎ **0800/225-050**). Passports for adults are NZ$80; for those under 16, NZ$40.

CUSTOMS
WHAT YOU CAN BRING IN

Every visitor over 21 years of age may bring in, free of duty, the following: (1) 1 liter of wine or hard liquor; (2) 200 cigarettes, 100 cigars (but not from Cuba), or 3 pounds of smoking tobacco; and (3) $100 worth of gifts. These exemptions are offered to travelers who spend at least 72 hours in the United States and who have not claimed them within the preceding 6 months. It is altogether forbidden to bring into the country foodstuffs (particularly fruit, cooked meats, and canned goods) and plants (vegetables, seeds, tropical plants, and the like). Foreign tourists may bring in or take out up to $10,000 in U.S. or foreign currency with no formalities; larger sums must be declared to U.S. Customs on entering or leaving, which includes filing form CM 4790. For

Driver's Licenses

The United States recognizes most foreign driver's licenses. You may want to get an international driver's license if your home license is not written in English.

more specific information regarding U.S. Customs, call your nearest U.S. embassy or consulate, or the **U.S. Customs Office** (☎ 202/927-1770; www.customs. ustreas.gov).

WHAT YOU CAN BRING HOME

U.K. citizens have a customs allowance of: 200 cigarettes; 50 cigars; 250g of smoking tobacco; 2 liters of still table wine; 1 liter of spirits or strong liqueurs (over 22% volume); 2 liters of fortified wine, sparkling wine, or other liqueurs; 60cc (ml) perfume; 250cc (ml) of toilet water; and £145 worth of all other goods, including gifts and souvenirs. People under 17 cannot have the tobacco or alcohol allowance. For more information, contact **HM Customs & Excise,** Passenger Enquiry Point, 2nd Floor Wayfarer House, Great South West Road, Feltham, Middlesex, TW14 8NP (☎ 0181/910-3744; from outside the U.K., 44/181-910-3744), or consult the Web site at www.open.gov.uk.

For a clear summary of **Canadian** rules, write for the booklet *I Declare,* issued by **Revenue Canada,** 2265 St. Laurent Blvd., Ottawa K1G 4KE (☎ 613/993-0534). Canada allows its citizens a CAN$500 exemption, and you're allowed to bring back duty-free 200 cigarettes, 2.2 pounds of tobacco, 40 imperial ounces of liquor, and 50 cigars. In addition, you're allowed to mail gifts to Canada from abroad at the rate of CAN$60 a day, provided they're unsolicited and don't contain alcohol or tobacco (write on the package "Unsolicited gift, under $60 value"). All valuables should be declared on the Y-38 form before departure from Canada, including serial numbers of valuables you already own, such as expensive foreign cameras. *Note:* The CAN$500 exemption can only be used once a year, and only after an absence of 7 days.

The duty-free allowance in **Australia** is A$400 or, for those under 18, A$200. Upon returning to Australia, citizens can bring in 250 cigarettes or 250 grams of loose tobacco, and 1,125ml of alcohol. If you're returning with valuable goods you already owned, such as foreign-made cameras, file form B263. A helpful brochure, available from Australian consulates or customs offices, is *Know Before You Go.* For more information, contact **Australian Customs Services,** GPO Box 8, Sydney NSW 2001 (☎ 02/9213-2000).

The duty-free allowance for **New Zealand** is NZ$700. Citizens over 17 can bring in 200 cigarettes, or 50 cigars, or 250 grams of tobacco (or all three if their combined weight doesn't exceed 250 grams); plus 4.5 liters of wine and beer, or 1.125 liters of liquor. New Zealand currency does not carry import or export restrictions. Fill out a certificate of export, listing the valuables you are taking out of the country; that way, you can bring them back without paying duty. Most questions are answered in a free pamphlet available at New Zealand consulates and customs offices: *New Zealand Customs Guide for Travellers, Notice no. 4.* For more information, contact **New Zealand Customs,** 50 Anzac Ave., P.O. Box 29, Auckland (☎ 09/359-6655).

INSURANCE

Although it's not required of travelers, health insurance is highly recommended. Unlike many European countries, the United States does not usually offer free or low-cost medical care to its citizens or visitors. Doctors and hospitals are expensive, and in most cases will require payment or proof of coverage before they render their services. Policies can cover everything from the loss or theft of your baggage and trip cancellation to the guarantee of bail in case you're arrested. Good policies will also cover the costs of an accident, repatriation, or death. See "Health & Insurance" in chapter 2 for more information.

Though lack of health insurance may prevent you from being admitted to a hospital in non-emergencies, don't worry about being left on a street corner to die—the American way is to fix you now and bill the living daylights out of you later.

INSURANCE FOR BRITISH TRAVELERS   Most big travel agents offer their own insurance, and will probably try to sell you their package when you book a holiday. Think before you sign. **Britain's Consumers' Association** recommends that you insist on seeing the policy and reading the fine print before buying travel insurance. **The Association of British Insurers** (☎ 0171/600-3333) gives advice by phone and publishes *Holiday Insurance,* a free guide to policy provisions and prices. You might also shop around for better deals. Try **Columbus Travel Insurance Ltd.** (☎ 0171/ 375-0011) or, for students, **Campus Travel** (☎ 0171/730-2101).

INSURANCE FOR CANADIAN TRAVELERS   Check with your provincial health-plan offices or call **HealthCanada** (☎ 613/957-2991) to find out the extent of your coverage and what documentation and receipts you must take home if you are treated in the United States.

MONEY

CURRENCY   The U.S. monetary system is painfully simple: The most common bills (all ugly, all green) are the $1 (colloquially, a "buck"), $5, $10, and $20 denominations. There are also $2 bills (seldom encountered), $50 bills, and $100 bills. The last two are usually not welcome as payment for small purchases. Note that a redesigned $100 and $50 bill were introduced in 1996, and a redesigned $20 bill in 1998. Expect to see redesigned $10 and $5 notes in 2000. Despite rumors to the contrary, the old-style bills are still legal tender.

There are six denominations of coins: 1¢ (1 cent, or a penny); 5¢ (5 cents, or a nickel); 10¢ (10 cents, or a dime); 25¢ (25 cents, or a quarter); 50¢ (50 cents, or a half dollar); and the rare $1 piece (the older, large silver dollar and newer, small Susan B. Anthony coin). A new gold $1 piece will be introduced by 2000.

Note: The foreign-exchange bureaus so common in Europe are rare even at airports in the United States, and non-existent outside major cities. It's best not to change foreign money (or traveler's checks denominated in a currency other than U.S. dollars) at a small-town bank, or even a branch in a big city. In fact, leave any currency other than U.S. dollars at home—it may prove a greater nuisance than it's worth.

TRAVELER'S CHECKS   Though traveler's checks are widely accepted, make sure that they're denominated in U.S. dollars. Foreign-currency checks are often difficult to exchange. The three traveler's checks that are most widely accepted are **Visa, American Express,** and **Thomas Cook.** Be sure to record the numbers of the checks, and keep that information separate in case they're lost or stolen. Most businesses are pretty good about taking traveler's checks, but you're better off cashing them in a bank (in small amounts, of course) and paying in cash. *Remember:* you'll need identification, such as a driver's license or passport, to change a traveler's check.

CREDIT CARDS & ATMS   Credit cards are the most widely used form of payment in the United States: **Visa** (BarclayCard in Britain), **MasterCard** (EuroCard in Europe, Access in Britain, Chargex in Canada), **American Express,** and others. There are, however, a handful of stores and restaurants that do not take credit cards, so be sure to ask in advance. Most businesses display stickers near the entrance to let you know which cards they accept.

It is strongly recommended that you bring at least one major credit card. Hotels, car-rental companies, and airlines usually require a credit-card imprint as a deposit against expenses, and in an emergency a credit card can be priceless.

Be sure to keep a copy of all your travel papers separate from your wallet or purse, and leave a copy with someone at home should you need it faxed in an emergency.

You'll find automated teller machines (ATMs) on just about every block. For detailed information on San Diego's ATMs, see "Money " in chapter 2.

SAFETY

While tourist areas are generally safe, crime is on the increase everywhere, and U.S. urban areas tend to be less safe than those in Europe or Japan. You should always stay alert. This is particularly true of large U.S. cities. It is wise to ask your hotel front-desk staff or the city's or area's tourist office if you're in doubt about which neighborhoods are safe.

Avoid deserted areas, especially at night, and don't go into public parks at night unless there's a concert or similar occasion that will attract a crowd. In **Balboa Park,** stay on designated walkways and away from secluded areas, day and night. In the **Gaslamp Quarter,** don't walk east of Fifth Avenue. San Diego's proximity to the international border contributes to its high rate of auto theft.

Avoid carrying valuables with you on the street, and don't display expensive cameras or electronic equipment. Hold on to your pocketbook, and place your billfold in an inside pocket. In theaters, restaurants, and other public places, keep your possessions in sight.

Remember also that hotels are open to the public, and in a large hotel, security may not be able to screen everyone entering. Always lock your room door—don't assume that once inside your hotel you are automatically safe and no longer need to be aware of your surroundings.

Driving safety is important, too; question your rental agency about personal safety, and ask for a traveler-safety brochure when you pick up your car. Ask at the agency for written directions to your destination, or a map with the route clearly marked. (Many agencies now offer the option of renting a cellular phone for the duration of your car rental; check with the rental agent when you pick up the car.) If possible, arrive and depart during daylight hours.

Recently, more and more crime has involved cars and drivers. If you drive off a highway into a doubtful neighborhood, leave the area as quickly as possible. If you have an accident, even on the highway, stay in your car with the doors locked until you assess the situation or until the police arrive. If you're bumped from behind on the street or are involved in a minor accident with no injuries, and the situation appears to be suspicious, motion to the other driver to follow you. Never get out of your car in such situations. Go directly to the nearest police precinct, well-lit service station, or 24-hour store.

Always try to park in well-lit and well-traveled areas. Never leave any packages or valuables in sight. If someone attempts to rob you or steal your car, don't try to resist the thief or carjacker. Report the incident to the police department immediately by calling ☎ **911.** This is a free call, even from pay phones.

2 Getting to the U.S.

The only direct international flights to San Diego are from Mexico and England. Other overseas travelers bound for San Diego will need to change planes at another U.S. gateway. If your port of entry is Los Angeles, you can fly to San Diego or take a train or bus. Unfortunately, the Los Angeles train and bus stations are a long way from Los Angeles International Airport (LAX), so it isn't convenient to use these modes of transportation to get to San Diego. However, if you're flying into L.A. and staying there a few days, taking the train or bus to San Diego makes a lot of sense.

Seven trains daily make the 2-hour, 58-minute trip. The one-way fare is $20. Union Station is in downtown Los Angeles at 800 Alameda St. The Los Angeles bus terminal is at Seventh and Alameda streets, and buses depart on the hour from 6am to 6pm daily, with some later departures; check with Greyhound for current schedules. The trip takes 2 hours and 45 minutes, and the one-way fare is $11.

In addition to the domestic U.S. airlines listed in chapter 2, many international carriers serve LAX and other U.S. gateways. These include **Aer Lingus** (☎ 01-705-3333 in Dublin; www.aerlingus.ie); **Air Canada** (☎ 888/247-2262 in Canada; www.air-canada.com); **Air New Zealand** (☎ 0800/737-000 in Auckland; www.airnz.com); **British Airways** (☎ 0345/222-111 in London; www.british-airways.com); **Canadian Airlines** (☎ 800/665-1177 in Canada; www.cdnair.ca); **Japan Airlines** (☎ 0354/89-1111 in Tokyo; www.jal.co.jp); and **Qantas** (☎ 13-13-13 in Australia; www.qantas.com.au).

Overseas visitors can take advantage of the Advance Purchase Excursion (APEX) reductions offered by all major U.S. and European carriers. For more money-saving airline advice, see "Getting There," in chapter 2.

IMMIGRATION & CUSTOMS CLEARANCE

Visitors arriving by air, no matter what the port of entry, should cultivate patience and resignation before setting foot on U.S. soil. Getting through immigration control may take as long as 2 hours on some days, especially on summer weekends, so be sure to have this guidebook or something else to read. Add the time it takes to clear customs, and you'll see that you should allow 2 to 3 hours for delays when you plan your connections between international and domestic flights.

In contrast, for the traveler arriving by car or rail from Canada, the border-crossing formalities have been streamlined to the vanishing point. People traveling by air from Canada, Bermuda, and some places in the Caribbean can sometimes clear customs and immigration at the point of departure, which is much quicker.

3 Getting Around the U.S.

BY PLANE Some large airlines (for example, Northwest and Delta) offer travelers on their transatlantic or transpacific flights special discount tickets under the name **Visit USA.** They allow mostly one-way travel from one U.S. destination to another at very low prices. These discount tickets are not on sale in the United States and must be purchased abroad in conjunction with your international ticket. This system is the best, easiest, and fastest way to see the United States at low cost. Obtain information well in advance from your travel agent or the office of the airline concerned, because the conditions attached can be changed without notice.

BY TRAIN International visitors can buy a **USA Railpass,** good for 15 or 30 days of unlimited travel on **Amtrak** (☎ 800/USA-RAIL; www.amtrak.com). The pass is available through many foreign travel agents. Prices in 1999 for a 15-day pass were $285 off-peak, $425 peak; a 30-day pass was $375 off-peak, $535 peak. (With a foreign passport, you can also buy passes at some Amtrak offices in the United States, including locations in Los Angeles, San Francisco, Chicago, New York, Miami, Boston, and Washington, D.C.) Reservations are generally required and should be made for each part of your trip as early as possible.

BY BUS   Although bus travel is often the most economical form of public transit for short hops between U.S. cities, it can also be slow and uncomfortable. It's certainly not an option for everyone, particularly when Amtrak, which is far more luxurious, offers similar rates. **Greyhound/Trailways** (☎ **800/231-2222;** www.greyhound.com), the sole nationwide bus line, offers an **Ameripass** for unlimited travel for 7 days ($199), 15 days ($299), 30 days ($409), or 60 days ($599). Passes must be purchased at a Greyhound terminal. Special rates are available for senior citizens and students.

BY CAR   The most cost-effective, convenient, and comfortable way to travel around the United States—especially California—is by car. For detailed information on automobile rentals in San Diego, see "Getting Around: By Car" in chapter 4. A comprehensive list of rental-car agencies, complete with Web sites and toll-free U.S. phone numbers, can be found in the Appendix at the end of this book.

Fast Facts: For the Foreign Traveler

Automobile Organizations   Auto clubs will supply maps, suggested routes, guidebooks, accident and bail-bond insurance, and emergency road service. The **American Automobile Association (AAA)** is the major auto club in the United States. If you belong to an auto club in your home country, inquire about AAA reciprocity before you leave. You may be able to join AAA even if you're not a member of a reciprocal club; to inquire, call AAA (☎ **800/922-8228** in the United States).

Business Hours   Banks and offices are usually open weekdays from 9am to 5pm. Stores, especially in shopping complexes, tend to stay open until about 9pm on weekdays and 6pm on weekends.

Climate   See "When to Go" in chapter 2.

Currency & Currency Exchange   See "Entry Requirements" and "Money" under "Preparing for Your Trip," above.

Drinking Laws   The legal age for purchase and consumption of alcoholic beverages is 21. Proof of age is required and often requested at bars, nightclubs, and restaurants, so it's always a good idea to bring ID when you go out. Supermarkets and convenience stores in California sell beer, wine, and liquor.

Do not carry open containers of alcohol in your car or any public area that isn't zoned for alcohol consumption. The police can, and probably will, fine you on the spot. And nothing will ruin your trip faster than getting a citation for DUI ("driving under the influence"), so don't even think about driving while intoxicated.

Electricity   Like Canada, the United States uses 110 to 120 volts AC (60 cycles), compared to 220 to 240 volts AC (50 cycles) in most of Europe, Australia, and New Zealand. If your small appliances use 220 to 240 volts, you'll need a 110-volt transformer and a plug adapter with two flat parallel pins. Downward converters that change 220–240 volts to 110–120 volts are difficult to find in the United States, so bring one with you.

Embassies & Consulates   All embassies are in Washington, D.C. Some consulates are in major U.S. cities, and most nations have a mission to the United Nations in New York City. If your country isn't listed below, call Washington, D.C., directory assistance (☎ **202/555-1212**) for the number of your national embassy.

The embassy of **Australia** is at 1601 Massachusetts Ave. NW, Washington, DC 20036 (☎ **202/797-3000;** www.austemb.org). The nearest consulate is at 2049 Century Park E., 19th Floor, Los Angeles, CA 90067 (☎ **310/229-4800**).

The embassy of **Canada** is at 501 Pennsylvania Ave. NW, Washington, DC 20001 (☎ **202/682-1740;** www.cdnemb-washdc.org). The nearest consulate is at 300 S. Grand Ave., 10th Floor, Los Angeles, CA 90071 (☎ **213/346-2700**).

The embassy of **Ireland** is at 2234 Massachusetts Ave. NW, Washington, DC 20008 (☎ **202/462-3939**). The nearest consulate is at 44 Montgomery St., Suite 3830, San Francisco, CA 94104 (☎ **415/392-4214**).

The embassy of **Japan** is at 2520 Massachusetts Ave. NW, Washington, DC 20008 (☎ **202/238-6700;** www.embjapan.org). The nearest consulate is at 50 Fremont St., San Francisco, CA 94105 (☎ **415/777-3533**).

The embassy of **New Zealand** is at 37 Observatory Circle NW, Washington, DC 20008 (☎ **202/328-4800;** www.emb.com/nzemb). The nearest consulate is at 12400 Wilshire Blvd., Suite 1150, Los Angeles, CA 90025 (☎ **310/207-1605**).

The embassy of the **United Kingdom** is at 3100 Massachusetts Ave. NW, Washington, DC 20008 (☎ **202/462-1340**). The nearest consulate is at 11766 Wilshire Blvd., Suite 400, Los Angeles, CA 90025 (☎ **310/477-3322**).

Emergencies   Call ☎ **911** to report a fire, to call the police, or to get an ambulance anywhere in the United States. This is a free call (no coins are required at public telephones).

If you encounter a travel-related problem, call the San Diego chapter of the **Traveler's Aid Society** (☎ **619/231-7361**), a nationwide, non-profit, social-service organization geared to helping travelers in difficult straits. Services might include reuniting families separated while traveling, providing food and shelter to people stranded without cash, or even emotional counseling.

Gasoline (Petrol)   Petrol is known as gasoline (or simply "gas") in the United States, and petrol stations are known as gas stations and service stations. Gasoline costs about half as much here as it does in Europe (about $1.20 per gallon at press time), and the posted price includes taxes. One U.S. gallon equals 3.8 liters or .85 imperial gallons.

Holidays   Banks, government offices, post offices, and many stores, restaurants, and museums are closed on the following national holidays: January 1 (New Year's Day), the third Monday in January (Martin Luther King, Jr. Day), the third Monday in February (Presidents' Day, Washington's Birthday), the last Monday in May (Memorial Day), July 4 (Independence Day), the first Monday in September (Labor Day), the second Monday in October (Columbus Day), November 11 (Veterans' Day or Armistice Day), the fourth Thursday in November (Thanksgiving Day), and December 25 (Christmas). Also, the Tuesday following the first Monday in November is Election Day, a federal-government holiday in presidential-election years (the next is 2000).

Legal Aid   The foreign tourist will probably never become involved with the American legal system. If you are "pulled over," or stopped for a minor infraction (of the highway code, for example—for speeding, maybe), never attempt to pay the fine directly to a police officer; this could be construed as attempted bribery, a much more serious crime. Pay fines by mail, or directly into the hands of the clerk of the court. If accused of a more serious offense, say and do nothing before consulting a lawyer. The burden is on the state to prove a person's guilt beyond a reasonable doubt, and everyone has the right to remain silent, whether he or she is suspected of a crime or is actually arrested. Once arrested, a person can make one telephone call to a party of his or her choice. Call your embassy or consulate.

Mail   If you aren't sure what your address will be in the United States, mail can be sent to you, in your name, c/o General Delivery, San Diego Post Office, 2535 Midway Dr., San Diego, CA 92138, USA. Pick up your mail there by taking bus no. 8 from downtown San Diego to Midway Drive at Barnett Avenue. Call ☎ **800/ 275-8777** for more information. The addressee must pick mail up in person and must produce proof of identity (driver's license or passport, for example). Most post offices will hold your mail for up to 1 month, and are open Monday to Friday from 8am to 5pm, and Saturday from 9am to 3pm. See also "Post Office" under "Fast Facts: San Diego" in chapter 4.

Generally found at intersections, mailboxes are blue with an eagle logo and carry the inscription U.S. MAIL. Domestic postage rates are 20¢ for a postcard and 33¢ for a letter. For international mail, a first-class letter of up to one-half ounce costs 60¢ (46¢ to Canada, 40¢ to Mexico); a first-class postcard costs 50¢ (40¢ to Canada, 35¢ Mexico); and a preprinted postal aerogramme costs 50¢.

Newspapers/Magazines   The daily *San Diego Union-Tribune* and *Los Angeles Times* and the weekly magazines *Newsweek* and *Time* cover world news and are available at newsstands. For newspapers from Europe and elsewhere, try **Seventh Near "B" Coffee and News,** 1146 Seventh Ave. near B Street (☎ **619/696-7071**), or **Paras Newsstand and Cigar Shop,** 3911 30th St. at University Avenue (☎ **619/296-2859**).

Taxes   In the United States there is no value-added tax (VAT) or other indirect tax at the national level. Sales tax is levied on goods and services by state and local governments, however, and is not included in the prices you'll see on merchandise. These taxes are not refundable. Sales tax in San Diego is 7.75%. Tax on hotel rooms is 10.5%.

Telephone & Fax   The telephone system in the United States is run by private corporations, so rates, especially for long-distance service and operator-assisted calls, can vary widely. Generally, hotel surcharges on long-distance calls are astronomical, so you're usually better off charging the call to a telephone charge card or a credit card—or using a **public pay telephone,** which you'll find clearly marked in most public buildings and private establishments as well as on the street. Convenience grocery stores and gas stations always have them. Many convenience groceries and packaging services sell **prepaid calling cards** in denominations up to $50; these can be the least expensive way to call home. Many public phones at airports now accept American Express, MasterCard, and Visa credit cards. **Local calls** made from public pay phones cost 25¢ or 35¢. Pay phones do not accept pennies, and few will take anything larger than a quarter.

Most long-distance and international calls can be dialed directly from any phone. **For calls within the United States and to Canada,** dial 1 followed by the area code and the seven-digit number. **For other international calls,** dial 011 followed by the country code, city code, and the telephone number of the person you are calling.

Calls to area codes **800, 888,** and **877** are toll-free. However, calls to numbers in area codes **700** and **900** (chat lines, bulletin boards, "dating" services, and so on) can be very expensive—usually 95¢ to $3 or more per minute, sometimes with minimum charges as high as $15 or more.

For **reversed-charge or collect calls,** and for person-to-person calls, dial 0 (zero, not the letter O) followed by the area code and number you want; an operator will come on the line to assist you.

For **local directory assistance** ("information"), dial 411; for long-distance information, dial 1, then the appropriate area code and 555-1212.

Most hotels have **fax machines** available for guests' use (be sure to ask about the charge to use it), and many places even have in-room fax machines. A less expensive way to send and receive faxes is to visit **Mail Boxes Etc.,** a national chain of office service stores. Locations in San Diego include downtown (501 W. Broadway, corner of Columbia Street; ☎ **619/232-0332**), Hillcrest (3707 5th Ave., 2 blocks south of University Avenue; ☎ **619/291-5678**), and Pacific Beach (1804 Garnet Ave.; ☎ **619/273-6661**).

Time   The continental United States is divided into **four time zones:** eastern standard time (EST), central standard time (CST), mountain standard time (MST), and Pacific standard time (PST). Alaska and Hawaii have their own zones. For example, noon in New York City (EST) is 11am in Chicago (CST), 10am in Denver (MST), 9am in Los Angeles (PST), 8am in Anchorage (AST), and 7am in Honolulu (HST).

Daylight saving time is in effect from 1am on the first Sunday in April through 1am the last Sunday in October, except in Arizona, Hawaii, part of Indiana, and Puerto Rico. Daylight saving time moves the clock 1 hour ahead of standard time.

For the correct time, call ☎ **619/853-1212.**

Tipping   Tipping is so ingrained in the American way of life that the annual income tax of tip-earning service personnel is based on how much they should have received relative to their employers' gross revenues. Accordingly, they may have to pay tax on a tip you didn't actually give them.

Here are some rules of thumb:

In hotels, tip **bellhops** at least $1 per bag ($2 to $3 if you have a lot of luggage) and tip the **maid or chamber staff** $1 per day. Tip the **doorman** or **concierge** only if he or she has provided you with some specific service (for example, calling a cab or obtaining difficult-to-get theater tickets). Tip the **valet parking attendant** $1 every time you get your car.

In restaurants, bars, and nightclubs, tip **service staff** 15% to 20% of the check, tip **bartenders** 10% to 15%, tip **checkroom attendants** $1 per garment, and tip **valet-parking attendants** $1 per vehicle. Tip the **doorman** only if he has provided you with some specific service (such as calling a cab). Tipping is not expected in cafeterias and fast-food restaurants.

Tip **cab drivers** 15% of the fare.

As for other service personnel, tip **skycaps** at airports at least $1 per bag ($2 to $3 if you have a lot of luggage), and tip **hairdressers** and **barbers** 15% to 20%.

Tipping ushers at movies and theaters, and gas-station attendants, is not expected.

Toilets   Rest rooms are easy to come by in San Diego, although you won't find public facilities on street corners. Instead, expect to find them in hotel lobbies and in public places, such as Horton Plaza and Seaport Village. Rest rooms in cafes and restaurants are for patrons only, but in an emergency you can just order a cup of coffee or simply ask to use the pay phone, usually conveniently positioned beside the rest rooms. Large hotels and fast-food restaurants are probably the best bet for good, clean facilities. If possible, avoid the toilets at parks and beaches, which tend to be dirty.

Getting to Know San Diego 4

San Diego is laid out in an easy-to-decipher manner, so learning the lay of the land is neither confusing nor daunting. Most San Diegans welcome visitors and are eager to answer questions and provide assistance; you'll feel like a local before you know it.

1 Orientation

ARRIVING
BY PLANE

San Diego International Airport/Lindbergh Field lies just north of downtown. The landing approach is right over the central business district, creating the familiar sight of planes threading through high-rise buildings on their way to the airport. A curfew (11:30pm to 6:30am) cuts down on noise in the surrounding residential areas. Planes may land during the curfew period, but they can't take off.

In 1998, the Port of San Diego completed a sorely needed 300,000-square-foot expansion of Lindbergh Field, so return visitors will be in for a surprise. The practical changes include an elevated pedestrian walkway between Terminal 2 and the parking area, and the renaming of the former East and West Terminals as 1 and 2. The addition onto the former West Terminal is known as the Terminal 2 Addition. Besides adding much-needed space to an airport that's grown awkwardly since the 1920s, the renovation brought dramatic pieces of local artwork, which are displayed in public spaces; there's even a slick, colorful brochure describing the art. The **Commuter Terminal,** half a mile away, remains unchanged; the "red bus" provides free service from the main airport to the Commuter Terminal.

General **information desks** with visitor materials, maps, and other services are in **Terminal 1,** near the United Airlines ticket counter, and in **Terminal 2** in the baggage-claim area and near the American Airlines ticket counter. You can **exchange foreign currency** at Travelex America (☎ **619/295-1501**), in Terminal 1 across from the United Airlines ticket counter. **Hotel reservation phones** and **car-rental courtesy phones** are in the baggage-claim areas of Terminals 1 and 2.

Getting into Town from the Airport
BY BUS   The new **Metropolitan Transit System (MTS) Route 992** provides service between the airport (there are stops at each terminal) and downtown San Diego. Buses run every 10 minutes on weekdays, every 15 minutes on weekends. The one-way fare is $2. The fare box

accepts $1 bills and coins (no change is made). Request a transfer if you're connecting to another bus or San Diego Trolley route downtown. Downtown, Route 992 stops on Broadway. The trip from the airport to downtown should take about 15 minutes.

At the **Transit Store,** 102 Broadway, at First Avenue (☎ **619/233-3004**), you can get information about greater San Diego's mass transit system (bus, rail, and ferry) and pick up free brochures, route maps, and timetables.

BY TAXI   Taxis line up outside both terminals and charge $7 to $10 for the trip to a downtown location, usually a 5- to 10-minute ride.

BY SHUTTLE   Several airport shuttles run regularly from the airport to downtown hotels; you'll see designated areas outside each terminal. The fare is $5 to $9 per person. The shuttles are a good deal for single travelers; two or more people traveling together might as well take a taxi. Companies that serve the whole county include **Cloud 9 Shuttle** (☎ **800/9-SHUTTLE** or 619/278-8877), **Coronado Livery** (☎ **619/ 435-6310**), and **Peerless Shuttle** (☎ **619/554-1700**). Coronado Livery is the least expensive to Coronado, and Cloud 9 is the cheapest to downtown.

BY LIMO   Chauffeur service is available from **Luxury Transportation of La Jolla** (☎ **858/459-9090**) and **Luxury Transportation** (☎ **619/270-6666**). A limo costs about as much as a taxi. These companies don't use stretch limos, but do have a fleet of well-kept Mercedes sedans.

BY CAR   If you are driving the short distance into the city from the airport, follow Harbor Drive to Broadway, the main east-west city street. For complete information on rental cars in San Diego, see "Getting Around," later in this chapter.

BY TRAIN

San Diego's **Santa Fe Station** is centrally located downtown, on Broadway between Front Street and First Avenue, within walking distance of most downtown hotels. Taxis line up outside the main door, the trolley station is across the street, and a dozen local bus routes stop on Broadway or Pacific Highway, one block away.

VISITOR INFORMATION

There are staffed information booths at both airport terminals, the train station, and the cruise-ship terminal.

In downtown San Diego, the Convention & Visitors Bureau's **International Visitor Information Center** (☎ **619/236-1212;** fax 619/230-7084; www.sandiego.org; e-mail: sdinfo@sandiego.org) is on First Avenue at F Street, street level at Horton Plaza. The multilingual staff offers brochures in English, French, German, Japanese, Portuguese, and Spanish. They can provide you with the glossy *San Diego Visitors Planning Guide.* It includes information on accommodations, dining, activities, attractions, tours, and transportation, and has excellent maps. Ask for the *Super Savings Coupon Book,* which is full of money-saving coupons. The center is open Monday through Saturday from 8:30am to 5pm year-round and Sunday from 11am to 5pm June through August; it is closed January 1, Thanksgiving, and December 25.

Some of the same materials are available at the **Mission Bay Visitor Information Center,** 2688 Mission Bay Dr. (☎ **619/276-8200**). You can also get pointers on recreational activities in the bay and beyond. From I-5, take the Clairemont Drive exit west to the end. There's plenty of parking; stop in between 9am and dusk.

The **Coronado Visitors Bureau,** 1047 B Ave. (☎ **800/622-8300** or 619/437-8788; fax 619/437-6006; www.coronado.ca.us; e-mail: corcvb@aol.com) dispenses maps, news letters, and information-packed brochures. It's open Monday through Friday from 9am to 5pm, Saturday 10am to 5pm, and Sunday 11am to 4pm.

Information on La Jolla is distributed by the **La Jolla Town Council,** 7734 Herschel Ave. (between Silverado and Kline streets) (☎ **858/454-1444**). The office is open Monday through Friday from 9:30am to 4:30pm.

Additional visitor information is available from the **Balboa Park Visitors Center,** 1549 El Prado (☎ **619/239-0512**), and **Old Town State Historic Park Headquarters,** 4002 Wallace St. (☎ **619/220-5422**).

For the latest on San Diego nightlife and entertainment, pick up the *Reader,* a free newspaper that comes out on Thursday and is available all over the city. Also check "Night and Day," the Thursday supplement in the *San Diego Union-Tribune.* For addresses of Web sites with plenty of up-to-the-minute information, see chapter 2, "Planning a Trip to San Diego."

CITY LAYOUT
MAIN ARTERIES & STREETS

It's not hard to find your way around downtown San Diego. Most streets run one way. First through Twelfth avenues alternate running north and south (Fifth Avenue is two-way in the Gaslamp Quarter only); A through K streets alternate running east and west. Broadway, the equivalent of D Street, is a two-way street, as are Market Street and Harbor Drive. East-west streets (north of A Street) bear the names of trees, in alphabetical order: Ash, Beech, Cedar, Date, and so on. Harbor Drive runs past the airport and along the waterfront, which is known as the Embarcadero. Ash Street and Broadway are the downtown arteries that connect with Harbor Drive. The Coronado Bay Bridge leading to Coronado is accessible from I-5, and I-5 north leads to Old Town, Mission Bay, La Jolla, and North County.

Balboa Park, home of the San Diego Zoo, and the Hillcrest and uptown areas lie northeast of downtown San Diego. The park and zoo are easily reached by way of Twelfth Avenue, which becomes Park Boulevard and leads to the parking lots. Fifth Avenue leads to Hillcrest and uptown (turn right onto University Avenue to get to the latter).

CORONADO   The main streets are Orange Avenue, where most of the hotels and restaurants are clustered, and Ocean Drive, which follows Coronado Beach.

DOWNTOWN   The major thoroughfares are Broadway (a major bus artery), Fourth and Fifth avenues (which run south and north, respectively), C Street (the trolley line), and Harbor Drive, which hugs the waterfront and passes the Maritime Museum, Seaport Village, and the Convention Center.

HILLCREST   In this area near Balboa Park, the main streets are University Avenue and Washington Street, both two-way running east and west, and Fourth and Fifth avenues.

LA JOLLA   The main avenues are Prospect and Girard, which are perpendicular to each other.

PACIFIC BEACH   Mission Boulevard is the main drag, and perpendicular to it are Grand and Garnet avenues and Pacific Beach Drive. East and West Mission Bay drives and Ingraham Street enable you to zip around the periphery of the bay or bisect it.

FINDING AN ADDRESS

It's easy to find an address on a downtown street running east-west. If the address is 411 Market St., for example, you'll find it between Fourth and Fifth avenues on Market; if it's 326 Broadway, it's between Third and Fourth avenues; if it's 1051 University Ave., it's between 10th and 11th avenues. Even numbers are on the north or west sides of streets; odd numbers are on the south or east sides of streets.

STREET MAPS

The **International Visitor Information Center,** at First Avenue and F Street (☎ 619/ 236-1212), provides the *San Diego Visitors Planning Guide,* which includes five free, easy-to-read maps. They cover downtown San Diego and Coronado (with arrows indicating traffic direction), Old Town, Balboa Park, La Jolla and Mission Bay, and San Diego County and vicinity.

The **Automobile Club of Southern California** has several locations, including 815 Date St. (☎ 619/233-1000). It distributes great maps, which are free to its members and to members of international auto clubs. The **Transit Store,** 102 Broadway, at First Avenue (☎ 619/233-3004), is a storehouse of bus and trolley maps, with a friendly staff on duty to answer specific questions.

Hotel receptionists can provide complimentary maps of the downtown area. You can buy maps of the city and vicinity at **Le Travel Store** at 745 Fourth Ave. or the **Upstart Crow** bookstore in Seaport Village.

If you're moving to San Diego or plan to spend a long time here, I suggest you buy the ***Thomas Bros. Guide,*** available at bookstores, drugstores, and large supermarkets. This all-encompassing book of maps deciphers San Diego street by street.

The Neighborhoods in Brief

In this guidebook, San Diego is divided into six areas, each with its own hotel and restaurant listings (see chapters 5 and 6).

Downtown   The business, shopping, dining, and entertainment heart of the city, the downtown area encompasses Horton Plaza, the Gaslamp Quarter, the Embarcadero (waterfront), and the Convention Center. The Maritime Museum, the downtown branch of the Museum of Contemporary Art, and the Children's Museum are also here. Visitors with business in the city center would be wise to stay downtown. This is also the best area for those attending meetings at the Convention Center. The **Gaslamp Quarter** is the center of a massive redevelopment kicked off in the mid-1980s with the opening of Horton Plaza; now, the once-seedy area is filled with trendy boutiques, restaurants, and nightspots. **Little Italy,** a small neighborhood along India Street between Cedar and Fir at the northern edge of downtown, is the best place to find gelato, espresso, pizza, and pasta.

Hillcreset/Uptown   At the turn of the century, the neighborhoods north of downtown were home to San Diego's white-collar elite (hence such sobriquets as Bankers Hill and Pill Hill, named for the area's many doctors). Hillcrest was the city's first self-contained suburb in the 1920s. Despite the cachet of being next to Balboa Park (home of the San Diego Zoo and numerous museums, including the Museum of Art, the Museum of Photographic Arts, and the Reuben H. Fleet Science Center) the area fell into neglect in the '60s and '70s. However, as the turn of the century looms once more, legions of preservation-minded residents—including an active and fashionable gay community—have restored Hillcrest's charms. I'd say Hillcrest is the local equivalent of L.A.'s West Hollywood or New York's SoHo. Centrally located and packed with the latest in stylish restaurants and avant-garde boutiques, Hillcrest also offers less expensive and more personalized accommodations than any other area in the city. Other uptown neighborhoods of interest are **North Park** and **Kensington.**

Old Town & Mission Valley   This area encompasses the Old Town State Historic Park, Presidio Park, Heritage Park, and numerous museums that recall the turn of the century and the city's beginnings. There's shopping and dining here, too—all aimed

Off the Beaten Path: Golden Hill

You don't think the trendy Gaslamp Quarter will be the last San Diego neighborhood to be rediscovered and gentrified, do you? If you like to explore, check out another old neighborhood that's quietly attracting history-minded fans . . . will it be the preservationists' next stop?

When the downtown we now call the Gaslamp Quarter was enjoying its turn-of-the-century heyday as the city's commercial center, the most convenient suburb was Golden Hill. Directly east of downtown, Golden Hill had the added advantage of being next to Balboa Park—it "wraps" around the southeast corner of the park. Homes here also enjoyed a sweeping view south to the bay, now mostly blocked by development. For a drive-by look at some oldies but goodies, visit Broadway, where finely preserved Victorians now serve as legal and medical offices; 28th Street along the park; and any other side street that catches your eye.

Some of the neighborhood's best Victorians and bungalows already show the caring touch of deep-pocketed architecture buffs, though plenty have fallen victim to the wrecking ball. Sandwiched between a natural *arroyo* (now the pathway of the 94 freeway) and vast Balboa Park, Golden Hill is an area where you're likely to see coyotes, opossums, and even red foxes trotting down quiet streets. You'll find (tie-) died-in-the-wool hippies, shacking up in unrestored shanties and hanging out at Santos Coffeehouse, whose Bohemian style is reminiscent of San Francisco's Haight-Ashbury.

Small stretches of retail interest lie at the intersection of Beech and 30th streets (Santos Coffeehouse, grassroots art galleries, and funky antique stores), and along 25th Street north of Broadway, home to several Mexican restaurants and the retro grill-your-own Turf Supper Club.

at tourists. Not far from Old Town lies the vast suburban sprawl of Mission Valley, home to San Diego's gigantic shopping centers. Between them is Hotel Circle, adjacent to I-8, where a string of moderately priced and budget hotels offer an alternative to the ritzier neighborhoods.

Mission Bay & the Beaches   Here's where they took the picture on the postcard you'll send home. Mission Bay is a watery playground perfect for water skiing, sailing, and windsurfing. The adjacent communities of Ocean Beach, Mission Beach, and Pacific Beach are known for their wide stretches of sand, active nightlife, and casual dining. Many San Diego singles live here, and once you've visited you'll understand why. The boardwalk, which runs from South Mission Beach through North Mission Beach to Pacific Beach, is a popular place for in-line skating, bike riding, and watching sunsets. This is the place to stay if you are traveling with beach-loving children or want to walk barefoot on the beach.

La Jolla   With an atmosphere that's a cross between Rodeo Drive and a Mediterranean village, this seaside community is home to an inordinate number of wealthy folks who could live anywhere. They choose La Jolla, surrounded by the beach, the University of California, San Diego, outstanding restaurants, pricey and traditional shops, and some of the world's best medical facilities. The wise tourist beds down here, taking advantage of the community's attributes without having to buy its high-priced real estate. The name is a compromise between Spanish and American Indian, as is the pronunciation (la-*hoy*-ya); it has come to mean "the jewel."

San Diego Neighborhoods

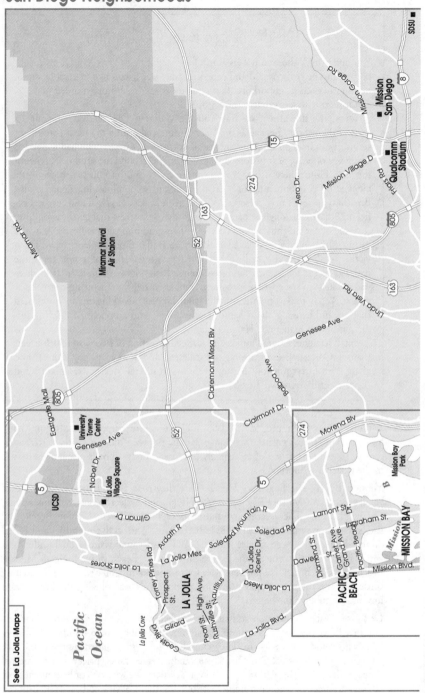

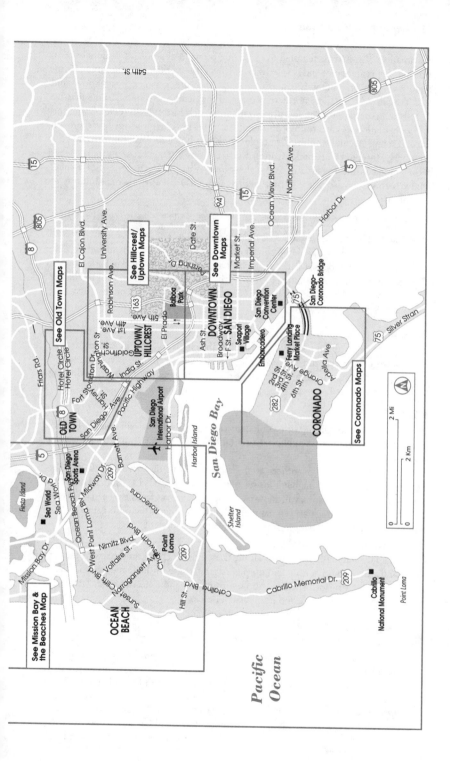

Pacific Ocean

San Diego Bay

See Mission Bay &
the Beaches Map

Fiesta Island

Mission Bay Dr

Sea World Dr

Sea World

San Diego
Sports Arena

Ocean Beach Fwy

West Point Loma Blvd

Midway Dr.

Nimitz Blvd.

Sunset Cliffs Blvd

Voltaire St.

Narragansett Ave.

Chatsworth Ave.

Rosecrans

Hill St.

Catalina Blvd.

OCEAN
BEACH

Point
Loma

Point Loma

Cabrillo Memorial Dr.

Cabrillo
National Monument

Shelter
Island

Barnett Ave.

Pacific Highway

Harbor Island

San Diego
International Airport

Harbor Dr.

San Diego – Ave.

Fort Stockton Dr.

Washington St.

India St.

Hancock St.

Friars Rd.

Hotel Circle

Hotel Circle

See Old Town Maps

OLD
TOWN

El Cajon Blvd.

University Ave.

Robinson Ave.

Goldfinch St.

Clifton St.

UPTOWN/
HILLCREST

See Hillcrest/
Uptown Maps

Balboa
Park

Pershing Dr.

Date St.

El Prado

1st Ave.

4th Ave.

5th Ave.

Ash St.

Broadway

F St.

Seaport
Village

Embarcadero

Ferry Landing
Market Place

DOWNTOWN
SAN DIEGO

See Downtown Maps

Market St.

Imperial Ave.

Ocean View Blvd.

National Ave.

San Diego
Convention Center

San Diego–
Coronado Bridge

Harbor Dr.

2rd St.

3rd St.

4th St.

6th St.

Orange Ave.

Adella Ave.

CORONADO

See Coronado Maps

Silver Stran

54th St.

0   2 Mi

0   2 Km

N

41

Coronado   You may be tempted to think of Coronado as an island. It does have an isolated, resort ambiance and is accessible only by ferry or bridge, but the city of Coronado is actually on a bulbous peninsula connected to the mainland by a narrow sand spit, the Silver Strand. The northern portion of the peninsula is home to the massive U.S. Naval Air Station. The southern sector has a rich history as an elite playground and a reputation as a charming community of suburbs. Quaint shops line the main street, Orange Avenue, and you'll find plenty of ritzy hotels and resorts, including the landmark **Hotel del Coronado.** Coronado has a lovely duned beach (one of the area's most popular), fine restaurants, and a downtown area that's reminiscent of a small Midwest town; it's also home to more retired admirals than any other community in the country.

2 Getting Around

San Diego has many walkable neighborhoods, from the historic downtown area, to Hillcrest and nearby Balboa Park, to the Embarcadero, to Mission Bay Park. You get there by car, bus, or trolley, and your feet do the rest. For inspiration, turn to chapter 8, "City Strolls." Always remember to cross the street at corners or in crosswalks; there's a $54 fine for jaywalking.

BY CAR
San Diegans complain of increasing traffic, but the city is still easy to navigate by car. Most downtown streets run one way, which may frustrate you until you learn your way around. Finding a parking space can be tricky, but some reasonably priced lots are fairly centrally located.

RENTALS
If you drive to San Diego with your own car, you'll want to rent one. While it's possible to get around by public transportation, having your own wheels is a big advantage.

   All the major firms have offices at the airport and in the larger hotels. See the Appendix in the back of the book for telephone numbers. **Avis** (☎ **800/331-1212**), like several other companies, will allow its cars into Mexico as far as Ensenada. Beyond Ensenada, the roads aren't as well maintained, and it's more difficult to get to the car should there be a breakdown or other problems (see chapter 11).

Saving Money on a Rental Car
Car rental rates vary even more than airline fares. Prices depend on the size of the car, where and when you pick it up and drop it off, the length of the rental period, where and how far you drive it, whether you buy insurance, and a host of other factors. A few key questions could save you hundreds of dollars.

Impressions

People in other places work hard to get somewhere, but in San Diego you're already there.
                    —Neil Morgan, associate editor, San Diego Union-Tribune

My first impulse was to get out in the street at high noon and shout four-letter words.
                    —Author Raymond Chandler, upon arriving
                    in the genteel village of La Jolla, circa 1949

- Are weekend rates lower than weekday rates? Ask if the rate is the same for pickup Friday morning, for instance, as it is for Thursday night. Reservations agents won't volunteer this information, so don't be shy about asking lots of questions.
- Does the agency assess a drop-off charge if you don't return the car to the same location where you picked it up?
- Are special promotional rates available? If you see an advertised price in your local newspaper, be sure to ask for that specific rate; otherwise you may be charged the standard cost. Terms change constantly.
- Are discounts available for members of AARP, AAA, frequent-flyer programs, or trade unions? If you belong to any of these organizations, you may be entitled to discounts of up to 30%.
- How much tax will be added to the rental bill? Local tax? State use tax?
- How much does the rental company charge to refill your gas tank if you return with the tank less than full? Though most rental companies claim these prices are "competitive," fuel is almost always cheaper in town. Try to allow enough time to refuel the car yourself before returning it.

Some companies offer "refueling packages," in which you pay for an entire tank of gas up front. The cost is usually fairly competitive with local prices, but you don't get credit for any gas remaining in the tank. If a stop at a gas station on the way to the airport will make you miss your plane, then by all means take advantage of the fuel-purchase option. Otherwise, skip it.

Kemwel Holiday Auto (KHA; ☎ 800/678-0678), a rental-car wholesaler, will search for the lowest price offered by the major agencies.

Demystifying Renter's Insurance

Before you drive off in a rental car, be sure you're insured. Hasty assumptions about your personal auto insurance or a rental agency's additional coverage could end up costing you tens of thousands of dollars, even if you are involved in an accident that was clearly the fault of another driver.

If you already hold a **private auto insurance** policy, you are most likely covered in the United States for loss of or damage to a rental car, and liability in case of injury to any other party involved in an accident. Be sure to find out whether you are covered in the area you are visiting, whether your policy extends to everyone who will be driving the car, how much liability is covered in case an outside party is injured in an accident, and whether the type of vehicle you are renting is included under your contract. (Rental trucks, sport-utility vehicles, and luxury vehicles or sports cars may not be covered.)

Most **major credit cards** (especially gold and platinum cards) provide some degree of coverage as well, provided they're used to pay for the rental. Terms vary widely, however, so be sure to call your credit card company directly before you rent.

If you are **uninsured,** your credit card will probably provide primary coverage as long as you decline the rental agency's insurance and as long as you rent with that card. This means that the credit card will cover damage or theft of a rental car for the full cost of the vehicle. (In a few states, however, theft is not covered; ask specifically about state law where you will be renting and driving.) If you already have insurance, your credit card will provide secondary coverage, which basically covers your deductible.

Note: Though they may cover damage to your rental car, *credit cards will not cover liability,* or the cost of injury to an outside party, damage to an outside party's vehicle, or both. If you do not hold an insurance policy, you may seriously want to consider purchasing additional liability insurance from your rental company, even if you decline collision coverage. Be sure to check the terms, however. Some rental agencies cover liability only if the renter is not at fault; even then, the rental company's obligation varies from state to state.

The basic insurance coverage offered by most car rental companies, known as the **Loss/Damage Waiver (LDW)** or **Collision Damage Waiver (CDW),** can cost as much as $20 a day. It usually covers the full value of the vehicle with no deductible if an outside party causes an accident or other damage to the rental car. In all states but California, you will probably be covered in case of theft as well. Liability coverage varies according to the company policy and state law, but the minimum is usually at least $15,000. If you are at fault in an accident, you will be covered for the full replacement value of the car, but not for liability. Some states allow you to buy additional liability coverage for such cases. Most rental companies will require a police report to process any claims you file, but your private insurer will not be notified of the accident.

Package Deals
Many packages are available that include airfare, accommodations, and a rental car with unlimited mileage. Compare these prices with the cost of booking airline tickets and renting a car separately to see if these offers are good deals.

PARKING
The **garage at Horton Plaza,** at G Street and Fourth Avenue, is free to shoppers for the first 3 hours. (The parking ticket must be validated by a merchant, or you must show your cinema or theater stub from Horton Plaza.) After the first 3 hours, it's $1 per half hour. A quick way to zip into Horton Plaza and avoid the ever-upward spiral is to enter the back way, off Third Avenue. The fenced-in lot adjacent to the Embarcadero, **Allright Parking,** 900 Broadway, at Harbor Drive (☎ **619/298-6944**), charges $3 to park between 5:30am and midnight. More convenient to downtown shopping and the Children's Museum is the open-air **lot on Market Street** between Front and First streets, where you can park all day on weekdays for $3, and weekends for $2.

Parking meters are plentiful in most areas: downtown and the Gaslamp Quarter, Hillcrest, and the beach communities. Posted signs indicate operating hours—generally 8am to 6pm, even on weekends. Be prepared with several dollars in quarters—most meters take no other coin, and 25¢ rarely buys more than 15 minutes, even on a 2-hour meter. Most unmetered areas have signs restricting street parking to 1 or 2 hours; count on vigilant chalking and ticketing during the regulated hours. Three-hour meters line Harbor Drive opposite the ticket offices for harbor tours; even on weekends, you have to feed them.

DRIVING RULES
California has a seatbelt law for both drivers and passengers, so buckle up before you venture out. You may turn right at a red light after stopping unless a sign says otherwise. Likewise, you can turn left on a red light from a one-way street onto another one-way street after coming to a full stop. Keep in mind when driving in San Diego that pedestrians have the right of way at all times, so stop for pedestrians who have stepped off the curb.

BY PUBLIC TRANSPORTATION
BY BUS
San Diego has an adequate bus system that will get you to where you're going—eventually. Most drivers are friendly and helpful. The system encompasses more than 100 routes in the greater San Diego area. The **Transit Store,** 102 Broadway, at First

Money-Saving Tip

The **Day Tripper pass** allows unlimited rides on MTS (bus) and trolley routes. Passes are good for 1, 2, 3, and 4 consecutive days, and cost $5, $8, $10, and $12, respectively. Day Trippers are for sale at the Transit Store and all Trolley Station automatic ticket vending machines.

Avenue (☎ **619/233-3004;** TTY/TDD ☎ 619/234-5005), dispenses passes, tokens, timetables, maps, brochures, and lost-and-found information. It issues ID cards for seniors 60 and older, and for travelers with disabilities, all of whom pay 75¢ per ride. Request a copy of the useful brochure *Your Open Door to San Diego,* which details the city's most popular tourist attractions and the buses that will take you to them. You may also call the number above and say where you are and where you want to go; the Transit Store staff will tell you the nearest bus stop and what time the next couple of buses will pass by. The office is open Monday through Friday from 8:30am to 5:30pm, Saturday and Sunday noon to 4pm. If you know your route and just need schedule information, call ☎ **619/685-4900** from any touch-tone phone. You can call between 5:30am and 8:30pm daily except Thanksgiving and Christmas. The line is often busy; the best times to call are from noon to 3pm and on weekends.

Bus stops are marked by rectangular blue signs every other block or so on local routes, farther apart on express routes. More than 20 bus routes pass through the downtown area. Most **bus fares** range from $1.75 to $2.25, depending on distance and type of service (local or express). Buses accept dollar bills, but the driver can't give change.

You can request a free transfer as long as you continue on a bus or trolley with an equal or lower fare (if it's higher, you pay the difference). Transfers must be used within 2 hours, and you can return to where you started.

Some of the most popular tourist attractions served by bus and rail routes are Balboa Park (Routes 1, 3, 7, 7A, 7B, and 25); the San Diego Zoo (Routes 7, 7A, and 7B); the Children's Museum, Convention Center, and Gaslamp Quarter (San Diego Trolley Orange Line); Coronado (Route 901); Horton Plaza (most downtown bus routes and the San Diego Trolley's Blue and Orange Lines); Old Town (San Diego Trolley's Blue Line); Cabrillo National Monument (Route 26 from Old Town Transit Center); Seaport Village (Route 7 and the San Diego Trolley's Orange Line); Sea World (Route 9 from the Old Town Transit Center); Qualcomm Stadium (San Diego Trolley Blue Line); and Tijuana (San Diego Trolley Blue Line to San Ysidro).

The Coronado Shuttle, bus Route 904, runs between the Coronado Island Marriott Hotel and the Old Ferry Landing and then continues along Orange Avenue to the Hotel del Coronado, Glorietta Bay, Loews, and back again. It costs 50¢ per person. Route 901 goes all the way to Coronado from San Diego and costs $1.75 for adults and 75¢ for seniors and children. Call ☎ **619/233-3004** for more information about this and other bus routes.

When planning your route, note that schedules vary and most buses do not run all night. Some stop at 6pm, while other lines continue to 9pm, midnight, and 2am— ask your bus driver for more specific information. On Saturdays some routes run all night.

BY TROLLEY

The San Diego Trolley routes serve downtown, the Mexican border (a 40-minute trip from downtown), Old Town, and the city of Santee, to the east. The recently completed Mission Valley extension carries sports fans to Qualcomm Stadium, major

San Diego Trolley System

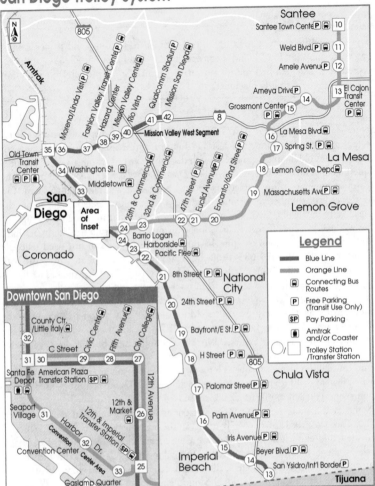

hotels, and shopping centers. Downtown, trolleys run along C Street (one block north of Broadway) and stop at Broadway and Kettner (America Plaza), Third Avenue (Civic Center), Fifth Avenue, and 12th Avenue (City College). Trolleys also circle around downtown's Bayside (parallel to Harbor Drive), with stops serving the Gaslamp Quarter, the Convention Center, Seaport Village, and the Santa Fe Depot.

Trolleys operate on a self-service fare-collection system; riders buy tickets from machines in stations before boarding. The machines list fares for each destination and dispense change. Tickets are valid for 3 hours from the time of purchase, in any direction. Fare inspectors board trains at random to check tickets. The bright-red trains run every 15 minutes during the day (every 10 minutes on the Blue Line, between Old Town and the border, during weekday rush hours) and every 30 minutes at night. Trolleys stop at each station for only 30 seconds. To open the door for boarding, push the lighted green button; to open the door to exit the trolley, push the lighted white button.

Trolley travel within the downtown area costs $1; the fare to the Mexican border from downtown is $2. Children under 5 ride free; seniors and riders with disabilities pay 75¢. For recorded transit information, call ☎ **619/685-4900.** To speak with a customer service representative, call ☎ **619/233-3004** (TTY/TDD 619/234-5005) daily from 5:30am to 8:30pm. The trolley generally operates daily from 5am to about 12:30am; the Blue Line, which goes to the border, runs 24 hours on Saturday.

Privately owned **Old Town Trolley Tours** (☎ **619/298-TOUR**) offers an alternative way to tour the city by trolley. If you'd like to hit the tourist high points in a short visit, without having to drive, it is a worthwhile option. The narrated tours cover a 30-mile route, including the highlights of areas such as Old Town, Downtown, Coronado, and Balboa Park. You can board and reboard the trolley at over a dozen stops every half hour. The fare is $24 for adults, $12 children 4 to 12, free for children under 4 (who must sit on an adult's lap).

BY TAXI

Half a dozen taxi companies serve the San Diego area. They do not charge standard rates, except from the airport into downtown, which costs about $8.50 with tip. Taxis don't cruise the streets as they do in other cities, so you have to call ahead for quick pickup. If you are at a hotel or restaurant, the front-desk attendant or maître d' will call for you. Among the local companies are **Orange Cab** (☎ **619/291-3333**), **San Diego Cab** (☎ **619/226-TAXI**), and **Yellow Cab** (☎ **619/234-6161**). The **Coronado Cab Company** (☎ **619/435-6211**) serves Coronado. In La Jolla, use **La Jolla Cab** (☎ **858/453-4222**).

BY TRAIN

San Diego's express rail commuter service, the **Coaster,** travels between the downtown Santa Fe Depot station and the Oceanside Transit Center, with stops at Old Town, Sorrento Valley, Solana Beach, Encinitas, and Carlsbad. Fares range from $2.75 to $3.50 each way, depending on how far you go. Eligible seniors and riders with disabilities pay half price. The trip between Oceanside and downtown San Diego takes just under an hour. Trains run Monday through Saturday; call ☎ **800/COASTER** for the current schedule.

Amtrak (☎ **800/USA-RAIL**) trains run daily between San Diego and Los Angeles. Trains to L.A. depart from the Santa Fe Depot and stop at Solana Beach and Oceanside. Some trains stop at San Juan Capistrano. A round-trip ticket to Solana Beach is $10, to Oceanside $15, to San Juan Capistrano $24, and to Los Angeles $40. The train also serves Disneyland (Anaheim); see chapter 11.

BY FERRY, WATER TAXI, OR BOAT

BY FERRY   There's regularly scheduled ferry service between San Diego and Coronado (☎ **619/234-4111** for information). Ferries leave from the Broadway Pier on the hour from 9am to 9pm Sunday through Thursday and from 9am to 10pm Friday and Saturday. They return from the Old Ferry Landing in Coronado to the Broadway Pier every hour on the 42-minute mark from 9:42am to 9:42pm Sunday through Thursday and from 9:42am to 10:42pm Friday and Saturday. The ride takes 15 minutes. Ferries also run from the Fifth Avenue Landing near the Convention Center to the Old Ferry Landing every hour on the half hour from 9:30am to 9:30pm Sunday through Thursday and from 9:30am to 10:30pm Friday and Saturday. The trip from Coronado to the Fifth Avenue Landing is every hour at the 18-minute mark from 9:18am to 9:18pm Sunday through Thursday and from 9:18am to 10:18pm Friday and Saturday. The fare is $2 for each leg of the journey (50¢ extra if you bring your bike). You can buy tickets in advance at the Harbor Excursion kiosk on Broadway Pier, the Fifth Avenue Landing in San Diego, or the Old Ferry Landing in Coronado.

BY WATER TAXI   Water taxis (☎ **619/235-TAXI**) will take you around most of San Diego Bay for $5. If you want to go to the southern part of the bay (to Loews Coronado Bay Resort, for example), the flat fee is $25.

You can call a taxi to pick you up from any landing in the bay, or go to the Harbor Excursion Dock at the foot of Broadway Pier, where taxis wait for passengers.

BY BOAT   Boat tours provide a great way to explore San Diego from one of its many bays, including Mission Bay and San Diego Bay. **Bahia Belle** (☎ **619/539-7779**), **Hornblower Invader Cruises** (☎ **619/234-8687**), and **San Diego Harbor Excursions** (☎ **619/234-4111**) offer narrated cruises of the local bays and drop off and pick up passengers at hotels along the way. Mission Bay cruises cost $6 per person; San Diego Harbor cruises run $12 for a 1-hour trip, $17 for 2 hours, and half-price for children.

BY BICYCLE

San Diego is flat enough for easy exploration by bicycle, and many roads have designated bike lanes. The San Diego Ridelink publishes a comprehensive map of the county detailing bike *paths* (separate rights-of-way for bicyclists), bike *lanes* (alongside motor vehicle ways), and bike *routes* (shared ways designated only by bike-symbol signs). The **San Diego Region Bike Map** is available at visitor centers; to receive a copy in advance, call ☎ **619/231-BIKE.**

Bikes are available for rent in most areas; see "Biking" in chapter 7 for suggestions. If you want to take your two-wheeler on a city bus, look for bike-route signs at the bus stop. The signs mean that the buses that stop here have bike racks. Let the driver know you want to stow your bike on the back of the bus, then board and pay the regular fare. With this service, you can bus the bike to an area you'd like to explore, do your biking there, then return by bus. Not all routes are served by buses with bike racks; call ☎ **619/233-3004** for information.

The San Diego Trolley has a **Bike-N-Ride** program that lets you bring your bike on the trolley for free. You'll need a bike permit before you board. Permits for bikers 16 and older cost $4 and are issued through the **Transit Store,** 102 Broadway, at First Avenue (☎ **619/234-1060**). Bikers must board at the back of the trolley car, where the bike-storage area is located; cars carry two bikes except during weekday rush hours, when the limit is one bike per car. Several trolley stops connect with routes for buses with bike racks. For more information, call the **Transit Information Line** (☎ **619/233-3004**).

Bikes are permitted on the ferry connecting San Diego and Coronado, which has 15 miles of dedicated bike paths.

Fast Facts: San Diego

Airport   See "Getting There," in chapter 2.

American Express   A full-service office is downtown at 258 Broadway (☎ **619/234-4455**).

Area Codes   Dial ☎ **619** to call most of San Diego, except for La Jolla, Del Mar, Rancho Sante Fe, and Rancho Bernardo, which received the new area code **858** during 1999. Use **760** to reach the remainder of San Diego County, including Encinitas, Carlsbad, Oceanside, Escondido, Ramona, Julian, and Anza–Borrego. Toward the end of 2000, the 619 area code will split further, with Coronado and the southern portion of San Diego County getting a new area code—**935**. Don't worry, though; this change doesn't go into effect until

December 8, 2000, and the rest of the city of San Diego will remain in the 619 area code.

Baby-sitters   A number of hotels will secure a bonded sitter for guests, or you can call **Marion's Child** (☎ 619/582-5029), whose sitters are bonded.

Business Hours   Banks are open weekdays from 9am to 4pm or later, and sometimes Saturday morning. Shops in shopping malls tend to stay open until about 9pm weekdays and until 6pm weekends.

Camera Repair   Both **George's Camera & Video,** 3827 30th St. (☎ 619/297-3544), and **Professional Photographic Repair,** 7910 Raytheon Rd. (☎ 619/277-3700), provide cameras and repair services. In La Jolla, try **Bob Davis' Camera Shop,** 7720 Fay St. (☎ 619/459-7355). Other good choices are **Nelson Photo Supply,** 1909 India St., at Fir Street (☎ 619/234-6621; fax 619/232-6153) and **Point Loma Camera Store,** 1310 Rosecrans St. (☎ 619/224-2719).

Car Rentals   See "Getting Around," earlier in this chapter.

Climate   See "When to Go," in chapter 2.

Dentists   For dental referrals, contact the San Diego County Dental Society at ☎ 800/201-0244, or call 800/DENTIST.

Doctors   Hotel Docs (☎ 800/468-3537 or 619/275-2663) is a 24-hour network of physicians, dentists, and chiropractors who claim they'll come to your hotel room within 35 minutes of your call. They accept credit cards, and their services are covered by most insurance policies. In a life-threatening situation, dial ☎ 911.

Driving Rules   See "Getting Around," earlier in this chapter.

Drugstores   See "Pharmacies," below.

Embassies & Consulates   See chapter 3, "For Foreign Visitors."

Emergencies   Call ☎ 911 for fire, police, and ambulance. The main police station is at 1401 Broadway, at 14th Street (☎ 619/531-2065 or 619/531-2000 for the hearing impaired).

Eyeglass Repair   Optometric Expressions, 55 Horton Plaza (☎ 619/544-9000), is at street level near the Westin Hotel; it's open Monday, Wednesday, and Friday from 8am to 6pm and Tuesday, Thursday, and Saturday from 9:30am to 6pm. **Optometry on the Plaza,** 287 Horton Plaza (☎ 619/239-1716), is open daily from 10am to 6pm (later during the summer). Both can fill eyeglass prescriptions, repair glasses, and replace contact lenses.

Hospitals   In Hillcrest, near downtown San Diego, **UCSD Medical Center–Hillcrest,** 200 W. Arbor Dr. (☎ 619/543-6400), has the most convenient emergency room. In La Jolla, **Thornton Hospital,** 9300 Campus Point Dr. (☎ 858/657-7600), has a good emergency room, and you'll find another in Coronado, at **Coronado Hospital,** 250 Prospect Place, opposite the Marriott Resort (☎ 619/435-6251).

Hot Lines   HIV Hot Line: ☎ 800/922-2437 (English) or 800/922-7432 (multilingual). Alcoholics Anonymous: ☎ 619/265-8762. Debtors Anonymous: ☎ 619/525-3065. Mental Health Crisis Line: ☎ 619/236-3339. Overeaters Anonymous: ☎ 619/563-4606. Traveler's Aid Society: ☎ 619/231-7361.

Information   See "Visitor Information," earlier in this chapter. For telephone directory assistance, dial ☎ 411.

Liquor Laws   The drinking age in California is 21. Beer, wine, and hard liquor are sold daily from 6am to 2am and are available in grocery stores.

Maps   See "City Layout," earlier in this chapter.

Newspapers/Magazines   The *San Diego Union-Tribune* is published daily, and its informative entertainment section, "Night & Day," is in the Thursday edition. The free alternative *Reader,* published weekly (on Thursday), is available at many shops, restaurants, theaters, and public hot spots; it's the best source for up-to-the-minute club and show listings. *San Diego* magazine is filled with entertainment and dining listings for an elite audience (that explains all the ads for face-lifts and tummy tucks). *San Diego Home-Garden Lifestyles* magazine highlights the city's homes and gardens, and includes a monthly calendar of events and some savvy articles about the restaurant scene. Both magazines are published monthly and sold at newsstands.

Pharmacies   Long's, Rite-Aid, and Sav-On sell pharmaceuticals and nonprescription products. Look in the phone book to find the one nearest you. If you need a pharmacy after normal business hours, the following branches are open 24 hours: **Sav-On Drugs,** 8831 Villa La Jolla Dr., La Jolla (☎ 858/457-4390), and 3151 University Ave., North Park; **Rite-Aid,** 535 Robinson Ave., Hillcrest (☎ 619/291-3703); **Long's Drug Store,** 5685 Balboa Ave., Clairemont (☎ 619/279-2753). Local hospitals also sell prescription drugs.

Police   The downtown police station is at 1401 Broadway (☎ 619/531-2000). Call ☎ 911 in an emergency.

Post Office   The downtown branch of the post office, 815 E St., between Eighth and Ninth avenues, is open Monday through Friday from 8:30am to 5pm, Saturday from 8:30am to noon. The more centrally located branch at 51 Horton Plaza, beside the Westin Hotel, is open Monday through Friday from 8am to 6pm, Saturday 9am to 5pm. For post office information, call ☎ 800/275-8777. See also "Business Hours" and "Mail," under "Fast Facts: For the Foreign Traveler," in chapter 3.

Rest Rooms   Horton Plaza and Seaport Village downtown, Balboa Park, Old Town State Historic Park in Old Town, and the Ferry Landing Marketplace in Coronado all have well-marked public rest rooms. In general, you won't have a problem finding one.

Safety   For suggestions on personal safety and driving safety tips, see "Safety" in chapter 3.

Smoking   Smoking is prohibited in nearly all indoor public places, including theaters, hotel lobbies, and enclosed shopping malls. In 1998, California enacted legislation prohibiting smoking in all restaurants and bars, except those with outdoor seating. Opponents immediately began preparing to appeal the law, so things may have changed by the time you visit; be sure to inquire before you light up, or if you're determined to avoid those who do.

Taxes   Sales tax in restaurants and shops is 7.75%. Hotel tax is 10.5%.

Taxis   See "Getting Around," earlier in this chapter.

Television   The main stations in San Diego are 6 (Fox), 8 (CBS), 10 (ABC), 7 or 39 (NBC), and 15 (PBS). Independent stations include channels 51 and 69. Channels 12, 19, and 52 offer programming in Spanish. Many hotels have cable TV.

Time Zone   San Diego, like the rest of the West Coast, is in the Pacific standard time zone, which is 8 hours behind Greenwich mean time. Daylight saving time is observed. To check the time, call ☎ **619/853-1212.**

Transit Information   Call ☎ **619/233-3004** (TTY/TDD 619/234-5005). If you know your route and just need schedule information, call ☎ **619/685-4900.**

Useful Telephone Numbers   For the latest San Diego arts and entertainment information, call ☎ **619/238-0700;** for half-price day-of-performance tickets, call ☎ **619/497-5000;** for a beach and surf report, call ☎ **619/221-8884.**

Weather   Call ☎ **619/289-1212.**

5 Tips on Accommodations

Where would you prefer to sleep? Over the water? On the beach? In historic surroundings? Facing the bay? With ocean views? Whatever your fancy, San Diego offers a variety of places to stay that range from pricey high-rise hostelries to inexpensive low-rise motels and some out-of-the-ordinary B&Bs.

In this chapter, I'll take you through all the options. For a list of my favorites in all kinds of categories, see "Best Hotel Bets" in chapter 1.

A note on air-conditioning: Unless you have a particular sensitivity to even mild heat, A/C is more a convenience than a necessity. In San Diego's temperate climate, ocean breezes cool the air year-round.

TIPS FOR SAVING ON YOUR HOTEL ROOM

A hotel's rack rate is the official published rate—we list these prices to help readers make a fair comparison. The truth is, hardly anybody pays these prices, and you can nearly always do better.

- **Don't be afraid to bargain.** Get in the habit of asking for a lower price than the first one quoted. Most rack rates include commissions of 10% to 25% or more for travel agents, which many hotels will cut if you make your own reservations and haggle a bit. Always ask politely whether a less expensive room is available, or whether any special rates apply to you. You may qualify for corporate, student, military, senior citizen, or other discounts. Be sure to mention membership in AAA, AARP, frequent-flyer and traveler programs, or trade unions, which may entitle you to special deals as well.
- **Remember the law of supply and demand.** Coastal and resort hotels are most crowded and therefore most expensive on weekends, so discounts are often available for midweek stays. Downtown and business hotels are busiest during the week; expect discounts over the weekend. Avoid high-season stays whenever you can: Planning your vacation just a week before or after official peak season can mean big savings.
- **Rely on a qualified professional.** Certain hotels give travel agents discounts in exchange for steering business their way, so if you're shy about bargaining, an agent may be better equipped to negotiate discounts for you.
- **Dial direct.** When booking a room in a chain hotel, call the hotel's local line and the toll-free number, and see where you get the best deal. A hotel makes nothing on a room that stays empty. The clerk who runs the place is more likely to know about vacancies and will often grant deep discounts in order to fill up.

- **Look into group or long-stay discounts.** If you come as part of a large group, you should be able to negotiate a bargain, because the hotel can guarantee occupancy in a number of rooms. Likewise, when you're planning a long stay (usually 5 days to a week), you'll qualify for a discount. As a rule, you will receive one night free after a 7-night stay.
- **Avoid excess charges.** When you book a room, ask whether the hotel charges for parking. Most hotels have free spaces, but many urban or beachfront hotels don't. Also, find out before you dial whether your hotel imposes a surcharge on local or long-distance calls. A pay phone, however inconvenient, may save you money.
- **Consider a suite.** If you are traveling with your family or another couple, you can pack more people into a suite (which usually comes with a sofa bed), and reduce your per-person rate. Remember that some places charge for extra guests, some don't.
- **Book an efficiency.** A room with a kitchenette allows you to grocery shop and eat some meals in. Especially during long stays with families, you're bound to save money on food this way.
- **Investigate reservation services.** These outfits usually work as consolidators, buying up or reserving rooms in bulk, and then dealing them out to customers at a profit. They do garner deals that range from 10 to 50% off, but remember, the discounts apply to rack rates—inflated prices that people rarely end up paying. You're probably better off dealing directly with a hotel; but if you don't like bargaining, this is certainly a viable option. Most of them offer online reservation services as well. Here are a few of the more reputable providers.
- **San Diego Hotel Reservations** (☎ 800/SAVE-CASH; www.savecash.com); **California Reservations** (☎ 800/576-0003; www.cal-res.com); **Accommodations Express** (☎ 800/950-4685; www.accommodationsxpress.com); **Hotel Reservations Network** (☎ 800/96HOTEL; www.180096HOTEL.com); **Quikbook** (☎ 800/789-9887, includes fax-on-demand service; www.quikbook.com); and **Room Exchange** (☎ 800/846-7000 in the United States, 800/486-7000 in Canada).
- Online, try booking your hotel through **Arthur Frommer's Budget Travel** (www.frommers.com), and save up to 50% on the cost of your room. **Microsoft Expedia** (www.expedia.com) features a "Travel Agent" that will also direct you to affordable lodgings.

Note: Rates given in this chapter do not include hotel tax, which is an additional 10.5%. Also, you'll notice that some listings mention a free airport shuttle. This is common in San Diego hotels, so before you take a taxi from the airport, check to see what your hotel offers.

LANDING THE BEST ROOM

Somebody has to get the best room in the house. It might as well be you.

Always ask for a corner room. They're usually larger, quieter, and closer to the elevator. They often have more windows and light than standard rooms, and they don't always cost more.

When you make your reservation, ask if the hotel is renovating; if it is, request a room away from the renovation work. Many hotels now offer rooms for non-smokers; if smoke bothers you, by all means ask for one. Inquire, too, about the location of restaurants, bars, and discos in the hotel—these could all be sources of irritating noise. If you aren't happy with your room when you arrive, talk to the front desk staff. If they have another room, they should be happy to accommodate you, within reason.

For the Web site addresses of the hotel chains mentioned in this chapter, see the Appendix at the end of the book.

BED & BREAKFASTS

Travelers who seek bed-and-breakfast accommodations will be pleasantly surprised by the variety and affordability of San Diego B&Bs (especially compared to the rest of California). The trend was late in coming to San Diego, but new establishments are popping up all the time. Many are traditional, strongly reflecting the personality of an on-site innkeeper and offering as few as two guest rooms; others accommodate more guests in a slickly professional way. More than a dozen are part of the close-knit **San Diego Bed & Breakfast Guild** (☎ **619/523-1300**), whose members work actively at keeping prices reasonable; many outstanding B&Bs remain under $100 a night.

1 Downtown

Visitors with business in the city center—including the Convention Center—will find the downtown area convenient. Keep in mind that our "downtown" heading includes hotels in the stylish Gaslamp Quarter, as well as properties conveniently located near the harbor and other leisure attractions.

VERY EXPENSIVE

Embassy Suites. 601 Pacific Hwy. (at N. Harbor Dr.), San Diego, CA 92101. ☎ **800/ EMBASSY** or 619/239-2400. Fax 619/239-1520. 337 suites. A/C TV TEL. $189–$300 suite. Rates include full breakfast and afternoon cocktail. Children under 12 stay free in parents' room. AE, DC, DISC, MC, V. Valet parking $12; indoor self-parking $9. Bus: 7. Trolley: Seaport Village.

What might seem like an impersonal business hotel is actually one of the better deals in town. It provides modern accommodations with lots of room for families or claustrophobes. Built in 1988, this neoclassical high-rise is topped with a distinctive neon bulls-eye that's visible from far away. Every room is a suite, with sofa beds in the living/dining areas and convenient touches like microwaves, coffeemakers, refrigerators, and hair dryers. All rooms open onto a 12-story atrium filled with palm trees, koi ponds, and a bubbling fountain; each also has a city or bay view. One block from Seaport Village and five blocks from downtown, the Embassy Suites is the second choice of Convention Center groups (after the pricier Hyatt Regency) and can be fully booked at unexpected times because of that.

Dining/Diversions: Barnett's Grand Cafe, which serves continental cuisine, looks onto the atrium and offers patio seating. Winning Streak Sports and Games Bar serves lunch and dinner, and has a large video screen, sports memorabilia, and video interactive trivia.

Amenities: Indoor pool (open 7am to 11pm), airport pickup, laundry, in-room movies, sauna, weight room, Jacuzzi, sundeck, meeting rooms, gift shop.

✪ **Hyatt Regency San Diego.** 1 Market Place (at Harbor Dr.), San Diego, CA 92101. ☎ **800/ 233-1234** or 619/232-1234. Fax 619/239-5678. 875 units. A/C MINIBAR TV TEL. $245–$290 double; from $500 suite. Extra person $25. Children under 12 stay free in parents' room. Packages and weekend rates available. AE, CB, DC, DISC, MC, V. Valet parking $16; self-parking $12. Trolley: Seaport Village.

The 40-story Hyatt Regency is generally the first choice of business travelers and convention groups, so the rack rates can be deceptively high—but don't let them scare you off if you want to stay in downtown's best modern high-rise. Weekend rates in partic-

Downtown San Diego Accommodations

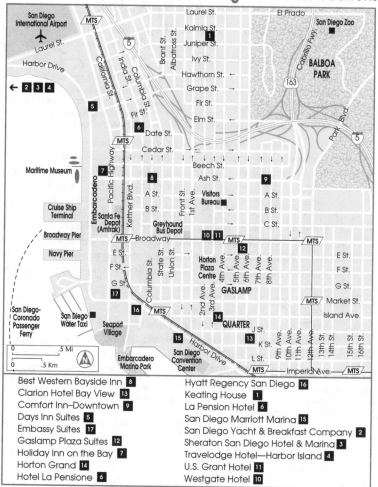

Best Western Bayside Inn **8**	Hyatt Regency San Diego **16**
Clarion Hotel Bay View **13**	Keating House **1**
Comfort Inn–Downtown **9**	La Pension Hotel **6**
Days Inn Suites **5**	San Diego Marriott Marina **15**
Embassy Suites **17**	San Diego Yacht & Breakfast Company **2**
Gaslamp Plaza Suites **12**	Sheraton San Diego Hotel & Marina **3**
Holiday Inn on the Bay **7**	Travelodge Hotel—Harbor Island **4**
Horton Grand **14**	U.S. Grant Hotel **11**
Hotel La Pensione **6**	Westgate Hotel **10**

ular can be a great deal.

While a behemoth with nearly 900 rooms can't offer very personalized service, you'll enjoy the amenities designed for those expense accounts. All the public spaces and guest rooms are light and airy, and boast stunning views over the city or sea. Built in 1992, the hotel (the tallest waterfront lodging on the West Coast) sports a limestone-and-marble neoclassical theme; guest rooms are quiet and furnished with high-quality but standard Hyatt-issue furnishings. (Trivia buffs: Did you know that virtually every Hyatt in the United States chooses from only *three* corporate-approved furniture styles?) Bathrooms have ample counter space and hair dryers. There's a club floor that provides upgraded service. More than 80% of the rooms are designated non-smoking, and the Hyatt gets kudos for superior service for travelers with disabilities (see "Best Hotel Bets," in chapter 1).

Dining: Sally's, a rather formal seafood restaurant, attracts locals as well as guests. There are two other less formal spots (all three offer alfresco dining) and two bars, including one with a spectacular 40-floor view.

Amenities: State-of-the-art health club and spa, third-story bay-view outdoor pool, whirlpool, concierge, 24-hour room service, six tennis courts, dry cleaning, laundry, shoeshine, newspaper delivery, in-room massage, baby-sitting, courtesy car, business center, car-rental desk, beauty salon, gift shop. Boat, water sports, and bicycle rentals.

San Diego Marriott Marina. 333 W. Harbor Dr. (at Front St.), San Diego, CA 92101-7700. ☎ **800/228-9290** or 619/234-1500. Fax 619/234-8678. 1,408 units. A/C MINIBAR TV TEL. $265–$300 double; from $500 suite. Children under 18 stay free in parents' room. Weekend rates, AARP discount, honeymoon and other packages available. Pets accepted. AE, CB, DC, DISC, MC, V. Valet parking $18; self-parking $13. Bus: 7. Trolley: Convention Center.

In the prosperous early '80s, long before San Diego's Convention Center was even a blueprint, this mirrored tower arose. Heck, with more than 1,400 rooms and multiple banquet and ballrooms, the Marriott *was* a convention center. Today it merely stands next door, garnering a large share of convention attendees. They're drawn by the scenic 446-slip marina, lush grounds, waterfall pool, and breathtaking bay-and-beyond views. The Marriott competes with the much newer Hyatt Regency, and guests benefit from constantly improved facilities and decor. Leisure travelers can also take advantage of greatly reduced weekend rates. Because the Marriott tends to focus on public features and business services, guest quarters are well maintained but plain, and standard rooms are on the small side. Hallway noise can sometimes be disturbing. Rooms have VCRs and in-room movies.

Dining: There are several restaurants, including the Yacht Club, a popular place for informal dining and dancing on the waterfront.

Amenities: Two lagoon-like outdoor pools, two whirlpools, fitness center, sauna, concierge, 24-hour room service, dry cleaning and laundry, newspaper delivery, six lighted tennis courts, bicycle and boat rentals, game room, business center with secretarial services, self-service laundry, car-rental desk, tour desk, hair salon, shops.

The Westgate Hotel. 1055 Second Ave. (between Broadway and C St.), San Diego, CA 92101. ☎ **800/221-3802** or 619/238-1818. Fax 619/557-3604. 223 units. A/C MINIBAR TV TEL. $184–$224 double; from $440 suite. Extra person $10. Children under 19 stay free in parents' room. Weekend rates and packages available. AE, DC, DISC, MC, V. Underground valet parking $10. Bus: 2. Trolley: Civic Center (C St. and Third Ave.).

It's hard not to compare the lavish Westgate with its equally elegant neighbor, the U.S. Grant. But whereas the latter came by its formality during an era when royal treatment was expected, the Westgate might be considered nouveau riche. It was built in 1970 by a wealthy financier whose wife toured Europe collecting the antiques that fill each guest room. Ultimately, the hotel became a money pit for C. Arnholt Smith, but not before it established a standard of luxury—including fruit baskets and deferential service—that today appeals mainly to European and Latin American travelers and dignitaries.

The lobby appears straight out of 18th-century France; it's a precise re-creation of a Versailles anteroom, featuring brocade upholstery, tapestries, luxurious Baccarat crystal chandeliers, and Persian rugs. If you're downtown for a night at the theater or symphony, the Westgate fills the bill, but casual tourists may find the formality a bit stifling.

Dining/Diversions: The Fontainebleau Room offers candlelight dining and bowing, white-gloved waiters; there's a more casual dining room, and a cocktail lounge with piano entertainment.

Amenities: Concierge; 24-hour room service; workout room; sundeck; business services; barbershop; gift shop; valet service; complimentary transportation to airport, downtown appointments, Sea World, and the zoo.

EXPENSIVE

Holiday Inn on the Bay. 1355 N. Harbor Dr. (at Ash St.), San Diego, CA 92101-3385. ☎ **800/ HOLIDAY** or 619/232-3861. Fax 619/232-4924. 580 units. A/C TV TEL. $139–$199 double; from $400 suite. Children under 18 stay free in parents' room. Packages and AARP and AAA discounts available. Pets accepted. AE, DC, MC, V. Parking $10. Bus: 22, 23, 992.

This high-rise is basic but well maintained, and located directly on the harbor near the Maritime Museum. It's only 1½ miles from the airport (you can watch planes landing and taking off), and two blocks from the train station and trolley. The rooms are decorated in California contemporary style; some offer harbor views and all have in-room movies. Bathrooms are generally small, but they have separate sinks with a lot of counter space.

Dining: The Elephant and Castle Restaurant, the San Diego branch of the world-famous Ruth's Chris Steakhouse, and Hazelwoods serve lunch and dinner. Elephant and Castle also serves breakfast.

Amenities: Outdoor heated pool, workout equipment, room service (6 to 11am and 5 to 11pm), baby-sitting, laundry, valet, self-service laundry.

Horton Grand. 311 Island Ave. (at Fourth Ave.), San Diego, CA 92101. ☎ **800/542-1886** or 619/544-1886. Fax 619/544-0058. www.hortongrand.com. 132 units. TV TEL. $139–$169 double; $209–$219 minisuite. Packages available. Children under 18 stay free in parents' room. Pets accepted; $50 fee. AE, DC, MC, V. Valet parking $10 overnight with unlimited in-out privileges. Bus: 1.

A cross between an elegant hotel and a charming inn, the Horton Grand combines two hotels that date from 1886—the Horton Grand and the Brooklyn Hotel (which for a time was the Kahle Saddlery Shop). Both were saved from demolition, moved to this spot, and connected by an airy atrium lobby filled with white wicker. The facade, with its graceful bay windows, is original.

Each room is unique and contains antiques and a gas fireplace (on a timer so you can fall asleep in front of it); even the bathrooms, complete with WC and pedestal sink, are genteel. Rooms overlook either the city or the fig tree–filled courtyard. Suites have a microwave, minibar, two TVs and telephones, a sofa bed, and a computer modem hookup. This is an old hotel, and sounds carry more than they might in a modern one; so if you're a light sleeper, request a room with no neighbors.

Dining/Diversions: Ida Bailey's restaurant, named for the well-loved madam whose establishment used to stand on this spot, serves breakfast, lunch, and dinner. It opens onto the hotel's courtyard, which is used for Sunday brunch on warm days. The Palace Bar serves afternoon tea Tuesday through Saturday from 2:30 to 5pm; there's live music Thursday through Saturday evenings and Sunday afternoons.

Amenities: Room service (7am to 10pm), access to nearby pool and weight room, concierge, dry cleaning, baby-sitting.

✪ **San Diego Yacht & Breakfast Company.** Marina Cortez, 1880 Harbor Island Dr., G-Dock, San Diego, CA 92101. ☎ **800/YACHT-DO** or 619/297-9484. Fax 619/295-9182. www.yachtdo.com. 12 vessels. TV TEL. May 15–Oct 15 and Dec 10–Jan 5 $135–$295 double; low season $115–$255 double. Extra person $25–$50. Discounts for multi-night stay. Rates include buffet breakfast at nearby Travelodge. AE, DISC, MC, V.

Here's an unusual opportunity to sleep on the water in your own power yacht, sailboat, or floating villa. You fall asleep to the gentle lapping of waves and awaken to the call of seagulls. The vessels are docked in a recreational marina on Harbor Island, near

Accommodations Farther Afield

If you're interested in staying in nearby Del Mar or Carlsbad—only 20 to 40 minutes from downtown San Diego—see "North County Beach Towns" in chapter 11, "Side Trips from San Diego."

---

the airport and close to downtown; for an additional charge you can even charter a private cruise aboard your "room" (power- and sailboats only).

The floating villas are 650 square feet and feel like modern condos. Each has one bedroom and 1½ bathrooms, and sleeps up to four. They have full kitchens, laundry facilities, comfortable furnishings, two TVs, a VCR, a stereo, and many other comforts. The well-kept power yachts have two staterooms, two heads, a full galley, VCR, stereo system, and TV. Serious sailors may prefer to sleep on a sailboat. They range in length from 25 to 45 feet and accommodate two to four people, but are best suited for one couple. Guests can use the pool at the marina. They receive a 20% discount at Harbor Island restaurants, and discounts on charter rates ($70 to $200 per hour) and on rentals of water toys (such as kayaks).

U.S. Grant Hotel. 326 Broadway (between Third and Fourth aves.), San Diego, CA 92101. ☎ **800/237-5029** or 619/232-3121. Fax 619/232-3626. 340 units. A/C MINIBAR TV TEL. $185–$205 double; from $255 suite. AAA, off-season, and weekend rates ($125–$185 double) available; off-season packages available. Children under 12 stay free in parents' room. Pets accepted. AE, CB, DC, MC, V. Parking $13. Bus: 2. Trolley: Civic Center (C St. and Third Ave.).

In 1910, Ulysses S. Grant, Jr. opened this stately hotel, now on the National Register of Historic Places, in honor of his father. Famous guests have included Albert Einstein, Charles Lindbergh, FDR, and JFK. Resembling an Italianate palace, the hotel is of a style more often found on the East Coast. An elegant atmosphere prevails, with age-smoothed marble, wood paneling, crystal chandeliers, and formal room decor that verges on stuffy. Guest rooms are quite spacious, as are the richly outfitted bathrooms, and include comforts like terry robes, hair dryers, and in-room movies. Extras in the suites make them worth the splurge; each has a fireplace and whirlpool tub, and rates include continental breakfast and afternoon cocktails and hors d'oeuvres. While the hotel has preserved a nostalgic formality, the surrounding neighborhood has become a hodgepodge of chic bistros, wandering panhandlers, and the visually loud Horton Plaza shopping center (Planet Hollywood looms large right across the street).

Dining/Diversions: The prestigious Grant Grill resembles an exclusive private club. In fact, in 1969, eight determined female San Diegans defied the "gentlemen only" lunch restriction, and a plaque in the restaurant honors their successful effort. The Grill's lounge features live blues and jazz, usually Thursday through Saturday nights. Afternoon tea is served in the lobby Tuesday through Saturday with soft piano music as a backdrop.

Amenities: Concierge, 24-hour room service, 24-hour fitness center with panoramic view of downtown, in-room exercise bike and rowing-machine rentals, access to San Diego Athletic Club, same-day laundry and dry cleaning (except Sunday), turndown service, baby-sitting, courtesy shuttle to and from the airport and to downtown attractions, limousine service, business services.

MODERATE

Best Western Bayside Inn. 555 W. Ash St. (at Columbia St.), San Diego, CA 92101. ☎ **800/**

341-1818 or 619/233-7500. Fax 619/239-8060. 122 units. A/C TV TEL. $104–$204 double; $114–$214 harbor-view double. Children under 12 stay free in parents' room. Rates include continental breakfast. Packages and fall, winter, spring weekend rates available. AE, CB, DC, DISC, MC, V. Free covered parking. Trolley: C Street and Kettner.

Though noisy downtown is just outside, this high-rise representative of reliable Best Western offers quiet lodgings. The hotel has an accommodating staff, and stunning city and harbor views. A mecca for business travelers, it's also close to more touristy downtown sites: It's an easy walk to the Embarcadero ("Bayview" would be a more accurate name for the hotel than "Bayside"), a bit farther to Horton Plaza, four blocks to the trolley stop, and five blocks to the train station. Rooms and bathrooms are basic chain-hotel issue, but are well maintained and feature brand-new bedding, towels, and draperies; all have balconies overlooking the bay or downtown (ask for the higher floors).

The hotel's restaurant, the Bayside Bar and Grill, serves breakfast, lunch, and dinner; meals are also available from room service, and many good restaurants and bars are nearby. In-room movies and complimentary airport transportation are provided. You can relax by the outdoor pool or in the Jacuzzi.

Clarion Hotel Bay View San Diego. 660 K St. (at Sixth Ave.), San Diego, CA 92101. ☎ **800/766-0234** or 619/696-0234. Fax 619/231-8199. 312 units. A/C TV TEL. $109–$139 double; $149–$169 suite. Children under 18 stay free in parents' room. Extra person $10. AARP, AAA, and off-season discounts available. AE, DC, DISC, MC, V. Parking $8. Bus: 1. Trolley: Gaslamp/Convention Center.

This relatively new entry on the San Diego hotel scene provides an affordable alternative for those attending meetings at the Convention Center—it's almost as close as the Marriott and the Hyatt, but considerably less expensive. Its location near the Gaslamp Quarter makes it a good choice for those who plan to enjoy the nightlife, but until the Quarter's gentrification spreads a couple of blocks farther south, the Clarion will remain in an industrial and commercial no-man's-land. All units are spacious, bright, and modern, and more than half offer views of San Diego Bay and the Coronado Bridge. Rooms have sliding glass doors and coffeemakers, and many have minibars.

The carpeted rooftop sundeck offers a great view as well as a Jacuzzi, sauna, workout room, and video arcade. Just off the marble-floored lobby is the Gallery Cafe, which serves breakfast, lunch, and dinner daily. There's a big-screen TV in the bar, and "Joey & Maria's Comedy Italian Wedding" dinner theater is popular on Friday and Saturday nights. Amenities include a concierge, room service (6am to 10pm), dry cleaning and laundry, in-room movies, and coin-operated washers and dryers.

Gaslamp Plaza Suites. 520 E. St. (corner of 5th Ave.), San Diego, CA 92101. ☎ **800/874-8770** or 619/232-9500. Fax 619/238-9945. 55 units. A/C TV TEL. $93–$139 double; $139–$179 suite. Rates include continental breakfast. AE, CB, DC, DISC, MC, V. Valet parking $11. Bus: 1, 3, 25. Trolley: Fifth Ave.

You can't get closer to the center of the vibrant Gaslamp Quarter than this impeccably restored late Victorian. At 11 stories, it was San Diego's first "skyscraper" in 1913. Built (at great expense) of Australian gumwood, marble, brass, and exquisite etched glass, this splendid building originally housed San Diego Trust & Savings. Various other businesses (jewelers, lawyers, doctors, photographers) set up shop here until 1988, when the elegant structure was placed on the National Register of Historic Places and reopened as a boutique hotel.

You'll be surprised at the timeless elegance, from the dramatic lobby and wide corridors to guest rooms furnished with European flair. Each bears the name of a writer (Emerson, Swift, Zola, Shelley, Fitzgerald, and so on). The bathrooms are impressive, with fine marble and tile, and each room is equipped with microwave, dinnerware, refrigerator, and VCR. Most rooms are spacious. Beware of the few cheapest rooms, however; they are uncomfortably small (although they do have regular-size bathrooms).

Gaslamp Plaza Suites sits atop popular Dakota Grill (see chapter 6), and hotel guests have the use of the nearby Westin fitness center for a nominal fee. Do remember where you are, and expect to hear some traffic and street noise, even in your room.

INEXPENSIVE

Inexpensive motels line Pacific Highway between the airport and downtown. The **Days Inn Suites** ($49 to $69), 1919 Pacific Hwy. at Grape Street (☎ **800/325-2525** or 619/232-1077), is within walking distance of the Embarcadero, the Maritime Museum, and the Harbor Excursion.

Comfort Inn–Downtown. 719 Ash St. (at Seventh Ave.), San Diego, CA 92101. ☎ **800/228-5150** or 619/232-2525. Fax 619/687-3024. 67 units. A/C TV TEL. $79–$84 double. Extra person $5. Children under 18 stay free in parents' room. AARP and AAA discounts, weekly rates available. Rates include continental breakfast. AE, DISC, MC, V. Free parking.

In the northern corner of downtown, this terrific value is popular with business travelers *without* expense accounts and vacationers who just need reliable, safe accommodations. The hotel is surprisingly quiet, partly because the landmark El Cortez Hotel across the street is closed while developers gather funds to transform it into upscale condos and shops. (Oddly enough, even boarded up, its distinctive profile is pleasant to gaze upon.) The Comfort Inn is smartly designed so rooms open onto exterior walkways surrounding the drive-in entry courtyard, lending an insular feel in this less-than-scenic corner of town. There are few frills here, but coffee is always brewing in the lobby, and there's also a Jacuzzi. The hotel operates a free shuttle to the airport and the train and bus stations.

✪ **Keating House.** 2331 Second Ave. (between Juniper and Kalmia sts.), San Diego, CA 92101. ☎ **800/995-8644** or 619/239-8585. Fax 619/239-5774. www.caliburnus.com/keating. 8 units, 3 with bathroom. $65–$95 double. Rates include full breakfast. AE, DISC, MC, V. Bus: 11. From the airport, take Harbor Dr. toward downtown; turn left on Laurel St., then right on Second Ave.

Keating House is a good choice if you'd like a B&B, because gracious owner Larry Vlassoff considers every detail for his guests' comfort. His grand Bankers Hill mansion, between downtown and stylish Hillcrest, has been meticulously restored. It contains splendid turn-of-the-century furnishings and appointments, and offers always-inventive breakfast treats, savvy restaurant recommendations, and a lovingly tended exotic garden. The downstairs entry, parlor, and dining room all have cozy fireplaces, and two rooms (each with a private bathroom) are in the secluded carriage house. In contrast to many B&Bs in Victorian-era homes, this one eschews dollhouse frills for a classy, sophisticated approach.

✪ **La Pensione Hotel.** 606 W. Date St. (at India St.), San Diego, CA 92101. ☎ **800/232-4683** or 619/236-8000. Fax 619/236-8088. www.lapensionehotel.com. 80 units. TV TEL. $60–$80 double. Packages available. AE, DC, DISC, MC, V. Limited free underground parking. Bus: 5. Trolley: County Center/Little Italy.

This place has a lot going for it: modern amenities, remarkable value, a convenient location within walking distance of the central business district, a friendly staff, and parking (a premium for small hotels in San Diego). The three-story La Pensione is built around a courtyard and feels like a small European hotel; in fact, it's the number one choice of foreign students attending the downtown Language Institute. The decor throughout is modern and streamlined, with plenty of sleek black and metallic surfaces, crisp white walls, and minimal furniture. Guest rooms, while not overly large, make the most of their space and leave you with room to move around. Each room offers a tub-shower combination, ceiling fan, microwave, and small refrigerator; try for a bay or city view rather than the concrete courtyard view. La Pensione is in San Diego's Little Italy and within walking distance of eateries (mostly Italian) and nightspots; there are two restaurants attached to the hotel.

2 Hillcrest/Uptown

Although they're certainly no longer a secret, the gentrified historic neighborhoods north of downtown are still something of a bargain. They're convenient to Balboa Park, with easy access to the rest of town. Filled with chic casual restaurants, eclectic shops, movie theaters, and sizzling nightlife, the area is also easy to navigate.

MODERATE

Balboa Park Inn. 3402 Park Blvd. (at Upas St.), San Diego, CA 92103. ☎ **800/938-8181** or 619/298-0823. Fax 619/294-8070. www.balboaparkinn.com. 26 units. TV TEL. $80–$95 double; $95–$135 suite; $125–$200 specialty suite. Children under 11 stay free in parents' room. Extra person $8. Rates include continental breakfast. AE, CB, DC, DISC, MC, V. Parking available on street. From I-5, take Washington St. east, follow signs to University Ave. E. Turn right at Park Blvd. Bus: 7, 7A/B.

Insiders looking for unusual, well-located accommodations head straight for this small pink inn at the northern edge of Balboa Park. It's a cluster of four Spanish Colonial–style former apartment buildings in a mostly residential neighborhood close to the trendy Hillcrest area. The hotel caters to a straight clientele as well as gay travelers drawn to Hillcrest's hip restaurants and clubs. All the rooms and suites are tastefully decorated; the "specialty suites," however, are over-the-top. There's the "Tara Suite," as in *Gone With the Wind;* the "Nouveau Ritz," which employs every art deco cliché, including mirrors and Hollywood lighting; and the "Greystoke" suite, a jumble of jungle, safari, and tropical themes with a completely mirrored bathroom and whirlpool tub. All rooms come with refrigerators and coffeemakers, and there's newspaper delivery Monday through Saturday. You can walk to Balboa Park attractions.

✪ **Sommerset Suites Hotel.** 606 Washington St. (at Fifth Ave.), San Diego, CA 92103. ☎ **800/ 962-9665** or 619/692-5200. Fax 619/692-5299. www.sommerset.com. 80 units. A/C TV TEL. $135–$195 double. Children under 12 stay free in parents' room. Discounts available. Rates include continental breakfast and afternoon refreshments. AE, DC, DISC, MC, V. Free covered parking. Take Washington St. exit off I-5. Bus: 16 or 25.

This all-suite hotel on a busy street was originally built as apartment housing for interns at the hospital nearby. It retains a residential ambiance and unexpected amenities like huge closets, medicine cabinets, and fully equipped kitchens in all rooms (executive suites even have dishwashers). There are poolside barbecue facilities, and a coin-operated laundry. The hotel has a personal, welcoming feel, from the friendly, helpful staff to the snacks, soda, beer, and wine served each afternoon. You'll even get a welcome basket with cookies and microwave popcorn. Rooms are comfortably furnished and have hair dryers, irons and ironing boards, and balconies. Be prepared for noise from the busy thoroughfare below, though. Several blocks of Hillcrest's chic restaurants and shops (plus a movie multiplex) are within easy walking distance. Guest services include a courtesy van to the airport, Sea World, the zoo, and other attractions within a 5-mile radius. *Note:* This hotel's rack rates are misleading; rooms can commonly be had for around $100.

INEXPENSIVE

The Cottage. 3829 Albatross St. (off Robinson Ave.), San Diego, CA 92103. ☎ **619/299-1564.** Fax 619/299-6213. 2 units. TV TEL. $65–$85 double; $85–$105 cottage. Extra person in cottage $10. Rates include continental breakfast. AE, DISC, MC, V.

Built in 1913, the two-room Cottage sits in a secret garden, a private hideaway tucked behind a homestead-style house, at the end of a residential cul-de-sac. There's an herb garden out front, birdbaths, and a flower-lined walkway. The cottage has king-size bed, a living room with a wood-burning stove and a queen-size sofa bed, and a charming kitchen with a coffeemaker. The guest room in the main house features a king-size bed. Both accommodations are filled with fresh flowers and antiques put to clever uses, and each has a private entrance. Owner Carol Emerick (she used to run an antique store—and it shows!) serves a scrumptious breakfast, complete with the morning paper. Guests are welcome to use the dining room and parlor in the main house, where they sometimes light a fire and rev up the 19th-century player piano. The Cottage is close to the cafes of Mission Hills and Hillcrest, and a short drive from Balboa Park.

Crone's Cobblestone Cottage Bed & Breakfast. 1302 Washington Place (2½ blocks west of Washington St. at Ingalls St.), San Diego, CA 92103. ☎ **619/295-4765.** 2 units. $85 double. Rates include continental breakfast. Minimum 2 nights. No credit cards; checks accepted. From I-5, take Washington St. exit east uphill. Make a U-turn at Goldfinch, then keep right at "Y" intersection onto Washington Place. Bus: 3.

After just one night at this magnificently restored Craftsman bungalow, you'll feel like an honored guest rather than a paying customer. Artist Joan Crone lives in the architectural award–winning addition to her 1913 home, which is a designated Historic Landmark. Guests have the run of the entire house, including a book-filled, wood-paneled den and antique-filled living room. Both cozy guest rooms have antique beds, goosedown pillows and comforters, and eclectic bedside reading. They share a full bathroom; the Eaton Room also has a private half-bath. Bookmaker and illustrator Crone lends a calm and literary aesthetic to the surroundings, aided by Sam, the cat, who peers in from his side of the house. The quiet, historic Mission Hills neighborhood, just blocks from Hillcrest and Old Town, is one of San Diego's best-kept secrets.

Park Manor Suites. 525 Spruce St. (between Fifth and Sixth aves.), San Diego, CA 92103. ☎ **800/874-2649** or 619/291-0999. Fax 619/291-8844. www.parkmanorsuites.com. 80 units. TV TEL. $69–$89 studio; $89–$129 1-bedroom suite; $139–$179 2-bedroom suite. Children under 12 stay free in parents' room. Extra person $15. Rates include continental breakfast. Weekly rates available. AE, DC, MC, V. Free parking. Bus: 1, 3, 25.

Popular with actors appearing at the Old Globe Theatre in neighboring Balboa Park, this eight-floor Italianate masterpiece was built as a full-service luxury hotel in 1926 on a prime corner overlooking the park. One of the original investors was the family of child actor Jackie Coogan. The Hollywood connection continued—the hotel became a popular stopping-off point for celebrities headed for Mexican vacations in the 1920s and '30s. Guest rooms are spacious and comfortable, featuring full kitchens, dining rooms, living rooms, and bedrooms with a separate dressing area. A few have glassed-in terraces; request one when you book. The overall feeling is that of a prewar East Coast apartment building, complete with steam heat and lavish moldings. Park Manor Suites does have its weaknesses: Bathrooms have mostly original fixtures and could use some renovation; and the rooftop banquet room, where a simple continental breakfast buffet is served, suffers from a bad '80s rehab with too many mirrors. But prices are quite reasonable for the trendy Hillcrest neighborhood; there's a restaurant on the ground floor, and laundry service is available.

Hillcrest/Uptown Accommodations

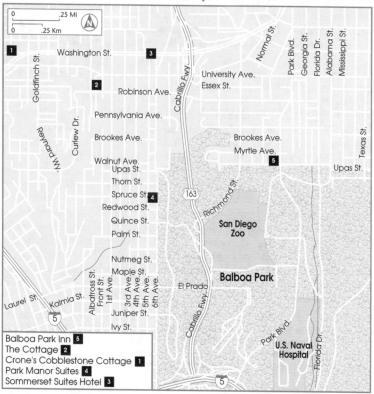

Balboa Park Inn **5**
The Cottage **2**
Crone's Cobblestone Cottage **1**
Park Manor Suites **4**
Sommerset Suites Hotel **3**

3 Old Town & Mission Valley

Old Town is a popular area for families because of its proximity to Old Town State Historic Park and other attractions that are within walking distance. **Hotel Circle,** on the way to Mission Valley, offers easy freeway access. Its many hotels cater to convention groups, sports fans heading to Qualcomm Stadium, families visiting the University of San Diego or San Diego State University, and leisure travelers drawn by the lower prices and competitive facilities.

MODERATE

Comfort Inn & Suites. 2485 Hotel Circle Place, San Diego, CA 92108. ☎ **800/647-1903** or 619/291-7700. Fax 619/297-6179. 200 units. A/C TV TEL. High season $89–$129 double. Extra person $10. Children under 18 stay free in parents' room. Rates include continental breakfast. Off-season discounts available. AE, CB, DC, DISC, MC, V. Free parking. From I-8, take Hotel Circle exit, follow signs for Hotel Circle north. Bus: 6.

This well-priced, modern, four-story motel at the western, or Old Town, end of Hotel Circle underwent a complete refurbishment in 1996. It enlarged rooms by doing away with balconies (many of which had opened onto the noisy freeway side anyway). Bathrooms are small but well equipped, and all have hair dryers. Rooms and suites are sparingly but adequately outfitted, with standard hotel-issue furnishings and coffeemakers. Suites are the way to go here; all have sleeper sofas in the living room, two TVs, a microwave, refrigerator, and separate vanity area. The heated outdoor pool and Jacuzzi adjoin the parking lot; there's a car-rental desk, game room, and washer and dryer. Stay away from the freeway side, and ask instead for a room looking toward the newly refurbished 18-hole public golf course across the street. The hotel doesn't have a restaurant, but offers room service at dinner from the steakhouse next door.

Hacienda Hotel. 4041 Harney St. (east of San Diego Ave.), San Diego, CA 92110. ☎ **800/ 888-1991** or 619/298-4707. Fax 619/298-4771. www.haciendahotel-oldtown.com. 170 units. A/C TV TEL. $135–$145 suite. Off-season discounts available. Children under 16 stay free in parents' room. AE, CB, DC, DISC, MC, V. Free underground parking. From I-5 take Old Town Ave. exit; turn left onto San Diego Ave. and right onto Harney St. Bus: 5, 5A.

Perched above Old Town, this Best Western all-suite hotel spreads over several levels. Walkways thread through courtyards with bubbling fountains, palm trees, and bougainvillea-trimmed balconies; but if you have trouble climbing stairs and hills, you'd be wise to stay elsewhere. Aside from that, the place is tops in its price range; every suite has rustic Mexican wood furniture, 20-foot ceilings, a refrigerator, microwave, coffeemaker, and VCR. The unremarkable Acapulco restaurant (yes, it's Mexican) atop the hotel serves breakfast, lunch, and dinner daily. Guests also have signing privileges next door at the Brigantine Restaurant and down the street at Cafe Pacifica (see "Old Town," in chapter 6). Amenities include a concierge (Monday through Friday), room service (6:30am to 2pm and 4 to 10pm), complimentary airport and train transportation, movie rentals with complimentary bag of microwave popcorn, heated outdoor pool and spa overlooking Old Town, fitness center, and coin-operated laundry.

Hanalei Hotel. 2270 Hotel Circle North, San Diego, CA 92108. ☎ **800/882-0858** or 619/297-1101. Fax 619/297-6049. www.hanaleihotel.com. 416 units. A/C MINIBAR TV TEL. $99–$160 double; $275–$375 suite. Extra person $10. Off-season, AARP, and AAA discounts and golf packages available. Pets accepted; $50 cleaning fee. AE, CB, DC, DISC, MC, V. Parking $6. From I-8, take Hotel Circle exit, follow signs for Hotel Circle N. Bus: 6.

My favorite hotel on Hotel Circle just emerged from a massive renovation and upgrade with its Polynesian theme splendidly intact. Its comfort-conscious sophistication sets it apart from the rest of the pack. Rooms are split between two high-rise towers, set far away from the freeway and cleverly positioned so that the balconies open onto the tropically landscaped pool courtyard or the luxurious links of a formerly private golf club on the Mission Valley floor. The heated outdoor pool is large enough for any luau, as is the oversized whirlpool beside it. The hotel boasts an unmistakable '60s vibe and Hawaiian ambiance—the restaurant and bar have over-the-top kitschy decor, with waterfalls, outrigger canoes, and more. But guest rooms sport contemporary furnishings and features like coffeemakers, hair dryers, irons, ironing boards, and in-room movies. Some have microwaves and refrigerators. There's an all-day casual coffee shop, plus a more expensive dinner-only restaurant. Services include free shuttle to Old Town and other attractions, laundry, and meeting facilities.

✪ Heritage Park Bed & Breakfast Inn. 2470 Heritage Park Row, San Diego, CA 92110. ☎ **800/995-2470** or 619/299-6832. Fax 619/299-9465. www.heritageparkinn.com. 12 units. $100–$235 double. Extra person $20. Rates include full breakfast and afternoon tea. AE, DC, DISC, MC, V. Free parking. Take I-5 to Old Town Ave., turn left onto San Diego Ave., then turn right onto Harney St.

This exquisite 1889 Queen Anne mansion is set in a "Victorian park"—an artfully arranged cobblestone cul-de-sac lined with historic buildings saved from the wrecking ball and assembled here, near Old Town, as a tourist attraction. Once inside, that unsettling "fishbowl" feeling subsides as you surrender to the pampering of afternoon tea, candlelight breakfast, and a number of romantic extras (champagne and chocolates, private in-room dinner) available for special celebrations. Like the gracious parlors and porches, each room is outfitted with meticulous period antiques and

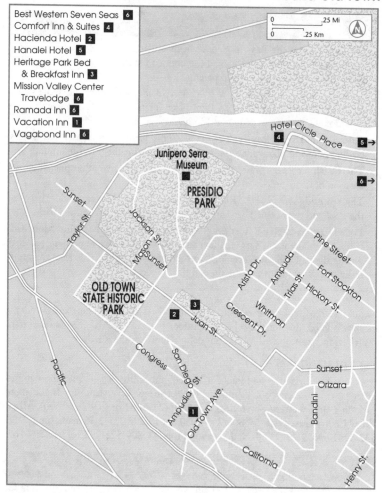

Best Western Seven Seas **6**
Comfort Inn & Suites **4**
Hacienda Hotel **2**
Hanalei Hotel **5**
Heritage Park Bed
  & Breakfast Inn **3**
Mission Valley Center
  Travelodge **6**
Ramada Inn **6**
Vacation Inn **1**
Vagabond Inn **6**

luxurious fabrics; the staff provides turn-down service. Although the fireplaces are all ornamental, some rooms have whirlpool baths. In the evenings, vintage films are shown in the Victorian parlor.

Vacation Inn. 3900 Old Town Ave., San Diego, CA 92110. ☎ **800/451-9846** or 619/ 299-7400. Fax 619/299-1619. 124 units. A/C TV TEL. June–Aug $110–$115 double; $130–$175 suite. Sept–May $84–$99 double; $114–$165 suite. Extra person $10. Children under 18 stay free in parents' room. Rates include continental breakfast and afternoon refreshments. AE, CB, DC, DISC, ER, MC, V. Free parking. Bus: 5, 5A.

Just a couple of easy walking blocks from the heart of Old Town, the Vacation Inn has a Colonial Spanish exterior that suits the neighborhood's theme. Inside you'll find better-than-they-have-to-be contemporary furnishings and surprising small touches that make this hotel an affordable option favored by business travelers and families alike. There's nothing scenic on the adjacent streets, so the hotel is smartly oriented toward the inside; request a room whose patio or balcony opens onto the pleasant courtyard. Rooms are thoughtfully and practically appointed, with coffeemakers, microwaves, refrigerators, and writing tables. The lobby, surrounded by French doors,

---

🛈 Family-Friendly Hotels

Holiday Inn on the Bay *(see p. 57)* Kids under 18 stay free, and so does the family pet. The hotel is well priced for strained family budgets, and even offers baby-sitting services for strained parents.

Catamaran Resort Hotel *(see p. 66)* Myriad sports facilities and a safe swimming beach make this resort an ideal place for families. Accommodations are comfortable, but not so posh that Mom and Dad need to worry.

Hilton San Diego Resort *(see p. 67)* This bay-front property has a kids' wading pool and playground, plus plenty of space for them to run around.

The Beach Cottages *(see p. 70)* Kids enjoy the informal atmosphere and the location near the beach.

The Sea Lodge *(see p. 73)* Right smack on the beach, kids can choose between the pool and the ocean. They can even eat in their swimsuits on the patio.

Loews Coronado Bay Resort *(see p. 80)* In the summer, the Commodore Kids Club, for children ages 4 to 12, provides supervised indoor and outdoor activities during the day and some evenings, too. Programs for older kids keep them out of harm's way without making them feel baby-sat.

---

features a large fireplace, several sitting areas, and a TV. Dry cleaning and laundry service are offered; the hotel also has an outdoor pool and Jacuzzi. The hotel entrance, on Jefferson Street, is hard to find but definitely worth the search.

INEXPENSIVE

Room rates at properties on Hotel Circle are significantly cheaper than those in many other parts of the city. You'll find a cluster of inexpensive chain hotels and motels, including **Best Western Seven Seas** (☎ **800/421-6662** or 619/291-1300), **Mission Valley Center Travelodge** (☎ **800/255-3050** or 619/297-2271), **Ramada Inn** (☎ **800/532-4241** or 619/291-6500), and **Vagabond Inn** (☎ **800/522-1555** or 619/297-1691).

4 Mission Bay & the Beaches

If you plan to enjoy the beach and aquatic activities, this part of town is the right spot. Some hotels are right on Mission Bay, San Diego's water playground; they're always good choices for families, especially those planning to visit Sea World. Ocean Beach, Mission Beach, and Pacific Beach provide a taste of the laid-back surfer lifestyle but can be unpredictable and raucous at times. Don't worry about missing out on the rest of San Diego; even though the beach communities are far removed in atmosphere, downtown is only a 10-minute drive.

VERY EXPENSIVE

Catamaran Resort Hotel. 3999 Mission Blvd. (4 blocks south of Grand Ave.), San Diego, CA 92109. ☎ **800/422-8386** or 619/488-1081; 800/233-8172 in Canada. Fax 619/488-1387. www.catamaranresort.com. 315 units. A/C TV TEL. $165–$225 double; from $265 suite; $190–$235 studio. Children under 18 stay free in parents' room. AE, CB, DC, DISC, MC, V. Valet parking $8; self-parking $6. Take Grand/Garnet exit off I-5 and go west on Grand Ave., then south on Mission Blvd. Bus: 34, 34A/B.

Ideally situated right on Mission Bay, the Catamaran has its own bay and ocean beaches, with water-sports facilities. Built in the 1950s, the hotel has been fully renovated to modern standards without losing its trademark Polynesian theme; the atrium lobby holds a 15-foot waterfall and full-size dugout canoe, and koi-filled lagoons meander through the property. After dark, torches blaze throughout the grounds, with numerous varieties of bamboo and palm sprouting; during the day, the resident tropical birds chirp away. Guest rooms—in a 13-story building or one of the six two-story buildings—have subdued South Pacific decor, and each has a balcony or patio. Tower rooms have commanding views of the bay, the San Diego skyline, La Jolla, and Point Loma. Studios and suites have kitchenettes, and every room has a coffeemaker, hair dryer, and movie channels. The Catamaran is within walking distance of Pacific Beach's restaurant and nightlife. It's also steps away from the bay's exceptional jogging and biking path, and you can rent bikes and jogging strollers at the hotel.

Dining/Diversions: The Atoll restaurant is an upscale hotel dining room, remarkable only for its romantic outdoor bayside seating. The large, lively Cannibal Bar hosts bands and videos. Moray's (named for the moray eels that inhabited its large aquarium until they became too aggressive) is an intimate piano bar.

Amenities: Outdoor heated pool, whirlpool spa, health club, concierge, room service (6:30am to 11pm), dry cleaning and laundry, nightly turn-down, baby-sitting, business center, lifeguard (summer only), supervised children's programs, car-rental desk, tour desk, gift shop.

Hilton San Diego Resort. 1775 E. Mission Bay Dr., San Diego, CA 92109. ☎ **800/ 445-8667,** 800/962-6307 in California and Arizona, or 619/276-4010. Fax 619/275-7991. 365 units. A/C MINIBAR TV TEL. Summer $205–$335 double; from $500 suite. Off-season $190–$285 double. Extra person $20. Children under 18 stay free in parents' room. Off-season discounts available. Pets under 25 lbs. accepted; $50 fee. AE, CB, DC, DISC, JCB, MC, V. Valet parking $10; free self-parking. Take I-5 to Sea World Dr. exit and turn north on E. Mission Bay Dr.

This sprawling Mediterranean-style resort occupies 18 acres on the east side of Mission Bay and is a quarter-mile from the Visitor Information Center. Room rates have skyrocketed in the past couple of years, but the place is consistently packed. Its main strength is the "no-brainer" aspect—within steps of your room are enough distractions and activities for the duration of your stay. They include a calm beach, tennis courts, charter boats, rental catamarans and water toys (like windsurfers and aquacycles), and an Olympic-plus-size pool. Guests have access to Mission Bay Park's trails and playgrounds, bike rentals, and a bevy of shops and restaurants. All rooms (contained in one eight-story tower and several low-rise buildings) have ceiling fans, a balcony or terrace, refrigerator, coffeemaker, iron and ironing board, hair dryer, makeup mirror, and in-room movies. Rooms are spacious and light, with large, elegant bathrooms and vaguely tropical pastel decor. Sea World is across the bay, and the ocean is 5 miles to the west.

Dining/Diversions: Three restaurants—a casual Southwestern bay-front cafe, a dinner-only Italian restaurant that serves gourmet pizzas, and a Mexican cantina serving tropical drinks and various nachos. The cantina features live entertainment and dancing at night.

Amenities: Giant swimming "lagoon," plus children's wading pool and four Jacuzzis; sauna; weight-training room; five lighted tennis courts; pro shop; putting green; playground; business center; massage; game arcade; meeting rooms; hair salon; concierge; room service (7am to 11pm); dry cleaning and laundry; baby-sitting; children's programs (summer only); free airport transportation.

✪ **Pacific Terrace Inn.** 610 Diamond St., San Diego, CA 92109. ☎ **800/344-3370** or 619/581-3500. Fax 619/274-3341. 73 units. A/C MINIBAR TV TEL. $195–$245 partial-view double; $255–$275 oceanfront double; from $280 suite. 10% AAA discount June 15–Sept 15 (25% Sept 16–June 14). Rates include continental breakfast. AE, CB, DC, DISC, MC, V. Free underground parking. Take I-5 to Grand/Garnet exit and follow Grand or Garnet west to Mission Blvd., turn right (north), then left (west) onto Diamond; inn is at the end of the street on the right. Bus: 34 or 34A.

This pink, condo-like building is the best modern hotel on the boardwalk, a luxury property that stands out from the casual beach pads in the area. With an upscale atmosphere and relaxed ambiance, the hotel provides more peace and quiet than most beachfront lodgings in this desirable but slightly raucous area.

The large, comfortable guest rooms come with balconies or terraces, refrigerators stocked with soft drinks, wall safes, VCRs, and in-room movies; bathrooms have hair dryers, cotton robes, and vanities with separate sinks. About half the rooms have kitchenettes, and top-floor rooms in this three-story hotel enjoy particularly nice views. Management keeps popcorn, coffee, and lemonade at the ready throughout the day; the pool and hot tub face a relatively quiet stretch of beach with fire rings for bonfires or barbecues.

Dining: Five local restaurants allow meals to be billed to the hotel; there's no restaurant on the premises.

Amenities: Outdoor heated pool, whirlpool, daily newspaper, dry cleaning, nightly turn-down, coin-operated laundry.

EXPENSIVE

Best Western Blue Sea Lodge. 707 Pacific Beach Dr., San Diego, CA 92109-5094. ☎ **800/ BLUE-SEA** or 619/488-4700. Fax 619/488-7276. www.bestwestern-bluesea.com. 100 units. TV TEL. Mid-June to mid-Sept $149–$179 double; up to $289 suite. Off-season $114–$139 double; up to $219 suite. Children under 13 stay free in parents' room. AAA and AARP discounts available. AE, CB, DC, DISC, MC, V. Underground and outdoor parking $3. Take I-5 to Grand/Garnet exit, follow Grand Ave. to Mission Blvd. and turn left, then turn right onto Pacific Beach Dr. Bus: 34.

The three-story Blue Sea Lodge is a reliable choice in a prime location. While I'd like to see more meticulous maintenance and decor upgrades, Best Western keeps up with the other bargain properties in the chain. And, despite the rates listed, this is a bargain. There are many ways to get a discount—including just asking. Outfitted in bright florals, each room has a balcony or patio; some have sunken tubs, or kitchenettes with coffeemakers. Rooms with full ocean views overlook the sand and have more privacy than those on the street, but the Pacific Beach boardwalk has never been known for quiet or solitude. Casual beach cafes and grills are nearby, along with several raucous Pacific Beach bars.

Amenities: The lobby offers coffee, tea, and a microwave for guests. The heated pool and Jacuzzi are steps from the beach.

✪ **Crystal Pier Hotel.** 4500 Ocean Blvd. (at Garnet Ave.), San Diego, CA 92109. ☎ **800/ 748-5894** or 619/483-6983. 26 cottages. TV. Cottages for 2–6 people $115–$305 mid-June to mid-Sept; $95–$250 mid-Sept to mid-June. 3-night minimum in summer. DISC, MC, V. Free parking. Take I-5 to Grand/Garnet exit; follow Garnet to the pier. Bus: 34 or 34A.

This historic property, which dates from 1927, offers a unique opportunity to sleep over the water. Built on a pier over the Pacific Ocean, the hotel offers self-contained cottages with breathtaking beach views. Most cottages date from 1936, and all have been completely renovated. Each comes with a private patio, living room, bedroom, and full kitchen, and has welcoming blue shutters and window boxes. The sound of waves is soothing, but the boardwalk action is only a few steps (and worlds) away. The quietest units are the farthest out on the pier. Guests drive right out and park beside their cottages, a real boon on crowded weekends. There are vending machines and movie rentals. Boogie boards, fishing poles, beach chairs, and umbrellas are also avail-

Accommodations in Mission Bay & the Beaches

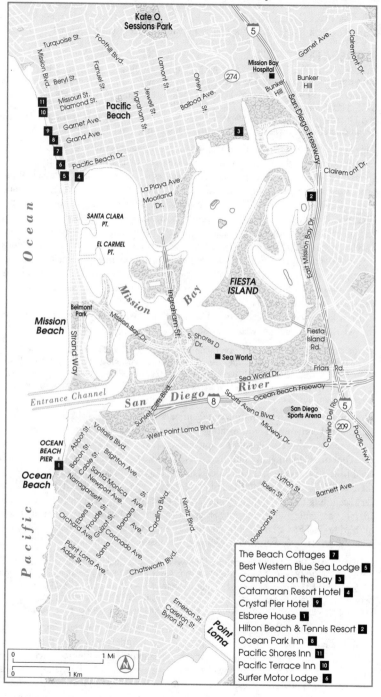

The Beach Cottages 7
Best Western Blue Sea Lodge 5
Campland on the Bay 3
Catamaran Resort Hotel 4
Crystal Pier Hotel 9
Elsbree House 1
Hilton Beach & Tennis Resort 2
Ocean Park Inn 8
Pacific Shores Inn 11
Pacific Terrace Inn 10
Surfer Motor Lodge 6

able. The office is open daily from 8am to 8pm. These accommodations book up fast. Besides being a restful place, the pier is a great place to watch the surfers at sunset.

MODERATE

The Beach Cottages. 4255 Ocean Blvd. (1 block south of Grand Ave.), San Diego, CA 92109-3995. ☎ **619/483-7440.** Fax 619/273-9365. 61 units, 17 cottages. TV TEL. July 1–Labor Day $95–$115 double; $125 studio for up to 4; $145–$190 apt for up to 6; $145–$180 cottage for up to 6; $220–$240 2-bedroom suite for up to 6. Off-season discounts and off-season weekly rates available. AE, CB, DC, DISC, MC, V. Free parking. Take I-5 to Grand/Garnet exit, go west on Grand Ave. and right on Mission Blvd. Bus: 34 or 34A.

This family-owned operation has a variety of guest quarters (most geared to the long-term visitor), but the cute little detached cottages steps from the sand give it real appeal. Most other units are perfectly adequate, especially for budget-minded families who want to log major hours on the beach, but stay away from the plain motel rooms—they're just dingy. All accommodations except the motel rooms have fully equipped kitchens. The Beach Cottages are within walking distance of shops and restaurants—look both ways for speeding cyclists before crossing the boardwalk—and have barbecue grills, shuffleboard courts, table tennis, and a laundry. The cottages themselves aren't pristine, but have a rustic charm that makes them popular with young honeymooners and those nostalgic for the golden age of laid-back California beach culture. With one or two bedrooms, each cottage sleeps up to six; each has a patio with tables and chairs.

To make a reservation, call between 9am and 9pm, when the office is open. Reserve the most popular cottages well in advance.

Ocean Park Inn. 710 Grand Ave., San Diego, CA 92109. ☎ **800/231-7735** or 619/483-5858. Fax 619/274-0823. 73 units. A/C TV TEL. Mid-May to mid-Sept $104–$214 double, $179–$304 suite; winter $89–$179 double, $124–$274 suite. Rates include continental breakfast. AE, DC, DISC, MC, V. Free indoor parking. Take Grand/Garnet exit off I-5; follow Grand Ave. to ocean. Bus: 34, 34A/B.

This modern oceanfront motor hotel offers attractive, spacious rooms with well-coordinated contemporary furnishings. Although the inn has a level of sophistication uncommon in this casual, surfer-populated area, you won't find solitude and quiet. The cool marble lobby and plushly carpeted hallways will help you feel a little insulated from the raucous scene outside, though. You can't beat the location (directly on the beach) and the view (ditto), and all rooms are equipped with refrigerators. Rates vary according to view, but all rooms have at least a partial ocean view. Units in front are most desirable, but it can get noisy directly above the boardwalk; try for the second or third floor. The Ocean Park Inn doesn't have its own restaurant, but the casual Firehouse Beach Cafe (see chapter 6, "Dining") is outside the front door.

Pacific Shores Inn. 4802 Mission Blvd. (between Law and Chalcedony sts.), San Diego, CA 92109. ☎ **800/826-0715** or 619/483-6300. Fax 619/483-9276. 55 units. TV TEL. June 15–Sept 15 $103–$108 double, $120 suite. Winter $63–$88 double, $73–$93 suite. Extra person $5. Children under 16 stay free in parents' room. Rates include continental breakfast. Pets up to 15 lbs. accepted; $25 fee. AE, DC, DISC, MC, V. Free parking. Bus: 34, 34A.

If the beach will be a large part of your San Diego vacation, you can't stay in a better location than the one enjoyed by this two-story contemporary motel at the north end of Pacific Beach. It's several blocks from the restaurants, but enjoys a quiet that you won't find at any of the places down the road—and the beach is just 100 yards away. The inn doesn't advertise ocean views, but rooms 23, 29, 31, 33, and 35 have them, and there's also a heated pool by the parking area. Half the units have kitchens; the others offer small refrigerators. The furniture is a little ragged, but carpets, drapes, and bedspreads are brand new. Ask for a room away from the street.

Surfer Motor Lodge. 711 Pacific Beach Dr. (at Mission Blvd.), San Diego, CA 92109. ☎ **800/787-3373** or 619/483-7070. Fax 619/274-1670. 52 units. TV TEL. June 15–Sept 15 $83–$122; winter $70–$93. Extra person $5. Weekly rates available off-season. AE, DC, MC, V. Free parking. Take I-5 to Grand/Garnet, then Grand Ave. to Mission Blvd.; turn left, then right onto Pacific Beach Dr. Bus: 34 or 34A.

Frankly, this property is looking pretty tired, but it's often booked solid during the summer because it offers moderately priced digs right on the boardwalk at the beach, as well as a heated pool. Most rooms in the four-story property have balconies and views and are cooled by ocean breezes, and many have kitchenettes. Hopefully management will consider sprucing the place up a bit, so it doesn't feel so haggard. On the premises is a coin-operated laundry. A popular restaurant serving three meals a day is adjacent.

INEXPENSIVE

Campland on the Bay. 2211 Pacific Beach Dr., San Diego, CA 92109-5699. ☎ **800/4-BAY-FUN** or 619/581-4260. Fax 619/581-4206. www.campland.com. 566 sites, most with hookup. Summer $25–$98 for up to 4 people; off-season $27–$68. Senior rates available. Weekly and monthly rates available off-season. Day use of facilities $5. Dogs accepted; $3 per day. MC, V. Take I-5 to Grand/Garnet exit, follow Grand to Olney and turn left; turn left again onto Pacific Beach Dr.

This bayside retreat is popular with a mixed crowd: RVers, campers (with or without vans), boaters, and their children and pets. At their fingertips are parks, a beach, a bird sanctuary, and a dog walk. Other facilities include pools, a Jacuzzi, catamaran and windsurfer rentals and lessons, bike and boat rentals, a game room, a cafe that serves three meals a day, a market, and a laundry. Planned activities include games and crafts for children; Sea World is 5 minutes away. Reserve popular spots at least six months in advance for spring and summer. The most desirable are the "Bayview" looking into the wildlife reserve. "Beachfront" sites are equally scenic, but noisy during the day.

Elsbree House. 5054 Narragansett Ave., San Diego, CA 92107. ☎ **619/226-4133.** www.oceanbeach-online.com/elsbree/b&b. 7 units. $95 double. 3-bedroom condo $1,250 per week. Room rate includes continental breakfast. MC, V. Bus: 35 or 23 to Narragansett Ave. and Cable St., 1½ blocks away. From airport, take Harbor Dr. west to Nimitz Blvd. to Lowell St., which becomes Narragansett Ave. Bus: 23, 35.

Katie and Phil Elsbree have turned this recently constructed Cape Cod–style building into an immaculate, exceedingly comfortable B&B half a block from the water's edge in Ocean Beach. One condo unit rents only by the week; the Elsbrees occupy another. Each of the six guest rooms has a patio or balcony. Guests share the cozy living room (with a fireplace and TV), breakfast room, and kitchen. Although other buildings on this tightly packed street block the ocean view, sounds of the surf and fresh sea breezes waft in open windows, and beautifully landscaped garden—complete with trickling fountain—runs the length of the house. This Ocean Beach neighborhood is eclectic, occupied by ocean-loving couples, dedicated surf bums, and a sometimes disturbing contingent of punk skater kids who congregate near the pier. Its strengths are proximity to the beach, a limited but pleasing selection of eateries that attract mostly locals, and some of the best antiquing in the city (along Newport Avenue).

5 La Jolla

Some consider La Jolla a jewel, and it's definitely the real thing, not a paste imitation.

You'll have a hard time finding bargain accommodations in this upscale, conservative community, but you'll get proximity to a beautiful coastline, as well as a compact downtown village that makes for delightful strolling.

Most of our choices are downtown, with two below the cliffs right on the beach. Chain hotels farther afield include a **Hyatt Regency,** 3777 La Jolla Village Dr. (☎ **800/ 233-1234** or 858/552-1234). It's a glitzy place whose contemporary decor includes lots of marble—Michael Graves received an American Institute of Architects Onion Award, which recognizes architectural flops, for the design. The **Marriott Residence Inn,** 8901 Gilman Dr. (☎ **800/331-3131** or 858/587-1770), is a good choice for those who want a fully equipped kitchen and more space. Both are near the University of California, San Diego.

A note on driving directions: To reach the places listed here, use the Ardath Road exit from **I-5 north** or the La Jolla Village Drive west exit from **I-5 south,** then follow individual directions.

VERY EXPENSIVE

✪ **Colonial Inn.** 910 Prospect St. (between Fay and Girard), La Jolla, CA 92037. ☎ **800/ 826-1278** or 858/454-2181. Fax 858/454-5679. www.colonialinn.com. 75 units. TV TEL. $180 double with village view, $205–$275 double with ocean view; from $300 suite. Off-season discounts available. Children under 18 stay free in parents' room. Pets under 20 lbs. accepted. AE, CB, DC, MC, V. Valet parking $7. Take Torrey Pines Rd. to Prospect Place and turn right. Prospect Place becomes Prospect St.

Possessed of an old-world European flair that's more London or Georgetown than sea-side La Jolla, the Colonial Inn has garnered accolades for the complete restoration of its polished mahogany paneling, brass fittings, and genteel library and lounge. Guest rooms are quiet and elegantly appointed, with beautiful draperies and traditional furnishings. The hotel is one block from the ocean. Guests who stay here instead of at the more expensive La Valencia, down the street, sacrifice air-conditioning for a ceiling fan, but gain elbow room (and save money). Numerous historic photos on the walls illustrate the inn's fascinating history; the reception desk has a printed sheet with more details of its beginnings as a full-service apartment hotel in 1913. Relics from the early days include oversized closets, meticulously tiled bathrooms, and heavy fire-proof doors suspended in the corridors. The guest rooms have amenities such as hair dryers and refrigerators; terry robes are available on request.

Dining/Diversions: Putnam's restaurant, a former drugstore, now features a popular bar in place of the soda fountain; the clubby dining room serves American and Continental cuisine. A large spray of fresh flowers is the focal point in the lounge, where guests gather in front of the fireplace for drinks.

Amenities: The outdoor heated pool, set in a landscaped garden, is open from

Important Area Code Changes

Dial **619** to call most of San Diego, except for La Jolla, Del Mar, Rancho Sante Fe, and Rancho Bernardo, which received the new area code **858** during 1999. Use **760** to reach the remainder of San Diego County, including Encinitas, Carlsbad, Oceanside, Escondido, Ramona, Julian, and Anza–Borrego. Toward the end of 2000, the 619 area code will split further, with Coronado and the southern portion of San Diego County getting a new area code—**935.** Don't worry, though, this change doesn't go into effect until December 8, 2000, and the rest of the city of San Diego will remain in the 619 area code.

sunup to sundown. Walking tours of La Jolla depart from the hotel (see chapter 7). Airport transportation is available for $9 one way. Room service, dry cleaning and laundry, turn-down service on request, baby-sitting, complimentary shoeshine, conference rooms.

☮ **La Valencia Hotel.** 1132 Prospect St. (at Herschel Ave.), La Jolla, CA 92037. ☎ **800/ 451-0772** or 858/454-0771. Fax 858/456-3921. www.lavalencia.com. 117 units. A/C MINIBAR TV TEL. $225–$550 double; from $625 suite. Extra person $15. AE, DC, DISC, MC, V. Valet parking $14. Take Torrey Pines Rd. to Prospect Place and turn right. Prospect Place becomes Prospect St.

It's not just La Valencia's distinctive pink stucco that brings to mind other gracious historic (and pink) hotels, like the Beverly Hills Hotel and Waikiki's Royal Hawaiian. Within its bougainvillea-draped walls and wrought-iron garden gates, this bastion of gentility does a fine job of resurrecting the elegance of its golden age, when celebrities like Greta Garbo and Charlie Chaplin vacationed alongside the world's moneyed elite. The cliff-top hotel has been the centerpiece of La Jolla since opening in 1926. Today, brides pose in front of the lobby's picture window (against a backdrop of La Jolla Cove and the Pacific), well-coifed ladies lunch in the dappled shade of the garden patio, and neighborhood cronies quaff libations in the clubby Whaling Bar, once a western Algonquin for literary inebriates. One chooses La Valencia for its history and unbeatably scenic location, but you won't be disappointed by the old-world standards of service and style. Rooms are lavishly furnished with rich fabrics and European antique reproductions, though some are on the dark side, and the 1920s bathrooms aren't huge. Rates vary wildly according to view. My advice is to get a cheaper room and enjoy the view from one of the many cozy lounges or serene garden terraces. Linens, towels, and bath accessories are of the finest quality, and rooms also have VCRs, for which you can rent videos.

Dining/Diversions: The elegant rooftop Sky Room serves French cuisine in an intimate setting; the Mediterranean Room and Tropical Patio serves California cuisine. There's also the legendary Whaling Bar & Grill (where Ginger Rogers and Charlton Heston once hung out) and adjoining Cafe La Rue.

Amenities: Outdoor heated pool, shuffleboard courts, Jacuzzi, concierge, 24-hour room service, dry cleaning and laundry, morning newspaper, nightly turn-down, in-room massage, baby-sitting, secretarial services, express checkout, small health club, sauna, access to tennis courts.

The Sea Lodge. 8110 Camino del Oro (at Avenida de la Playa), La Jolla, CA 92037. ☎ **800/ 237-5211** or 858/459-8271. Fax 858/456-9346. 128 units. A/C TV TEL. Mid-June to mid-Sept $189–$399 double, $429 suite; off-season $139–$269 double, $319–$329 suite. Children under 12 stay free in parents' room. Extra person $15. AE, DC, DISC, MC, V. Free covered parking. Take La Jolla Shores Dr., turn left onto Avenida de la Playa, turn right on Camino del Oro.

This three-story, 1960s hotel in a mainly residential enclave is under the same management as the La Jolla Beach & Tennis Club next door. It has an identical on-the-sand location, minus the country club ambiance—there are no reciprocal privileges. Most rooms have some view of the ocean, and the rest look out on the pool or a tiled courtyard. From the Sea Lodge's beach you can gaze toward the top of the cliffs, where La Jolla's village hums with activity (and relentless traffic). The rooms are pretty basic, priced by view and size. Bathrooms feature separate dressing areas with large closets; and all rooms are outfitted with coffeemakers, refrigerators, hair dryers, irons, and ironing boards. Balconies or patios are standard, and some rooms have fully equipped kitchenettes. Like the "B&T," the Sea Lodge is popular with families but also attracts business travelers looking to balance meetings with time on the beach or the hotel's two tennis courts.

Dining: The unremarkable restaurant serves three meals a day; it's convenient, but there are better restaurants in the surrounding neighborhood (see chapter 6, "Dining").

Amenities: Lighted tennis courts, heated outdoor pool with whirlpool and kids' pool, fitness room, laundry and dry cleaning, baby-sitting.

EXPENSIVE

The Bed & Breakfast Inn at La Jolla. 7753 Draper Ave. (near Prospect), La Jolla, CA 92037. ☎ **800/582-2466** or 858/456-2066. www.InnLaJolla.com. 15 units. A/C TEL. $109–$225 double, $250 suite. Rates include full breakfast and afternoon wine and cheese. Extra person $25. AE, MC, V. Take Torrey Pines Rd. to Prospect Place and turn right. Prospect Place becomes Prospect St.; proceed to Draper Ave. and turn left.

A 1913 Cubist house designed by prominent local architect Irving Gill—and once occupied by John Philip Sousa and his family—is the setting for this genteel and elegant B&B. Reconfigured for this purpose, the house has lost none of its charm, and appropriately un-frilly period furnishings add to the sense of history. The inn also features lovely enclosed gardens and a cozy library and sitting room. Fresh fruit, sherry, fresh-cut flowers, and terry robes await in every room, some of which feature a fireplace or ocean view. The furnishings are tasteful and cottage-style, with plenty of historic photos of La Jolla.

Dining: The gourmet breakfast is served wherever you desire—dining room, patio, sundeck, or in your room. Picnic baskets (extra charge) are available with a day's notice.

Empress Hotel of La Jolla. 7766 Fay Ave. (at Silverado), La Jolla, CA 92037. ☎ **888/369-9900** or 858/454-3001. Fax 858/454-6387. www.empress-hotel.com. 73 units. A/C TV TEL. $139–$199 double; $349 suite. Extra person $10. Children under 18 stay free in parents' room. Rates include continental breakfast. Off-season and long-stay discounts available. AE, DC, DISC, MC, V. Valet parking $7. Take Torrey Pines Rd. to Girard Ave., turn right, then left on Silverado St.

The Empress Hotel offers spacious quarters with traditional furnishings a block or two from La Jolla's main drag and the ocean. It's quieter here than at the Colonial Inn or the Prospect Park Inn, and you'll sacrifice little other than direct ocean views. (Many rooms on the top floors afford a partial view.) If you're planning to explore La Jolla on foot, the Empress is a good base, and it exudes a classiness many comparably priced chains lack. Rooms are tastefully decorated (and frequently renovated), and equipped with refrigerators, hair dryers, coffeemakers, irons and ironing boards, and robes. Bathrooms are of average size but exceptionally well appointed, and four "Empress" rooms have sitting areas with full-size sleeper sofas.

Amenities: Room service, valet, laundry service, fitness room with spa and sauna. On nice days, breakfast is set up on a serene sundeck.

◆ La Jolla Beach & Tennis Club. 2000 Spindrift Dr., La Jolla, CA 92037. ☎ **800/624-CLUB** or 858/454-7126. Fax 858/456-3805. www.ljbtc.com. 90 units. TV TEL. Mid-June to mid-Sept $165–$289 double; from $229 suite. Off-season $129–$239 double; from $189 suite. Children under 12 stay free in parents' room. Extra person $20. AE, DC, MC, V. Take La Jolla Shores Dr., turn left on Paseo Dorado, and follow to Spindrift Dr.

Pack your best tennis whites for a stay at La Jolla's private "B&T" (as it's locally known), where CEOs and MDs come to relax and recreate. Surprisingly, rates for the club's overnight accommodations aren't that much higher than at the sister hotel next door, but the exclusive atmosphere and extensive amenities are far superior. Guest rooms are unexpectedly plain and frill-free, though they are equipped with hair dryers,

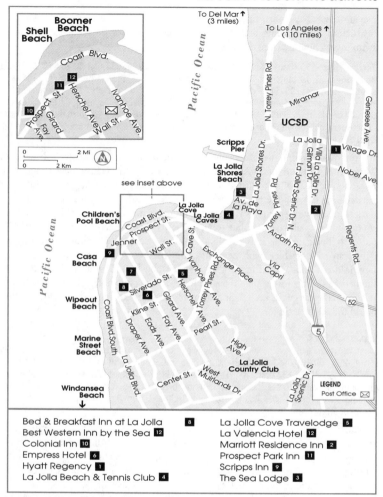

Bed & Breakfast Inn at La Jolla **8**
Best Western Inn by the Sea **12**
Colonial Inn **10**
Empress Hotel **6**
Hyatt Regency **1**
La Jolla Beach & Tennis Club **4**

La Jolla Cove Travelodge **5**
La Valencia Hotel **12**
Marriott Residence Inn **2**
Prospect Park Inn **11**
Scripps Inn **9**
The Sea Lodge **3**

coffeemakers, irons, and ironing boards. Most have well-stocked full kitchens that are ideal for families or longer stays. This historic property was founded in the 1920s, when original plans included constructing a private yacht harbor. Today it's known primarily for tennis. The beach is popular here; the staff sets up comfy sand chairs and umbrellas, and races to supply club members and guests with fluffy towels, beverages, and snacks. Kayaks and water-sport equipment can be rented; there's even a sand croquet court. Surprisingly, there's no room service; besides the on-site dining options, several cozy neighborhood trattorias are two blocks away.

Dining: There's a casual dining room and seasonal beach hut, but don't leave without peeking into the distinctive Marine Room, where waves literally smash against the windows inches away from well-coifed diners. The menu is pricey, but for the price of a cocktail you can enjoy the same astounding view.

Amenities: 12 championship tennis courts and a tennis shop, 9-hole pitch-and-putt course that winds around a lagoon along the stately entry drive, jogging path, playground, table tennis, fitness room, elegant Olympic-size swimming pool, swim instruction, dry cleaning and laundry, turn-down service on request, baby-sitting, swim instruction, massage therapist, coin laundry.

Scripps Inn. 555 Coast Blvd. S. (at Cuvier), La Jolla, CA 92037. ☎ **858/454-3391.** Fax 858/456-0389. 14 units. TV TEL. Memorial Day–Labor Day $155–$200 double, $185–$300 suite; off-season $135–$155 double, $165–$200 suite. Extra person $10. Children under 5 stay free in parents' room. Weekly and monthly rates available off-season. Rates include continental breakfast. AE, DISC, MC, V. Free parking. Take Torrey Pines Rd., turn right on Prospect Place, veer right (downhill) onto Coast Blvd. If you miss the turn, drive through town and turn right at the museum.

It's not easy to find this meticulously maintained inn, tucked away behind the Museum of Contemporary Art, but you're rewarded with seclusion even though the attractions of La Jolla are just a short walk away. Only a small, grassy park comes between the inn and the beach, cliffs, and tide pools; the view from the second-story deck seems to hypnotize guests, who gaze out to sea indefinitely. Rates vary depending on ocean view (all have one, but some are better than others); aside from Room 14, currently being remade into an ultra-deluxe apartment, they're furnished in "early-American comfortable," with new bathroom fixtures and appointments. All rooms have fold-out sofas and refrigerators; two have wood-burning fireplaces, and four have kitchenettes. The inn supplies beach towels, firewood, and French pastries each morning. Repeat guests keep their favorite rooms for up to a month each year, so book ahead for the best choice.

MODERATE

Best Western Inn by the Sea. 7830 Fay Ave. (between Prospect and Silverado sts.), La Jolla, CA 92037. ☎ **800/462-9732,** 800/526-4545 in California and Canada, or 858/459-4461. Fax 858/456-2578. 132 units. A/C TV TEL. $129–$199 double; $175–$450 suite. Off-season discounts available. Rates include continental breakfast. AE, CB, DC, DISC, MC, V. Free parking. Take Torrey Pines Rd. to Prospect Place and turn right. Prospect Place becomes Prospect St.; proceed to Fay Ave. and turn left.

Occupying an enviable location at the heart of La Jolla's charming village, this independently managed property puts guests just a short walk from the cliffs and beach. The low-rise tops out at five stories, with the upper floors enjoying ocean views (and the highest room rates). The Best Western and the more formal Empress, a block away, offer a terrific alternative to pricier digs nearby. Rooms here are Best Western standard issue—freshly maintained, but nothing special. All rooms do have balconies, though, and refrigerators are available at no extra charge; other amenities include a heated pool and whirlpool, free daily newspaper and local phone calls, and room service from the attached IHOP.

Prospect Park Inn. 1110 Prospect St. (at Coast Blvd.), La Jolla, CA 92037. ☎ **800/433-1609** or 858/454-0133. Fax 858/454-2056. 23 units. A/C TV TEL. $120–$185 double; from $275 suite. Rates include continental breakfast and afternoon refreshments. Off-season discounts available. AE, CB, DC, DISC, JCB, MC, V. Free indoor parking ½ block away. Take Torrey Pines Rd. to Prospect Place and turn right. Prospect Place becomes Prospect St.

This place is a real gem. It's a small property, next door to La Valencia, that offers charming rooms, some with narrow ocean views. Built in 1947 as a boarding house for women, this spotless boutique hotel feels more European than Californian—it has a sparse but functional lobby, a stairway (there's no elevator in the three-story building), and an unexpected combination of frugality and comfort. Fresh fruit and beverages are offered in the library area every afternoon, and breakfast is served on the sundeck, which has a great ocean view. Prospect Park Inn enjoys essentially the same location as La Valencia and the Colonial Inn—the beach, park, shops, and restaurants are within steps—at much lower prices. Beach towels and chairs are provided free of charge for guests.

INEXPENSIVE

La Jolla Cove Travelodge. 1141 Silverado St. (at Herschel Ave.), La Jolla, CA 92037. ☎ **800/ 578-7878** or 858/454-0791. Fax 858/459-8534. 30 units. A/C TV TEL. $59–$98 double (subject to availability). AE, DC, MC, V. AARP and AAA discounts available. Free off-street parking. Take Torrey Pines Rd. and turn right on Herschel Ave.

While the name is deceptive—the Cove is a 10-minute walk away—this motel is a good value in tony La Jolla. Fitting in with the village's retro feel, the exterior seems unchanged from the 1940s; though rooms have been diligently updated, no one will thrill to the basic motel decor, which features cinder-block walls and small, basic bathrooms. But somehow, the place seems less dreary because it's surrounded by the glamour of La Jolla. Rooms have coffeemakers; some have kitchenettes and microwaves. Management provides the daily newspaper. There isn't a pool, but there is a modest sundeck on the third floor with a view of the ocean, which is about three-quarters of a mile away.

6 Coronado

The "island" (really a peninsula) of Coronado is a great escape. It offers quiet, architecturally rich streets; a small-town, navy-oriented atmosphere, and laid-back vacationing on one of the state's most beautiful and welcoming beaches. Choose a hotel on the ocean side for a view of Point Loma and the Pacific, or stay facing the city for a spectacular skyline vista (especially at night). You may feel pleasantly isolated here, so it isn't your best choice if you're planning to spend lots of time in more central parts of the city.

   A Note on Driving Directions: To reach the places listed here, take I-5 to the Coronado Bridge, then follow individual directions. If you have a passenger, stay in the far right lanes to avoid paying the bridge toll.

VERY EXPENSIVE

✪ **Hotel del Coronado.** 1500 Orange Ave., Coronado, CA 92118. ☎ **800/468-3533** or 619/435-8000. Fax 619/522-8238. www.hoteldel.com. 700 units. MINIBAR TV TEL. From $200 standard; from $245 deluxe; from $330 ocean view; from $435 oceanfront; from $500 suite. Packages available. Children under 18 stay free in parents' room. AE, CB, DC, DISC, MC, V. Valet parking $16; self-parking $12. From Coronado Bridge, turn left onto Orange Ave. Bus: 901. Ferry: from Broadway Pier.

Opened in 1888 and designated a National Historic Landmark in 1977, the "Hotel Del," as it's affectionately known, is the last of California's grand old seaside hotels. Legend has it that the Duke of Windsor met his duchess here, and Marilyn Monroe frolicked around the hotel in *Some Like It Hot.* This monument to Victorian grandeur boasts tall cupolas, red turrets, and gingerbread trim, all spread out over 26 acres. Rooms run the gamut from compact to extravagant, and all are packed with antique charm; most have custom-made furnishings. The best rooms have balconies fronting the ocean and large windows that take in one of the city's finest white-sand beaches. If you're a stickler for detail, ask to stay in the original building rather than in the contemporary tower additions.

   During the shelf life of this guide—and probably the next edition, too—the hotel will be undergoing painstaking restoration. Purists will rejoice to hear that historical accuracy is paramount; as the infrastructure is upgraded, public spaces and Victorian

A Hotel with History:
Scenes from the Hotel del Coronado

San Diego's romantic Hotel del Coronado is an unmistakable landmark, filled with enchanting and colorful memories.

Several familiar names helped shape the hotel. In 1887, it was among the first buildings with Thomas Edison's new invention, electric light; the building had its own electrical power plant, which supplied the entire city of Coronado until 1922. Author L. Frank Baum, a frequent guest, designed the Crown Dining Room's elegant crown-shaped chandeliers. Baum wrote several of the books in his beloved *Wizard of Oz* series in Coronado, and many believe he modeled the Emerald City's geometric spires after the Del's conical turrets.

The hotel has played host to royalty and celebrities as well. The first visiting monarch was Kalakaua, Hawaii's last king, who spent Christmas here in 1890. But the best-known royal guest was Edward, Prince of Wales (later Edward VIII, then Duke of Windsor). He came to the hotel in April 1920, the first British royal to visit California. Of the many lavish social affairs held during his stay, at least two were attended by Wallis Simpson (then navy-wife Wallis Warfield), 15 years before her official introduction to the prince in London. Speculation continues about whether their love affair, which culminated in his abdication of the throne, might have begun right here.

America's own "royalty" often visited the hotel. In 1927, San Diego's beloved son Charles Lindbergh was honored here following his historic 33½-hour solo flight across the Atlantic. Hollywood stars, including Mary Pickford, Greta Garbo, Charlie Chaplin, and Esther Williams, have flocked to the Del. Director Billy Wilder filmed *Some Like It Hot* at the hotel; longtime staffers remember seeing stars Marilyn Monroe, Tony Curtis, and Jack Lemmon romping on the beach. The hotel has also hosted 10 U.S. presidents. And some guests have never left: the ghost of Kate Morgan, whose body was found in 1892 where the tennis courts are today, supposedly still roams the halls.

Visitors and guests intrigued by the hotel's past can stroll through the lower-level History Gallery, a mini-museum of hotel memorabilia.

wing rooms are being returned to their turn-of-the-century splendor. Inquire when you book, so you can avoid construction areas, enjoy vintage rooms before they're worked on, or take advantage of just-completed improvements. Even if you don't stay here, don't miss a stroll through the grand, wood-paneled lobby or along the pristine wide beach.

Dining/Diversions: The hotel has nine dining areas; the most charming is the Prince of Wales Grill, newly remodeled from a dark, clubby room to a golden-hued salon with ocean views. The upscale menu puts a Pacific Rim twist on Continental favorites. The sunny, breezy Ocean Terrace offers alfresco bistro fare; cocktails and afternoon tea are served in the wood-paneled lobby and adjoining conservatory lounge. There's music and dancing nightly, ranging from quiet piano tinkling to amplified dance music.

Amenities: Two outdoor pools, whirlpools, massage, six tennis courts, bicycle rental, concierge, 24-hour room service, turn-down service, laundry and dry cleaning, valet, baby-sitting, beauty salon and spa, limousine service, guided tours of the hotel (they're fun), 24-hour deli, children's activities, airport shuttle ($10), shopping arcade, signature shop with appealing logo items.

Coronado Island Marriott Resort. 2000 Second St. (at Glorietta Blvd.), Coronado, CA 92118. ☎ **800/228-9290** or 619/435-3000. Fax 619/435-3032. http://marriotthotels.com/ SANCI. 300 units. A/C MINIBAR TV TEL. $195–$325 double; from $395 suite; from $495 villa. Children under 12 stay free in parents' room. Packages available. AE, CB, DC, MC, V. Valet parking $15; self-parking $11. From Coronado Bridge, turn right onto Glorietta Blvd., take first right to hotel. Bus: 901. Ferry: from Broadway Pier.

We're happy to see the new management (Marriott International Inc.) fulfilling its promise to get this former Le Meridien back to high-end status. Elegance and luxury here are understated—without a lot of flash, guests just seem to get whatever they need, be it a lift downtown (by water taxi from the private dock), a tee time at the neighboring golf course, or a prime appointment at the property's spa.

Enduring appeals of the property remain: Its waterfront location, view of the San Diego skyline (but within easy distance of Coronado shopping and dining); casual, airy architecture; lushly planted grounds filled with preening exotic birds; and a wealth of sporting and recreational activities. Guest rooms are generously sized and attractively furnished—actually *decorated*—in colorful French country style; they feature balconies or patios, coffeemakers, hair dryers, and irons and ironing boards. The superbly designed bathrooms hold an array of toiletries and plush bathrobes. Watch this low-key, comfortable Marriott give competitor Loews a run for its money.

Dining/Diversions: L'Escale, a Mediterranean brasserie, serves breakfast, lunch, and dinner. The hotel's cocktail lounge is worth a visit for its jazzy, moody ambiance.

Amenities: Sporting a new contemporary image, the Spa intends to be Marriott's main attraction; clients can choose from Swiss beauty treatments, Hawaiian and Asian holistic therapies, and expanded fitness, yoga, and tennis programs. Other features include three outdoor heated pools (including a lap pool), two outdoor whirlpools, six lighted tennis courts, bicycle rental, water sports, a jogging trail and bike path, concierge, 24-hour room service, laundry, valet, turn-down service, baby-sitting, business center, complimentary shuttle to Horton Plaza, airport shuttle ($9 each way).

Glorietta Bay Inn. 1630 Glorietta Blvd. (near Orange Ave.), Coronado, CA 92118. ☎ **800/283-9383** or 619/435-3101. Fax 619/435-6182. www.gloriettabayinn.com. 100 units. A/C TV TEL. Mansion $225–$245 double, $275–$425 suite; annex $135–$225 double, from $245 suite. Children under 19 stay free in parents' room. Extra person $10. Rates include continental breakfast. AE, MC, V. Free parking. From Coronado Bridge, turn left on Orange Ave. After 2 miles, turn left onto Glorietta Blvd.; inn is across the street from the Hotel del Coronado.

Right across the street and somewhat in the (figurative) shadow of the Hotel del Coronado, this pretty white hotel consists of the charmingly historic John D. Spreckels mansion (1908) and two younger, motel-style buildings. Only 11 rooms are in the mansion, which boasts original fixtures, a grand staircase, and old-fashioned wicker furniture; the guest rooms are also decked out in antiques, and have a romantic and nostalgic ambiance.

Rooms in the modern annexes are less expensive but much plainer. All units are equipped with refrigerators, coffeemakers, in-room movies, and hair dryers; some have kitchenettes. Wherever your room is, you'll gather for breakfast on the main house's sunny veranda. In addition to offering rental bikes and boat rentals on Glorietta Bay across the street, the hotel is within easy walking distance of the beach, golf, tennis, water sports, shopping, and dining. Rooms in the mansion get booked early, but are worth the extra effort and expense.

Dining: Only continental breakfast is available.

Amenities: Heated swimming pool, whirlpool, in-room movies, laundry and dry cleaning, baby-sitting, coin laundry.

😊 **Loews Coronado Bay Resort.** 4000 Coronado Bay Rd., Coronado, CA 92118. ☎ **800/ 81-LOEWS** or 619/424-4000. Fax 619/424-4400. 437 units. A/C MINIBAR TV TEL. $235–$285 double; from $425 suite. Children under 18 stay free in parents' room. Packages available. Pets under 25 lbs. accepted. AE, CB, DC, DISC, MC, V. Valet parking $14; covered self-parking $12. From Coronado Bridge, go left onto Orange Avenue, continue 8 miles down Silver Strand Hwy. Turn left at Coronado Bay Rd., entrance to the resort.

This luxury resort opened in 1991 on a secluded 15-acre peninsula, slightly removed from downtown Coronado and San Diego. It's perfect for those who prefer a self-contained resort in a get-away-from-it-all location, and is surprisingly successful in appealing to business travelers, convention groups, vacationing families, and romance-minded couples. All units offer terraces that look onto the hotel's private 80-slip marina, the Coronado Bay Bridge, or San Diego Bay. A private pedestrian underpass leads to nearby Silver Strand Beach. Rooms boast finely appointed marble bathrooms, plus VCRs, for which you can rent videos. At press time Loews was in the midst of refurnishing the guest rooms, which had become far too outdated and worn for a hotel of this caliber.

Dining: Azzura Point, facing the San Diego skyline, has Mediterranean decor and sophisticated California-Mediterranean cuisine. There's also a casual cafe, lobby lounge, poolside bar and grill, and specialty food market.

Amenities: A highlight here is the **Gondola Company** (☎ **619/429-6317**), which offers romantic and fun gondola cruises through the canals of tony Coronado Cays. The seasonal Commodore Kids Club, for children 4 to 12, offers supervised half-day, full-day, and evening programs with meals. Other features include three outdoor swimming pools; a fitness center with saunas and whirlpools; five lighted tennis courts and a pro shop; bicycle, skate, and water-sports rentals; concierge; 24-hour room service; laundry/valet; newspaper delivery; turn-down service; in-room massage; baby-sitting; business center; fax machines in suites; car-rental desk; beauty salon.

MODERATE

El Cordova Hotel. 1351 Orange Ave. (at Adella Ave.), Coronado, CA 92118. ☎ **800/229-2032** or 619/435-4131. Fax 619/435-0632. 40 units. TV TEL. $95 double; $115–$125 studio with kitchen; $145–$185 1-bedroom suite; $220–$295 2-bedroom suite. Children under 12 stay free in parents' room. Weekly and monthly rates available off-season. AE, DC, DISC, MC, V. No off-street parking. From Coronado Bridge, turn left onto Orange Ave. Parking available on street.

This Spanish hacienda across the street from the Hotel del Coronado began life as a private mansion in 1902. By the 1930s it had become a hotel, the original building augmented by a series of attachments housing retail shops along the ground-floor arcade. Shaped like a baseball diamond and surrounding a courtyard with meandering tiled pathways, flowering shrubs, a swimming pool, and patio seating for Miguel's Cocina Mexican restaurant, El Cordova hums pleasantly with activity.

Each room is a little different from the next—some sport a Mexican colonial ambiance, while others evoke a comfy beach cottage. All feature ceiling fans and brightly tiled bathrooms, but lack the frills that command exorbitant rates. El Cordova has a particularly inviting aura, and its prime location makes it a popular option; I advise reserving several months in advance, especially for the summer. Facilities include a heated pool, barbecue area with a picnic table, and a laundry room.

Coronado Accommodations

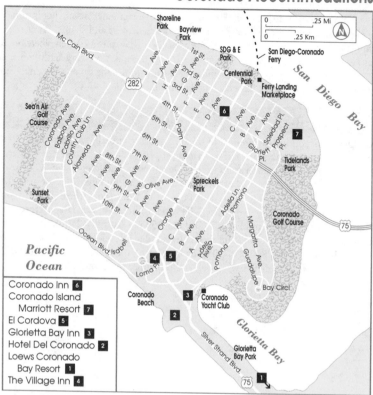

Coronado Inn **6**
Coronado Island
　Marriott Resort **7**
El Cordova **5**
Glorietta Bay Inn **3**
Hotel Del Coronado **2**
Loews Coronado
　Bay Resort **1**
The Village Inn **4**

INEXPENSIVE

Coronado Inn. 266 Orange Ave. (corner of 3rd St.), Coronado, CA 92118. ☎ **800/598-6624** or 619/435-4121. www.coronadoinn.com. 30 units (most with shower only). A/C TV TEL. Memorial Day through Labor Day $98–$125 up to 4 people; winter $85–$110. Rates include continental breakfast. Discounts available. Pets accepted; $10 per night. AE, MC, V. Free parking. From Coronado Bridge, stay on 3rd St.

Well-located and terrifically priced, this renovated 1940s courtyard motel has such a friendly ambiance; it's like staying with old friends. Iced tea, lemonade, and fresh fruit are even provided poolside on summer days. It's still a motel, though—albeit with brand-new paint and fresh tropical floral decor—so rooms are pretty basic. The six rooms with bathtubs also have small kitchens. There are laundry facilities on the property, and refrigerators and microwaves are available. Rooms close to the street are noisiest, so ask for one toward the back. The Coronado shuttle stops a block away; it serves the shopping areas and Hotel Del.

The Village Inn. 1017 Park Place (at Orange Ave.), Coronado, CA 92118. ☎ **619/435-9318.** 14 units. Summer $90–$95 double; winter and weekly rates available. Rates include continental breakfast. AE, MC, V. Parking available on street. From Coronado Bridge, turn left onto Orange Ave., then right on Park Place.

Its location a block or two from Coronado's main sights—the Hotel Del, the beach, shopping, and cafes—is this inn's most appealing feature. Historic charm runs a close second; a plaque outside identifies the three-story brick-and-stucco hotel as the once-chic Blue Lantern Inn, built in 1926. The charming vintage lobby sets the mood in this European-style hostelry; each simple but well-maintained room holds antique dressers and armoires, plus lovely Battenberg lace bedcovers and shams. Front rooms enjoy the best view, and coffee and tea are available all day in the kitchen where breakfast is served. The appealing inn's only Achilles' heel is tiny, tiny bathrooms, so cramped that you almost have to stand on the toilet to use the small-scale sinks. Surprisingly, some bathrooms have been updated with whirlpool tubs.

7 Near the Airport

San Diego's airport has the unusual distinction of being virtually *in* downtown. While locals grouse about the noise and decreased property values, it's good news for travelers: Most of the accommodations in the "Downtown," "Hillcrest," and "Old Town" (including Hotel Circle) neighborhoods are only 5 to 10 minutes from the airport.

For those who must stay as close as possible to the airport, there are two good choices literally across the street. The 1,045-room **Sheraton San Diego Hotel and Marina,** 1380 Harbor Island Dr. (☎ **800/325-3535** or 619/291-2900), offers rooms from $150 to $280. At the 208-room **Travelodge Hotel–Harbor Island,** 1960 Harbor Island Dr. (☎ **800/255-3050** or 619/291-6700), rooms go $129 to $149. Both Hotels offer a marina view, a pool, and proximity to downtown San Diego.

Dining 6

The city's dining scene, once a bastion of rich Continental and heavy American cuisine, has come into its own during the past decade. The explosion of a transplant population and the diversification of San Diego neighborhoods have sparked a new spirit of experimentation and style. An improved economy helped, too, motivating folks to step out and exercise their palates. The restaurant scene races to keep up with current trends and desires. One positive sign is that the culinary bible, the *Zagat Survey*, now publishes an edition exclusively for San Diego and its environs.

San Diego offers terrific seafood, far more so than in the equally oceanfront Los Angeles, for example. Whether at unembellished market-style restaurants that let freshness take center stage or at upscale restaurants that feature extravagant presentations, the ocean's bounty is everywhere.

Those traditional mainstays, American and Continental cuisine, are (metaphorically speaking) still carrying their share of the weight in San Diego. But, with increasing regularity, they're mating with lighter, more contemporary, often ethnic styles. The movement is akin to the eclectic "fusion" cuisine that burst onto the scene in the early 1990s. That's not to say traditionalists will be disappointed—San Diego still has the most clubby steak-and-potatoes stalwarts on the West Coast.

If you love Italian food, you're in luck. Not only does San Diego boast a strong contingent of old-fashioned Sicilian-style choices, but these days you can't turn a corner without running into a trattoria. The Gaslamp Quarter corners the market, with upscale Northern Italian bistros on virtually every block. Hillcrest, La Jolla, and other neighborhoods also boast their fair share. They cater mostly to locals, and their menus usually include gourmet pizzas baked in wood-fired ovens, a trend that shows no signs of slowing down (see "Only in San Diego," at the end of this chapter).

Ethnic foods are rising in popularity even as this book is being written. Number 1 on everyone's list of favorites is Mexican—a logical choice given the city's history and location. You'll find lots of highly Americanized fare along with a few hidden jewels, like Palenque and Berta's, that serve true south-of-the-border cuisine. The most authentic Mexican food may be the humble fish taco (see "Only in San Diego," at the end of this chapter). The Baja import, faithfully re-created by Rubio's, has become San Diego's favorite fast food. Asian cuisine runs a close second, with Thai and Vietnamese restaurants starting to catch

A Note on Smoking

In January 1998, California law made it illegal to smoke in all restaurants and bars, except in outdoor seating. Almost immediately, opponents scrambled to appeal the legislation, so the situation may have changed by the time you visit—be sure to inquire before you light up.

---

up with Chinese and Japanese. Many intrepid chefs fuse Asian ingredients and preparations with more familiar Mediterranean or French menus, and sushi bars are on the rise.

In this chapter, restaurants are indexed by cuisine as well as by location and price category. *Note:* For a list of my favorites in all kinds of categories, see "Best Dining Bets" in chapter 1.

For diners on a budget, the more expensive San Diego restaurants are accommodating if you want to order a few appetizers instead of a main course, and many offer more reasonably priced lunch menus. Dress tends to be pretty casual, even in pricey places; some notable exceptions are La Jolla's more expensive restaurants and the hotels on Coronado, where jeans are a no-no and gentlemen generally wear jackets.

A note on parking: Unless a listing specifies otherwise, drivers can expect to park within 2 or 3 blocks of the restaurants listed here. If you can't find a free or metered space on the street, you can seek out a garage or lot (see "Getting Around: By Car" in chapter 4).

1 Restaurants by Cuisine

AMERICAN

Bay Beach Cafe (Coronado, *M*)
Chart House (Coronado, La Jolla, *E*)
Corvette Diner (Hillcrest/Uptown, *I*)
Croce's Restaurant & Nightclubs (Downtown, *E*)
Dakota Grill and Spirits (Downtown, *M*)
Firehouse Beach Cafe (Pacific Beach, *I*)
The Green Flash (Pacific Beach, *M*)
Hard Rock Cafe (La Jolla, *I*)
Hob Nob Hill (Hillcrest/Uptown, *M*)
Kansas City Barbecue (Downtown, *I*)
Karl Strauss Downtown Brewery & Grill (Downtown, La Jolla, *M*)
Kono's Surf Club (Pacific Beach, *I*)
Rhinoceros Cafe & Grill (Coronado, *M*)

BREAKFAST

The Cottage (La Jolla, *I*)
Brockton Villa (La Jolla, *I*)
Café Lulu (Downtown, *I*)
Hob Nob Hill (Hillcrest/Uptown, *M*)

Kono's Surf Club (Pacific Beach, *I*)
The Mission (Pacific Beach, *I*)
Old Town Mexican Cafe (Old Town, *I*)
Primavera Pastry Caffé (Coronado, *I*)

CALIFORNIA

Azzura Point (Coronado, *E*)
Brockton Villa (La Jolla, *M*)
Cafe Pacifica (Old Town, *E*)
California Cuisine (Hillcrest/ Uptown, *E*)
The Cottage (La Jolla, *I*)
D'Lish (La Jolla, *I*)
George's at the Cove (La Jolla, *E*)
George's Ocean Terrace and Cafe/Bar (La Jolla, *M*)
Mixx (Hillcrest/Uptown, *M*)
Prince of Wales Grill (Coronado, *E*)
Qwiig's (Ocean Beach, *E*)
Wolfgang Puck Cafe (Mission Valley, *M*)

Key to abbreviations: *E* = Expensive; *M* = Moderate; *I* = Inexpensive

CHINESE

Mandarin House (Hillcrest, Pacific Beach, La Jolla, *I*)
Panda Inn (Downtown, *M*)

COFFEE & TEA

Garden House Coffee & Tea (Old Town, *I*)
The Mission (Pacific Beach, *I*)
Newbreak Coffee Co. (Hillcrest/Uptown, Ocean Beach, *I*)
Pannikin (See "Java Joints in La Jolla" box)
The Secret Garden (See "Java Joints in La Jolla" box)
Wall Street Cafe (See "Java Joints in La Jolla" box)

CONTINENTAL

Thee Bungalow (Ocean Beach, *E*)
Top O' the Cove (La Jolla, *E*)

DESSERTS

Extraordinary Desserts (Hillcrest/Uptown, *I*)

ECLECTIC

Chameleon Cafe & Lizard Lounge (Coronado, *I*)
Croce's Restaurant & Nightclubs (Downtown, *E*)

ENGLISH

Princess Pub & Grille (Downtown, *I*)

FRENCH

Cafe Eleven (Hillcrest, *M*)
Chez Loma (Coronado, *E*)
Laurel (Hillcrest/Uptown, *E*)
Liaison (Hillcrest/Uptown, *M*)
Thee Bungalow (Ocean Beach, *E*)

INTERNATIONAL

The Mission (Pacific Beach, *I*)
Mixx (Hillcrest/Uptown, *M*)

ITALIAN

D'Lish (La Jolla, *I*)
Filippi's Pizza Grotto (Downtown, Pacific Beach, and other locations, *I*)
Fio's (Downtown, *E*)
Old Spaghetti Factory (Downtown, *I*)
Osteria Panevino (Downtown, *M*)
Primavera Ristorante (Coronado, *E*)
Trattoria Acqua (La Jolla, *E*)

JAPANESE/SUSHI

Cafe Japengo (La Jolla, *E*)
Ichiban (Hillcrest/Uptown, *I*)
Sushi Ota (Mission Bay, *M*)

LATIN AMERICAN

Berta's Latin American Restaurant (Old Town, *M*)

LIGHT FARE

Bread & Cie. Bakery and Cafe (Hillcrest/Uptown, *I*)
Kensington Coffee Company (Coronado, *I*)
Newbreak Coffee Co. (Hillcrest/Uptown, Ocean Beach, *I*)
Primavera Pastry Caffé (Coronado, *I*)

MEDITERRANEAN

Bread & Cie. Bakery and Cafe (Hillcrest/Uptown, *I*)
Laurel (Hillcrest/Uptown, *E*)

MEXICAN

Casa de Bandini (Old Town, *M*)
Casa de Pico (Old Town, *I*)
Old Town Mexican Cafe (Old Town, *I*)
Miguel's Cocina (Coronado, *M*)
Palenque (Pacific Beach, *I*)

MOROCCAN

Marrakesh (La Jolla, *E*)

PACIFIC RIM

Azzura Point (Coronado, *E*)
Cafe Japengo (La Jolla, *E*)
Peohe's (Coronado, *E*)

SEAFOOD

Anthony's Star of the Sea Room (Downtown, *E*)
Bay Beach Cafe (Coronado, *M*)
Brigantine Seafood Grill (Old Town, Coronado, *E*)

The Fish Market/Top of the Market
  (Downtown, *E*)
Peohe's (Coronado, *E*)

SOUTHWESTERN

Croce's Restaurant & Nightclubs
  (Downtown, *E*)
Dakota Grill and Spirits
  (Downtown, *M*)

THAI

Celadon (Hillcrest/Uptown, *M*)
Spice & Rice Thai Kitchen
  (La Jolla, *M*)

VEGETARIAN

Café Lulu (Downtown, *I*)
The Vegetarian Zone
  (Hillcrest/Uptown, *I*)

2 Downtown

Downtown dining tends to be more formal than elsewhere, because of the business clientele and evening theater- and opera-goers. Once the domain of high-priced and highfalutin Continental and American restaurants, downtown was turned on its ear when chic spots began filling the Gaslamp Quarter's restored Victorian buildings. If you stroll down Fifth Avenue between E Street and K Street, you'll find a month's worth of restaurants, all packed with a hip local crowd. The Embarcadero, a stretch of waterfront along the bay, is also home to several great eating spots, all of which capitalize on their bay views.

EXPENSIVE

Anthony's Star of the Sea Room. Harbor Dr. and Ash St. ☎ **619/232-7408.** Reservations required. Jacket and tie suggested. Main courses $16.50–$32.50. AE, CB, DC, MC, V. Daily 5:30–10:30pm. Closed major holidays. Valet parking $4. Bus: 2. Trolley: America Plaza or Seaport Village. SEAFOOD.

An institution since 1965, Anthony's specializes in service, style, and seafood—all superbly delivered under the attentive eye of manager and maître d' Mario Valerio, who has been with the restaurant since it opened. The "newest" waiter has worked here for more than 25 years. The restaurant is set over the water on pilings, and its arched window wall and raised booths ensure that all diners can enjoy the view. Candles glow and crystal glistens, setting the stage for white-gloved and silver-domed-platter service that seems pretentious for all but the most special occasions. Popular appetizers are clams Genovese tossed with béchamel sauce and topped with Parmesan cheese, and lobster scampi della casa. Other seafood dishes that get top billing are baked sole à l'admiral (stuffed with lobster, shrimp, and crab) and swordfish, both prepared for two. Come with a hearty appetite—portions are quite large.

✪ **Croce's Restaurants & Nightclubs.** 802 Fifth Ave. (at F St.). ☎ **619/233-4355.** www.croces.com. Reservations not accepted; call for same-day "priority seating" (before walk-ins). Main courses $14–$23. AE, DC, DISC, MC, V. Daily 5pm–midnight. Valet parking $6 with validation. Bus: 3, 5, 16, or 25. Trolley: Gaslamp Quarter. AMERICAN/SOUTHWESTERN/ECLECTIC.

Ingrid Croce, widow of singer-songwriter Jim, was instrumental in the resurgence of the once-decayed Gaslamp Quarter, and her establishment has expanded to fill every corner of this 1890 Romanesque building. Croce's is the primary restaurant, featuring a menu that fuses Southern soul food and Southwestern spice with Asian flavors and Continental standards. Croce's West is more casual in ambiance, but not in price; the menu is virtually identical save for a few more Southwestern touches (a jalapeño here, an avocado there). Add the raucous Top Hat Bar & Grille and the intimate Jazz Bar, and the complex is the hottest ticket in town, with crowds lining up for dinner tables and nightclub shows.

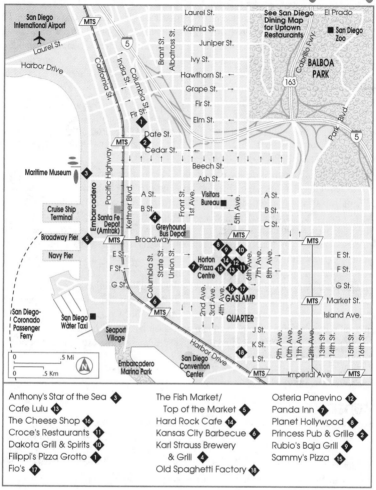

Anthony's Star of the Sea ◆3
Cafe Lulu ◆13
The Cheese Shop ◆16
Croce's Restaurants ◆11
Dakota Grill & Spirits ◆10
Filippi's Pizza Grotto ◆1
Fio's ◆17

The Fish Market/
    Top of the Market ◆5
Hard Rock Cafe ◆14
Kansas City Barbecue ◆6
Karl Strauss Brewery
    & Grill ◆4
Old Spaghetti Factory ◆18

Osteria Panevino ◆12
Panda Inn ◆7
Planet Hollywood ◆8
Princess Pub & Grille ◆2
Rubio's Baja Grill ◆9
Sammy's Pizza ◆15

An evening in the Gaslamp Quarter isn't complete without at least strolling by the Croce's corner; expect a festive good time any night of the week. Those who dine at the full-service restaurants can enter the two nightspots (see chapter 10 for a full listing) without paying the cover charge.

✪ **Fio's.** 801 Fifth Ave. (at F St.). ☎ **619/234-3467.** www.fioscucina.com. Reservations recommended for dinner. Main courses $11–$25. AE, DC, DISC, MC, V. Mon–Thurs 5–10:30pm, Fri–Sat 5–11pm, Sun 5–10pm. Valet parking $6 with validation. Bus: 3, 5, 16, or 25. Trolley: Gaslamp Quarter. NORTHERN ITALIAN.

Fio's has been *the* spot to see and be seen in the Gaslamp Quarter since it opened, and it's the granddaddy of the new wave of trendy Italian restaurants. Set in an 1881 Italianate Victorian that once housed chic Marston's department store, Fio's has a sophisticated ambiance and is *always* crowded. Once cutting-edge, the upscale trattoria menu is now practiced and consistently superior. It features jet-black linguini tossed with the freshest seafood, delicate angel hair pasta perfectly balanced with basil and pine nuts, and gourmet pizzas served at regular tables and the special pizza bar. The menu pleases both light eaters (with antipasti and pastas) and heartier palates—the impressive list of meat entrees includes mustard-rosemary rack of lamb, veal shank on saffron risotto, and delicately sweet hazelnut-crusted pork loin with Frangelico and peaches. If you stop by without a reservation, you can sit at the elegant cocktail bar and order from the complete menu.

The Fish Market/Top of the Market. 750 N. Harbor Dr. ☎ **619/232-FISH** (Fish Market), or 619/234-4TOP (Top of the Market). www.thefishmarket.com. Reservations not accepted at the Fish Market, recommended for Top of the Market. Main courses $9–$25 (Fish Market); $15–$32 (Top of the Market). AE, CB, DC, DISC, MC, V. Daily 11am–10pm. Valet parking $4. Bus: 7/7B. Trolley: Seaport Village. SEAFOOD.

The red building perched on the end of the G Street Pier at the Embarcadero houses two of San Diego's most popular seafood restaurants: The Fish Market and its pricier cousin, Top of the Market. Both offer superb fresh seafood and menus that change daily. The chalkboard out front tells you what's freshest, be it Mississippi catfish, Maine lobster, Canadian salmon, or Mexican yellowtail. The ground-level Fish Market, a market and casual restaurant, has oyster and sushi bars and a cocktail lounge. Upstairs, the elegant Top of the Market looks like a private club, with teakwood touches, mounted fish trophies, and historic photographs. The panoramic view encompasses the bay, the Coronado Bay Bridge, and, sometimes, aircraft carriers (the restaurant provides binoculars). Besides seafood, you can order homemade pasta and choose from a wine list as extensive as the menu. This lofty place inspires some to dress up and make a reservation, but you can also drop by just to have a drink and enjoy the view. Outdoor seating is directly above the water. You can spend a moderate amount downstairs, and a lot more upstairs.

There is another Fish Market Restaurant in **Del Mar** at 640 Via de la Valle (☎ **858/755-2277**).

MODERATE

Dakota Grill and Spirits. 901 Fifth Ave. (at E St.). ☎ **619/234-5554.** Reservations recommended. Main courses $9–$18. AE, DC, DISC, MC, V. Mon–Fri 11:30am–2:30pm; Mon–Thurs 5–10pm, Fri–Sat 5–11pm, Sun 5–9pm. Valet parking (after 5pm) $5; self-parking in the area $7. Bus: 3, 5, 16, or 25. Trolley: Gaslamp Quarter. AMERICAN/SOUTHWESTERN.

This downtown business lunch favorite is always busy and noisy; the Southwestern cowboy kitsch matches the cuisine but can be a little too theme-y for some. Little pistols on the menu indicate the most popular items, which include shrimp tasso (sautéed with Cajun ham and sweet peas in ancho chili cream), spit-roasted chicken with orange chipotle glaze or Dakota barbecue sauce, and mixed grill served with roasted garlic and grilled red potatoes. When the kitchen is on, Dakota's innovation makes it one of San Diego's best, but an occasional dud results from the overzealous combination of too many disparate ingredients. Still, it's not losing any ground as one of the Gaslamp Quarter's star eateries, and the raucous, casual atmosphere fits the lively cuisine. A pianist plays weekend nights.

Karl Strauss Downtown Brewery & Grill. 1157 Columbia St. (between B and C sts.). ☎ **619/ 234-BREW** (2739). Main courses $7–$15. MC, V. Sun–Wed 11:30am–10pm (beer and wine until 11pm), Thurs–Sat 11:30am–midnight (beer and wine until 1am). Bus: 5. Trolley: America Plaza. AMERICAN.

Brewmaster Karl Strauss put San Diego on the microbrewery map with this unpretentious factory setting. The smell of hops and malt wafts throughout, and the stainless-steel tanks are visible from the bar. Brews, all on tap, range from pale ale to amber lager. Five-ounce samplers are 85¢ each; if you like what you taste, 12-ounce glasses, pints, and hefty schooners stand chilled and ready. There's also non-alcoholic beer, and wine by the glass. Accompaniments include Cajun fries, hamburgers, German sausage with sauerkraut, fish-and-chips, and other greasy bar food, but that's secondary to the stylish suds. Beer-related memorabilia and brewery tours are available. (For more information, see "Pitcher This: San Diego's Microbreweries," in chapter 10.)

Osteria Panevino. 722 Fifth Ave. (between F and G sts.). ☎ **619/595-7959.** Reservations recommended. Main courses $9–$21. AE, CB, DC, DISC, MC, V. Sun–Thurs 11:30am–10pm, Fri–Sat 11:30am–11:30pm. Valet parking $6. Bus: 3, 5, 16, or 25. Trolley: Gaslamp Quarter. ITALIAN.

Expertly prepared, intricate dishes set Osteria Panevino apart from the Gaslamp Quarter's ubiquitous trattorias. The setting is welcoming, a New York–like space with bare brick walls and a small sidewalk-seating area. The unselfconscious atmosphere belies the sophistication of the menu, which peaks with homemade pastas in rich, complex sauces. Antipasti are so satisfying that they are almost minimeals; I recommend mozzarella wrapped in prosciutto and baked over sautéed spinach, or filet mignon carpaccio topped with hearts of palm, avocado, goat cheese, and olive oil. Fish and meat entrees are equally enticing, bathed in rich reduction sauces and accented with inventive flavors. A good wine list is made better with special themed trios of 2-ounce tastings. Sometimes the hostess, clad in evening gown and heels, warmly greets passersby from the doorway like a high-class circus barker. The atmosphere is cozy or crowded, depending on how close you like to be to your fellow diners.

✪ **Panda Inn.** Horton Plaza (top floor). ☎ **619/233-7800.** Reservations recommended. Main courses $8–$18. AE, DC, DISC, JCB, MC, V. Sun–Thurs 11am–10pm, Fri–Sat 11am–10:30pm. Trolley: American Plaza. CHINESE.

Circus-like Horton Plaza holds many restaurants, but this stylish, upscale choice is on the opposite end of the spectrum from your average Hot-Dog-on-a-Stick. Its elegant interior—decorated with modern art and Chinese pottery—matches the gourmet selection of Mandarin and Szechuan dishes. Standouts include lemon scallops, honey-walnut shrimp, and enoki-mushroom chicken. The dining room has a view of the city skyline, and the lounge area has a full bar. Some will find the location convenient for shopping and movie-going, while others will be irritated at dealing with parking and the crowded shopping mall maze—Panda Inn is really one of San Diego's best, though.

INEXPENSIVE

✪ **Café Lulu.** 419 F St. (near Fourth Ave.). ☎ **619/238-0114.** Main courses $3–$7. No credit cards. Sun–Thurs 9am–2am, Fri and Sat 9am–4am. Bus: 3, 5, 16, or 25. Trolley: Gaslamp Quarter. VEGETARIAN.

Smack-dab in the heart of the Gaslamp Quarter, Café Lulu aims for a hip, Bohemian mood despite its location half a block from commercial Horton Plaza. Ostensibly a coffee bar, the cafe makes a terrific choice for casual dining; if the stylishly metallic interior is too harsh for you, watch the street action from a sidewalk table. The food is health conscious, prepared with organic ingredients and no meat. Soups, salads, cheese melts, and veggie lasagne are on the menu; breads come from the incomparable Bread & Cie., uptown (see the entry later in this chapter). Eggs, granola, and waffles are served in the morning, but anytime is the right time to try one of the inventive coffee drinks, like cafe Bohème (mocha with almond syrup) or cafe L'amour (iced latte with a hazelnut tinge). Beer and wine are also served.

✪ **Filippi's Pizza Grotto.** 1747 India St. (between Date and Fir sts.), Little Italy. ☎ **619/232-5095.** Main courses $4.75–$12.50. AE, DC, DISC, MC, V. Sun–Thurs 11am–10pm, Fri–Sat 11am–11pm. Free parking. Bus: 5. Trolley: County Center/Little Italy. ITALIAN.

The Chain Gang

San Diego's branch of the ubiquitous **Planet Hollywood,** 197 Horton Plaza, corner of Broadway and 5th Avenue (☎ **619/702-STAR;** www.planethollywood.com), is in the heart of the Gaslamp Quarter, downtown. There's nearly always a line of folks waiting to eat here and ogle the movie memorabilia; the staff regularly pacifies diners with free movie posters and theater passes.

You'll find the **Hard Rock Cafe's** rock 'n' roll memorabilia–and great burgers–in the Gaslamp Quarter at 801 4th Ave. (☎ **619/615-7625;** www.hardrock.com) and in La Jolla at 909 Prospect St., La Jolla (☎ **619/454-5101**).

Think Little Italy, and this is the picture that comes to mind. To get to the dining area, decorated with Chianti bottles and red-checked tablecloths, you walk through an Italian grocery store and deli strewn with cheeses, pastas, wines, bottles of olive oil, and salamis. You might even end up eating behind shelves of canned olives, but don't feel bad—this has been a tradition since 1950. The intoxicating smell of pizza wafts into the street; Filippi's has more than 15 varieties (including vegetarian), plus Old World spaghetti, lasagne, and other pasta. Children's portions are available, and kids will feel right at home.

The original of a dozen branches, this Filippi's has free parking; other locations include 962 Garnet Ave., **Pacific Beach** (☎ **619/483-6222**); Kearny Mesa; East Mission Valley; and Escondido.

Kansas City Barbecue. 610 W. Market St. ☎ **619/231-9680.** Reservations accepted only for parties of 8 or more. Main courses $8.75–$11.50. MC, V. Daily 11am–1am. Trolley: Seaport Village. AMERICAN.

Kansas City Barbecue's honky-tonk mystique was fueled by its appearance as the fly-boy hangout in the movie *Top Gun.* Posters from the film share wall space with county-fair memorabilia, old Kansas car tags, and a photograph of official "bar wench" Carry Nation. This homey dive is right next to the railroad tracks and across from the tony Hyatt Regency. The spicy barbecue ribs, chicken, and hot links are slow-cooked over an open fire and served with sliced Wonder bread and your choice of coleslaw, beans, fries, onion rings, potato salad, or corn on the cob. The food is okay, but the atmosphere is the real draw.

Old Spaghetti Factory. 275 Fifth Ave. (at K St.). ☎ **619/233-4323.** Main courses $4.25–$8.10. DISC, MC, V. Mon–Fri 11:30am–2pm and 5–10pm, Sat–Sun noon–10pm. Bus: 1. Trolley: Gaslamp Quarter. ITALIAN.

It's lively, it's family-friendly, and it's a great deal—no wonder folks are always waiting for tables. The menu is basic spaghetti-and-meatball fare; for the price of a main course, you also get salad, sourdough bread, ice cream, and coffee or tea (with refills). Table wines are available by the glass or decanter. Part of a chain that always has creative settings; the restaurant is in a former printing factory, with some tables enclosed in a 1917 trolley car. The decor is lavish early bordello—fun for adults and stimulating for kids, who can frolic in the small play area.

Princess Pub & Grille. 1665 India St. (at Date St.). ☎ **619/702-3021.** www.princesspub.com. Main courses $6–$11. DISC, MC, V. Daily 11:30am–1am. Bus: 5. Trolley: Santa Fe Depot. ENGLISH.

This local haunt is great for Anglophiles and others hungry for a ploughman's plate, Cornish pasty, steak-and-kidney pie, fish-and-chips, or bangers in hefty portions. Formerly known as the Princess of Wales, the bar still has photos and commemorative plates of Princess Diana hanging everywhere, along with flags from England, a well-worn dartboard, and a photo of the Queen Mother downing a pint. You can usually find a copy of the *Union Jack* (a newspaper published in the United States for British expats), too. Among the English beers available are Bass, Fuller's, and Watney's. For a taste of Ireland, order a Guinness; the Princess also serves hard Devon cider. Friday and Saturday nights are particularly busy.

3 Hillcrest/Uptown

Hillcrest and the other fashionable uptown neighborhoods are jam-packed with great food for any palate (and any wallet). Some are old standbys filled nightly with loyal regulars; others are cutting-edge experiments that might be gone next year. Ethnic food, French food, health-conscious bistro fare, retro comfort food, specialty cafes and bakeries, California cuisine (as in the restaurant of the same name)—they're all done with the panache you'd expect in the trendiest part of town.

If none of the listings below appeals to you, here are more: **Cafe Eleven,** 1440 University Ave. (☎ 619/260-8023), is a dinner-only country French restaurant, and a good value. The word's out, so you'll need a reservation for the dining room or garden-patio tables. Nearby, **Ichiban,** 1449 University Ave. (☎ **619/299-7203**), is where locals on the run stop in for a fix of sushi, teriyaki bowls, or yakisoba noodles. It's fast, cheap, and no-frills—and the food is great.

EXPENSIVE

California Cuisine. 1027 University Ave. (east of 10th St.). ☎ **619/543-0790.** Reservations recommended for dinner. Main courses $13–$20; 3-course theater menu (daily 5–7pm) $20. AE, DISC, MC, V. Tues–Fri 11am–10pm, Sat–Sun 5–10pm. Bus: 8, 11, 16, or 25. CALIFORNIA.

While this excellent restaurant's name is no longer as cutting-edge as when it opened in the early '80s, the always-creative menu keeps up with contemporary trends. A quiet, understated dining room and delightfully romantic patio set the stage as the smoothly professional and respectful staff proffers fine dining at moderate prices to a casual crowd.

The menu changes daily and contains mouth-watering appetizers like sesame-seared ahi with hot-and-sour raspberry sauce, or caramelized onion and Gruyère tart on balsamic baby greens. Main courses are, more often than not, stacked in trendy towers, and their flavors are composed with equal care: Blackened beef tenderloin sits atop sun-dried mashed potatoes surrounded by bright tomato puree, and Chilean sea bass is poached in saffron broth with tangy capers and buttery Yukon gold potatoes. Early birds and bargain seekers will appreciate the theater menu, which is a great deal. Parking can be scarce along this busy stretch of University. You'll spot the light-strewn bushes in front of the restaurant.

✪ **Laurel.** 505 Laurel St. (at Fifth Ave.). ☎ **619/239-2222.** Reservations recommended. Main courses $15–$22. AE, CB, DC, DISC, JCB, MC, V. Sun–Thurs 5–10pm, Fri–Sat 5–11pm. Valet parking $4. Bus: 1, 3, or 25. FRENCH/MEDITERRANEAN.

Given its sophisticated decor, pedigreed chefs, prime Balboa Park location, and well-composed menu of country French dishes with a Mediterranean accent, it's no wonder this relatively new restaurant was an instant success. It's also popular with theatergoers, offering shuttle service to the Old Globe followed by an after-performance dessert. Live piano music adds to the glamour of dining in this swank room on the ground floor of a new office building. Start by choosing from an extensive selection of tantalizing appetizers, including saffron-tinged red pepper–and–shellfish soup, veal sweetbreads with portabella mushrooms and grainy mustard sauce, and warm caramelized onion and Roquefort tart. Main courses include crisp Muscovy duck confit, roasted salmon with tangy red-beet vinaigrette, and venison in a rich shallot–port wine sauce. One of the most stylish choices near often-funky Hillcrest, Laurel has an almost New York ambiance coupled with moderate prices.

MODERATE

Celadon. 3628 Fifth Ave. (between Brookes and Pennsylvania aves.). ☎ **619/295-8800.** Reservations recommended. Main courses $8–$15. AE, MC, V. Mon–Fri 11:30am–2pm; Mon–Sat 5–10pm. Bus: 1, 3, or 25. THAI.

Celadon fills a niche with moderately priced yet elegant dining. When it opened in the mid-'80s, this sleek, modern eatery was a pioneer, bringing gourmet Thai to a city unfamiliar with the cuisine. Because the restaurant is still known for beautifully prepared and presented dishes, it seems unfair to grouse about the dated mauve decor. Specialties include shrimp in spicy, creamy coconut sauce; sautéed scallops in "burnt" sauce with a touch of garlic; *mee krob*, caramelized noodles with chicken and shrimp; and vegetarian pad Thai with deep-fried tofu. Appetizers range from sweet and savory to hot and spicy; a favorite is Bangkok summer salad, composed of roasted pork with cilantro, mint, and lime juice.

Hob Nob Hill. 2271 First Ave. (at Juniper St.). ☎ **619/239-8176.** Breakfast and lunch menu items $3.25–$8.55; dinner main courses $8–$14. AE, DC, DISC, MC, V. Daily 7am–9pm. Bus: 1, 3, or 25. AMERICAN.

This homey coffee shop and deli began as a 14-stool lunch counter in 1944, and has grown into one of the most popular neighborhood hangouts in the city. At any given time it's a sure bet no patron lives farther than 5 miles away; this is no "destination" restaurant. You'll find comfort food at its best, priced reasonably enough for many regulars to dine here more often than in their own homes. The career waitresses are accustomed to plenty of hobnobbing professionals conducting power breakfasts over beef hash, oatmeal with pecans, or fried eggs with thick, hickory-smoked bacon. Stick-to-your-ribs meals appear at lunch and dinner—old favorites like chicken and dumplings, roast turkey, prime rib, or liver grilled with onions. It's a great place to bring the kids, especially on Sunday, when many local families observe a multigeneration dinner tradition.

Liaison. 2202 Fourth Ave. (at Ivy St.). ☎ **619/234-5540.** Main courses $10.75–$19.75; fixed-price dinner $46 per couple. AE, CB, DC, DISC, MC, V. Tues–Sun 5–10:30pm. Bus: 1, 3, or 25. FRENCH.

The cuisine and decor at this cozy, inviting cafe evoke a Gallic farmhouse kitchen. It has stone walls, blue-and-white tablecloths, candlelit tables, and copper pots hanging from the rafters. Conveniently located for Balboa Park theater-goers, this fave has a hearty French country menu that includes lamb curry, medallions of pork or beef, coquilles St. Jacques, roast duckling à l'orange, salmon with crayfish butter, and more. The nightly fixed price dinner—pâté, soup, salad, main course, dessert, and wine for two—is a great deal. The house specialty dessert costs extra: a Grand Marnier chocolate or amaretto soufflé for two, at $5 per person. Ooh la la!

Mixx. 3671 Fifth Ave. (at Pennsylvania Ave.). ☎ **619/299-6499.** Reservations recommended, especially on weekends. Main courses $11–$19. AE, CB, DC, DISC, MC, V. Sun–Thurs 5–10pm, Fri–Sat 5–11pm. Bus: 1, 3, or 25. CALIFORNIA/INTERNATIONAL.

Aptly named for its subtle global fusion fare, Mixx embodies everything good about Hillcrest dining: an attractive, relaxing room; a sophisticated crowd; thoughtfully composed dinners; and polished, friendly service. It's easy to see why hip locals gravitate to

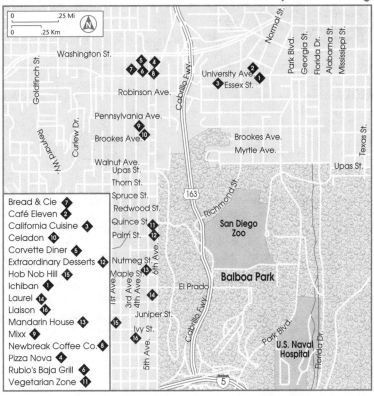

Bread & Cie 7
Café Eleven 2
California Cuisine 3
Celadon 10
Corvette Diner 5
Extraordinary Desserts 12
Hob Nob Hill 15
Ichiban 1
Laurel 14
Liaison 16
Mandarin House 13
Mixx 9
Newbreak Coffee Co. 8
Pizza Nova 4
Rubio's Baja Grill 6
Vegetarian Zone 11

Mixx's wood-paneled street-level cocktail lounge and the often-jovial dining room above. Menu standouts include a starter of pepper-seared ahi over ginger-jicama slaw, duck and wild mushroom ravioli, and pepper filet mignon on truffle mashed potatoes with an armagnac, cream, and port wine reduction. Even carnivores should check out chef Josh McGinnis' surprisingly inventive nightly vegetarian special. Prepared, plated, and presented with finesse, one meal here will quickly convince you that Mixx cares about style, substance, *and* value. Allow time to search for that elusive Hillcrest parking space!

INEXPENSIVE

✪ **Bread & Cie. Bakery and Cafe.** 350 University Ave. (between Third and Fourth sts.). ☎ **619/683-9322.** Sandwiches and light meals $3–$6. No credit cards. Mon–Fri 7am–7pm, Sat 7am–6pm, Sun 8am–6pm. Bus: 8, 11, or 16. LIGHT FARE/MEDITERRANEAN.

Delicious aromas permeate this cavernous Hillcrest bakery, where the city's most unusually flavored breads are baked before your eyes all day long. The traditions of European artisan bread-making and attention to the fine points of texture and crust quickly catapulted Bread & Cie. to local stardom. Mouthwatering favorites include anise and fig, black olive, *panella dell'uva* (grape bread), and rye currant (weekends only). Even the relatively plain sourdough batard is tart, chewy perfection. Ask for a free sample, or order one of the many Mediterranean-inspired sandwiches on the bread of your choice. Try tuna niçoise on potato dill; mozzarella, roasted peppers, and olive tapenade on rosemary olive oil; or roast turkey with hot pepper cheese on

San Diego's Cyber Cafes

If you're looking to log some online time while in San Diego, check out the plugged-in coffee houses featured in chapter 10, "San Diego After Dark."

jalapeño. The specialty coffee drinks make a perfect accompaniment to a light breakfast of fresh scones, muffins, and fruit turnovers. Seating is at bistro-style metal tables in full view of the busy ovens.

Corvette Diner. 3946 Fifth Ave. (between Washington St. and University Ave.). ☎ **619/542-1001.** Reservations not accepted. Main courses $4.50–$9.95. AE, DC, DISC, MC, V. Sun–Thurs 11am–10pm, Fri–Sat 11am–midnight. Valet parking free weekdays, $4 evening and weekend. Bus: 1, 3, or 25. AMERICAN.

Time travel back into the rockin' '50s at this theme diner, where the jukebox is loud, the gum-snapping waitresses slide into your booth to take your order, and the decor is vintage Corvette to the highest power. Equal parts *Happy Days* hangout and Jackrabbit Slim's (from *Pulp Fiction*), the Corvette Diner is a comfy time warp in the midst of trendy Hillcrest, and the eats ain't bad, either. Burgers, sandwiches, appetizer munchies, blue-plate specials, and salads share the menu with a *very* full page of fountain favorites. Beer and wine are served, and there's a large bar in the center of the cavernous dining room. The party jumps a notch at night, with DJs and even a magician providing more entertainment (on top of the already entertaining atmosphere).

۞ Extraordinary Desserts. 2929 Fifth Ave. (between Palm and Quince sts.). ☎ **619/294-7001.** Desserts $2–$6. MC, V. Mon–Thurs 8:30am–11pm, Fri 8:30am–midnight, Sat 11am–midnight, Sun 2–11pm. Bus: 1, 3, or 25. DESSERTS.

If you're a lover of sweets—heck, if you've ever eaten a dessert at all—you owe it to yourself to visit this unique cafe. Chef and proprietor Karen Krasne's name features prominently on the sign, as well it should: Krasne's talent surpasses the promise of her impressive pedigree, which includes a *Certificate de Patisserie* from Le Cordon Bleu in Paris. Dozens of divine creations are available daily, and even the humble carrot cake is savory enough to wow naysayers. Others include a raspberry linzer torte layered with white-chocolate buttercream; Grand Marnier chocolate cheesecake on a brownie crust, sealed with bittersweet ganache; and 24-karat chocolate praline dacquoise—crunchy chocolate praline mousse balanced by Frangelico-soaked hazelnut meringues and coated with dark chocolate and gold leaf. Originally educated in Hawaii, Krasne likes to incorporate island touches like macadamia nuts, ultra-fresh coconut, passion fruit, and pure Kona coffee. Her Parisian experience is also represented; the shop sells tea and accoutrements from the fine salon Mariage Frères. If you're trying to moderate your diet, eat at the Vegetarian Zone next door (see below)—it helps justify dessert!

Mandarin House. 2604 Fifth Ave. (at Maple St.). ☎ **619/232-1101.** Reservations recommended. Most main courses $6.50–$10. AE, DC, MC, V. Mon–Sat 11am–10pm, Sun 2–10pm. Bus: 1, 3, or 25. CHINESE.

Practiced Mandarin and Szechuan fare at reasonable prices is the prevailing theme of this Hillcrest mainstay, the bulk of whose business is local takeout. The dining room is comfortable, quiet, and softly lit; I'd gladly trade the bland pastel decor, though, for the kitschy red lacquer–and–dragon style usually associated with the classic Chinese restaurant. It would certainly be in keeping with the ornate Polynesian cocktails Mandarin House serves in specialty glasses (hula girls, Buddhas, and so forth); sweet and not too potent, they're a bargain at $3.75. The comprehensive menu probably contains your favorite dish—there are several show-stopping sizzling platters, and a nice selection of meat-free choices. Anything marked hot and spicy can have its heat turned down (or up) a notch according to taste. While vegetable and chicken dishes are evenly good, those featuring beef or pork don't always use the best grade of meat.

Mandarin House also has locations in **La Jolla,** at 6765 La Jolla Blvd. (☎ **858/ 454-2555**), and **Pacific Beach,** at 1820 Garnet Ave. (☎ **619/273-2288**).

Newbreak Coffee Co. 523 University Ave. ☎ **619/295-1600.** Menu items $1.25–$5. No credit cards. Mon–Thurs 6am–11pm, Fri 6am–midnight, Sat 7am–midnight, Sun 7am–11pm. Bus: 1 or 3. COFFEE & TEA/LIGHT FARE.

It changes ownership—and names—too often to keep track, but this centrally located coffeehouse is essential to the Hillcrest scene. Ocean Beach's Newbreak Coffee Company recently took over from the San Diego coffee gurus Pannikin, but changed little else. The large, casual main lounge is strewn with newspapers and people at leisure, enjoying Newbreak's gourmet bagel spreads, light sandwiches, scones, sweets, and coffee fresh from the in-store roaster. Those seeking solitude can be found nestled in the cozy upstairs lounge, and even busy Hillcrest residents stop in for freshly ground coffee sold by the pound.

There's a branch in **Ocean Beach,** at 1830 Sunset Cliffs Blvd. (☎ **619/226-4471**).

✪ **The Vegetarian Zone.** 2949 Fifth Ave. (between Palm and Quince sts.). ☎ **619/ 298-7302,** or 619/298-9232 for deli and takeout. Reservations not accepted. Main courses $5–$10. AE, DC, DISC, MC, V. Mon–Thurs 11:30am–9pm, Fri 11:30am–10pm, Sat 8:30am–10pm, Sun 8:30am–9pm; deli, daily 10am–9pm. Free parking. Bus: 1, 3, or 25. VEGETARIAN.

San Diego's only strictly vegetarian restaurant is a real treat, and word has gotten around—it's nearly always crowded, and everyone knows about it. Even if you're wary of tempeh, tofu, and meat substitutes, there are plenty of veggie ethnic selections on the menu. Greek spinach-and-feta pie has crispy edges and buttery phyllo layers; Indian turnovers are sweet and savory, flavored with pumpkin and curry; and the Mediterranean roasted-vegetable sandwich is accented with smoky mozzarella cheese. If you're ordering salad, don't miss the tangy miso-ginger dressing. In business since 1975, the Vegetarian Zone has opened a deli next door. There's seating indoors and on a casual patio; soothing music creates a pleasant ambiance enjoyed by trendy Hillcrest types, business lunchers, and the health-conscious from all walks of life. Wine is served by the glass. In case you feel deserving of a treat after such a healthful meal, the heavenly Extraordinary Desserts (see above) is next door.

4 Old Town

Visitors usually have at least one meal in the Old Town area. San Diego's oldest historic district is also its most touristy, and most restaurants here follow suit—Mexican food and bathtub-size margaritas are the big draw, as are mariachi music and colorful decor. For a change of pace, try Cafe Pacifica or Berta's; the Garden House also offers a pleasant respite.

EXPENSIVE

Brigantine Seafood Grill. 2444 San Diego Ave. ☎ **619/298-9840.** Reservations recommended on weekends. Main courses $7.95–$29.95; early-bird special (Sun–Thurs 5–7pm) $10–$14. AE, CB, DC, MC, V. Mon–Thurs 11am–10:30pm, Fri–Sat 11am–11pm, Sun 10am–10:30pm. Bus: 5/5A. Trolley: Old Town. SEAFOOD.

The Brigantine is best known for its oyster-bar happy hour from 4 to 7pm (until 9:30pm on Mondays). Beer, margaritas, and food are heavily discounted, and you can expect standing room only. Early-bird dinners include seafood, steak, or chicken served with several side dishes and bread. The food is good but not great; it's above average for a chain, but the congenial atmosphere seems the primary draw. Inside, the decor is upscale and nautical; outside, there's a pleasant patio with a fireplace to take the chill off the night air. At lunch, you can get everything from crabcakes or fish-and-chips to fresh fish or pasta. Lunch specials come with sourdough bread and two side dishes. The bar and oyster bar are open daily until midnight.

There's also a Brigantine Seafood Grill on **Coronado,** at 1333 Orange Ave. (☎ **619/435-4166**).

Cafe Pacifica. 2414 San Diego Ave. ☎ **619/291-6666.** www.cafepacifica.com. Reservations recommended. Main courses $12–$22. AE, CB, DC, DISC, MC, V. Mon–Sat 5:30–10pm, Sun 5–9:30pm. Valet parking $4. Bus: 5/5A. Trolley: Old Town. CALIFORNIA.

You can't tell a book by its cover: Inside this cozy Old Town casita, the decor is cleanly contemporary (but still romantic) and the food anything but Mexican. Established in 1980 by the now revered duo of Kipp Downing and Deacon Brown, Cafe Pacifica serves upscale, imaginative seafood and produces kitchen alumni who go on to enjoy local fame. Among the temptations on the menu are crab-stuffed portabella mushroom topped with grilled asparagus, anise-scented bouillabaisse, and daily fresh-fish selections served grilled with your choice of five sauces. Signature items include Hawaiian ahi with shiitake mushrooms and ginger butter, griddled mustard catfish, and the "Pomerita," a pomegranate margarita. Patrons tend to dress up, though it's not required. To avoid the crowds, arrive in the early evening.

MODERATE

✪ **Berta's Latin American Restaurant.** 3928 Twiggs St. (at Congress St.). ☎ **619/ 295-2343.** Main courses $5–$7 at lunch, $11–$13 at dinner. AE, MC, V. Daily 11am–10pm (lunch menu till 3pm). Bus: 5/5A. Trolley: Old Town. LATIN AMERICAN.

Berta's is a welcome change from the nacho-and-fajita joints that dominate Old Town dining, though it can attract as large a crowd on weekends. Housed in a charming, basic cottage tucked away on a side street, Berta's faithfully re-creates the sunny flavors of Central America, where slow cooking mellows the heat of chiles and other spices. Everyone starts with a basket of fresh flour tortillas and mild salsa verde, which usually vanishes before you're done contemplating such mouthwatering dishes as Guatemalan *chilimal,* a rich pork-and-vegetable casserole with chiles, tomatoes, cornmeal masa, coriander, and cloves. Try the Salvadoran *pupusas* (at lunch only)—dense corn-mash turnovers with melted cheese and black beans, their texture perfectly offset with crunchy cabbage salad and one of Berta's special salsas. Or opt for a table full of Spanish-style *tapas,* grazing alternately on crispy empanadas (filled turnovers), strong Spanish olives, or *Pincho Moruno,* skewered lamb and onion redolent of spices and red saffron.

Casa de Bandini. 2754 Calhoun St. (opposite Old Town Plaza). ☎ **619/297-8211.** Reservations not accepted. Main courses $6–$15. AE, CB, DC, DISC, MC, V. Daily 11am–9pm (till 10pm in summer). Free parking. Bus: 5/5A. Trolley: Old Town. MEXICAN.

As much an Old Town tradition as the mariachi music that's played here on weekends, Casa de Bandini is the most picturesque of several Mexican restaurants with predictable food and birdbath-size margaritas. It fills the nooks and crannies of an adobe hacienda built in 1823 for Juan Bandini, a local merchant and politician. The superbly renovated enclosed patio has iron gates, flowers blooming around a bubbling fountain, and umbrella-shaded tables for year-round alfresco dining. Some of the dishes are gourmet Mexican, others simple south-of-the-border fare. The crowd consists mainly of out-of-towners, but the ambiance and towering tostada salads draw a lunchtime crowd. The setting makes this restaurant extra-special, and makes it worth a mediocre meal.

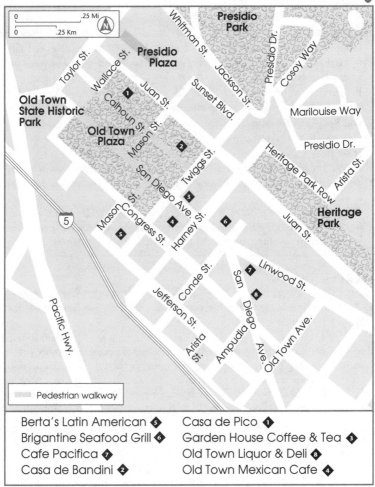

Berta's Latin American ❺
Brigantine Seafood Grill ❻
Cafe Pacifica ❼
Casa de Bandini ❷
Casa de Pico ❶
Garden House Coffee & Tea ❸
Old Town Liquor & Deli ❽
Old Town Mexican Cafe ❹

Casa de Pico. 2754 Calhoun St. ☎ **619/296-3267.** Reservations not accepted. Main courses $5–$14. AE, DC, MC, V. Sun–Thurs 10am–9pm, Fri–Sat 10am–9:30pm. Free parking. Bus: 5/5A. Trolley: Old Town. MEXICAN.

The heartbeat of Bazaar del Mundo, Casa de Pico has a carnival atmosphere and a colorful courtyard complete with fountain, flags, umbrellas, and mariachis who will serenade your table on request. The restaurant sits on the original site of the home of General Pío Pico, the last governor of Mexican California. Diagrammed explanations of Mexican dishes on the menu are a tip-off to the touristy element, but plenty of visitors are eager to dine at the heart of Old Town's historic center. A selection of bodacious margaritas helps keep things lively. The menu holds no surprises to anyone familiar with enchiladas, tacos, and burritos; a popular selection is the Mexican sampler, "La Especial de Juan," with chimichangas, enchiladas, and fajitas. To avoid standing in line for a table, try coming here before 5pm or after 8pm Sunday through Thursday.

⊕ Family-Friendly Restaurants

Filippi's Pizza Grotto *(see p. 89)*   Children's portions are available, and kids will feel right at home at this red-checked vinyl–tablecloth joint. The pizzas are among the best in town.

Planet Hollywood *(see p. 90)*   Your kids can sip a "Home Alone" while they drink in the decor, which includes more than 300 pieces of movie memorabilia.

Old Spaghetti Factory *(see p. 90)*   Kids get special attention here, and even their own toys. There's a play area, too.

Hard Rock Cafe *(see p. 90)*   Besides the great burgers, salads, and sandwiches, the family can also enjoy the wide range of rock memorabilia exhibited here. The casual atmosphere, blaring music, and friendly staff will make the kids feel right at home.

Corvette Diner *(see p. 94)*   Resembling a 1950s diner, this place appeals to teens and preteens. Parents will have fun reminiscing, and kids will enjoy the burgers and fries or other short-order fare, served in sock-hop surroundings.

INEXPENSIVE

Garden House Coffee & Tea. 2480 San Diego Ave. ☎ **619/220-0723.** Menu items $1–$3. No credit cards. Mon–Thurs 7am–6pm, Fri–Sat 7am–9pm, Sun 7am–7:30pm (shorter hours in winter). Bus: 5/5A. Trolley: Old Town. COFFEE & TEA.

Set off San Diego Avenue along a brick walkway beside the Whaley House, this gourmet shop in an old wooden cottage is always good for a cup of fresh-brewed coffee (any variation or size). You get 10¢ off if you bring your own cup the way the locals do; refills are half price. Muffins and pastries are also available. While it's mostly a takeout place, there are a few chairs on the porch, and some benches nearby. This is a great place to rest in the shade of the wizened pepper trees. It's next to the Old Town Drug Store Museum.

✪ Old Town Mexican Cafe. 2489 San Diego Ave. ☎ **619/297-4330.** Reservations accepted only for parties of 10 or more. Main courses $7.50–$11.50. AE, DISC, MC, V. Sun–Thurs 7am–11pm, Fri–Sat 7am–midnight; bar service until 2am. Bus: 5/5A. Trolley: Old Town. MEXICAN.

This place is so popular that it's become an Old Town tourist attraction in its own right. It keeps expanding into additional colorful dining rooms and outdoor patios, but the wait for a table is still often 30 to 60 minutes. Pass the time gazing in from the sidewalk as tortillas are hand-patted the old-fashioned way, soon to be a hot-off-the-grill treat accompanying every meal. Once inside, order what some consider the best margarita in town, followed by one of the cafe's two specialties: carnitas, the traditional Mexican dish of deep-fried pork served with tortillas, guacamole, sour cream, beans, and rice; or rotisserie chicken with the same trimmings. It's loud and crowded and the *cerveza* flows like, well, beer, but this Old Town mainstay is best in the city for traditional Mexican.

5 Mission Bay & the Beaches

Generally speaking, restaurants at the beach exist primarily to provide an excuse for sitting and gazing at the water. Because this activity is most commonly accompanied by steady drinking, it stands to reason that the food isn't often remarkable. We've tried to balance the most scenic of these typical hangouts with places actually known for outstanding food—with a little effort, they can be found.

Noteworthy beach spots include **Kono's Surf Club Cafe,** 704 Garnet Ave., Pacific Beach (☎ **619/483-1669**), a Hawaiian-themed boardwalk breakfast shack that's cheap and delicious. A plump Kono's breakfast burrito provides enough fuel for a day of surfing or sightseeing. Additional locations of several restaurants described elsewhere in this chapter: **Mandarin House,** 1820 Garnet St., in Pacific Plaza, Pacific Beach (☎ **619/273-2288**); **Filippi's Pizza Grotto,** 962 Garnet St., Pacific Beach (☎ **619/483-6222**); and **Newbreak Coffee Co.,** 1830 Sunset Cliffs Blvd., Ocean Beach (☎ **619/226-4471**).

EXPENSIVE

Thee Bungalow. 4996 W. Point Loma Blvd. (at Bacon St.), Ocean Beach. ☎ **619/224-2884.** www.theebungalow.com. Reservations recommended. Main courses $14–$23; early-bird specials $10–$13. AE, DC, DISC, MC, V. Mon–Thurs 5:30–9:30pm, Fri–Sat 5–10pm, Sun 5–9pm. Free parking. Bus: 26 or 34B. FRENCH/CONTINENTAL.

This small cottage stands alone at the edge of Robb Field near the Ocean Beach channel, a romantic hideaway beckoning diners for consistently good Continental cuisine augmented by a well-chosen, well-priced wine list. By far the fanciest restaurant in laid-back Ocean Beach, Thee Bungalow endears itself to the local crowd with daily early-bird specials ($10–$13). The house specialty is crispy roast duck, served with your choice of sauce (the best are black cherry or spiced pepper rum), ideally followed by one of the decadent, made-to-order dessert soufflés for two (chocolate or Grand Marnier). Another menu standout is *osso buco*–style lamb shank adorned with shallot–red-wine puree. Equally appealing first courses include brie and asparagus baked in puff pastry, and warm chicken salad (stuffed with sun-dried tomatoes and basil, then presented with feta cheese and fruit, it also doubles as a light meal). There's always a sampler plate featuring house-made pâtés with Dijon, cornichons, capers, and little toasts.

Qwiig's. 5083 Santa Monica St. (at Abbott St.), Ocean Beach. ☎ **619/222-1101.** Reservations suggested. Main courses $12–$21. AE, MC, V. Mon–Fri 11:30am–9pm, Sat 5–10pm, Sun 5–9pm. Bus: 23 or 35. CALIFORNIA.

It's taken more than a sunset view overlooking the Ocean Beach Pier to keep this upscale bar and grill going since 1985; the restaurant owes its consistent popularity to first-rate food served without pretense. Every table faces the sea, but the best view is from slightly elevated crescent-shaped booths (ask for one when reserving). Even the after-work crowd that gathers at the bar to munch on fried calamari, artichokes, and oysters can see to the pier; only sushi bar patrons in the corner miss out on the view.

Large and welcoming, Qwiig's hums pleasantly with conversation and serves food that's better than any other view-intense oceanfront spot in this area. The fresh-fish specials are most popular—choices often include rare ahi with braised spinach and sesame-sherry sauce, and Chilean sea bass with lime, tequila, and roasted garlic. Several seafood pastas are offered. Meat and poultry dishes include prime rib, an outstanding ½-pound burger, and nightly specials that always shine. Wines are well matched to the cuisine, and there are imaginative special cocktails each night. The restaurant got its strange name from a group of Ocean Beach surfers nicknamed "qwiigs."

MODERATE

The Green Flash. 701 Thomas Ave. (at Mission Blvd.), Pacific Beach. ☎ **619/270-7715.** Reservations recommended. Main courses $10–$20; sunset specials Sun–Thurs 4:30–7pm. AE, CB, DC, DISC, MC, V. Mon–Thurs 8am–9:30pm, Fri 8am–10pm, Sat 7:30am–10pm, Sun 7:30am–9:30pm. Bus: 34/34A. AMERICAN.

Known throughout Pacific Beach for its location and hip, local clientele, the Green Flash serves reasonably good (and typically beachy) food at decent prices. The menu includes plenty of grilled and deep-fried seafood, straightforward steaks, and giant main-course salads. You'll also find platters of shellfish (oysters, clams, shrimp) and ethnic appetizers. On the glassed-in patio, locals congregate every evening to catch a glimpse of the optical phenomenon for which this boardwalk hangout is named. It has something to do with the color spectrum at the moment the sun disappears below the horizon, but the scientific explanation becomes less important—and the decibel level rises—with every round of drinks.

✪ **Palenque.** 1653 Garnet Ave. (at Jewell St.), Pacific Beach. ☎ **619/272-7816.** Reservations not accepted. Main courses $4–$8 at lunch, $9–$15 at dinner. AE, MC, V. Daily 11:30am–2:30pm; Sun–Thurs 5–9pm, Fri–Sat 5–10pm. Bus: 27. MEXICAN.

Often described as a hole-in-the-wall and a hidden treasure, this casual, family-run restaurant is both—and well worth the search. Behind a foliage-laden fence on busy Garnet Avenue, Palenque has a pleasant outdoor patio and casual dining room where piñatas and paper birds dangle from the thatched, skylit ceiling. You'll start with crispy chips accompanied by two homemade salsas whose fresh perfection is representative of every dish on the menu. From earthy *mole* sauce (the best in San Diego) and freshly patted corn tortillas to carafes of refreshing lemonade, everything tastes as if it was lovingly prepared by your Mexican grandma. Drawing on regional traditions from Mexico's interior, the menu features a long list of unique appetizers that are good for sharing, plus exceptionally good layered enchiladas. At dinner, meats like *tinga poblano* (pork flavored with chipotle peppers), beef *panile* (with peanut-pasilla chile sauce), and chicken *mole poblano* are served platter-style with tortillas and all the fixings. Some dishes pack quite a spicy kick.

✪ **Sushi Ota.** 4529 Mission Bay Dr. (at Bunker Hill), Mission Bay. ☎ **619/270-5670.** Reservations recommended on weekends. Main courses $8–$15; sushi $2.50–$8. AE, MC, V. Tues–Fri 11:30am–2pm; daily 5:30–10:30pm. JAPANESE.

If you like statistics, you should know that chef-owner Yukito Ota's masterful sushi garnered a nearly perfect food rating in the San Diego *Zagat Survey.* This sophisticated, traditional restaurant (no Asian fusion here) is a minimalist bento box with stark white walls and black furniture, softened by indirect lighting. The sushi menu is short, because savvy regulars look first to the 8 to 10 daily specials posted behind the counter. The city's most experienced chefs, armed with nimble fingers and very sharp knives, turn the day's fresh catch into artful little bundles accented with mounds of wasabi and ginger. The rest of the varied menu features seafood, teriyaki-glazed meats, feather-light tempura, and a variety of small appetizers perfect to accompany a large sushi order.

This restaurant is difficult to find, mainly because it's hard to believe that such outstanding dining would hide behind a Laundromat and convenience store in the rear of a mini-mall that's perpendicular to the street. It's also in a nondescript part of Pacific Beach, nearer to I-5 than the ocean, but none of that should discourage you from seeking it out.

INEXPENSIVE

Firehouse Beach Cafe. 722 Grand Ave., Pacific Beach. ☎ **619/272-1999.** Reservations recommended on weekends. Main courses $6–$13. AE, DISC, MC, V. Sun–Thurs 7am–9pm, Fri–Sat 7am–10pm. Free parking. Bus: 34/34A. AMERICAN.

Ceiling fans stir the air in this cheerful, comfortably crowded place, and there's pleasant rooftop dining with an ocean view if you're lucky enough to snag a seat. Just off the Pacific Beach boardwalk, the cafe sees a lot of foot traffic and socializing locals.

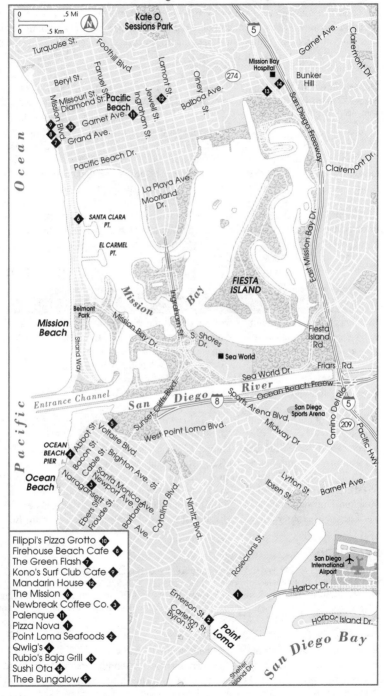

Filippi's Pizza Grotto ⑩
Firehouse Beach Cafe ⑧
The Green Flash ⑦
Kono's Surf Club Cafe ⑨
Mandarin House ⑫
The Mission ⑥
Newbreak Coffee Co. ③
Palenque ⑪
Pizza Nova ①
Point Loma Seafoods ②
Qwiig's ④
Rubio's Baja Grill ⑬
Sushi Ota ⑭
Thee Bungalow ⑤

Those in the know go for great breakfasts—choices include Mexican-style eggs and breakfast burritos, French toast, and omelets. During happy hour (4 to 6pm), you'll find bargain prices on drinks and finger-lickin' appetizers. The rest of the menu is adequate, running the gamut from fish tacos to Tex-Mex fajitas to lasagne and all-American burgers.

The Mission. 3795 Mission Blvd. (between Pacific Beach Dr. and Mission Bay Way), Mission Beach. ☎ **619/488-9060.** Menu items $4.50–$8. AE, MC, V. Mon–Fri 7am–3pm, Sat–Sun 7am–4pm. Bus: 27, 34, 34A, or 34B. COFFEEHOUSE/INTERNATIONAL.

Located alongside the funky surf shops, bikini boutiques, and alternative galleries of Bohemian Mission Beach, the Mission is this neighborhood's central meeting place. But it's good enough to attract more than just locals, and now has an upscale sister location east of Hillcrest that serves dinner. At the beach, the menu features all-day breakfasts (from traditional pancakes to nouvelle egg dishes and Latin-flavored burritos and quesadillas), plus light lunch sandwiches and salads. Standouts include tamales and eggs with tomatillo sauce, chicken-apple sausage with eggs and a mound of rosemary potatoes, and cinnamon French toast with blackberry puree. Seating is casual, comfy, and conducive to lingering (tons of students, writers, and diarists hang out here), if only with a soupbowl-size caffe latte.

The other location is in **North Park,** at 2801 University Ave. (☎ **619/220-8992**).

6 La Jolla

As befits an upscale community with time (and money) on its hands, La Jolla seems to have more than its fair share of good restaurants. Happily, they are mostly affordable, and more ethnically diverse than you might expect in a community that still supports a haberdashery called "The Ascot Shop." While many restaurants are clustered in the village, on Prospect Street and the few blocks directly east, you can also cruise down La Jolla Boulevard or up by the La Jolla Beach & Tennis Club for additional choices.

Branches of establishments described elsewhere in this chapter include **Mandarin House,** 6765 La Jolla Blvd. (☎ **858/454-2555**)—it has bad rest rooms; get takeout—and the reliable **Chart House,** 1270 Prospect St. (☎ **858/459-8201**).

La Jolla restaurants don't serve very late. If you get hungry after the traditional dinner hour, head for **Karl Strauss Brewery & Grill,** 1044 Wall St. (☎ **858/551-BREW**), where the kitchen stays open until 9pm Monday through Wednesday, 10pm on Thursday and Sunday, and 11pm on Friday and Saturday (see "Pitcher This: San Diego's Microbreweries," in chapter 10 for more information). The Hard Rock Cafe also stays open late.

EXPENSIVE

Cafe Japengo. At the Hyatt Regency La Jolla, 8960 University Center Lane. ☎ **858/450-3355.** Reservations recommended. Main courses $12–$20. AE, DC, DISC, MC, V. Mon–Fri 11:30am–2:30pm; Sun–Thurs 5–10pm, Fri–Sat 5–10:30pm. Sushi bar open till 11pm Mon–Thurs, 11:30pm Fri–Sat. Valet parking $3, validated self-parking free. From I-5, take La Jolla Village Dr. E. PACIFIC RIM/SUSHI.

Despite being contrived and self-conscious, Cafe Japengo is worth a trip for the food alone. With subdued lighting and a highly stylized Asian atmosphere, this restaurant is the best of several attached to the Golden Triangle's behemoth Hyatt Regency Hotel. The beautiful people know they look even more so among the warm woods and leafy shadows here, so there's lots of posing and people-watching. It's always packed; patrons come from all over the county for Japengo's Pacific Rim fusion cuisine, which incorporates South American and even European touches.

Important Area Code Changes

Dial **619** to call most of San Diego, except for La Jolla, Del Mar, Rancho Sante Fe, and Rancho Bernardo, which received the new area code **858** during 1999. Use **760** to reach the remainder of San Diego County, including Encinitas, Carlsbad, Oceanside, Escondido, Ramona, Julian, and Anza–Borrego. Toward the end of 2000, the 619 area code will split further, with Coronado and the southern portion of San Diego County getting a new area code—**935**. Don't worry, though, this change doesn't go into effect until December 8, 2000, and the rest of the city of San Diego will remain in the 619 area code.

Some offerings, like the pot-stickers in tangy coriander-mint sauce or lemongrass-marinated swordfish, are superb; others, like the seared ahi "Napoleon," suffer from extra ingredients that just make the dish fussy. Sushi here is the same way; Japengo features the finest and freshest fish, but churns out enormously popular "specialty" rolls (combinations wrapped in even more ingredients, often drenched in sauce and garnished even further). The dramatic, colorfully presented inventions are enormously popular, but sushi purists will be happiest sticking to the basics.

George's at the Cove. 1250 Prospect St. ☎ **858/454-4244.** Reservations recommended. Main courses $9–$15 at lunch, $21–$31 at dinner. AE, DC, DISC, MC, V. Mon–Fri 11:30am–2:30pm, Sat–Sun 11:30am–3pm; Mon–Thurs 5:30–10pm, Fri–Sat 5–10:30pm, Sun 5–10pm. Valet parking $5–$6. CALIFORNIA.

You'll find host and namesake George Hauer at his restaurant's door most nights; he greets loyal regulars by name, and his confidence assures newcomers that they'll leave impressed with this beloved La Jolla tradition. Voted most popular in the *Zagat* restaurant survey, George's wins consistent praise for impeccable service, gorgeous views of the cove, and outstanding California cuisine.

The menu, in typical San Diego fashion, presents many inventive seafood options. Appetizers range from baked Carlsbad mussels to phyllo-wrapped prawns flavored with cumin and ginger. The healthful smoked chicken, broccoli, and black-bean soup is a mainstay. Main courses combine many flavors with practiced artistry; applewood-smoked and cedar-roasted king salmon is paired with crisp polenta and subtle nuances of ginger, and tenderloin filet is wrapped in bacon and finished with a gorgonzola-tinged reduction. As an alternative to dinner's pricey main courses, try the tasting menu, which offers a seasonally composed five-course sampling for around $38 per person; or try the more reasonably priced lunch menu. The informal Ocean Terrace Cafe (see below) is upstairs.

Marrakesh. 634 Pearl St. (at Draper Ave.). ☎ **858/454-2500.** Reservations recommended on weekends. Main courses $15–$19.95; 5-course "feasts" $16.50–$23. AE, CB, DC, DISC, MC, V. Sun–Thurs 5–10pm, Fri–Sat 5–11pm. Free parking. MOROCCAN.

One of several Southern California Marrakesh locations, this "total experience" restaurant evokes its origins in the 1960s, when many of its ilk were inspiring decorators with banquette seating and ethnic prints. Step inside and you enter a Moroccan palace, where guests eat in the traditional style—fingers only, no utensils—at low tables in tent-like surroundings. The padded walls and seats are rich with dark tapestries and North African prints. Exotic mood music, soft lighting, and (on weekends only) a strolling belly dancer complete the experience—along with authentic Moroc-can fare that's available à la carte or as a complete feast. Appetizers include Middle Eastern tabouleh and hommus, as well as traditional Moroccan bastilla (a pastry filled with chicken, egg, and crushed almonds, then topped with powdered sugar and cinnamon).

There's also a seafood bastilla. Most dinners feature brochettes of beef, lamb, chicken, or seafood, while the "feasts" offer choices of lemon chicken, lamb in honey sauce, quail, rabbit, or fish stew. Finish with a simple dessert of fruit, nuts, and baklava. While some consider food-as-entertainment passé, Marrakesh is still a great choice for the uninitiated or a festive group meal.

✪ **Top O' the Cove.** 1216 Prospect St. ☎ **858/454-7779.** www.topofthecove.com. Reservations recommended. Jackets suggested for men at dinner. Main courses $10–$17 at lunch, $25–$32 at dinner; Sun brunch $18.50. AE, CB, DC, MC, V. Mon–Sat 11:30am–10:30pm, Sun 10:30am–10:30pm. Valet parking $5. CONTINENTAL.

Always voted "most romantic" in annual diner surveys, Top O' the Cove is traditionally where San Diegans go for special occasions—first dates, marriage proposals, anniversaries. They're banking that its timeless elegance will enhance the evening's mood, and they're rarely disappointed. The finely proportioned historic cottage is one of the last remaining along Prospect Street, and it's shaded by 100-year-old Australian fig trees. Fireplaces glow on chilly evenings, and a gazebo and patio make the perfect setting for balmy summer dining or Sunday brunch.

The menu is peppered with French names, but the cuisine has distinct California overtones, often with Asian flavors (blackened ahi sashimi, salmon spring rolls, pan-seared tuna with wasabi). Classic standouts include green-peppercorn tenderloin dressed with Cognac and cream, veal piccata, medallion of elk with wine-shallot sauce, and fresh swordfish prepared differently each day. Sorbet is served between courses. Lunch is lighter, with salads and sandwiches joining selections from the dinner menu. The dessert specialty is a bittersweet-chocolate box filled with cream and fruit in a raspberry sauce—try it with a liqueur-laced house coffee. Aficionados will thrill to the extensive wine list, but its steep markup threatens to spoil the mood.

✪ **Trattoria Acqua.** 1298 Prospect St., on Coast Walk. ☎ **858/454-0709.** www. trattoriaacqua.com. Reservations recommended. Main courses $13–$22. AE, MC, V. Daily 11:30am–2:30pm; Sun–Thurs 5–9:30pm, Fri–Sat 5–10:30pm. Validated self-parking free. ITALIAN.

Nestled on tiled terraces close enough to catch ocean breezes, this excellent Northern Italian spot has a more relaxed ambiance than similarly sophisticated Gaslamp Quarter trattorias. Rustic walls and outdoor seating shaded by flowering vines evoke a romantic Tuscan villa. A mixed crowd of suits and well-heeled couples gather to enjoy expertly prepared seasonal dishes; every table starts with bread served with an indescribably pungent Mediterranean spread. Acqua's pastas (all available as appetizers or main courses) are as good as it gets—rich, heady flavor combinations like spinach, chard, and four-cheese gnocchi, or veal-and-mortadella tortellini in fennel cream sauce. Other specialties include *saltimbocca con funghi* (veal scaloppini with sage, prosciutto, and forest-mushroom sauce), cassoulet (traditional Toulouse-style duck confit, sausage, and braised lamb baked with white beans, tomato, and fresh thyme), and *salmone al pepe* (roasted peppercorn-crusted Atlantic salmon served over lentils with sherry-and-shallot vinaigrette). The well-chosen wine list has received *Wine Spectator* accolades several years in a row.

MODERATE

✪ **Brockton Villa.** 1235 Coast Blvd. (across from La Jolla Cove). ☎ **858/454-7393.** Reservations recommended (call by Thurs for Sun brunch). Breakfast $4–$7.25; dinner main courses $10–$20. AE, DISC, MC, V. Mon 8am–3pm, Tues–Sun 8am–9pm (later in summer). BREAKFAST/CALIFORNIA.

In a restored 1894 beach bungalow, this charming cafe has a history as intriguing as its varied, eclectic menu. Named for an early resident's hometown (Brockton, Mass.),

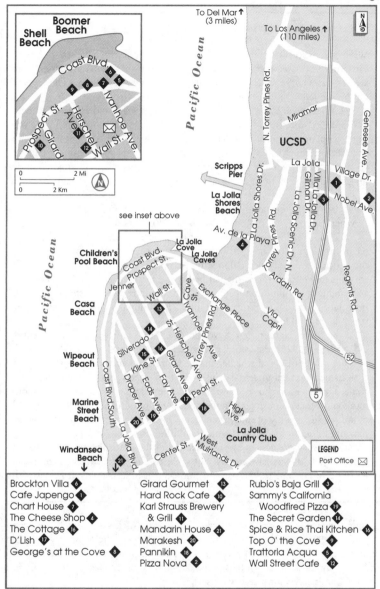

Brockton Villa 🔶6
Cafe Japengo 🔶1
Chart House 🔶7
The Cheese Shop 🔶4
The Cottage 🔶16
D'Lish 🔶17
George's at the Cove 🔶8

Girard Gourmet 🔶13
Hard Rock Cafe 🔶10
Karl Strauss Brewery
  & Grill 🔶11
Mandarin House 🔶21
Marakesh 🔶20
Pannikin 🔶18
Pizza Nova 🔶2

Rubio's Baja Grill 🔶3
Sammy's California
  Woodfired Pizza 🔶19
The Secret Garden 🔶14
Spice & Rice Thai Kitchen 🔶15
Top O' the Cove 🔶9
Trattoria Acqua 🔶5
Wall Street Cafe 🔶12

the cottage is imbued with the spirit of artistic souls drawn to this breathtaking perch overlooking La Jolla Cove. Rescued by the trailblazing Pannikin Coffee Company in the 1960s, the restaurant is now independently run by a Pannikin alum.

The biggest buzz is at breakfast, when you can enjoy inventive dishes such as soufflé-like "Coast Toast" (the house take on French toast) and Greek "steamers" (eggs scrambled with an espresso steamer, then mixed with feta cheese, tomato, and basil). The dozens of coffee drinks include the "Keith Richards"—four shots of espresso topped with Mexican hot chocolate (Mother's Little Helper indeed!). Lunch stars

Java Joints in La Jolla

While cafes specializing in espresso, latte, and cappuccino have sprung up all over San Diego, no other area caters to java hounds the way La Jolla does. Here are a few area coffeehouses that serve up caffeine as well as charm. (They appear on the "La Jolla Dining" map.)

The **Wall Street Cafe,** 1044 Wall St., between Girard and Herschel avenues (☎ **858/551-1044**), used to be a bank. Today the rest rooms are in the old vault, so patrons who use the facilities must pass through the huge door that once secured much of La Jolla's money. Local businesspeople pop in for cups to go or for lunch, while the midmorning and afternoon crowd lingers a little longer and has time to sit and read. Live entertainment, such as light jazz or a mellow guitar, makes this a particularly popular place on Friday and Saturday nights between 8pm and midnight. The cafe also serves beer and wine.

When it opened in 1968, the **Pannikin,** 7467 Girard Ave., near Pearl Street (☎ **858/454-5453**), was La Jolla's first coffeehouse, and, in some ways, it still seems frozen in 1968. Long-haired men ponder chess moves on the porch, and the notice board touts meditation seminars. This is a favored hangout of UCSD students and faculty. Inside the old house, the fireplace and communal seating are conducive to impromptu intellectual discussions. Some customers wander next door to the D. G. Wills bookstore. The Pannikin's retail store across the street draws loyal locals.

At the **Secret Garden,** 928 Silverado Ave., between Fay and Girard avenues (☎ **858/551-0928**), the weekday customers are almost all regulars. Many work or work out nearby, and whether they're wearing ties or tights, the staff knows their names and their preferred drinks—it's the "Cheers" of the local coffeehouse scene. This is a good choice for early risers: The official opening time is 7am, but locals know that they can get a fresh hot cup anytime after 6:15am. The weekend crowd consists mainly of shoppers taking a coffee break. (Stairs into the cottage may hinder access for travelers with disabilities.)

No matter where you enjoy your java, mind the time limit for your parking spot. La Jolla doesn't have meters, but street parking in the village is restricted to 1 or 2 hours, and zealous parking-enforcement officers dole out tickets with regularity.

include homemade soups and salads, plus unusual sandwiches like turkey meat loaf on toasted sourdough bread with spicy tomato-mint chutney. The constantly expanding dinner menu includes salmon *en croute* (wrapped in prosciutto, Gruyère, and sage, with a grainy mustard sauce), plus pastas, stews, and grilled meats. Steep stairs from the street limit access for wheelchair users.

George's Ocean Terrace and Cafe/Bar. 1250 Prospect St. ☎ **858/454-4244.** Reservations not accepted. Main courses $10–$15 at lunch, $9.50–$14.95 at dinner. AE, DC, DISC, MC, V. Sun–Thurs 11am–10pm, Fri–Sat 11am–10:30pm. Valet parking $5–$6. CALIFORNIA.

The legendary main dining room at George's (see above) has won numerous awards for its haute cuisine. But George's also accommodates those seeking good food and a spectacular setting with a more reasonable price tag—the upstairs Ocean Terrace and Cafe prepares similar dishes as well as new creations in the same kitchen as the high-priced fare. The two areas offer indoor and outdoor seating overlooking La Jolla Cove, and the same great service as the main dining room. For dinner, you can choose from several seafood or pasta dishes, or have something out of the ordinary like George's

To See . . . Perchance to Eat

Incredible ocean views, a sweeping skyline, and sailboats fluttering along the shore—it's the classic backdrop for a memorable meal. So where can you find the best views?

Downtown, the **Fish Market** and its pricier cousin **Top of the Market** overlook San Diego Bay, and the management even provides binoculars for getting a good look at aircraft carriers and other vessels. Across the harbor in Coronado, the **Bay Beach Cafe** and **Peohe's** offer panoramic views of the San Diego skyline, and the tony **Prince of Wales Grill** at the Hotel Del looks onto the sand and surf. In Pacific Beach, the **Green Flash** is just steps from the sand, and the **Firehouse Beach Cafe's** lofty deck provides another perspective of the same scene. Nearby, the **Atoll** (☎ 619/539-8635), in the Catamaran Resort Hotel, has a romantic patio facing tranquil Mission Bay. In La Jolla, **George's at the Cove** and **Top O' the Cove** are near the water, but **Brockton Villa** actually offers the La Jolla Cove as advertised on every postcard stand in town.

If you want to get up close and personal, grab your gold card and head to the **Marine Room** (☎ 858/539-8635), where Sea World technology (yes, Sea World) helped build the windows that withstand the crashing tide each day. It's at the La Jolla Beach & Tennis Club.

meat loaf served with mushroom-and-corn mashed potatoes. The award-winning smoked chicken, broccoli, and black-bean soup appears on both menus.

Spice & Rice Thai Kitchen. 7734 Girard Ave. ☎ **858/456-0466.** Reservations recommended. Main courses $7–$13. AE, MC, V. Mon–Thurs 11am–3pm and 5–10pm, Fri 11am–3pm and 5–11pm, Sat 5–11pm, Sun 5–10pm. THAI.

A fairly recent entry into the La Jolla mix, this stylish Thai restaurant is a couple of blocks from the village's tourist crush—far enough to ensure effortless parking. The lunch crowd consists of shoppers and curious tourists, while dinner is quieter; all the local businesses have shut down and many diners are going to the old-fashioned Cove movie theater next door. The food is excellent, with polished presentations and expert renditions of the classics like pad Thai, satay, curry, and glazed duck. The starters often sound as good as the entrees—consider making a grazing meal of house specialties like "gold bags" (minced pork, vegetables, and herbs wrapped in crispy rice paper and served with earthy plum sauce) or minced roast duck spiced with chiles and lime juice; spicy calamari is flavored with ginger, cilantro, lime, and chili sauce. The romantically lit covered front patio has a secluded garden feel, and inside tables also have indirect lighting. I'm predicting this all-around satisfying insider's secret will soon explode with popularity.

INEXPENSIVE

✪ **The Cottage.** 7702 Fay Ave. (at Kline St.). ☎ **858/454-8409.** www.cottagelajolla.com. Reservations accepted for dinner only. Breakfast and lunch $5–$7; dinner main courses $7–$12. AE, DISC, MC, V. Daily year-round 7:30am–3pm; May 15–Sept 30 Tues–Sat 5–9:30pm. BREAKFAST/CALIFORNIA.

La Jolla's best—and friendliest—breakfast is served at this turn-of-the-century bungalow on a sunny village corner. Newly modernized, the cottage is light and airy, but most diners opt for tables outside, where a charming white picket fence encloses the trellis-shaded brick patio. Omelets and egg dishes feature Mediterranean, Asian, or classic American touches; my favorite has creamy mashed potatoes, bacon, and melted cheese folded inside. The Cottage bakes its own muffins, breakfast breads, and—you can quote me on this—the best brownies in San Diego. While "breakfast" dishes are served all day, toward lunch the kitchen begins turning out freshly made, healthful soups, light meals, and sandwiches. Summer dinners (never heavy, always tasty) are a delight, particularly when you're seated before dark on a balmy seaside night.

D'Lish. 7514 Girard Ave. (at Pearl St.). ☎ **858/459-8118.** Reservations recommended on weekends. Main courses $7–$11. AE, DC, DISC, MC, V. Sun–Thurs 11:30am–10pm, Fri–Sat 11:30am–11pm. Free underground parking. ITALIAN/CALIFORNIA.

Located on one of La Jolla's busiest intersections (in what some consider the ugliest building in town), D'Lish is a casual crowd-pleaser. The menu offers something for everyone. The specialty is pizza—the trendy, wood-fired variety. There's also an impressive selection of equally inventive pastas, and you could just as easily choose a steak grilled with wild mushrooms, Santa Fe chicken wrap with chipotle and salsa, or meal-sized Thai chicken salad. The service is friendly and polished, even when the place is packed, and the food is reliably good enough to make up for the lack of atmosphere. Booths and tables are clustered downstairs around a wide bar, and on an upstairs mezzanine that tends to be stuffy in summer's heat.

7 Coronado

Rather like the conservative, old-school navy aura that pervades the entire "island," Coronado's dining options are reliable and often quite good, but the restaurants aren't breaking new culinary ground.

Some notable exceptions are the resort dining rooms, which seem to be waging a little rivalry over who can attract the most prestigious, multiple–award-winning executive chef. If you're in the mood for a special-occasion meal that'll knock your socks off, consider **Azzura Point,** in Loews Coronado Bay Resort, or the **Prince of Wales Grill** at the Hotel del Coronado. Of course, such culinary expertise doesn't come cheap. And if you seek ethnic or funky food, better head back across the bridge. Mexican fare (gringo-style, but well practiced) is served on the island at popular **Miguel's Cocina,** inside El Cordova hotel (☎ 619/437-4237). A branch of the **Brigantine Seafood Grill** (see "Old Town," above) is at 1333 Orange Ave. (☎ 619/435-4166).

EXPENSIVE

The Chart House. 1701 Strand Way. ☎ **619/435-0155.** Reservations recommended. Main courses $9–$25. AE, CB, DC, DISC, MC, V. Daily 5–10pm. Free parking. Bus: 901. AMERICAN.

Perched at the edge of Glorietta Bay, this restaurant resembles a cupola that must have escaped from the Hotel del Coronado, up the hill. It has been here, in the Del's former boathouse, since 1968. The upscale Chart House chain is known for restoration of historic structures, and this project is a beauty; it holds 38 antique tables and the largest collection of Tiffany lamps in Southern California (about 20 at last count). Enjoy dinner on the deck in summer or in the upstairs lounge; the mahogany, teak, and stained-glass bar came from Atlanta and dates from 1880.

The fare is straightforward—seafood and steaks, with plenty of fresh-fish specials daily. Tourist-oriented and overpriced by local standards, the Chart House still guarantees the best prime rib or Australian lobster tail you'll find. The view from the restaurant encompasses Glorietta Bay, the Coronado Yacht Club, and the Coronado Bay Bridge.

There's also a branch in **La Jolla,** at 1270 Prospect St. (☎ 858/459-8201).

Chez Loma. 1132 Loma (off Orange Ave.). ☎ **619/435-0661.** Reservations recommended. Main courses $18–$26. AE, DC, MC, V. Daily 5–10pm; Sun 10am–2pm. Bus: 901. FRENCH.

Coronado's Wide World of Hors D'Oeuvres: A Cocktail Hour Tip

If you're longing for great appetizers that are more sophisticated than popcorn shrimp and potato skins, then the new **Chameleon Cafe & Lizard Lounge,** 1301 Orange Ave., Coronado (☎ **619/437-6677**), is your answer. It's the latest venture of chef Ken Irvine, the local superstar of Chez Loma fame. The casual, eclectic eatery is half cocktail lounge—fitting, because the menu is half appetizers. The "first plates" range in price from $4 to $9, and are generously sized and suitable for sharing. Relax and watch the activity along Orange Avenue while nibbling on Asian delicacies (lobster-crab pot-stickers, smoked salmon–and–avocado sushi), Southwestern spice (goat-cheese tamales, pork empanadas), or Mediterranean standards (grilled pizzas with smoked chicken and fontina cheese or portabella mushrooms). The bar features premium vodkas and aged tequilas; we recommend eschewing the restaurant's pricier main courses and having a "grazing" meal in the bar, which stays open from lunchtime till closing.

You'd be hard pressed to find a more romantic dining spot than this intimate Victorian cottage filled with antiques and subdued candlelight. The house dates from 1889, the French-Continental restaurant from 1975. Tables are scattered throughout the house and on the enclosed garden terrace; an upstairs wine salon, reminiscent of a Victorian parlor, is a cozy spot for coffee or conversation.

Among the creative entrees are salmon with smoked-tomato vinaigrette, and roast duckling with green-peppercorn sauce. All main courses are served with soup or salad, rice or potatoes, and fresh vegetables. California wines and American microbrews are available. Follow dinner with a creamy crème caramel or Kahlúa crème brûlée. Chez Loma's service is attentive, the herb rolls addictive, and early birds enjoy specially priced meals.

Peohe's. 1201 First St. (Ferry Landing Marketplace). ☎ **619/437-4474.** Reservations recommended. Main courses $7–$15 at lunch, $16–$29 at dinner. AE, CB, DC, DISC, MC, V. Mon–Sat 11:30am–2:30pm, Sun 10:30am–2:30pm; Mon–Thurs 5:30–9pm, Fri 5:30–10pm, Sat 5–10pm, Sun 4:30–9pm. Bus: 901 or 904. PACIFIC RIM/SEAFOOD.

With over-the-top Polynesian decor of which Disneyland would be proud, Peohe's is definitely touristy and definitely overpriced—but there's no denying the awesome view across the bay or the excellent Hawaiian-style seafood and Pacific Rim–accented cuisine. Every table in the giant, light- and plant-filled atrium has a view; there are even better tables on the wooden deck at the water's edge. Dinner main courses include acclaimed crunchy coconut shrimp; island-style halibut sautéed with banana, macadamia nuts, and Frangelico liqueur; and rack of New Zealand lamb with Hunan barbecue sauce. Lunchtime options include more casual sandwiches and salads, and the tropical fantasy desserts are delectably rich. For those who love theme restaurants and Polynesian kitsch, Peohe's is a worthwhile splurge.

Primavera Ristorante. 932 Orange Ave. ☎ **619/435-0454.** Reservations recommended. Main courses $8–$12 at lunch, $13–$27 at dinner. AE, CB, DC, DISC, MC, V. Mon–Fri 11am–2:30pm; daily 5–10:30pm. Bus: 901. ITALIAN.

Located among the most fashionable Orange Avenue businesses, Primavera is the only Italian restaurant worth noting on Coronado. Residents of this conservative enclave continue to rave about the excellent fare, which noncommittally straddles the line between traditional Northern Italian and the trendy variety in evidence at San Diego's newer trattorias. The restaurant's unremarkable pastel tapestry decor brings banquet rooms to mind, but that hardly seems to matter, considering the reliably excellent food and polished service—albeit at somewhat steep prices. Old-fashioned is represented by seven traditional veal dishes, the most intriguing of which pairs tender medallions and scampi sautéed with wild mushrooms and shallots in Madeira sauce. Saffron-seafood risotto or spinach tortellini under porcini mushroom and tomato-cream sauce will appeal to more contemporary tastes. If you have room for dessert, Primavera is known for perfectly balanced tiramisu. Look for plenty of button-down military types and well-coifed socialites in the dinner crowd; at lunch, you'll see shoppers, military bigwigs who get to leave the base, and escapees from the "mainland."

MODERATE

Bay Beach Cafe. 1201 First St. (Ferry Landing Marketplace). ☎ **619/435-4900.** Reservations recommended for dinner on weekends. Main courses $9–$18; pub menu $6–$10. AE, DISC, MC, V. Mon–Fri 7–10:30am and 11am–4pm, Sat–Sun 7–11:30am and noon–4pm; daily 5–10:30pm. Free parking. Bus: 901 or 904. AMERICAN/SEAFOOD.

This loud, friendly gathering place isn't on the beach at all, but enjoys a prime perch on San Diego Bay. Seated indoors or on a glassed-in patio, diners gaze endlessly at the city skyline, which is dramatic by day and breathtaking at night. The cafe is quite popular at happy hour, when the setting sun glimmers on downtown's mirrored high-rises. The ferry docks at a wooden pier a few steps away, discharging passengers into the complex of gift shops and restaurants with a New England fishing-village theme. At the Bay Beach Cafe, the food takes a back seat to the view, but the pub menu of burgers, sandwiches, salads, and appetizers is inexpensive and satisfying. Dinner entrees aren't quite good enough for the price.

Rhinoceros Cafe & Grill. 1166 Orange Ave. ☎ **619/435-2121.** Main courses $8.95–$17.95. AE, DISC, MC, V. Mon–Fri 11am–2:45pm, Sat–Sun 8am–2:45pm; daily 5–9pm. Bus: 901. AMERICAN.

With its quirky name and something-for-everyone menu, this light, bright bistro is a welcome addition to the Coronado dining scene. It's more casual than it looks from the street and offers large portions, though the kitchen is a little heavy-handed with sauces and spices. At lunch, every other patron seems to be enjoying the popular penne à la vodka in creamy tomato sauce; favorite dinner specials are monkfish cioppino over spaghettini, Southwestern-style meat loaf, and simple herb-roasted chicken. Plenty of crispy fresh salads balance out the menu. There's a good wine list, or you might decide to try Rhino Chaser's American Ale.

INEXPENSIVE

Kensington Coffee Company. 1106 First St. ☎ **619/437-8506.** Menu items $1.50–$4.50. AE, DISC, MC, V. Daily 6am–11pm. Bus: 901 or 904. LIGHT FARE.

Dropping by here is a great way to start or end the day—or take a break. This popular coffee and tea emporium at the island's east end features five fresh brews daily, and specialty espresso drinks. Munchies include bagels, croissants, filled pastries, muffins, and scones—plus tempting brownies and cakes. Light fare, such as burritos and salads, is served at lunchtime. Tables are set up outdoors and in, scattered amongst displays of coffee and tea paraphernalia, gifts, and postcards. The friendly staff knows almost everyone by name and is extra nice to newcomers.

Primavera Pastry Caffé. 956 Orange Ave. ☎ **619/435-4191.** Main courses $4–$6. No credit cards. Daily 6:30am–6pm. Bus: 901. SANDWICHES/LIGHT FARE.

If the name sounds familiar, it's because this fantastic little cafe—the best of its kind on the island—is part of the family that includes Primavera Ristorante, up the street.

Coronado Dining

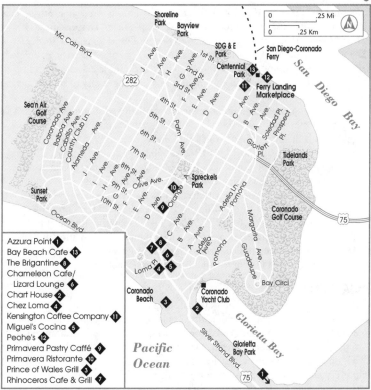

Azzura Point ❶
Bay Beach Cafe ⑬
The Brigantine ❽
Chameleon Cafe/
  Lizard Lounge ❻
Chart House ❷
Chez Loma ❹
Kensington Coffee Company ⑪
Miguel's Cocina ❺
Peohe's ⑫
Primavera Pastry Caffé ❾
Primavera Ristorante ⑩
Prince of Wales Grill ❸
Rhinoceros Cafe & Grill ❼

In addition to fresh-roasted coffee and espresso drinks, it serves omelets and other breakfast treats (till 1:30pm), burgers and deli sandwiches on the delicious house bread, and a daily fresh soup. It's the kind of spot where half the customers are greeted by name. Locals rave about the "Yacht Club" sandwich, a croissant filled with yellowfin tuna, and the breakfast croissant, topped with scrambled ham and eggs and cheddar cheese. I can't resist Primavera's fat, gooey cinnamon buns.

8 Only in San Diego

WOOD-FIRED PIZZA

It all started with Wolfgang Puck, that crafty Austrian chef who dazzled Hollywood restaurant-goers at Spago and went on to build a dynasty of California cuisine. By now, everyone is familiar with the building block of that empire; heck, you can even get it in the frozen-food section. We're talking about pizza, of course. Not the marinara-and-pepperoni variety found in other pizza meccas like New York and Chicago—for a whole generation of Californians, pizza will always mean barbecued chicken, tomato-basil, or goat cheese and sun-dried tomato. Gourmet pizzas appear to have overtaken the traditional variety in popularity, and kitchens all over San Diego stoke their wood-fired ovens to keep up with the demand.

Most of the Italian restaurants in this chapter feature at least a handful of individual-size pizzas. **D'Lish** in La Jolla (☎ 858/459-8118) has almost 20 eclectic topping variations borrowed from various ethnic cuisine. Always tops in San Diego polls is **Sammy's California Woodfired Pizza,** at 770 Fourth Ave., at F Street, in the Gaslamp Quarter (☎ **619/230-8888**); 702 Pearl St., at Draper Street, La Jolla (☎ **858/456-8018**); and 12925 El Camino Real, at Del Mar Heights Road, Del Mar (☎ **858/259-6600**). Conveniently located and always frustratingly crowded, Sammy's serves creations like duck sausage, potato garlic, or Jamaican jerk shrimp atop 10-inch rounds. It also excels at enormous salads, making it easy to share a meal and save a bundle.

A similar menu is available at **Pizza Nova,** a similarly stylish minichain with a similarly vibrant atmosphere. Despite being alike, each chain thrives by covering the neighborhoods the other doesn't. You'll find Pizza Nova at 3955 Fifth Ave., north of University Avenue, Hillcrest (☎ **619/296-6682**); 5120 N. Harbor Dr., west of Nimitz Boulevard, Point Loma (☎ **619/226-0268**); and 8650 Genesee Ave., at Nobel Drive, in La Jolla's Golden Triangle (☎ **858/458-9525**).

If you're a purist, or unfamiliar with this trend's granddaddy, head to Mission Valley and San Diego's new branch of **Wolfgang Puck Cafe,** 1640 Camino del Rio N., in Mission Valley Center (☎ **619/295-9653**). Like its cousins throughout Southern California, the casual cafe has dizzying decor, loud music, and an army of fresh-faced staffers ferrying much more than pizza. (Another of Puck's excellent signature dishes is bacon-wrapped meat loaf served on a bed of mashed potatoes.)

BAJA FISH TACOS

One of San Diego's culinary ironies is that, although the city is conscious of its Hispanic roots—not to mention within visual range of the Mexican border—it's hard to find anything other than gringo-ized combo plates in most local Mexican restaurants.

Perhaps the most authentic recipes are those at humble **Rubio's Baja Grill.** Actually, it's not so humble anymore, since proprietor Ralph Rubio began branching out into every corner of Southern California with his enormously successful yet deceptively simple fare. You can now find Rubio's in Phoenix, Las Vegas, and Los Angeles, and even edging out hot dogs in the stands at Qualcomm Stadium. In 1983, it was an achievement for local surfer Rubio to come in off the beach just long enough to open a tiny walk-up taco stand on busy Mission Bay Drive.

After years of scarfing down cheap beers and fish tacos in the Mexican fishing village of San Felipe, Ralph secured the "secret" recipe for this quintessential Baja treat: batter-dipped, deep-fried fish fillets folded in corn tortillas and garnished with shredded cabbage, salsa, and tangy *crema* sauce. Thatched-roof shacks along Baja's beach roads sell the tacos, and in the past decade they've taken this side of the border by storm. The menu at Rubio's has expanded to include beefy *carne asada,* marinated pork carnitas, chargrilled mahimahi, and homemade guacamole, all accented by the distinctively Baja flavors of fresh lime and cilantro. Unlike the food at your average McDrive-thru, at Rubio's you can wash it all down with an icy-cold beer. Because many of the newer locations have a homogenous fast-food look to them, it's fun to stop by the original stand, at 4504 E. Mission Bay Dr., at Bunker Hill Street (☎ **619/272-2801**), if you're in the neighborhood.

Rubio's also has locations in the **Gaslamp Quarter,** 901 Fourth St., at E Street (☎ **619/231-7731**); **Hillcrest,** 3900 Fifth Ave., at University Avenue (☎ **619/299-8873**); **La Jolla,** 8855 Villa La Jolla Dr., at Nobel Drive (☎ **858/546-9377**); **Pacific Beach,** 910 Grand Ave. (☎ **619/270-4800**); and **Point Loma,** 3555 Rosecrans St., at Midway Drive (☎ **619/223-2631**).

PICNIC FARE

San Diego's benign climate lends itself to dining alfresco. An excellent spot to pick up sandwiches is the **Cheese Shop,** a gourmet deli with locations downtown at 401 G St.

(☎ **619/232-2303**) and in La Jolla Shores at 2165 Avenida de la Playa (☎ **858/ 459-3921**). Other places to buy picnic fare include **Girard Gourmet,** 7837 Girard Ave., La Jolla (☎ **858/454-3321**); **Boudin Sourdough Bakery and Cafe** and the **Farmer's Market,** both in Horton Plaza; and **Old Town Liquor and Deli,** 2304 San Diego Ave. (☎ **619/291-4888**).

Another spot that's very popular with San Diegans is **Point Loma Seafoods,** on the water's edge in front of the Municipal Sportfishing Pier, at 2805 Emerson near Scott Street, south of Rosecrans and west of Harbor Drive (☎ **619/223-1109**). There's a fish market here, and you can pick up seafood sandwiches, fresh sushi, and salads to go. If you decide to make your own sandwiches, the best bread in the county comes from **Bread & Cie. Bakery and Cafe,** 350 University Ave., Hillcrest (☎ **619/683-9322**), and **Primavera Pastry Caffé,** 956 Orange Ave., Coronado (☎ **619/435-4191**).

7

Exploring San Diego

You won't run out of things to see and do in San Diego. The San Diego Zoo, Sea World, and the Wild Animal Park are the three top drawing cards, but many other activities—lots of them free!—also await.

Suggested Itineraries

If You Have 1 Day

With only one day in San Diego, you'll have to choose between two major draws: the Zoo and Sea World. Get there when the gates open to maximize your time, and make sure to allow time to enjoy lunch at an ocean-view restaurant in Ocean Beach, Pacific Beach, or La Jolla. In the afternoon, shoppers will want to do a little antiquing in Ocean Beach or Hillcrest, or stroll the boutiques of La Jolla if that was the chosen lunch spot. If shopping isn't your style, spend some time walking along the boardwalk or the Embarcadero, perhaps stopping to tour the vessels that make up the Maritime Museum. Either way, finish the day in the Gaslamp Quarter, which always promises a lively evening street scene. Choose from dozens of excellent restaurants, and stick around for some live music after dinner—if you have the energy!

If You Have 2 Days

With 2 full days in the city, you can devote each one to a separate major attraction. In addition to the Zoo and Sea World, consider spending several hours strolling through the rest of Balboa Park, enjoying the great architecture and peeking into a couple of its fantastic museums. Some, such as the Automotive Museum, the Model Railroad Museum, the Mingei International Museum, the Museum of Man, and the Museum of San Diego History, won't take more than 30 to 60 minutes. Or, if the weather is too perfect to believe, forgo an organized attraction, rent some recreational gear (bikes, skates, kayaks—they're all available), and spend several hours soaking up the sun on beautiful Mission Bay.

If You Have 3 Days

Plan the first 2 days as above, reserving the third for an excursion to the Wild Animal Park in the morning. When you return to the city, ride the ferry to Coronado for a tour of the majestic Hotel del Coronado and dinner on the island. Take a sunset walk along the beach before or after dinner.

If You Have 4 Days or More

On your fourth day, visit the Cabrillo National Monument in the morning. Spend the rest of the day enjoying the outdoors San Diego is famous for—assemble a picnic for the beach, or, if you haven't visited Balboa Park's Prado, take your picnic there and then catch an exciting OMNIMAX movie at the Fleet Science Center. Another option for Day 4 would be to take the trolley into Tijuana, and spend the day shopping there and sampling south-of-the-border flavors. With an extended stay comes the opportunity to indulge your own passion. For example, play one of San Diego's challenging golf courses; take kayak lessons on a North County beach; treat the kids to a day at LEGOLAND in Carlsbad; or poke around a historic house museum (like the Marston House, Villa Montezuma, or the William Heath Davis House).

1 The Three Major Animal Parks

Looking for wild times? San Diego supplies them as no other city can. Its world-famous zoo is home to more than 4,000 animals, many of them rare and exotic. A sister attraction, the San Diego Wild Animal Park, offers another 2,500 creatures representing 275 species in an *au naturel* setting. And Shamu and his friends form a veritable chorus line at Sea World—waving their flippers, waddling across an ersatz Antarctica, and blowing killer-whale kisses—in more than a dozen shows a day.

✪ **San Diego Zoo.** Park Blvd. and Zoo Place, Balboa Park. ☎ **619/234-3153.** TDD 619/233-9639. www.sandiegozoo.org. Admission $16 adult, $7 children 3–11, military in uniform free. Deluxe package (admission, guided bus tour, round-trip Skyfari aerial tram) $24 adults, $21.60 seniors 60 and over, $13 children. Combination Zoo and Wild Animal Park package (deluxe zoo package, Wild Animal Park admission) $35.15 adults, $20.75 children; valid for 5 days from date of purchase. DISC, MC, V. Daily year-round 9am–4pm (grounds close at 5pm); summer 9am–9pm (grounds close at 10pm). Bus: 7/7B.

More than 4,000 animals reside at this world-famous zoo, which was founded in 1916 with a handful of animals originally brought here for the 1915–16 Panama–California International Exposition. Many of the buildings you see in surrounding Balboa Park were built for the exposition. The zoo's founder, Dr. Harry Wegeforth, a local physician and lifelong animal lover, once braved the fury of an injured tiger to toss medicine into its roaring mouth.

In the early days of the zoo, "Dr. Harry" traveled around the world and bartered native Southwestern animals such as rattlesnakes and sea lions for more exotic species. The loan of two giant pandas from the People's Republic of China is a twist on the long-standing tradition—instead of exchanging exotic species, the San Diego Zoo agreed to pay $1 million for each year that the pandas are here, to aid the conservation effort in China. (See "Panda-monium," below.)

The zoo is also an accredited botanical garden, representing more than 6,000 species of flora from many climate zones, all installed to help simulate the animals' native environments.

The giant pandas are the big attention-getters, but the zoo has many other rare and exotic species: cuddly koalas from Australia, long-billed kiwis from New Zealand, wild Przewalski horses from Mongolia, lowland gorillas from Africa, and giant tortoises from the Galapagos. Of course, the zoo's regulars—lions, elephants, giraffes, tigers, and bears—prowl around as well, and the zoo is home to a great number of tropical birds. Most of the animals are housed in barless, moated enclosures that resemble their natural habitats. The habitats include Australasia, Tiger River, Sun Bear Forest, two of the world's largest walk-through bird aviaries, Flamingo Lagoon, Gorilla Tropics, Hippo Beach, and Polar Bear Plunge.

Money-Saving Tip

If you plan to go to both the Zoo and the Wild Animal Park, you might want to consider buying a **Zoological Society Membership,** which costs $68 for two adults living in the same household. Membership gives each cardholder unlimited entrance to the Zoo and Wild Animal Park, plus two adult-admission passes, six discounted admission passes, and four two-fer bus tickets, plus a subscription to *Zoo News* magazine. A **Koala Club** membership for a child costs $15 and provides unlimited entry for a year. If you don't buy the annual pass the best discount is the one for **AAA members.** The next best deal is using the coupons in the **Super Savings Coupon Book** available from the International Visitor Information Center.

The zoo offers two types of bus tours. Both provide a narrated overview and allow you to see 75% of the park. On the **35-minute guided bus tour,** you get on the bus and complete a circuit around the zoo. It costs $4 for adults, $3 for kids 3 to 11, and is included in the deluxe package. The **Kangaroo Bus Tour** allows you to get on and off the bus as many times as you want at any of the eight stops—you can even go around more than once. It costs $8 for adults and $5 for children. In general, it's better to take the tour early in the morning or late in the afternoon, when the animals are more active. The last tour starts an hour before closing—it's not as crowded as the others, but you won't see the elephants because it's their feeding time. Call the **Bus Tour Hot Line** (☎ 619/685-3264) for information about these tours, as well as Spanish-language tours, a comedy tour, and signed tours for the hearing impaired.

You can also get an aerial perspective from the **Skyfari,** which costs $1 per person each way. The ride lasts about 5 minutes—but, because it doesn't get particularly close to the animals, it's better for a bird's-eye view of Balboa Park and a survey of the zoo.

The **Children's Zoo** is scaled to a youngster's viewpoint. There's a nursery with baby animals and a petting area where kids can cuddle up to sheep, goats, and the like. The resident wombat is a special favorite here.

Wild Animal Park. 15500 San Pasqual Valley Rd., Escondido. ☎ **760/747-8702.** TDD 760/738-5067. www.sandiegozoo.org. Admission $19.95 adults, $17.95 seniors 60 and over, $12.95 children 3–11, free for children under 3 and military in uniform. Combination Zoo and Wild Animal Park package (includes deluxe zoo package) $35.15 adults, $20.75 children; valid for 5 days from date of purchase. DISC, MC, V. Daily 9am–4pm (grounds close at 5pm); extended hours during summer and Festival of Lights in December. Parking $3 per car. Take I-15 to Via Rancho Pkwy.; follow signs for about 3 miles.

Just 30 miles north of San Diego, in the San Pasqual Valley, the Wild Animal Park transports you to the African plains and other landscapes. Some 3,200 animals, many of them endangered species, roam freely over the park's 1,800 acres. In a reversal of roles, the humans are enclosed here instead of the animals. This living arrangement encourages breeding colonies, so it's not surprising that more than 80 white rhinoceroses have been born here. Several species of rare animals that had vanished from the wild, such as cheetahs and Przewalski wild horses, have been reintroduced to their natural habitats from stocks bred by the park. Approximately 650 baby animals are born every year in the park, which also serves as a botanical preserve with more than 2 million plants, including 300 endangered species.

The best way to see the animals is by riding the 5-mile **monorail** (included in the price of admission); for the best views, sit on the right-hand side. During the 50-minute ride, you'll pass through areas resembling Africa and Asia, and you'll learn interesting tidbits—did you know that rhinos are susceptible to sunburn and mosquito bites? Trains leave every 20 minutes; you can watch informative videos while you wait in the stations.

San Diego Area Attractions

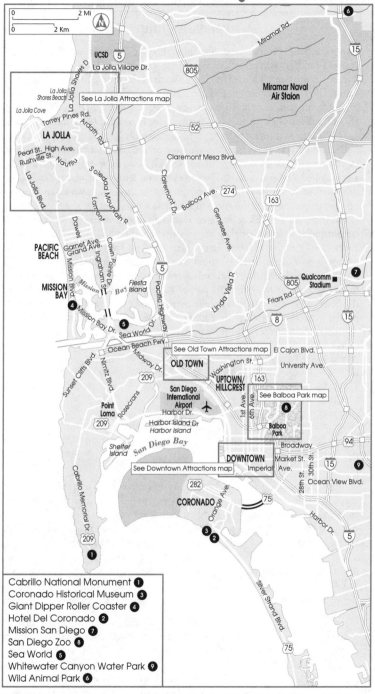

Cabrillo National Monument **1**
Coronado Historical Museum **3**
Giant Dipper Roller Coaster **4**
Hotel Del Coronado **2**
Mission San Diego **7**
San Diego Zoo **8**
Sea World **5**
Whitewater Canyon Water Park **9**
Wild Animal Park **6**

Panda-monium

Two giant pandas from China, Shi Shi (a 13-year-old male) and Bai Yun (a 3-year-old female), arrived at the San Diego Zoo in late 1996 after 3 years of intense negotiation with the U.S. Department of the Interior, the Wolong Giant Panda Conservation Centre, and the Chinese government. They are the only pair of giant pandas in the United States (the National Zoo in Washington, D.C., houses a single male, who's been in fragile health). Only about 15 giant pandas live in zoos outside China and North Korea.

Because giant pandas are endangered and protected under the Convention on International Trade in Endangered Species (CITES), importing Shi Shi and Bai Yun required a federal permit. The zoo's previous requests had been denied, but this time the powers-that-be were convinced that this project would make a significant contribution to the effort to save wild pandas.

Giant pandas are among the rarest mammals in the world—fewer than 1,000 remain in the wild, where they live in dense bamboo and coniferous forests at altitudes of 5,000 to 10,000 feet. Their numbers have dwindled due to the destruction of their natural habitat and poaching. Illegal hunting is still a problem even though the Chinese government has imposed life sentences on those convicted of the crime. As part of the agreement to get the pandas here, the San Diego Zoo agreed to contribute $1 million each year to wild-panda habitat protection projects in China. The projects were established to help double the number of existing panda preserves and create protected wildlife corridors connecting the areas.

You needn't worry that the pandas will be gone before you get here: The loan is for a period of 12 years. During that time, scientific study of their breeding and behavior patterns will take place. (Any baby pandas born at the zoo will belong to the People's Republic of China.)

Shi Shi, who weighs 230 pounds, was born in the wild and taken to the Wolong Giant Panda Conservation Centre after he was found critically wounded—probably from a fight with another male panda. Bai Yun was born at the Wolong center on September 7, 1991, and was raised by her mother, Dong Dong.

Giant pandas are related to both bears and raccoons. They are bear-like in shape, with striking black-and-white markings, and have unique front paws that enable them to grasp stalks of bamboo. Bamboo makes up about 95% of their diet, and they eat 20 to 40 pounds of food every day. This takes them 10 to 16 hours, so there's a pretty good chance that you'll see them eating.

Because of the exhibit's enormous popularity and the fact that the pandas are not always on display, the zoo provides a panda-viewing hot line (☎ **888/MY-PANDA**). Call before you go.

If you'd like to get a little closer to the animals, the park offers several alternative ways to explore the area. On the 1¾-mile **Kilimanjaro self-guided safari walk,** you'll see tigers, elephants, and cheetahs close up, as well as the Australian rain forest and views of East Africa. You can also journey into the **Heart of Africa** (the park's newest feature) on a ¾-mile self-guided trail that takes walkers through dense forest, flourishing wetlands, sprawling savannas, and open plains to discover Africa's biodiversity. It encompasses 30 acres and is home to about 300 animals representing nearly 30 species. Photographers will get a click out of **photo caravan tours,** which venture into the field enclosures. The photo tours run Wednesday through Sunday, and they cost $65 or $90 depending on the tour. Stroller and wheelchair rentals are available. Take a jacket along; it can get cold in the open-air monorail.

The most intriguing development at the Wild Animal Park is the **Roar and Snore** program, which runs from May through September. It offers a chance to camp out in the park compound and observe the nocturnal movements of rhinos, tigers, and other animals, which are often more active at night than during the day. The park provides equipment, the camp staff sets up tents, and dinner is cooked for you on a camp stove—well, an industrial-strength version. The camping is secondary, though, to the opportunity to sit around the campfire listening to tales of animal behavior, then be lulled to sleep (or from it, for the skittish) by the extraordinary animal calls emanating from every corner of the park. In the morning, enjoy a pancake breakfast, monorail ride, and Heart of Africa visit, and spend the rest of the day exploring the park. The camp-overs take place on Friday, Saturday, and Sunday nights; some are restricted to adults, while others are family events. Prices are $87.50 for adults, $67.50 for kids 8 to 11; children under 8 are not permitted. To request Roar and Snore information by mail, call ☎ **760/738-5049;** reservations can be made by calling ☎ **800/934-CAMP.**

Sea World. 500 Sea World Dr., Mission Bay. ☎ **619/226-3901.** TDD 619/226-3907. www.seaworld.com. Admission $38 adults, $29 children 3–11, free for children under 3. DISC, JCB, MC, V. Parking $6 per car, $3 per motorcycle, $8 per RV. Guided 90-min. behind-the-scenes tours, $8 adults, $7 children 3–11. Ticket sales stop ½ hr. before closing. June–Aug daily 9am–10pm; Sept–May daily 10am–5pm. Bus: 9. By car from I-5, take Sea World Dr. exit; from I-8, take W. Mission Bay Dr. exit to Sea World Dr.

One of the best-promoted attractions in California, Sea World may be your main reason for coming to San Diego. The 150-acre, multimillion-dollar aquatic playground is a showplace for marine life, made politically correct with a nominally "educational" atmosphere. Several successive 4-ton black-and-white killer whales have functioned as the park's mascot, Shamu. At its heart, Sea World is a family entertainment center where the performers are dolphins, otters, sea lions, walruses, and seals. Shows run continuously throughout the day, while visitors can rotate through the various theaters.

The 2-acre hands-on area called **Shamu's Happy Harbor** encourages kids to handle things—and features everything from a pretend pirate ship, with plenty of netted towers, to tube crawls, slides, and chances to get wet. The newest attraction is **Wild Arctic,** a virtual-reality trip to the frozen North, complete with polar bears, beluga whales, walruses, and harbor seals. Other draws include **Baywatch at Sea World,** a water-ski show named for the popular TV show, and **Shamu Backstage,** where visitors can get up close and personal with killer whales.

The **Dolphin Interaction Program** creates an opportunity for people to meet bottlenose dolphins. Although the program stops short of allowing you to swim with the dolphins, it does offer the opportunity to wade waist-deep, and plenty of time to stroke the mammals and give commands like the trainers. This 2-hour program (1 hour of education and instruction, 15 minutes of wet-suit fitting, 45 minutes in the water with the dolphins) costs $125 per person, which includes admission to Sea World on the day of your program, as well as another day within a week. Space is limited to eight people per day, so reservations are required. Participants must be age 13 or older.

Although Sea World is best known as Shamu's home, the facility also plays an important role in rescuing and rehabilitating beached animals found along the West Coast—including more than 300 seals, sea lions, marine birds, and dolphins in a year. Following the successful rescue and 1998 release of a young California gray whale, Sea

World turned its attention to the manatee, an unusual aquatic mammal rarely seen outside Florida's tropical waters. At press time, the manatees were on display at the park.

2 San Diego's Beaches

San Diego County is blessed with 70 miles of sandy coastline and more than 30 beaches that attract surfers, snorkelers, swimmers, and sunbathers. In summer, the beaches teem with locals and visitors alike. The rest of the year, when the water is cooler, they are popular places to walk and jog, and surfers don wet suits to pursue their passion.

Here's a list of San Diego's most accessible beaches, each with its own personality and devotees. They are listed geographically from south to north. If you are interested in others, *The California Coastal Access Handbook,* published by the California Coastal Commission, is helpful; it's available at most area bookstores for $17.95, or you can order it through your local bookseller. All California beaches are public to the mean high-tide line, and this publication tells you how to get to each one.

Exploring tide pools—areas that retain water after the tide has gone out, providing homes for a plethora of sea creatures—can be a lot of fun. You can get a tide chart free or for a nominal charge from many surf and diving shops, including **Emerald City Surf & Sport,** 1118 Orange Ave., Coronado, and **San Diego Divers Supply,** 5701 La Jolla Blvd., La Jolla.

Note: All beaches are good for swimming unless otherwise indicated.

IMPERIAL BEACH

Half an hour south of San Diego by car or trolley, and only a few minutes from the Mexican border, lies Imperial Beach. Besides being popular with surfers, it plays host to the annual U.S. Open Sandcastle Competition each August. The world-class sand creations range from sea scenes to dragons to dinosaurs.

✪ CORONADO BEACH

Lovely, wide, and sparkling white, this beach is conducive to strolling and lingering, especially in the late afternoon. It fronts Ocean Boulevard and is especially pretty in front of the Hotel del Coronado. The islands visible from here, "Los Coronados," are 18 miles away and belong to Mexico.

OCEAN BEACH

The northern end of Ocean Beach Park is officially known as "Dog Beach," and is one of only two in San Diego where your pooch can roam freely on the sand (and frolic with several dozen other people's pets). Surfers generally congregate around the Ocean Beach Pier, mostly in the water but often at the snack shack on the end. Rip currents are strong here and discourage most swimmers from venturing beyond waist depth. Facilities at the beach include rest rooms, showers, picnic tables, and plenty of metered parking lots. To reach the beach, take West Point Loma Boulevard all the way to the end.

BONITA COVE/MARINER'S POINT AND MISSION POINT

Facing Mission Bay in South Mission Beach, with calm waters, grassy areas for picnicking, and playground equipment, these spots are perfect for families.

PACIFIC BEACH

There's always some action at Mission Beach, particularly along **Ocean Front Walk,** a paved promenade featuring a human parade akin to that at L.A.'s Venice Beach boardwalk. It runs along Ocean Boulevard (just west of Mission Boulevard), north of Pacific Beach Drive. Pacific Beach is the home of **Tourmaline Surfing Park,** where the sport's old guard gathers to surf waters where swimmers are prohibited.

In case you want to be welcomed there.

We're here to see that you're always welcomed at establishments everywhere. That's why millions of people carry the American Express® Card – for peace of mind, confidence, and security, around the world or just around the corner.

do more

Cards

In case you're running low.

We're here to help with more than 190,000 Express Cash locations around the world. In order to enroll, just call American Express at 1 800 CASH-NOW before you start your vacation.

do more AMERICAN EXPRESS

Express Cash

And in case you'd rather be safe than sorry.

We're here with American Express® Travelers Cheques. They're the safe way to carry money on your vacation, because if they're ever lost or stolen you can get a refund, practically anywhere or anytime. To find the nearest place to buy Travelers Cheques, call 1 800 495-1153. Another way we help you do more.

do more

Travelers Cheques

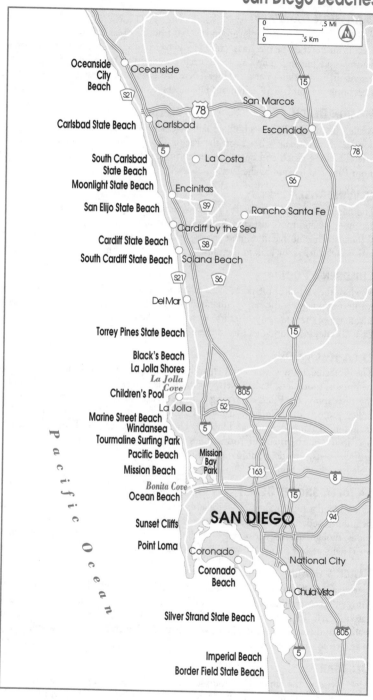

Oceanside City Beach
Oceanside

Carlsbad State Beach
Carlsbad
La Costa

South Carlsbad State Beach
Moonlight State Beach
Encinitas
San Elijo State Beach
Rancho Santa Fe
Cardiff by the Sea
Cardiff State Beach
South Cardiff State Beach
Solana Beach

San Marcos
Escondido

Del Mar

Torrey Pines State Beach

Black's Beach
La Jolla Shores
La Jolla Cove
Children's Pool
La Jolla
Marine Street Beach
Windansea
Tourmaline Surfing Park
Pacific Beach
Mission Beach
Mission Bay Park
Bonita Cove
Ocean Beach

SAN DIEGO

Sunset Cliffs
Point Loma
Coronado
National City
Coronado Beach
Chula Vista

Silver Strand State Beach

Imperial Beach
Border Field State Beach

Pacific Ocean

0 .5 Mi
0 .5 Km

✪ MISSION BAY PARK

In this 4,600-acre aquatic playground, you'll find 27 miles of bayfront, 17 miles of oceanfront beaches, picnic areas, children's playgrounds, and paths for biking, roller-skating, and jogging. The bay lends itself to windsurfing, sailing, riding personal watercraft, water-skiing, and fishing. There are dozens of access points; one of the most popular is off I-5 at Clairemont Drive, where there's a visitor information center.

MISSION BEACH

While Mission Bay Park is a body of salt water surrounded by land and bridges, Mission Beach is actually a beach on the Pacific Ocean. Surfing is popular year-round here. The long beach and boardwalk extend from Pacific Beach Drive south to Belmont Park and beyond to the jetty.

✪ WINDANSEA

The fabled locale of Tom Wolfe's *Pump House Gang,* Windansea is legendary to this day among California's surf elite. Reached by way of Bonair Street (at Neptune Place), Windansea has no facilities, and street parking is first-come, first-served. Come to surf, watch surfers, or soak in the camaraderie and party atmosphere.

CHILDREN'S POOL

Much of the sand near the point of La Jolla's peninsula is cordoned off for the resident sea lion population; the rest is inhabited by curious shutterbugs and families taking advantage of the same calm conditions that keep the sea lions around. The beach is at Coast Boulevard and Jenner Street; there's limited free street parking.

✪ LA JOLLA COVE

The protected, calm waters—praised as the clearest along the California coast—attract swimmers, snorkelers, scuba divers, and families. There's a small sandy beach, and on the cliffs above, the **Ellen Browning Scripps Park.** The cove's "look but don't touch" policy protects the colorful Garibaldi, California's state fish, plus other marine life, including abalone, octopus, and lobster. The unique Underwater Park stretches from here to the northern end of Torrey Pines State Reserve and incorporates kelp forests, artificial reefs, two deep submarine canyons, and tidal pools. La Jolla Cove is accessible from Coast Boulevard.

LA JOLLA SHORES BEACH

The wide, flat mile of sand at La Jolla Shores is popular with joggers, swimmers, and beginning body and board surfers, as well as families. Weekend crowds can be enormous, though, quickly occupying both the sand and the metered parking spaces in the lot. There are rest rooms, showers, and picnic areas here.

BLACK'S BEACH

The area's unofficial (and illegal) nude beach, it lies between La Jolla Shores Beach and Torrey Pines State Beach. Located below some steep cliffs, it is out of the way and not easy to reach. To get here, take North Torrey Pines Road, park at the Glider Port, and walk from there. *Note:* Although the water is shallow and pleasant for wading, this area is known for its rip currents.

DEL MAR

After a visit to the famous fairgrounds that are home to the Del Mar Thoroughbred Club, you may want to make tracks for the beach, a long stretch of sand backed by grassy cliffs and a playground area. Del Mar is about 15 miles from downtown San Diego (see chapter 11).

NORTHERN SAN DIEGO COUNTY

Those inclined to venture farther north in San Diego County won't be disappointed. Pacific Coast Highway leads to some inviting beaches, such as these in Encinitas: peaceful **Boneyards Beach, Swami's Beach** for surfing, and **Moonlight Beach,** popular with families and volleyball buffs. Farthest north is Oceanside, which has one of the West Coast's longest wooden piers, wide sandy beaches, and several popular surfing areas.

3 Attractions in Balboa Park

Balboa Park's 1,174 acres encompass walkways, gardens, historic buildings, restaurants, an ornate pavilion with the world's largest outdoor organ, a high-spouting fountain, an OMNIMAX theater, a nationally acclaimed theater, and the world-famous zoo (see section 1 of this chapter for a complete listing). The park's most distinctive features are the architectural beauty of the Spanish-Moorish buildings lining El Prado, its main street, and the outstanding and diverse museums contained within it.

Free **tram** transportation within the park runs Monday through Friday from 8am to 5pm and Saturday and Sunday from 11am to 4pm. Ask at the Visitor Center about free walking and museum **tours.** I've also mapped out a **walking tour** in chapter 8.

✪ **San Diego Aerospace Museum.** Pan-American Plaza. ☎ **619/234-8291.** www.aerospacemuseum.org. Admission $6 adults, $2 children 6–17, free for active military with ID and children under 6. Free 4th Tues of each month. Sept–May daily 10am–4:30pm; June–Aug daily 10am–5:30pm (last admission ½ hour before closing). Closed Thanksgiving, Dec 25. Bus: 7/7B, 16, or 25.

The Aerospace Museum, with its International Aerospace Hall of Fame, provides an overview of the nation's air and space history, from the days of hot-air balloons to the space age. It emphasizes local aviation history, including the construction here of the *Spirit of St. Louis*. The cylindrical Ford Building, built by the Ford Motor Company for the California Pacific International Exposition of 1935, houses the museum. Behind-the-scenes restoration tours are available.

Museum of Art. 1450 El Prado. ☎ **619/232-7931.** www.sdmart.com. Admission $8 adults; $6 seniors 65 and over, military, and students with ID; $3 children 6–17; free for children under 6. Admission to traveling exhibits varies. Free 3rd Tues of each month. Tues–Sun 10am–4:30pm. Bus: 7/7B, 16, or 25.

This museum has outstanding collections of Italian Renaissance and Dutch and Spanish baroque art, along with contemporary paintings and sculptures. The Grant–Munger Gallery on the ground floor features works by Monet, Toulouse-Lautrec, Renoir, Pissarro, van Gogh, and Dufy. Upstairs in the Fitch Gallery is El Greco's *Penitent St. Peter* and in the Gluck Gallery, Modigliani's *Boy with Blue Eyes* and Braque's *Coquelicots*. The traveling exhibit *Norman Rockwell: Pictures For The American People* will run in the fall of 2000. The museum has a shop, sculpture garden, and cafe with outdoor seating. Its rotunda features a striking Spanish-style tile staircase.

Money-Saving Tip

Many Balboa Park attractions are free on certain days; see "Free of Charge & Full of Fun," later in this chapter. If you plan to visit all or most of the museums in the park, consider buying the **Passport to Balboa Park.** The $19 passport, which represents a $56 value, is a coupon booklet that allows one entrance to each of 11 museums and is valid for a week. You can buy yours at any participating museum, the Balboa Park Visitor Center, or the Times Arts Tix Booth in Horton Plaza.

Museum of Photographic Arts. 1649 El Prado. ☎ **619/238-7559.** Admission $4 adults, free for children under 13 with adult. Free 2nd Tues of each month. Daily 10am–5pm. Bus: 7/7B, 16, or 25.

This is one of the few museums in the country dedicated exclusively to photographic arts, and the exhibits span the 150-year history of the medium. The extensive permanent collection of 3,600 images includes work by Edward Weston, Duane Michals, Ansel Adams, Max Yavno, Manual Alvarez Bravo, Mary Ellen Mark, Margaret Bourke-White, Sebastiao Salgado, and many others. There are also six to eight changing exhibitions every year.

Natural History Museum. 1788 El Prado. ☎ **619/232-3821.** www.sdnhm.org. Admission $6 adults, $5 seniors and active-duty military, $3 children 6–17, free for children under 6. Free 1st Tues of each month. Daily 9:30am–4:30pm, open later in summer. Bus: 7/7B, 16, or 25.

The museum focuses on the flora, fauna, and mineralogy of the Southwest. Kids marvel at the animals they find here and enjoy exploring the Desert Lab, home to live snakes and tarantulas. Upcoming exhibits include **"Dinosaurs of the Lost World"** (March 3 to September 4, 2000).

Reuben H. Fleet Science Center. 1875 El Prado. ☎ **619/238-1233.** www.rhfleet.org. Admission to Science Center $5 adults, $4 seniors 65 and over, $3 kids 3–12. Free to all 1st Tues of each month. Combination tickets available for admission plus Space Theater, SciTours, or Planetarium. MC, V. Mon–Tues 9:30am–6pm, Wed–Thurs and Sun 9:30am–9pm, Fri–Sat 9:30am–10pm. Bus: 7/7B, 16, or 25.

The Reuben H. Fleet Science Center houses the world's first OMNIMAX theater, a 76-foot tilted-dome screen that shows breathtaking IMAX/OMNIMAX films. The Science Center features five galleries with hands-on exhibits as intriguing for grown-ups as kids, and in 1998 it added **SciTours,** a simulator ride that explores space and the worlds of science and biology. To avoid waiting in line, you can buy tickets in advance; this is especially useful on weekends, which tend to be busy.

Museum of Man. 1350 El Prado. ☎ **619/239-2001.** www.museumofman.org. Admission $5 adults, $4.50 seniors, $3 children 6–17, free for children under 6. Free 3rd Tues of the month. Daily 10am–4:30pm. Bus: 16 or 25.

In a landmark building just inside the park entrance at the Cabrillo Bridge, this museum is devoted to anthropology, with an emphasis on the peoples of North and South America. Favorite exhibits include life-size replicas of a dozen varieties of *Homo sapiens,* from Cro-Magnon and Neanderthal to Peking Man. Don't overlook the annex across the street, which houses more exhibits. The museum's annual **Indian Fair,** held in June, features American Indians from the Southwest demonstrating tribal dances and selling ethnic food, arts, and crafts.

Mingei International Museum. 1439 El Prado, in the House of Charm. ☎ **619/ 239-0003.** Admission $5 adults, $2 children 6–17 and students with ID, free for children under 6. AE, MC, V. Free 3rd Tues of each month. Tues–Sun 10am–4pm.

This museum (pronounced Min-gay—"art of the people" in Japanese) offers changing exhibitions celebrating human creativity. It's manifested in textiles, costumes, jewelry, toys, pottery, paintings, and sculpture—all crafted from natural materials. Displays represent countries all over the world. Martha Longenecker, a potter and professor emeritus of art at San Diego State University, founded the museum in 1977. It is one of only two major museums in the United States devoted to folk crafts on a worldwide scale (the other is in Santa Fe, New Mexico).

San Diego Automotive Museum. 2080 Pan American Plaza. ☎ **619/231-2886.** Admission $6 adults, $5 seniors and active military, $2 children 6–15, free for children under 6. Free

Balboa Park

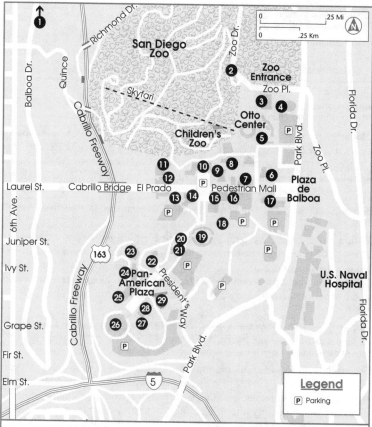

Alcazar Gardens ⑬
Balboa Park Club ㉓
Botanical Building ⑧
Carousel ④
Casa de Balboa ⑯
   Hall of Champions Sports Museum
   Museum of Photographic Arts
   Museum of San Diego History
   Model Railroad Museum
Casa del Prado ⑦
Federal Building ㉙
Hall of Nations ⑳
House of Charm ⑭
   Mingei International Museum
   San Diego Art Institute
House of Hospitality ⑮
   Balboa Park Visitors Center
   Terrace on the Prado
House of Pacific Relations
 International Cottages ㉒
Japanese Friendship Garden ⑱
Marston House Museum ①

Municipal Museum ㉘
Museum of Art ⑩
Museum of Man ⑫
Natural History Museum ⑥
Palisades Building ㉔
   Marie Hitchcock Puppet Theater
Reuben H. Fleet Science Center ⑰
San Diego Aerospace Museum ㉖
San Diego Automotive Museum ㉕
San Diego Miniature Railroad ③
San Diego Zoo ②
Simon Edison Centre
  for the Performing Arts ⑪
   Old Globe Theatre
   Cassius Carter Centre Stage
   Lowell Davies Festival Theatre
Spanish Village Art Center ⑤
Spreckels Organ Pavilion ⑲
Starlight Bowl ㉗
Timken Museum of Art ⑨
United Nations Building ㉑

125

Activities Farther Afield

To find information on attractions in nearby Del Mar, Carlsbad, Encinitas, and Oceanside—only 20 to 40 minutes from downtown San Diego—turn to "North County Beach Towns" in chapter 11, "Side Trips from San Diego."

4th Tues of each month. MC, V. Sept 5–May 31 daily 10am–4:30pm, June 1–Sept 4 daily 10am–5:30pm. Last admission ½ hour before closing. Bus: 7/7B, 16, or 25.

Classic, antique, and exotic cars and motorcycles are on display here in changing shows. The museum has an extensive gift shop and a full automotive research library. On your visit you might see a 1927 Bentley, a 1931 Duesenberg Model J, a 1931 Rolls-Royce Phaeton, and the late actor Steve McQueen's 1953 Allard, as well as the ill-fated 1948 Tucker and 1981 DeLorean.

Botanical Building and Lily Pond. El Prado. Free admission. Fri–Wed 10am–4pm. Bus: 7/7B, 16, or 25.

Within a serene park, ivy, ferns, orchids, impatiens, begonias, and other plants— about 1,200 tropical and flowering varieties—are sheltered beneath the domed lath house. The building, part of the 1915 Panama–California Exposition, measures 250 feet long by 75 feet wide by 60 feet high, and is one of the world's largest wood lath structures. The lily pond out front attracts sun worshipers and street entertainers.

Hall of Champions. 2133 Pan American Plaza. ☎ **619/234-2544.** Admission $5 adults, $3 seniors 65 and older and military, $1 children 6–17, free for children under 6. Free 2nd Tues of each month. Daily 10am–4:30pm. Bus: 7/7B, 16, or 25.

One of the country's few multisport museums, Hall of Champions has been popular with sports fans since 1961. The museum highlights more than 40 professional and amateur sports. More than 25 exhibits surround a centerpiece statue, the *Discus Thrower.* One particularly interesting exhibit is devoted to athletes with disabilities. The museum moved to this spacious new location in 1999.

House of Pacific Relations International Cottages. Adjacent to Pan-American Plaza. ☎ **619/234-0739.** Free admission; donations welcome. Sun 12:30–4:30pm, 4th Tues of each month 11:30am–3pm. Bus: 7/7B, 16, or 25.

This cluster of one- and two-room cottages disseminates information about the culture, traditions, and history of 31 countries. Light refreshments are served, and outdoor lawn programs are presented March through October.

Japanese Friendship Garden. Adjacent to the Organ Pavilion. ☎ **619/232-2780.** Admission $2 adults; $1 seniors 65 and older, military, people with disabilities, and children 7–17; $5 family; free for children under 7. Free 3rd Tues of each month. Tues and Fri–Sun 10am–4pm. Bus: 7/7B, 16, or 25.

Of the 11½ acres designated for the garden, only an acre—a beautiful, peaceful one— has been developed. The garden's Information Center shows a model of the future installation, San-Kei-En (Three-Scenery Garden). It will eventually include a shallow lake with a shoreline of Japanese irises; a pastoral scene, such as a meadow abloom with springtime trees; and a rushing mountain waterfall and a stream filled with colorful koi. A self-guided tour is available at the main gate. From the gate, a crooked path (to confound evil spirits, who move only in a straight line) threads its way to the information center in a Zen-style house; here you can view the most ancient kind of garden, the sekitei, made only of sand and stone. Refreshments are served on a Japanese-style deck to the left of the entrance. Japanese holidays are celebrated here, and the public is invited.

Marston House Museum. 3525 Seventh Ave. (northwest corner of Balboa Park at Balboa Dr. and Upas St.). ☎ **619/298-3142.** Guided tour $3, $5 in combination with Villa Montezuma, free for children under 13. Fri–Sun noon–4:30pm (last tour at 3:45pm). Bus: 1, 3, 16, or 25.

The noted San Diego architect Irving Gill designed this house in 1905 for George Marston, a local businessman and philanthropist. A classic example of Craftsman-style architecture, reminiscent of Frank Lloyd Wright's work, the house is now managed by the San Diego Historical Society. Some of its interesting features are wide hallways, brick fireplaces, and redwood paneling. Opened to the public in 1991, it contains few original pieces, but does exhibit Roycroft, Stickley, and Lampert furniture and is slowly being furnished with Craftsman-era pieces or copies as funds become available. Tours take about 45 minutes. Enter at the left. There's a small bookstore and gift shop.

○ **Model Railroad Museum.** Casa de Balboa Building, El Prado. ☎ **619/696-0199.** www.sdmodelrailroadm.com. Admission $3 adults, free for children under 15. Senior, student, and military (with ID) discounts. Free 1st Tues of each month. Tues–Fri 11am–4pm, Sat–Sun 11am–5pm. Bus: 7, 7A/B, 16, or 25.

Four permanent, scale-model railroads depict Southern California's transportation history and terrain, including San Diego County's Grand Canyon, the Carriso Gorge. Children will enjoy the hands-on Lionel trains, and train buffs of all ages will appreciate the interactive multimedia exhibits. The gift shop sells rail-related items, including toys, mugs, signs, and kids' overalls and shirts.

Museum of San Diego History. 1649 El Prado, in Casa del Balboa. ☎ **619/232-6203.** Admission $4 adults, $3 seniors and military with ID, $3 for groups of 10 or more, $1.50 children 5–12, free for children under 5. Free 2nd Tues of each month. Tues–Sun 10am–4:30pm. Bus: 7/7B, 16, or 25.

A good place to start if you are a newcomer to San Diego, the recently remodeled museum offers permanent and changing exhibits on topics related to the history of the region, from pioneer outposts in the 1800s to the present day. Many of the museum's photographs depict Balboa Park and the growth of the city. Docent tours are available; call ☎ **619/232-6203,** ext. 117, for information and reservations. Books about San Diego's history are available in the gift shop.

Spreckels Organ Pavilion. South of El Prado. ☎ **619/226-0819.** Free 1-hr. concerts Sun year-round; free Summer Festival concerts July–Aug, 8pm Mon and 6:15pm Tues–Thurs. Bus: 7/7B, 16, or 25.

Given to San Diego citizens in 1914 by brothers John D. and Adolph Spreckels, the ornate, curved pavilion houses a magnificent organ with 4,445 individual pipes. They range in length from less than a half-inch to more than 32 feet. With only brief interruptions, the organ has been in continuous use in the park, and today visitors can enjoy free hour-long concerts on Sundays at 2pm. There's seating for 2,400.

Timken Museum of Art. 1500 El Prado. ☎ **619/239-5548.** gort.ucsd.edu/sj/timken. Free admission. Tues–Sat 10am–4:30pm, Sun 1:30–4:30pm. Closed Sept. Bus: 7/7B, 16, or 25.

Called the "Jewel of the Park," this museum houses the Putnam Foundation's collection of 19th-century American paintings and works by European old masters, as well as an outstanding display of Russian icons.

4 More Attractions

DOWNTOWN & BEYOND

In downtown San Diego, you can wander in the **Gaslamp Quarter** (see "Walking Tour 1," in chapter 8) or the **Horton Plaza** shopping center. You can shop for hours, stroll, snack or dine, enjoy free entertainment, see a movie, and people-watch—all within a unique and colorful architectural framework. The Gaslamp Quarter, San Diego's trendiest area, consists of 16 or so blocks of restored historic buildings. It gets its name from the old-fashioned street lamps that line the sidewalks.

Seaport Village is a shopping and dining complex on the waterfront. It was designed to look like a New England seaport community. The views across the water are terrific.

✪ **Cabrillo National Monument.** 1800 Cabrillo Memorial Dr., Point Loma. ☎ **619/ 557-5450.** www.nps.gov/cabr. Admission $5 per vehicle, $2 for walk-ins, free for children under 17 and American citizens age 62 and older with Golden Age Passport. Daily 9am–5:15pm. Take I-5 or I-8 to Highway 209/Rosecrans St. and follow signs. Bus: 26.

Breathtaking views mingle with the early history of San Diego, which began when Juan Rodríguez Cabrillo arrived in 1542. His statue dominates the tip of Point Loma, which is also a vantage point for watching migrating gray whales en route from the Arctic Ocean to Baja California from December through March. The restored lighthouse (1855) allows a glimpse of what life was like here in the past century. The road into the monument passes Fort Rosecrans National Cemetery, with row after row of white markers. National Park Service rangers lead walks at the monument, and there are tide pools that beg for exploration. Free 30-minute films on Cabrillo, tide pools, and California gray whales are shown on the hour daily from 10am to 4pm. Cabrillo National Monument welcomes almost 1.2 million visitors annually, making it one of the country's most visited national monuments. Only a half-hour ride from downtown, the trip is worth your time. Gray Line tours also offers an excursion to the monument (see section 8 of this chapter for details).

Children's Museum of San Diego. 200 W. Island Ave. ☎ **619/233-KIDS.** Admission $6 adults and children, $3 seniors, free for children under 2. Tues–Fri 10am–3pm, Sat–Sun 10am–4pm. Trolley: Convention Center; museum is a block away. All-day parking (across the street) about $3.

This interactive attraction, which encourages participation, is a home away from home for kids. It provides ongoing supervised activities, as well as a monthly special celebration, recognizing important issues such as earth awareness or African-American history. The indoor-outdoor art studio is a big draw for kids ages 2 to 10. There is also a theater with costumes for budding actors to don, plus an observation walk above the exhibits that kids climb on and exit by way of a spiral slide. The museum shop is filled with toys, games, crafts, and books. School groups come in the morning, so you might want to schedule your visit for the afternoon.

Firehouse Museum. 1572 Columbia St. (at Cedar St.). ☎ **619/232-FIRE.** Admission $2 adults, $1 seniors and military in uniform, $1 youths 13–17, free for children under 13. Wed–Fri 10am–2pm, Sat–Sun 10am–4pm. Bus: 5, 16, or 105.

Appropriately housed in San Diego's oldest firehouse, the museum features shiny fire engines, including hand-drawn and horse-drawn models, a 1903 steam pumper, and memorabilia such as antique alarms, fire hats, and foundry molds for fire hydrants. There's also a small gift shop.

✪ **Maritime Museum.** 1306 N. Harbor Dr. ☎ **619/234-9153.** www.sdmaritime.com. Admission $5 adults, $4 seniors over 62 and youths 13–17, $2 children 6–12, free for children under 6. Daily 9am–8pm. Bus: 2. Trolley: America Plaza.

This unique museum consists of a trio of fine ships: the full-rigged merchant vessel *Star of India* (1863), whose impressive masts are an integral part of the San Diego cityscape; the gleaming white San Francisco–Oakland steam-powered ferry *Berkeley* (1898), which worked round-the-clock to carry people to safety following the 1906 San Francisco

Downtown San Diego Attractions

Children's Museum of San Diego ⑥
Convention Center ⑦
Firehouse Museum ②
Horton Plaza ⑨
Maritime Museum ③
Museum of Contemporary Art, Downtown ④

San Diego Zoo ①
Seaport Village ⑤
Villa Montezuma ⑩
Walkabout International ⑪
William Heath Davis House ⑧

earthquake; and the sleek *Medea* (1904), one of the world's few remaining large steam yachts. You can board and explore each vessel, and from April through October you can watch movies on deck (see chapter 10, "San Diego After Dark").

Museum of Contemporary Art, Downtown (MCA). 1001 Kettner Blvd. (at Broadway). ☎ **619/234-1001.** Admission $2 adults; $1 students, military with ID, and seniors; free for children under 13. Free 1st Tues and Sun of each month. Tues–Sat 10am–5pm, Sun noon–5pm. Parking $2 with validation at America Plaza Complex. Trolley: America Plaza.

MCA Downtown is the second location of the Museum of Contemporary Art, San Diego (the first is in La Jolla). Two large and two smaller galleries present changing exhibitions of nationally and internationally distinguished contemporary artists. Lectures and tours for adults and children are also offered. There's a gift shop and bookstore on the premises.

Villa Montezuma. 1925 K St. (at 20th Ave.). ☎ **619/239-2211.** Admission $3 adults, $5 in combination with Marston House (in Balboa Park), free for children under 13. Sat–Sun noon–4:30pm. Bus: 3, 3A, 4, 5, 16, or 105 to Market and Imperial sts. By car, follow K St.

This stunning mansion just east of downtown was built in 1887 for internationally acclaimed musician and author Jesse Shepard. Lush with Victoriana, it features more stained glass than most churches have; windows depict Mozart, Beethoven, Sappho, Rubens, St. Cecilia (patron saint of musicians), and other notables. The striking ceilings are of Lincrusta Walton—pressed canvas coated with linseed oil, a fore-runner of linoleum, which never looked this good. Shepard lived here with his life companion, Lawrence Tonner, for only 2 years and died in obscurity in Los Angeles in 1927. The San Diego Historical Society painstakingly restored the house, which is on the National Register of Historic Places, and furnished it with period pieces. Unfortunately, the neighborhood is not as fashionable as the building, but it's safe to park your car in the daytime. If you love Victorian houses, don't miss this one for its quirkiness.

William Heath Davis House Museum. 410 Island Ave. (at Fourth Ave.). ☎ **619/ 233-4692.** www.gqhf.com. Admission $2. Mon–Fri 10am–2pm, Sat 10am–4pm, Sun noon–4pm. Call ahead to verify hours. Bus: 1, 3, or 3A. Trolley: Gaslamp Quarter/Convention Center W.

Shipped by boat to San Diego in 1850 from Portland, Maine, this is the oldest struc-ture in the Gaslamp Quarter. It is a well-preserved example of a prefabricated "saltbox" family home, and has remained structurally unchanged for over 120 years. A museum, on the first and second floors, is open to the public, as is the small park adjacent to the house. The house is also home to the Gaslamp Quarter Historical Foundation, which sponsors walking tours of the quarter every Saturday at 11am for $5 (see "Orga-nized Tours," later in this chapter).

OLD TOWN

The birthplace of San Diego—indeed, of California—Old Town takes you back to the Mexican California, which existed here until the mid-1800s.

"Walking Tour 3" in chapter 8 goes through Old Town. In addition, free walking tours leave daily at 10:30am and 2pm from **Seeley Stables Visitor Center** (☎ **619/ 220-5422**), at the head of the pedestrian walkway that is the continuation of San Diego Avenue.

Admission to all museums, open daily from 10am to 5pm, is free. Seven of the park's 20 structures are original; the rest are reconstructed. All museums are free, although donations are welcome. They're accepted at the Park Headquarters; La Casa de Estudillo, which depicts the living conditions of a wealthy family in 1872; and Seeley Stables, named after A. L. Seeley, who ran the stagecoach and mail service in these parts from 1867 to 1871. The stables have two floors of wagons, carriages, stage-coaches, and other memorabilia, including washboards, slot machines, and hand-worked saddles, as well as a 17-minute slide show.

On weekdays during the school year, Old Town buzzes with fourth graders.

Heritage Park. 2455 Heritage Park Row (corner of Juan and Harney sts.). ☎ **619/694-3049.** Free admission. Daily 9:30am–3pm. Bus: 4 or 5/105.

This 7.8-acre county park contains seven original 19th-century houses moved here from other places and given new uses. Among them are a bed-and-breakfast, a doll shop, and a gift shop. The most recent addition is the small synagogue, placed near the park's entrance in 1989. A glorious coral tree crowns the top of the hill.

Junípero Serra Museum. 2727 Presidio Dr., Presidio Park. ☎ **619/297-3258.** Admission $5 adults, $4 seniors and students, $2 children 6–17, free for children under 6. Fri–Sun 10am–4:30pm. Take Interstate 8 to the Taylor St. exit. Turn right on Taylor, then left on Pre-sidio Dr.

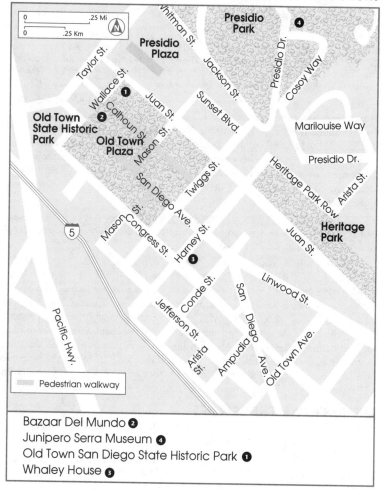

0 | .25 Mi
0 | .25 Km

Presidio Park

Presidio Plaza

Whitman St.

Jackson St.

Presidio Dr.

Cosoy Way

Taylor St.

Wallace St.

Calhoun St.

Juan St.

Sunset Blvd.

Marilouise Way

Old Town State Historic Park

Old Town Plaza

Mason St.

San Diego Ave.

Twiggs St.

Presidio Dr.

Heritage Park Row

Arista St.

5

Mason St.

Congress St.

Harney St.

Heritage Park

Juan St.

Conde St.

Linwood St.

San Diego Ave.

Pacific Hwy.

Jefferson St.

Arista St.

Ampudia St.

Old Town Ave.

Pedestrian walkway

Bazaar Del Mundo ❷
Junipero Serra Museum ❹
Old Town San Diego State Historic Park ❶
Whaley House ❸

Perched on a hill above Old Town, the stately mission-style building overlooks the hill-side where California began. Here, in 1769, the first mission and first non-native settlement on the west coast of the United States and Canada were founded. The museum's exhibits introduce visitors to California's origins and to the Native American, Spanish, and Mexican people who first called this place home. On display are their belongings, from cannons to cookware; a Spanish furniture collection; and one of the first paintings brought to California, which survived being damaged in an Indian attack. The mission remained San Diego's only settlement until the 1820s, when families began to move down the hill into what is now Old Town. You can also watch an ongoing archaeological dig uncovering more of the items used by early settlers. From the 70-foot tower, visitors can compare the spectacular view with historic photos to see how this land has changed over time.

The museum is in Presidio Park, called the "Plymouth Rock of the Pacific." The large cross in the park was made of floor tile from the Presidio ruins. Sculptor Arthur Putnam made the statues of Father Serra, founder of the missions in California. Climb up to **Inspiration Point,** as many have done for marriage ceremonies, for a sweeping view of the area.

Mission Basilica San Diego de Alcala. 10818 San Diego Mission Rd., Mission Valley. ☎ **619/281-8449.** Admission $2 adults, $1 seniors and students, 50¢ children under 13. Free Sun and for daily services. Daily 9am–5pm; mass daily 7am and 5:30pm. Take I-8 to Mission Gorge Rd. to Twain Ave. Bus: 6, 16, 25, 43, or 81.

Established in 1769, this was the first link in a chain of 21 missions founded by Spanish missionary Junípero Serra. In 1774, the mission was moved to its present site for agricultural reasons, and to separate Native American converts from the fortress that included the original building. A few bricks belonging to the original mission can be seen in Presidio Park in Old Town. Mass is said daily in this active Catholic parish. Other missions in the San Diego area include Mission San Luis Rey de Francia in Oceanside, Mission San Antonia de Pala near Mount Palomar, and Mission Santa Ysabel near Julian.

Whaley House. 2482 San Diego Ave. ☎ **619/298-2482.** Admission $4 adults, $3 seniors over 60, $2 children 5–18, free for children under 5. June–Sept daily 10am–5pm, Oct–May Wed–Mon 10am–5pm. Closed on major holidays.

In 1856, this striking two-story brick house (the first one in these parts) one block from Old Town State Historic Park was built for Thomas Whaley and his family. Whaley was a New Yorker who arrived via San Francisco, where he had been lured by the gold rush. The house is one of only two authenticated haunted houses in California, and 10,000 schoolchildren visit each year to see for themselves. Apparently, four spirits haunt the house, and other paranormal phenomena have taken place. Exhibits include a life mask of Abraham Lincoln, one of only six made; the spinet piano used in the movie *Gone With the Wind;* and the concert piano that accompanied Swedish soprano Jenny Lind on her final U.S. tour in 1852. Director June Reading will make you feel at home, in spite of the ghosts.

MISSION BAY & THE BEACHES

This is a great area for walking, jogging, in-line skating, biking, and boating. See the appropriate headings in "Outdoor Pursuits," below.

Giant Dipper Roller Coaster. 3190 Mission Blvd. ☎ **619/488-1549.** Ride on the Giant Dipper $3. MC, V. Sun–Thurs 11am–10pm, Fri–Sat 11am–11pm. Take I-5 to the Sea World exit, and follow W. Mission Bay Park to Belmont Park.

A local landmark for 70 years, the Giant Dipper is one of two surviving fixtures from the original Belmont Amusement Park (the other is the Plunge swimming pool). After sitting dormant for 15 years, the vintage wooden roller coaster, with more than 2,600 feet of track and 13 hills, underwent extensive restoration and reopened in 1991. If you're in the neighborhood (especially with older kids), it's worth a stop. You must be 50 inches tall to ride the roller coaster. You can also ride on the Giant Dipper's neighbor, the Liberty Carousel ($1).

LA JOLLA

The area's most scenic spot—star of postcards for over 100 years—is **La Jolla Cove** and **Ellen Browning Scripps Park** on the cliff above it. Both are on Coast Boulevard. The park is a boat-free zone, with protected undersea flora and fauna that draws many scuba divers and other visitors. Swimming, sunning, picnicking, barbecuing, reading, and strolling along the oceanfront walkway are all ongoing activities. The unique 6,000-acre **San Diego–La Jolla Underwater Park,** established in 1970, stretches from La Jolla Cove to the northern end of Torrey Pines State Reserve. It can be reached from La Jolla Cove or La Jolla Shores.

La Jolla Attractions

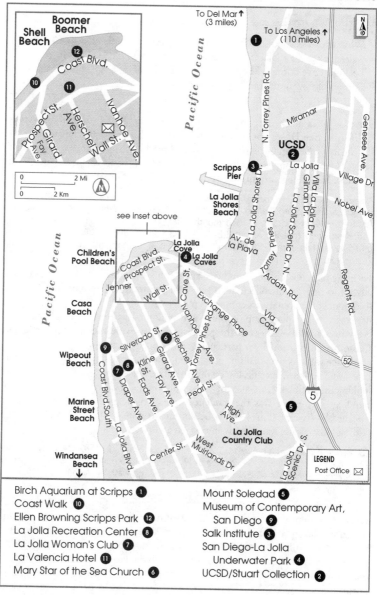

Birch Aquarium at Scripps ❶
Coast Walk ❿
Ellen Browning Scripps Park ⑫
La Jolla Recreation Center ❽
La Jolla Woman's Club ❼
La Valencia Hotel ⑪
Mary Star of the Sea Church ❻

Mount Soledad ❺
Museum of Contemporary Art,
  San Diego ❾
Salk Institute ❸
San Diego-La Jolla
  Underwater Park ❹
UCSD/Stuart Collection ❷

For a scenic drive, follow La Jolla Boulevard to Nautilus Street and turn east to get to **Mount Soledad,** which offers a 360° view of the area. The cross on top, erected in 1954, is 43 feet high and 12 feet wide.

Highlights in town include **Mary Star of the Sea,** 7727 Girard (at Kline), a beautiful Roman Catholic church; and the **La Valencia Hotel,** 1132 Prospect St., a fine example of Spanish Colonial structure. The **La Jolla Woman's Club,** 7791 Draper Ave.; the adjacent **Museum of Contemporary Art, San Diego;** the **La Jolla Recreation Center;** and **The Bishop's School** are all examples of village buildings designed by architect Irving Gill.

Insider's Tip

While droves of folks stroll the sidewalks adjacent to the San Diego–La Jolla Underwater Park and La Jolla Cove, only a few know about Coast Walk. It starts near the
La Jolla Cave & Shell Shop, 1325 Coast Blvd. (☎ **858/454-6080**), and affords a
wonderful view of the beach and beyond.

At La Jolla's north end, you'll find the 1,200-acre, 15,000-student **University of
California, San Diego** (UCSD), which was established in 1960. The campus features
the Stuart Collection of public sculpture and the Birch Aquarium at Scripps Institution of Oceanography (see individual listings, below). Louis Kahn designed the **Salk
Institute for Biological Studies,** 10010 North Torrey Pines Rd.

Museum of Contemporary Art, San Diego. 700 Prospect St. ☎ **858/454-3541.**
www.mcasandiego.org. Admission $4 adults, $2 students and seniors, free for children under
12; free 1st Tues and Sun of each month. Tues, Thurs–Sat 10am–5pm, Wed 10am–8pm,
Sun noon–5pm. Take the Ardath Rd. exit off I-5 north or the La Jolla Village Dr. west exit
off I-5 south. Take Torrey Pines Rd. to Prospect Place and turn right. Prospect Place becomes
Prospect St.

Focusing primarily on work produced since 1950, the museum is known internationally for its permanent collection and thought-provoking exhibitions. The MCA's collection of contemporary art comprises more than 3,000 works of painting, sculpture,
drawings, prints, photography, video, and multimedia works. The holdings include
every major art movement of the past half-century, with a strong representation by
California artists. You'll see particularly noteworthy examples of minimalism, light
and space work, conceptualism, installation, and site-specific art—the outside sculptures were designed specifically for this site. The museum is perched on a cliff overlooking the Pacific Ocean, and the views from the galleries are gorgeous. The original
building on the site was the residence of the legendary Ellen Browning Scripps,
designed by Irving Gill in 1916. It became an art museum in 1941, and the original
Gill building facade was recently uncovered and restored.

✪ Birch Aquarium at Scripps. 2300 Expedition Way. ☎ **858/534-FISH.** Admission
$7.50 adults, $6.50 seniors, $4 children 3–17, free for children under 3. Parking $3. AE, MC,
V. Daily 9am–5pm. Take I-5 to La Jolla Village Dr. exit, go west 1 mile, and turn left at Expedition Way. Bus: 34.

The Birch Aquarium is operated by Scripps Institution of Oceanography, at the University of California, San Diego. This beautiful facility is both an aquarium and a
museum. The aquarium is to the right of the entrance, the museum to the left. To
make the most of the self-guided experience, be sure to pick up a visitor guide from
the information booth just inside the entrance, and take time to read the text on each
of the exhibits. The aquarium affords close-up views of the Pacific Northwest, the California coast, Mexico's Sea of Cortez, and the tropical seas, all presented in 33 marine-
life tanks. The giant kelp forest is particularly impressive (keep an eye out for a tiger
shark or an eel swimming through). Be sure to notice my favorite sea creatures: the
fanciful white anemones and the ethereal moon jellies (which look like parachutes).
The rooftop demonstration tide pool not only shows visitors marine coastal life but
offers an amazing view of Scripps Pier, La Jolla Shores Beach, the village of La Jolla,
and the ocean. Free tide-pool talks are offered on weekends, which is also when the
aquarium is most crowded.

The museum section has numerous interpretive exhibits on current and historic
research at the Scripps Institution, which was established in 1903 and became part
of the university system in 1912. You'll learn what fog is and why salt melts snow;

the number of supermarket products with ingredients that come from the sea (toothpaste, ice cream, and matches, to name a few) might surprise you; and you can feel what an earthquake is like and experience a 12-minute simulated submarine ride. The bookstore is well stocked with textbooks, science books, educational toys, gifts, and T-shirts.

A series of **"Seaside Explorations,"** such as the La Jolla Coast Walk, Tidepooling Adventures, and Running with Grunion, are offered. Call ☎ **858/543-6691** for information and prices.

Stuart Collection. University of California, San Diego (UCSD). ☎ **858/534-2117.** Free admission. From La Jolla, take Torrey Pines Rd. to La Jolla Village Dr., turn right, go 2 blocks to Gilman Dr. and turn left into the campus; in about a block the information booth will be visible on the right.

Consider the Stuart Collection a work in progress on a large scale. Through a 1982 agreement between the Stuart Foundation and UCSD, the still-growing collection consists of site-related sculptures by leading contemporary artists throughout the 1,200 acres of the campus. Among the 12 diverse sculptures on view are Niki de Saint-Phalle's *Sun God,* a jubilant 14-foot-high fiberglass bird on a 15-foot concrete base. Nicknamed "Big Bird," it's been made an unofficial mascot by the students, who use it as the centerpiece of their annual celebration, the Sun God Festival. Also in the collection are Alexis Smith's *Snake Path,* a 560-foot-long slate-tile pathway that winds up the hill from the Engineering Mall to the east terrace of the University Library; and Terry Allen's *Trees,* three eucalyptus trees encased in lead. One tree emits songs, and another poems and stories, while the third stands silent in a grove of trees the students call "The Enchanted Forest." Pick up a brochure and map with marked sculpture locations from the information booth at the Northview Drive or Gilman Drive entrance to the campus. Guides, parking permits, and general information are also available.

CORONADO

It's hard to miss one of Coronado's most famous landmarks: the **Coronado Bay Bridge.** Completed in 1969, this five-lane bridge spans 2 miles across the bay, linking San Diego and Coronado. When it opened, it put the commuter ferries out of business, although in 1986 passenger ferry service restarted. Crossing the bridge by car or bus is a thrill because you can see Mexico, the San Diego skyline, Coronado, the naval station, and San Diego Bay. The bridge's middle section floats, so that if it's destroyed in wartime, naval ships will still have access to the harbor and sea beyond. From San Diego to Coronado, vehicles with solo occupants pay a $1 toll; there's no charge if two or more people are in the car or if you're traveling from Coronado to San Diego. Bus 901 from downtown will also take you over the bridge.

Coronado Historical Museum. 1126 Loma Ave. ☎ **619/435-7242.** Free admission. Wed–Sat 10am–4pm, Sun noon–4pm. Follow Orange Ave. to Loma Ave. and turn right; it's on the left side beside Chez Loma restaurant.

In the Thomson House (ca. 1898), this little museum goes back to the Coronado of yesteryear. It holds photographs of the Hotel Del in its infancy; the old ferries;

Impressions

Let Coronado wear her crown
As Empress of the Sea;
Nor need she fear her earthly peer
Will e'er discovered be.

—L. Frank Baum, 1905

and Tent City, a seaside campground for middle-income vacationers from 1900 to 1939. Other memorabilia include army uniforms, old postcards, and even recorded music. You'll learn about the island's military aviation history during World Wars I and II.

⊗ **Hotel del Coronado.** 1500 Orange Ave., Coronado. ☎ **619/435-6611.** Free admission. Bus: 901. Ferry: Broadway Pier. Then ½-hr. walk, or take a bus or the Coronado trolley, or rent a bike.

Built in 1888, this turreted Victorian seaside resort remains an enduring, endearing national treasure. Whether you stay here, dine here, dance here, or simply wander through on a tour of its grounds and photo gallery, prepare to be enchanted. See "A Hotel with History: Scenes from the Hotel del Coronado," in chapter 5 for more details.

5 Free of Charge & Full of Fun

It's easy to get charged up on vacation—$10 here, $5 there, and pretty soon your credit-card balance looks like the national debt. To keep that from happening, we offer this list of free San Diego activities. In addition, scan the lists of "Outdoor Pursuits," "Spectator Sports," and "Special-Interest Sightseeing," below, and the "San Diego Calendar of Events" in chapter 2. Many events listed in these sections, such as the U.S. Open Sandcastle Competition, are free. San Diego also has numerous parades, such as the Holiday Bowl Parade and the Parade of Lights, both in December.

DOWNTOWN & BEYOND

It doesn't cost a penny to stroll around the Gaslamp Quarter, which is full of restaurants, shops, and historic buildings, or along the Embarcadero (waterfront), and around the shops at Seaport Village or Horton Plaza. And don't forget: Walkabout International offers free guided walking tours (described below). **Centre City Development Corporation's Downtown Information Center** (☎ **619/235-2222**) offers free trolley tours of the downtown area on the first and third Saturdays of the month from 10am to noon (see "Trolley Tours," below).

If you'd rather drive around, ask for the map of the **52-mile San Diego Scenic Drive** when you're at the International Visitor Information Center.

The downtown branch of the Museum of Contemporary Art, San Diego, is free on the first Tuesday and Sunday of each month. Another fun activity is the **Sunset Cinema,** discussed in "Only in San Diego" in chapter 10. And you can fish free of charge from any municipal pier. The **Children's Park,** across the street from the Children's Museum of San Diego, is free, as are all parks in San Diego.

BALBOA PARK

The **San Diego Zoo** is free to all on the first Monday of October (Founders Day), and children under 12 enter free every day during October.

All the **museums** in Balboa Park are open to the public without charge 1 day a month. Here's a list of the free days:

> **1st Tuesday of each month:** Natural History Museum, Reuben H. Fleet Science Center, Model Railroad Museum.
> **2nd Tuesday:** Museum of Photographic Arts, Hall of Champions, Museum of San Diego History.
> **3rd Tuesday:** Museum of Art, Museum of Man, Mingei International Museum of World Folk Art, Japanese Friendship Garden.
> **4th Tuesday:** San Diego Aerospace Museum, San Diego Automotive Museum.

These Balboa Park attractions are always free: The Botanical Building and Lily Pond, House of Pacific Relations International Cottages, and Timken Museum of Art.

Free 1-hour Sunday concerts and free Summer Festival concerts are given at the Spreckels Organ Pavilion.

OLD TOWN & BEYOND

Explore **Heritage Park, Presidio Park,** or **Old Town State Historic Park.** There's free entertainment (mariachis and folk dancers) at the **Bazaar del Mundo,** 2754 Calhoun (☎ **619/296-3161**), on Saturday and Sunday. **Mission Trails Regional Park,** which offers hiking trails and an interpretive center, is at the east end of Highway 52.

MISSION BAY, PACIFIC BEACH & BEYOND

Walk along the beach or around the bay—it's free, fun, and good for you. (See "Hiking/Walking" in "Outdoor Pursuits," later in this chapter.)

LA JOLLA

Enjoy free outdoor **concerts** at Scripps Park on Sundays from 2 to 4pm, mid-June through mid-September (☎ **858/525-3160**).

Anytime is a good time to walk around the La Jolla Cove, Ellen Browning Scripps Park, and Torrey Pines State Reserve, or watch the fur-seal colony at Seal Rock or the Children's Pool. If you're a diver, check out the 6,000-acre San Diego–La Jolla Underwater Park, which stretches from La Jolla Cove to the northern end of Torrey Pines State Reserve.

If you like arts and crafts, you'll love the **La Jolla Arts Festival,** held the last weekend in September. It's also fun to meander around the campus of the University of California, San Diego (UCSD) and view the Stuart Collection of Outdoor Sculpture. The La Jolla branch of the Museum of Contemporary Art, San Diego, is free on the first Tuesday and Sunday of each month.

For the best vista, follow the "Scenic Drive" signs to Mount Soledad and a 360° view of the area.

CORONADO

Drive across the Coronado Bay Bridge (free for two or more people in a car) and take a self-guided tour of the Hotel del Coronado's grounds and photo gallery. Take a walk on the beach and continue to the Coronado Historical Museum.

FARTHER AFIELD: ARCO TRAINING CENTER

Free tours of the ARCO Training Center in Chula Vista are given year-round. This is the country's first warm-weather, year-round, multisport Olympic training complex. It's on the western shore of Lower Otay Reservoir in Chula Vista, and is one of three United States Olympic Committee training centers. (The others are in Colorado Springs, Colorado, and Lake Placid, New York.) Visitors see a 6-minute film about the Olympic movement, followed by a narrated tour (1.5-mile walk) of the 150-acre campus. The hour-long tours are available Monday through Saturday from 9am to 3:30pm, Sunday noon to 3:30pm. Call ☎ **619/482-6222** for more information.

To get here, take I-805 south to Telegraph Canyon Road, then go east about 7 miles until you reach a sign directing you to turn right; follow this road to the visitor center.

6 Especially for Kids

If you didn't know better, you would think that San Diego was designed by parents planning a long summer vacation. Activities abound for toddlers to teens. Dozens of public parks, 70 miles of beaches, and myriad museums are just part of what awaits kids and families. For up-to-the-minute information about activities for children, pick up a free copy of the monthly *San Diego Family Press;* its calendar of events is geared toward family activities and kids' interests. The **International Visitor Information Center,** at First Avenue and F Street (☎ **619/236-1212**), is always a great resource.

THE TOP ATTRACTIONS

- **Balboa Park** *(see p. 123)* has street entertainers and clowns that always rate high with kids. They can usually be found around El Prado on weekends. The Natural History Museum and the Reuben H. Fleet Science Center, with its hands-on exhibits and IMAX/OMNIMAX theater, draw kids like magnets.
- **The San Diego Zoo** *(see p. 115)* appeals to children of all ages, and the double-decker bus tours bring all the animals into easy view of even the smallest visitors.
- **Sea World** *(see p. 119),* on Mission Bay, entertains everyone with killer whales, pettable dolphins, and plenty of penguins—the park's penguin exhibit is home to more penguins than are in all other zoos combined. Try out the new family adventure land, "Shamu's Happy Harbor," where everyone is encouraged to explore, crawl, climb, jump, and get wet in more than 20 interactive areas; or brave a raging river in Shipwreck Rapids.
- **The Wild Animal Park** *(see p. 116)* brings geography classes to life when kids find themselves gliding through the wilds of Africa and Asia in a monorail.

OTHER ATTRACTIONS

- **Children's Museum of San Diego** *(see p. 128)* provides a wonderful interactive and imagination-probing experience.
- **Children's Park** *(see p. 136)* is across the street from the Children's Museum. The park holds grassy knolls, trees, lighted pathways, and a 200-foot-diameter pond with a spray fountain. Children's Park is a 1996 addition to Martin Luther King, Jr. Promenade—a 12-acre park that faces Harbor Drive and includes a walkway with landscaping and benches. Fifteen granite pavers along the walkway focus on Dr. King's philosophy.
- At **Seaport Village** *(see p. 128),* children can enjoy an old-fashioned carousel.
- **Old Town State Historic Park** *(see p. 131)* has a one-room schoolhouse that rates high with kids. They also love the haunted Whaley House, just outside the park. *(See also p. 166.)*
- **Birch Aquarium at Scripps** *(see p. 134),* in La Jolla, is an aquarium that lets kids explore the realms of the deep and learn about life in the sea.
- **La Jolla Cove** *(see p. 122)* provides a place for kids to splash around in tranquil waters.
- **LEGOLAND** *(see p. 204),* in Carlsbad, is a brand-new theme park primarily for children; kids can see impressive models built entirely with LEGO blocks. There are also rides, refreshments, and LEGO and DUPLO building contests.

WET & WILD

White Water Canyon Water Park. 2052 Otay Valley Rd., Chula Vista. ☎ **619/ 661-7373.** www.whitewatercanyon.com. Admission $21.99; children under 48 in. tall $15.99; free for children under 3. Parking $4. Memorial Day to mid-June Sat–Sun 10am–6pm; mid-June to Labor Day daily 10am–6pm. From I-805 south, take the Otay Valley Rd./Main St. exit; turn left and continue 2½ miles.

Located 7 miles south of downtown, this 25-acre water park has a Western gold-mining town theme. Features include 16 water slides, a wave pool, a children's pool with minislides, and "Jumping Water Jets." Fort White Water, a four-story interactive play structure, has shallow pools, slides, water cannons, cargo nets, and a floating lily-pad bridge across the pool. **Still Water River** is a leisurely inner-tube ride along a 1,200-foot river. There are shaded structures throughout, food and picnic facilities, a ballpark, and sand volleyball pits.

THAT'S ENTERTAINMENT

San Diego Junior Theatre is in Balboa Park's Casa del Prado Theatre (☎ **619/239-8355;** www.juniortheatre.com). The productions—shows like *Peter Pan* and *Little Women*— are acted and managed by kids 8 to 18; ticket prices are $5 to $7 for kids and $7 to $9 for adults. Sunday afternoon is a great time for kids in **Balboa Park.** They can visit both the outdoor Spreckels Organ Pavilion for a free concert (the mix of music isn't too highbrow for a young audience) and the House of Pacific Relations to watch folk dancing on the lawn and experience food from many nations. Or get a taste of Punch and Judy at **Marie Hitchcock Puppet Theatre,** in Balboa Park's Palisades Building (☎ **619/685-5045**). Shows are given Wednesday to Friday at 10 and 11:30am and Saturday and Sunday at 11am, 1, and 2:30pm. These cost $2 for adults, $1.50 for children over 2, free for children under 2.

7 Special-Interest Sightseeing

FOR ARCHITECTURE BUFFS

Lovers of period houses will enjoy walking through the Victorian **Villa Montezuma** and the Craftsman-style **Marston House Museum** (described earlier in this chapter). The **Gaslamp Quarter** walking tour (see chapter 8) will lead you past the area's restored Victorian commercial buildings.

Downtown high-rises of particular interest include the **Hyatt Regency San Diego, the Emerald–Shapery Center** at 400 W. Broadway, and **One America Plaza** at 600 W. Broadway. This last building is 498 feet high, which is 24 inches under the maximum height allowed by the FAA. Some people say San Diego's new skyline resembles the contents of a toolbox: a straight screwdriver, a Phillips screwdriver, and a cluster of Allen wrenches. Take a look and see what you think.

While you're in the central business district, the 12-by-12-foot **scale model** of the city at the Centre City Development Corporation's Downtown Information Center, 225 Broadway (☎ **619/235-2200**), might be of interest.

Students of architecture will also want to see the Louis Kahn–designed **Salk Institute** and the classic buildings created by **Irving Gill** (see "La Jolla," in section 4 of this chapter). La Jolla's **Wall Street Cafe** and **Brockton Villa** (both described in chapter 6, "Dining") have won architectural awards for excellence.

In contrast, the Hyatt Regency San Diego received a Major Raw Onion (an award given for architectural flops)—the same year the Salk Institute was lambasted for adding an extension that compromised Louis Kahn's design. Not far from the Salk Institute, the Michael Graves–designed **Hyatt Regency La Jolla** has also garnered an Onion. For further information on San Diego architecture, phone the AIA (☎ **619/232-0109**).

FOR GARDENERS

San Diego is a gardener's paradise, thanks in part to the efforts and inspiration of Kate Sessions. In Balboa Park, visit the Japanese Friendship Garden, the Botanical Building and Lily Pond, and the rose and desert gardens (across the road from Plaza de Balboa).

And when you're at the San Diego Zoo and Wild Animal Park, you'll notice that both are outstanding botanical gardens. Many visitors who admire the landscaping at the zoo don't realize that the plantings have been carefully developed over the years. The 100 acres were once scrub-covered hillsides with few trees. Today, towering eucalyptus and graceful palms, birds-of-paradise, and hibiscus are just a few of the 6,500 botanical species from all over the world that flourish here, providing a beautiful garden setting as well as dinner for some animals. In fact, the plant collection is worth more than the zoo's animals.

In North County, garden enthusiasts will want to visit the 30-acre **Quail Botanical Gardens** (see chapter 11). If you'd like to take plants home with you, visit some of the area's nurseries, including the one started in 1910 by Kate Sessions, **Mission Hills Nursery,** 1525 Fort Stockton Dr., San Diego (☎ 619/295-2808). **Walter Andersen's Nursery,** 3642 Enterprise St., San Diego (☎ 619/224-8271), is also a local favorite. See chapter 11 for information on nurseries in North County. Flower growing is big business in this area, and plant enthusiasts could spend a week just visiting the retail and wholesale purveyors of everything from pansies to palm trees. The **San Diego Floral Association,** in the Casa del Prado in Balboa Park (☎ 619/232-5762), may also be able to provide information.

FOR MILITARY BUFFS

The public is welcome at the Broadway Pier, near the intersection of Broadway and Harbor Drive, where a navy ship is in port and open for free tours most Saturdays and Sundays from 1 to 4pm (☎ 619/532-1430, ext. 9).

You can also attend a recruit parade at the Marine Corps Recruit Depot (MCRD), off Pacific Coast Highway, most Fridays at 10am (☎ 619/524-1765). Old Town Trolley Tours (☎ 619/298-TOUR) is the only company allowed on San Diego military bases. On its Friday morning tour to North Island Naval Air Station, passengers get a close-up look at any aircraft carriers that are in port. The tour lasts 2 to 3 hours and allows an opportunity to purchase military memorabilia.

FOR WINE LOVERS

Visit **Orfila Vineyards** (☎ 760/738-6500; www.orfila.com), near the Wild Animal Park in Escondido. Italian-born wine-maker Leon Santoro is a veteran of Napa Valley (Louis Martini and Stag's Leap). Besides producing excellent Chardonnay and Merlot, the winery also makes several Rhone and Italian varietals, including sangiovese. Tours and tastings are offered daily from 10am to 6pm. The property includes a park-like picnic area and a shop.

If you have time to go farther afield, the wineries along Rancho California Road in **Temecula,** just across the San Diego County line, are open for tours and tastings. For details, see chapter 11.

8 Organized Tours

It's almost impossible to get a handle on the diversity of San Diego in a short visit, but one way to maximize your time is to take an organized tour that introduces you to the city. Many are creative, not as touristy as you might fear, and allow you a great deal of versatility in planning your day.

Centre City Development Corporation's Downtown Information Center (☎ 619/235-2222) offers free downtown residential walking tours for five or more people Saturdays from 1pm to 3pm. The tours require reservations and start at 225 Broadway,

Suite 160. Go inside to see models of the Gaslamp Quarter and the downtown area. The office is open Monday through Saturday from 9am to 5pm.

BAY EXCURSIONS

Bahia Belle. 998 W. Mission Bay Dr. ☎ **619/539-7779**. www.sternwheelers.com. Tickets $6 adults, $3 children under 12. June and Sept Wed–Sat 6:30pm–12:30am; July–Aug Wed–Sun 6:30pm–12:30am; Oct 1–Nov 30 and Jan 1–May 31 Fri–Sat 7:30pm–12:30am. Children accompanied by an adult allowed until 9:30pm; after 9:30pm, 21 or over only (with valid ID).

Cruise Mission Bay and dance under the moonlight aboard this festive stern-wheeler. It picks up passengers at the dock of the Bahia Hotel, 998 W. Mission Bay Dr., on the half hour from 7:30pm (6:30 in summer) to 12:30am, and at the Catamaran Resort Hotels, 3999 Mission Blvd., on the hour from 8pm (7pm in summer) to midnight.

Hornblower Cruises & Events. 1066 N. Harbor Dr. ☎ **619/234-8687** for info, or 619/686-8715 for tickets. www.hornblower.com. Tickets start at $49 for dinner cruise, $33.50 for brunch cruise; half price for children. Harbor tours $12–$17.

This company offers 1- and 2-hour narrated tours of San Diego Bay. Nightly dinner cruises with music and dancing run from 7 to 9pm, Sunday brunch cruises from 11am to 1pm. Whale-watching trips are offered in the winter.

✪ **Gondola di Venezia.** 1010 Santa Clara Place, Mission Bay. ☎ **619/221-2999**. Tickets $72 per couple; $17 for each additional passenger. Located east of Mission Blvd.

This unique business operates from Santa Clara Point, plying the calm waters of Mission Bay in gondolas crafted according to centuries-old designs from Venice. It features all the trimmings, right down to the striped-shirt–clad gondolier with ribbons waving from his (or her) straw hat. Mediterranean music plays while you and up to three friends recline with snuggly blankets, and the company will even provide antipasto appetizers and chilled wine glasses and ice for the beverage of your choice (BYOB). A 1-hour cruise for two is $72, and expanded packages are available. Hours of operation are noon to midnight daily, year-round. Reservations are necessary.

San Diego Harbor Excursion. 1050 N. Harbor Dr. (foot of Broadway). ☎ **800/442-7847** or 619/234-4111. Tickets $12 for 1 hr., $17 for 2 hrs.; half price for children.

The company offers daily 1- and 2-hour narrated tours of the bay, plus dinner cruises. In the winter, it runs whale-watching excursions. The narrators have been with the company for at least 5 years. Times and frequency vary seasonally.

BUS TOURS

Note: Both of these bus companies pick up passengers at most area hotels.

San Diego Mini Tours (☎ **619/477-8687**) offers city sightseeing tours, including a "Grand Tour" that covers San Diego, Tijuana, and a 1-hour harbor cruise. It also runs trips to the San Diego Zoo, Sea World, Disneyland, Universal Studios, Tijuana, Rosarito Beach, and Ensenada. Prices range from $26 to $62 for adults, $14 to $44 for children under 12, and include admissions. Multiple tours can be combined for discounted rates.

Gray Line San Diego (☎ **800/331-5077** or 619/491-0011; www.graylinesandiego. com) offers city sightseeing, including tours of Cabrillo National Monument, Sea World, and La Jolla. Other trips go farther afield, to the Wild Animal Park, wine country, and Tijuana and Ensenada, Mexico. Prices range from $24 to $56 for adults and $10 to $35 for children.

TROLLEY TOURS

San Diego's most comprehensive, and most popular, tour is the narrated **Old Town Trolley** (☎ 619/298-TOUR). The 30-mile route has more than a dozen stops. You can get off at any of them, explore at leisure, and reboard when you please (a bus-cum-trolley passes each stop every half hour). Stops include the Embarcadero, downtown area, Horton Plaza, Gaslamp Quarter, Coronado, San Diego Zoo, Balboa Park, Heritage Park, and Presidio Park. The tour costs $20 for adults, $8 for children 6 to 12, and is free for children under 5, for one complete loop, no matter how many times you hop on or off the trolley. One loop takes 90 minutes; once you've finished the circuit, you can't go around again. It's a good idea to start early in the day. Old Town Trolley Tours offers tours to Naval Air Station North Island on Friday morning.

Centre City Development Corporation's Downtown Information Center (☎ 619/235-2222) offers free trolley tours of the downtown area on the first and third Saturdays of the month from 10am to noon.

WHALE WATCHING

As it is everywhere along the coast, whale watching is an eagerly anticipated wintertime activity in San Diego. If you've ever been lucky enough to spot one of these gentle behemoths swimming gracefully and purposefully through the ocean, you'll understand the thrill. When they pass the San Diego shores, California gray whales are more than three-quarters of the way from Alaska to their breeding grounds at the southern tip of Baja—or just beginning the trip home to their rich Alaskan feeding grounds (with calves in tow). Mid-December to mid-March is the best time to see the migration, and there are several ways to view the spectacular parade.

The easiest is to grab a pair of binoculars and head to a good land-bound vantage point. **Cabrillo National Monument,** on Point Loma peninsula, offers a glassed-in observatory and educational whale exhibits. Each January the rangers conduct a special "Watch Weekend" featuring presentations by whale experts, programs for children, and entertainment. The monument is open daily 10am to 5pm, and admission is $5 per car; call ☎ 619/557-5450 for more information.

In La Jolla, the **Birch Aquarium at Scripps Institution of Oceanography** celebrates the gray whale season with "WhaleFest" throughout January and February. A variety of educational activities and whale exhibits are planned, and the aquarium's outdoor plaza offers an excellent vantage point for spotting the mammals from shore. Aquarium admission is $7.50 for adults, $6.50 for seniors, and $4 for kids 3 to 17. Daily hours are 9am to 5pm; call ☎ 858/534-3474 for further information.

If you want to get a closer look, head out to sea on one of the excursions that locate and follow gray whales, taking care not to disturb their journey. **Classic Sailing Adventures** (☎ 800/659-0141 or 619/224-0800) offers two trips per day (8:30am and 1pm); each lasts 4 hours and carries a maximum of six passengers. Sailing is less distracting to the whales, but more expensive; tickets are $50 per person, including beverages and snacks.

Companies that offer traditional, engine-driven expeditions include **Hornblower Cruises** and **San Diego Harbor Excursions** (see "Bay Excursions," above). Excursions are generally 3 hours, and fares run around $19 for adults, with discounts for kids.

The **San Diego Natural History Museum** begins offering naturalist-led half-day whale-watching trips in January aboard the 88-passenger *Pacific Queen.* Your guide will discuss whale behavior and biology, as well as sea birds, harbor seals, sea lions, and other coastal life. Passengers must be 12 years or older, and fares are $49 to $66 for non-museum members. For an excursion schedule and preregistration, call ☎ **619/ 232-3821,** ext. 203.

WALKING TOURS

Walkabout International, 835 Fifth Ave., Room 407 (☎ **619/231-7463**), sponsors more than 100 free walking tours every month. They're led by volunteers in the San Diego area. A lively guide known as Downtown Sam, who retired from the Air Force in 1972, leads downtown tours, which are particularly popular with retired San Diegans eager for exercise and camaraderie. He's easy to spot, in walking shorts and a cap with a button proclaiming "No thanks, I'd rather walk." Sam's Saturday-morning tours draw 20 to 40 people, and they end with a stop for coffee or a meal. Sam also leads a 1½-hour downtown theme tour at 11am on Tuesday, focusing on bookstores, shopping, pubs, thrift shops, bank lobbies—you name it.

On Saturday from 1 to 3pm, the **Centre City Development Corporation,** 225 Broadway, Suite 160 (☎ **619/235-2222**), offers free walking tours that focus on downtown-area development. Reservations are required.

Coronado Touring, 1110 Isabella Ave., Coronado (☎ **619/435-5993** or 619/435-5444), provides upbeat, informative 90-minute walking tours of Coronado, including the Hotel del Coronado. Enthusiastic guides Nancy Cobb and Gerry MacCartee have been doing this since 1980, so they know their subject well. Tours leave at 11am on Tuesday, Thursday, and Saturday from the Glorietta Bay Inn, 1630 Glorietta Blvd. (near Orange Avenue). The price is $7.

At the **Cabrillo National Monument** on the tip of Point Loma, rangers often lead free walking tours (see "More Attractions," earlier in this chapter). The **Gaslamp Quarter Association** offers tours of the quarter on Saturday at 11am for a $5 donation. Tours leave from William Heath Davis House, 410 Island Ave. (☎ **619/233-5227**).

Docents at **Torrey Pines State Reserve** in La Jolla lead guided nature walks on weekends (see "Hiking/Walking" under "Outdoor Pursuits," below).

You can explore La Jolla by taking walking and shopping tours conducted by **La Jolla Walking Tours** (☎ **858/453-8219**). These leave from the Colonial Inn, 910 Prospect St., on Friday and Saturday at 10am and cost $9.

Volunteers from the **Natural History Museum** (☎ **619/232-3821,** ext. 203) lead nature walks throughout San Diego County.

9 Outdoor Pursuits

See section 2 of this chapter for a complete rundown of San Diego's beaches, and section 8 for details on whale-watching excursions.

BALLOONING

For a balloon's-eye glimpse of the area at sunrise or sunset, followed by champagne and hors d'oeuvres, contact **Skysurfer Balloon Company** (☎ **800/660-6809** or 858/481-6800) or **California Dreamin'** (☎ **800/373-3359** or 760/438-3344). The balloon rides provide sweeping vistas of the Southern California coast, rambling estates, and golf courses. They cost about $145 per person. You may also be interested in the **Temecula Balloon and Wine Festival** held in late April. Call ☎ **909/676-4713** for information.

BIKING

Most major thoroughfares offer bike lanes. To receive a great map of San Diego County's bike lanes and routes, call **Ride Link Bicycle Information** (☎ **619/231-BIKE** or

619/237-POOL). You might also want to talk to the **City of San Diego Bicycle Co-ordinator** (☎ **619/533-3110**) or the **San Diego Bicycle Coalition** (☎ **619/685-7742**). For more practical information on biking on city streets, turn to "Getting Around: By Bicycle" in chapter 4. Always remember to wear a helmet; it's the law.

The Mission Bay and Coronado areas, in particular, are good for leisurely bike rides. The boardwalk in Pacific Beach and Mission Beach can get very crowded, especially on weekends. Coronado has a 16-mile round-trip bike trail that starts at the Ferry Landing Marketplace and follows a well-marked route around Coronado to Imperial Beach.

RENTALS, ORGANIZED BIKE TOURS & OTHER TWO-WHEEL ADVENTURES

Downtown, call **Bike Tours San Diego,** 509 Fifth Ave. (☎ **619/238-2444**), which offers free delivery. In Mission Bay there's **Hamel's Action Sports Center,** 704 Ventura Place, off Mission Boulevard at Ocean Front Walk (☎ **619/488-8889**), and **Hilton San Diego Resort,** 1775 E. Mission Bay Dr. (☎ **619/276-4010**). In La Jolla, try **La Jolla Sports and Photo,** 2199 Avenida de la Playa (☎ **858/459-1114**). In Coronado, check out **Bikes and Beyond,** 1201 First St. at the Ferry Landing Marketplace (☎ **619/435-7180**), which also offers surrey and skate rentals. Expect to pay $5 to $6 for bicycles, $15 to $25 for surreys (pedal-powered carriages).

Adventure Bike Tours, 333 W. Harbor Dr., in the San Diego Marriott Marina (☎ **619/234-1500**, ext. 6514), conducts bicycle tours from San Diego to Coronado. The cost of about $40 includes ferry fare and equipment. The company offers a guided tour around the bay (the Bayside Glide) for $22 per person and rents bikes for $8 an hour, $18 for half a day, or $25 for a full day. In-line skates are also for hire.

For a downhill thrill of a lifetime, take the **Palomar Plunge.** From the top of Palomar Mountain to its base is a 5,000-foot vertical drop, stretched over 16 miles. Or try the **Desert Descent,** a 12-mile, 3,700-foot descent down the Montezuma Valley Grade to the desert floor, followed by a tour of the Visitor Center and a delicious lunch. For about $80 per person, **Gravity Activated Sports** (☎ **800/985-4427** or 760/742-2294; www.gasports.com) supplies the mountain bike, helmet, gloves, souvenir photo, and T-shirt. The company also offers a bike tour through the Temecula wine region.

Adventurous cyclists might like to participate in the **Rosarito–Ensenada 50-Mile Fun Bicycle Ride,** held every April and September just across the border in Mexico. This event attracts more than 8,000 riders of all ages and abilities. It starts at the Rosarito Beach Hotel and finishes in Ensenada. For information, contact Bicycling West, Inc. (☎ **619/583-3001**; www.adventuresports.com/bike/rosarito/welcome.htm).

BOATING

Club Nautico, a concession at the San Diego Marriott Marina, 333 W. Harbor Dr. (☎ **619/233-9311**), provides guests and non-guests with an exhilarating way to see the bay. It rents 20- to 27-foot offshore powerboats by the hour, half day, or full day. Rentals start at $89 an hour. The company allows boats to be taken into the ocean, and also offers diving, water-skiing, and fishing packages.

Seaforth Boat Rental, 1641 Quivira Rd., Mission Bay (☎ **619/223-1681**; www.seaforth-boat-rental.com/seaforth), has a wide variety of boats for bay and ocean. It rents 15- to 135-horsepower powerboats for $45 to $90 an hour, 14- to 30-foot sailboats for $20 to $45 an hour, and ski boats and personal watercraft for $65 an hour. Half- and full-day rates are available. Canoes, pedal boats, and rowboats are available for those who prefer a slower pace.

Outdoor Pursuits in the San Diego Area

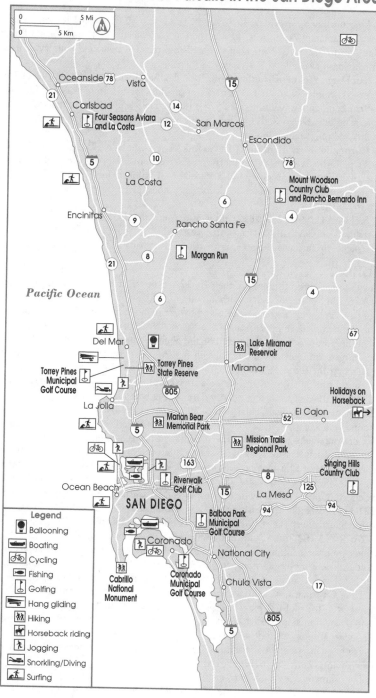

Legend

- 🎈 Ballooning
- 🚤 Boating
- 🚲 Cycling
- 🐟 Fishing
- ⛳ Golfing
- ✈ Hang gliding
- 🚶 Hiking
- 🐴 Horseback riding
- 🏃 Jogging
- 🤿 Snorkling/Diving
- 🏄 Surfing

Mission Bay Sportcenter, 1010 Santa Clara Place (☎ 619/488-1004), rents sailboats, catamarans, sailboards, kayaks, personal watercraft, and motorboats. Prices range from $12 to $72 an hour, with discounts for 4-hour and full-day rentals. Instruction is available.

San Diego Yacht & Breakfast Club, 1880 Harbor Island Dr. (☎ 619/298-6623), rents kayaks for $20 an hour, 3-horsepower dinghies for $15 an hour, Windriders for $40 an hour, and Waverunners for $65 an hour. Half- and full-day rentals are available. **The San Diego Sailing Club,** at the same address and phone number, rents yachts and offers sailing lessons.

Coronado Boat Rental, 1715 Strand Way, Coronado (☎ 619/437-1514), rents powerboats with 90- and 110-horsepower motors for $55 to $90 an hour, with half- and full-day rates; and 14- to 30-foot sailboats for $25 to $45 an hour. It also rents personal watercraft, ski boats, canoes, pedal boats, fishing skiffs, and charter boats.

Sail USA (☎ 619/298-6822) offers custom-tailored skippered cruises on a 34-foot Catalina sloop. A half-day bay cruise costs $275 for six passengers. Full-day and overnight trips are also available, as are trips to Ensenada and to Catalina.

FISHING

For information on fishing, call the **City Fish Line** (☎ 619/465-3474). Anglers of any age can fish free of charge without a license off any municipal pier in California. Public fishing piers are on Shelter Island (where there's a statue dedicated to anglers), Ocean Beach, and Imperial Beach.

Fishing charters depart from Harbor and Shelter islands, Point Loma, the Imperial Beach pier, and Quivira Basin in Mission Bay (near the Hyatt Islandia Hotel). Participants over the age of 16 need a California fishing license.

For sportfishing, you can go out on a large boat for about $25 for half a day or $35 to $85 for three-quarters to a full day. To charter a boat for up to six people, the rates run about $550 for half a day and $850 for an entire day, more in summer. Call around and compare prices. Summer and fall are excellent times for excursions. Locally, the waters around Point Loma are filled with bass, bonito, and barracuda; the Coronado Islands, which belong to Mexico but are only about 18 miles from San Diego, are popular for abalone, yellowtail, yellowfin, and big-eyed tuna. Some outfitters will take you farther into Baja California waters. The following outfitters offer short or extended outings with daily departures: **H & M Landing,** 2803 Emerson (☎ 619/222-1144); **Islandia Sportfishing,** 1551 W. Mission Bay Rd. (☎ 619/222-1164); **Lee Palm Sportfishers** (☎ 619/224-3857); **Point Loma Sportfishing,** 1403 Scott St. (☎ 619/223-1627); and **Seaforth Boat Rentals,** 1641 Quivira Rd. (☎ 619/233-1681).

For freshwater fishing, San Diego's lakes and rivers are home to bass, channel and bullhead catfish, bluegill, trout, crappie, and sunfish. Most lakes have rental facilities for boats, tackle, and bait, and they also provide picnic and (usually) camping areas.

Lake Cuyamaca, 45 minutes from San Diego near Julian, is 5,000 feet above sea level, set in the midst of pines and cedars, and filled with trout year-round. It's open daily from sunrise to sunset; there are motorboat and rowboat rentals and a small charge for fishing (☎ 619/447-8123).

For more information on fishing in California, contact the **California Department of Fish and Game** (☎ 619/467-4201).

For fishing in Mexican waters, including the area off the Coronado Islands, angling permits are required. Contact the **Mexican Department of Fisheries,** 2550 Fifth Ave., Suite 101, San Diego, CA 92103-6622 (☎ 619/233-6956).

GOLF

With nearly 80 courses, 50 of them open to the public, San Diego County offers golf enthusiasts innumerable opportunities to play their game. Courses are diverse—some have vistas of the Pacific, others views of country hillsides or desert landscapes.

M & M Tee Times (☎ **800/867-7397** or 858/456-8366; www.torreypines.com) can arrange tee times for you at most golf courses. And where else but San Diego can you practice your golf swing in the middle of the central business district? **Metro Golf Harborside,** 801 W. Ash St. at Pacific Highway (☎ 619/239-GOLF), is open from 7am to 10pm Monday to Friday, 8am to 10pm on Saturday, and 9am to 9pm on Sunday. It offers 80 tees, a putting and chipping area, night lighting, a pro shop, and golf instruction. Club rental is available at $1 each; a large bucket of balls costs $6, a small bucket costs $3.

✪ Balboa Park Municipal Golf Course. 2600 Golf Course Dr. (off Pershing Dr. or 26th St. in southeast corner of the park), San Diego. ☎ **619/570-1234** (automated tee times) or 619/239-1660 (pro shop).

Everybody has a humble municipal course like this at home, with a bare-bones 1940s clubhouse where old guys hold down lunch counter stools for hours after the game—and players take a few more mulligans than they would elsewhere. Surrounded by the beauty of Balboa Park, this 18-hole course features mature, full trees; fairways sprinkled with eucalyptus leaves; and distractingly nice views of the San Diego skyline. It's so convenient and affordable that it's the perfect choice for visitors who want to work some golf into their vacation rather than the other way around. The course even rents clubs. Non-resident greens fees are $30 weekdays, $35 weekends; cart rental is $20, pull carts $5. Reservations are suggested at least a week in advance.

Coronado Municipal Golf Course. 2000 Visalia Row, Coronado. ☎ **619/435-3121.**

This is the first sight that welcomes you as you cross the Coronado Bay Bridge (the course is to the left). It is an 18-hole, par-72 course overlooking Glorietta Bay, and there's a coffee shop, pro shop, and driving range. Two-day prior reservations are strongly recommended; call anytime after 7am. Greens fees are $20 to walk and $32 to ride for 18 holes; $10 to walk and $17 to ride after 4pm. Club rental is $15, and pull-cart rental is $4.

Four Seasons Resort Aviara Golf Club. 7447 Batiquitos Dr., Carlsbad. ☎ **760/603-6900.** From I-5 northbound, take the Aviara Pkwy. exit east to Batiquitos Dr. Turn right and continue 2 miles to the clubhouse.

Uniquely landscaped to incorporate natural elements compatible with the protected Batiquitos Lagoon nearby, Aviara doesn't infringe on the wetlands bird habitat. The course is 7,007 yards from the championship tees, laid out over rolling hillsides with plenty of bunker and water challenges. Casual duffers may be frustrated here. Greens fees are $175 (including mandatory cart), and there are practice areas for putting, chipping, sand play, and driving. The pro shop is fully equipped, as is the clubhouse. Golf packages are available for guests of the Four Seasons.

Morgan Run. 5690 Cancha de Golf, Rancho Santa Fe. ☎ **858/756-3255.** Take I-5 north to Via De la Valle exit east. After about 5 miles, signs will direct you to turn right on Cancha de Golf.

Formerly Whispering Palms, these three 9-hole courses (one par 35; two par 36) are part of a resort, but you don't have to stay there to play. Course architect Jay Morrish redesigned one of the courses in 1995. There's also a driving range. Greens fees are $65 during the week and $80 on weekends, including a cart.

Mount Woodson Country Club. 16422 N. Woodson Dr., Ramona. ☎ **760/788-3555.** Take I-5 north to Poway Road exit; at the end of Poway Road, turn left (north) onto Route 67 and drive 3¾ miles to Archie Moore Road; turn left. Entrance is on the left.

One of San Diego County's dramatic golf courses, Mount Woodson is a par-70, 6,180-yard course on 150 beautiful acres. The award-winning 18-hole course, which opened in 1991, meanders up and down hills, across bridges, and around granite boulders. Elevated tees provide striking views of Ramona and Mount Palomar, and on a clear day you can see for almost 100 miles. It's easy to combine a game of golf with a weekend getaway to Julian (see chapter 11). Greens fees for 18 holes are $45 to $48 Monday through Thursday, $50 to $55 Friday, $65 to $70 on Saturday and Sunday. Lower twilight rates are available. Mount Woodson is about 40 minutes north of San Diego.

Rancho Bernardo Inn. 17550 Bernardo Oaks Dr., Rancho Bernardo. ☎ **800/426-0966** or 858/485-8880. www.golfuniversity.com. From I-15 north, exit at Rancho Bernardo Rd. Head east to Bernardo Oaks Dr., turn left, and continue to the resort entrance.

Home to Ken Blanchard's Golf University of San Diego since 1992, Rancho Bernardo has a mature 18-hole, 72-par championship course with terrains, water hazards, sand traps, lakes, and waterfalls. Lessons or 1-hour clinics with a pro, 2- to 4-day schools through the Golf University with meals and lodging included, and a standard golf package are available. Greens fees are $65 during the week and $80 Friday through Sunday, including a cart. Twilight rates (after 2pm) are $35 weekdays and $45 weekends.

Riverwalk Golf Club. 1150 Fashion Valley Rd., Mission Valley. ☎ **619/698-GOLF.** Take I-8 to Hotel Circle south, turn on Fashion Valley Rd.

Designed by Ted Robinson and Ted Robinson, Jr., these links meander along the Mission Valley floor. Replacing the private Stardust Golf Club, the course reopened in 1998, sporting a slick, upscale new clubhouse, four lakes with waterfalls (in play on 13 of the 27 holes), open, undulating fairways, and one peculiar feature—trolley tracks! The bright red trolley speeds through now and then, but doesn't prove too distracting. Non-resident greens fees, including cart, are $75 Monday through Thursday, $85 Friday and Sunday, and $95 Saturday (fees for residents are $30 less).

Singing Hills. 3007 Dehesa Rd., El Cajon. ☎ **800/457-5568** or 619/442-3425. Take Calif. 94 to the Willow Glen exit. Turn right and continue to the entrance.

The only resort in Southern California offering 54 holes of golf (two championship courses and a par-54 executive course), Singing Hills has taken advantage of the area's natural terrain. Mountains, natural rock outcroppings, and aged oaks and sycamores add character to individual holes. In 1997, this course made the *Golf for Women* magazine Top Fairways list as one of the courses that "best meet women golfers' needs." Singing Hills is the home of the 19-year-old School of Golf for Women. The golf courses are part of the Singing Hills Resort, but non-guests are welcome. Greens fees are $35 Monday through Thursday, $37 Friday, and $42 Saturday and Sunday for the two par-72 courses, and $14 on the shorter course. Cart rental costs $20. The resort offers a variety of good-value packages.

✪ Torrey Pines Golf Course. 11480 Torrey Pines Rd., La Jolla. ☎ **858/552-1784** for information, 858/570-1234 to book a tee time, 858/452-3226 for the pro shop.

Two gorgeous 18-hole championship courses are on the coast between La Jolla and Del Mar, only 15 minutes from downtown San Diego. Home of the Buick Invitational

Tournament, these municipal courses are very popular. Both overlook the ocean; the north course is more picturesque, the south course more challenging.

Tee times are taken by computer, starting at 5am, up to 7 days in advance by telephone only. Confirmation numbers are issued, and you must have the number and photo identification with you when you check in with the starter 15 minutes ahead of time. If you're late, your time may be forfeited.

Insider's tip: Single golfers stand a good chance of getting on the course if they just turn up and wait for a threesome. The locals also sometimes circumvent the reservation system by spending the night in a camper in the parking lot. The starter lets these diehards on before the reservations made by the computer go into effect at 7:30am.

Golf professionals are available for lessons, and the pro shop rents clubs. Greens fees for out-of-towners are $48 during the week and $52 Saturday, Sunday, and holidays for 18 holes; $26 for 9 holes. After 4pm April through October and after 3pm November through March, the 18-hole fee is only $26. Cart rental is $28. San Diego city and county residents pay much less.

HANG GLIDING
If you have a U.S. Hang Gliding Association rating card, you can soar above the cliffs and coast at Torrey Pines State Reserve, about 4 miles north of La Jolla. For information about lessons or gear, contact the **Hang Gliding Center** (☎ 858/450-9008).

HIKING/WALKING
San Diego's mild climate makes it a great place to walk or hike most of the year, and the options are diverse. Walking along the water is particularly popular. The best **beaches** for walking are La Jolla Shores, Mission Beach, and Coronado, but pretty much any shore is a good choice. You can also walk around Mission Bay on a series of connected footpaths. If a four-legged friend is your walking companion, head for Dog Beach in Ocean Beach or Fiesta Island in Mission Bay—two of the few areas where dogs can legally go unleashed. Coast Walk in La Jolla offers supreme surf-line views (see "La Jolla" under "More Attractions," above).

The **Sierra Club** sponsors regular hikes in the San Diego area, and non-members are welcome to participate. There's always a Wednesday mountain hike, usually in the Cuyamaca Mountains, sometimes in the Lagunas; there are evening and day hikes as well. Most are free. For a recorded message about upcoming hikes, call ☎ 619/299-1744, or call the office (☎ 619/299-1743) weekdays from noon to 5pm or Saturday from 10am to 4pm.

Torrey Pines State Reserve in La Jolla (☎ 858/755-2063) offers hiking trails with wonderful ocean views and a chance to see the rare torrey pine. To reach it, use North Torrey Pines Road. Trail access is free; parking costs $4 per car, $3 for seniors. Guided nature walks are available on weekends.

The **Bayside Trail** near Cabrillo National Monument also affords great views. Drive to the monument and follow signs to the trail.

Mission Trails Regional Park, 8 miles northeast of downtown, offers a glimpse of what San Diego looked like before development. Located between Highway 52 and I-8 and east of I-15, rugged hills, valleys, and open areas provide a quick escape from the urban bustle. A visitor and interpretive center (☎ 619/668-3275) is open daily from 9am to 5pm. Access is by way of Mission Gorge Road.

Marian Bear Memorial Park, a.k.a. San Clemente Canyon (☎ 619/581-9952 for park ranger), is a 10-mile, round-trip trail that runs directly underneath Highway 52. Most of the trail is flat, hard-packed dirt, but some areas are rocky. There are benches and places to sit and have a quiet picnic. From Highway 52 west, take the Genesee South exit; at the light, make a U-turn and an immediate right into the parking lot. From Highway 52 east, exit at Genesee and make a right at the light, then an immediate right into the parking lot.

Lake Miramar Reservoir has a 5-mile, paved, looped trail with a wonderful view of the lake and mountains. Take I-15 north and exit on Mira Mesa Boulevard. Turn right on Scripps Ranch Boulevard, then left on Scripps Lake Drive, and make a left at the Lake Miramar sign. Parking is free, but the lot closes at 6:30pm. There's also a wonderful walkway around **Lake Murray.** Take the Lake Murray Boulevard exit off I-8 and follow the signs.

The **Coronado bike trail** (see "Biking," above) is also a great place to walk. For additional hiking-trail information, see "Julian," in chapter 11.

Volunteers from the **Natural History Museum** (☎ **619/232-3821,** ext. 203) lead nature walks throughout San Diego County.

HORSEBACK RIDING

Jim and Suzanne Miller of **Holidays on Horseback** (☎ **619/445-3997;** fax 619/659-6097), 40 miles east of San Diego in Descanso, offer trail rides in the mountains of the Cuyamaca Rancho State Park, which has 135 miles of wilderness trails. Excursions take 1½ to 9 hours. Riders pass through beautiful scenery that includes native chaparral, live oak, and manzanita. The Millers have 12 horses; all are experienced, gentle trail horses suitable for every riding level. A 4-hour ride with a picnic lunch on the trail costs $65. American Express, Discover, MasterCard, and Visa are accepted.

JOGGING/RUNNING

An invigorating route downtown is along the wide sidewalks of the Embarcadero, stretching around the bay. One of my favorite places to jog is the sidewalk that follows the east side of Mission Bay. Start at the Visitor Information Center and head south past the Hilton to Fiesta Island. A good spot for a short run is La Jolla Shores Beach, where there's hard-packed sand even when it isn't low tide. The beach at Coronado is also a good place for jogging, as is the shore at Pacific Beach and Mission Beach—just watch your tide chart to make sure you won't be there at high tide.

Safety note: Avoid secluded areas of Balboa Park, even in broad daylight.

SCUBA DIVING & SNORKELING

San Diego Divers Supply, 4004 Sports Arena Blvd. (☎ **619/224-3439**) and 5701 La Jolla Blvd. (☎ **858/459-2691**), will set you up with scuba and snorkeling equipment. The **San Diego–La Jolla Underwater Park,** especially the La Jolla Cove, is the best spot for scuba diving and snorkeling. For more information, see "San Diego Beaches," earlier in this chapter. The Underwater Pumpkin Carving Contest, held at Halloween, is a fun local event. For information, call ☎ **858/565-6054.**

SKATING

Gliding around San Diego, especially the Mission Bay area, on in-line skates is the quintessential Southern California experience. In Mission Beach, rent a pair of regular or in-line skates from **Skates Plus,** 3830 Mission Blvd. (☎ **619/488-PLUS**), or **Hamel's Action Sports Center,** 704 Ventura Place, off Mission Boulevard at Ocean Front Walk (☎ **619/488-8889**). In Pacific Beach, try **Pacific Beach Sun and Sea,** 4539 Ocean Blvd. (☎ **619/483-6613**). In Coronado, go to **Mike's Bikes,** 1343

Orange Ave. (☎ **619/435-7744**), or **Bikes and Beyond,** 1201 First St. and at the Ferry Landing (☎ **619/435-7180**). Be sure to ask for protective gear.

If you'd rather ice-skate, try the **Ice Capades Chalet** at University Towne Center, La Jolla Village Drive at Genesee Street (☎ **858/452-9110**).

SURFING

With its miles of beaches, San Diego is a popular surf destination. Some of the best spots include Windansea, La Jolla Shores, Pacific Beach, Mission Beach, Ocean Beach, and Imperial Beach. In North County, you might consider Carlsbad State Beach and Oceanside.

If you didn't bring your own board, they are available for rent at stands at many popular beaches. Many local surf shops also rent equipment; they include **La Jolla Surf Systems,** 2132 Avenida de la Playa, La Jolla Shores (☎ **858/456-2777**), and **Emerald Surf & Sport,** 1118 Orange Ave., Coronado (☎ **619/435-6677**).

For surfing lessons, with all equipment provided, check with **Kahuna Bob's Surf School** (☎ **760/721-7700**) or **San Diego Surfing Academy** (☎ **800-477-SURF;** www.surfSDSA.com).

SWIMMING

Most San Diego hotels have pools, and there are plenty of other options for the visitor. Downtown, head to the **YMCA,** 500 W. Broadway, between Columbia and India streets (☎ **619/232-7451**). There's a $10 day-use fee for non-YMCA members; towels are supplied. It's open Monday through Friday from 5:45am to 9pm, Saturday from 8am to 5pm. In Balboa Park, you can swim in the **Kearns Memorial Swimming Pool,** 2229 Morley Field Dr. (☎ **619/692-4920**). The fee for using the public pool is $2 for adults; call for seasonal hours and laps-only restrictions. In Mission Bay, you'll find the famous indoor **Plunge,** 3115 Oceanfront Walk, (☎ **619/488-3110**), part of Belmont Park since 1925. Pool capacity is 525, and there are 10 lap lanes and a viewing area inside. It's open to the public Monday through Friday from 6 to 8am, noon to 1pm, and 2:30 to 8pm, and Saturday and Sunday from 8am to 4pm. Admission is $2.50 for adults, $2.25 for children.

In La Jolla you can swim at the **Jewish Community Center,** 4126 Executive Dr. (☎ **858/457-3161**). It has an ozone pool (kept clean by an ozone generator), instead of the typical chlorinated pool. It is open to the public Monday through Thursday from 6:30am to 7:30pm, Friday from 6:30am to 6pm, Saturday from 11am to 6pm, and Sunday from 10am to 6pm. Admission is $5 for adults, $3 for children under 17.

Swimmers may want to compete in (or watch) a rough-water swim. These include the **Oceanside Rough Water Swim** (☎ **760/941-0946**) and the **La Jolla Rough Water Swim** (☎ **858/456-2100**), both held in early September.

TENNIS

There are 1,200 public and private tennis courts in San Diego. Public courts include the **La Jolla Tennis Club,** 7632 Draper, at Prospect (☎ **858/454-4434**), which is free and open daily from dawn until the lights go off at 9pm. At the **Balboa Tennis Club,** 2221 Morley Field Dr., in Balboa Park (☎ **619/295-9278**), court use is free, but reservations are required. The courts are open Monday through Friday from 10am to 8pm, Saturday and Sunday 8am to 6pm. The brand-new **Barnes Tennis Center,** 4490 W. Point Loma Blvd., near Ocean Beach and Sea World (☎ **619/221-9000;**

www.tennissandiego.com) has 20 lighted hard courts and four clay courts; they're open every day from 8am to 9pm. Court rental is $5 to $10 an hour, instruction an additional $12 to $14 per hour.

10 Spectator Sports

AUTO RACING

The **Score Baja 500,** held in June, is an annual off-road car, motorcycle, and truck loop race that starts and ends in Ensenada. The **Score Baja 1,000** takes place in November. For information, call ☎ **818/583-8068.**

BASEBALL

The **San Diego Padres,** led to the National League championship in 1998 by stars Tony Gwynn and Trevor Hoffman, play from April through October at **Qualcomm Stadium,** 9449 Friars Rd., in Mission Valley (☎ **619/283-4494** for schedules and information; 619/29-PADRES for tickets). The **Padres Express** bus (☎ **619/233-3004** for information) costs $5 round-trip and picks up fans at several locations throughout the city, beginning 2 hours before the game. The bus operates only for home games on Friday, Saturday, and Sunday. Tickets are readily available.

BOATING

San Diego has probably played host to the America's Cup for the last time, but several other boating events of interest are held here. They include the **America's Schooner Cup,** held every March or April (☎ **619/223-3138**), and the **Annual San Diego Crew Classic,** held on Mission Bay every April (☎ **619/488-0700**). The Crew Classic rowing competition draws teams from throughout the United States and Canada. The **Wooden Boat Festival** is held on Shelter Island every May (☎ **619/574-8020**). Approximately 90 boats participate in the festival, which features nautical displays, food, music, and crafts.

FISHING TOURNAMENTS

Enthusiasts will want to attend the **Day at the Docks** event, held at the San Diego Sportfishing Landing, Harbor Drive and Scott Street, in Point Loma, every April. For information, call ☎ **619/294-7912.**

FOOTBALL

San Diego's professional football team, the **San Diego Chargers,** plays at **Qualcomm Stadium,** "The Q," 9449 Friars Rd., Mission Valley (☎ **619/280-2111**). The season runs from August through December. The Chargers Express bus (☎ **619/233-3004** for information) costs $5 round-trip and picks up passengers at several locations throughout the city, beginning 2 hours before the game. The bus operates for all home games.

The collegiate **Holiday Bowl,** held at Qualcomm Stadium every December, pits the Western Athletic Conference champion against a team from the Big 10. For information, call ☎ **619/283-5808.**

GOLF

San Diego is the site of some of the country's most important golf tournaments, including the **Buick Invitational,** held in February at Torrey Pines Golf Course in La Jolla (☎ **800/888-BUICK** or 858/281-4653). The **HGH Pro-Am Golf Classic** takes place at Carlton Oaks Country Club in September (☎ **619/448-8500**).

HORSE RACING

Live Thoroughbred racing takes place at the **Del Mar Race Track** (☎ 858/755-1141 for information; ☎ **619/792-4242** for the ticket office; www.dmtc.com) from late July through mid-September. Post time for the nine-race program is 2pm (except the first four Fridays of the meet, when it's 4pm); there is no racing on Tuesdays. Admission to the clubhouse is $6; to the grandstand, $3. Bing Crosby and Pat O'Brien founded the track in 1937, and it has entertained stars such as Lucille Ball and Desi Arnaz, Dorothy Lamour, Red Skelton, Paulette Goddard, Jimmy Durante, and Ava Gardner. Del Mar's 1993 season marked the opening of a new $80-million grandstand, built in the Spanish mission style of the original structure. The new grandstand features more seats, better race viewing, and a centrally located scenic paddock. The $1-million Pacific Classic, featuring the top horses in the country, is held the second weekend in August (see chapter 11).

HORSE SHOWS

The **Del Mar National Horse Show** takes place at the Del Mar Fairgrounds from late April to mid-May. Olympic-caliber and national championship riders participate. For information, call ☎ **858/792-4288** or 858/755-1161.

ICE HOCKEY

The **San Diego Gulls** of the West Coast Hockey League skate at the San Diego Sports Arena from late October into March. For schedules, tickets, and information, call ☎ **619/224-4625** or 619/224-4171.

JAI ALAI

Experience the excitement of this fast-action game at the **Caliente Fronton Palace,** or Jai Alai Palace (☎ **619/260-0454** in San Diego, 85-36-87 in Tijuana), in downtown Tijuana. For details, see chapter 11.

MARATHONS/TRIATHLONS

San Diego is a wonderful place to run or watch a marathon because the weather is usually mild. The **San Diego Marathon** takes place in January. It's actually in Carlsbad, 35 miles north of San Diego, and stretches mostly along the coastline. For more information, contact the **San Diego Track Club** (☎ **858/452-7382**) or **In Motion** (☎ **619/792-2900**).

Another popular event is the **La Jolla Half Marathon,** held in April. It begins at the Del Mar Fairgrounds and finishes at La Jolla Cove. For information, call ☎ **858/454-1262.**

The **America's Finest City Half Marathon** is held in August every year. The race begins at Cabrillo National Monument, winds through downtown, and ends in Balboa Park. For information, call ☎ **619/297-3901.**

The **San Diego International Triathlon,** held in the middle of June, includes a 1,000-meter swim, 30-kilometer bike ride, and 10K run. It starts at Spanish Landing on Harbor Island. For information, call ☎ **619/627-9111** or 619/687-1000.

POLO

The public is invited to watch polo matches on Sundays from June through October at the **Rancho Santa Fe Polo Club,** 14555 El Camino Real, Rancho Santa Fe (☎ **858/481-9217**). Admission is $5.

SOCCER

The **San Diego Sockers,** popular members of the Continental Indoor Soccer League, play from June through September at the San Diego Sports Arena, 3500 Sports Arena Blvd. (☎ **619/224-GOAL**). Admission is $5 to $12.50.

SOFTBALL

The highlight of many San Diegans' summer is the softball event known as the **World Championship Over-the-Line Tournament,** held on Fiesta Island in Mission Bay on the second and third weekends of July. For more information, see the "San Diego Calendar of Events," in chapter 2.

TENNIS

San Diego plays host to some major tennis tournaments, including the **Toshiba Ten-nis Classic,** held at the La Costa Resort and Spa in Carlsbad. The tournament is usually held between late July and early August. For tickets, call ☎ **619/438-LOVE;** for information, ☎ **619/436-3551.**

City Strolls 8

San Diego lends itself to strolling, and the four walking tours in this chapter will give you a sense of the city as well as a look at some of its most appealing sights and structures. Wandering a city's streets and parks gives you insights that are hard to come by any other way—and the exercise can't be beat, especially under the warm (but usually not unbearably hot) Southern California sun.

Walking Tour 1
The Gaslamp Quarter

Start: Fourth Avenue and E Street, at Horton Plaza.
Finish: Fourth Avenue and F Street.
Time: Approximately 1½ hours, not including shopping and dining.
Best Times: During the day.
Worst Times: Evenings, when the area's popular restaurants and nightspots attract big crowds.

A National Historic District covering 16½ city blocks, the Gaslamp Quarter contains many Victorian-style commercial buildings built between the Civil War and World War I. The quarter—set off by electric versions of old gas lamps—lies between Fourth Avenue to the west, Sixth Avenue to the east, Broadway to the north, and L Street and the waterfront to the south. The blocks are noticeably short; developer Alonzo Horton knew corner lots were desirable to buyers, so he created more of them. This tour hits some highlights of buildings along Fourth and Fifth avenues. If it whets your appetite for more, the Gaslamp Quarter Foundation, 410 Island Ave. (☎ **619/233-4692,** or hot line 619/233-4691), offers a 2-hour walking tour ($5) on Saturdays at 11am. Other tours are available; see "Organized Tours" in chapter 7. The book *San Diego's Historic Gaslamp Quarter: Then and Now,* by Susan H. Carrico and Kathleen Flanagan, makes an excellent, lightweight walking companion. It has photos, illustrations, and a map.

The tour begins at:

1. **Horton Plaza,** a colorful conglomeration of shops, eateries, and architecture—and a tourist attraction. Ernest W. Hahn, who planned and implemented the redevelopment and revitalization of downtown San Diego, built the plaza in 1985. This core project, which covers 11½ acres and 6½ blocks in the heart of downtown, represents the successful integration of public and private funding.

The ground floor at Horton Plaza is home to the 1906 Jessop Street Clock. The timepiece has 20 dials, 12 of which tell the time in places throughout the world. Designed by Joseph Jessop, Sr., and built primarily by Claude D. Ledger, the clock stood outside Jessop's Jewelry Store on Fifth Avenue from 1927 until being moved to Horton Plaza in 1985. In 1935, when Mr. Ledger died, the clock stopped; it was restarted, but it stopped again 3 days later—the day of his funeral.

In front of Horton Plaza is:

2. **Horton Plaza Park.** Its centerpiece is a fountain designed by well-known local architect Irving Gill and modeled after the choragic monument of Lysicrates in Athens. Dedicated October 15, 1910, it was the first successful attempt to combine colored lights with flowing water. On the fountain's base are bronze medallions of Juan Rodríguez Cabrillo, Father Junípero Serra, and Alonzo Horton, three men who were important to San Diego's development.

Walk along Horton Plaza, down Fourth Avenue, to the:

3. **Balboa Theatre,** at the southwest corner of Fourth Avenue and E Street. Constructed in 1924, the Spanish Renaissance–style building has a distinctive tile dome, striking tile work in the entry, and two 20-foot-high ornamental waterfalls inside. In the past, the waterfalls ran at full power during intermission; however, when turned off, they would drip and irritate the audience. The ship mosaic at Fourth and E depicts Balboa discovering the Pacific Ocean in 1513. In the theater's heyday, plays and vaudeville took top billing. It's currently closed, awaiting renovation.

Cross Fourth Avenue and proceed along E Street to Fifth Avenue. The tall, striking building to your left is the:

4. **Watts-Robinson Building,** built in 1913. One of San Diego's first skyscrapers, it once housed 70 jewelers. Currently a hotel, the building is gradually being converted into time-share units. Take a minute to look inside at the marble wainscoting, tile floors, ornate ceiling, and brass ornamentation.

Return to the southwest corner of Fifth Avenue. To your right, at 837 Fifth Ave., is the unmistakable "grand old lady of the Gaslamp," the twin-towered baroque revival:

5. **Louis Bank of Commerce.** You can admire the next few buildings from the west side of the street and then continue south from here. Built in 1888, this proud building was the first in San Diego made of granite. It once housed a 24-hour ice-cream parlor for which streetcars made unscheduled stops; an oyster bar frequented by Wyatt Earp; and a number of upstairs rooms inhabited by ladies of the night. After a fire in 1903, the original towers of the building, with eagles perched atop them, were removed.

Next door, at 831 Fifth Ave., is the Romanesque revival:

6. **Nesmith-Greely Building,** also built in 1888, with its 12-foot-wide entry. Clara Shortridge Foltz, the first woman admitted to the California State Bar and the founder of the Woman's Bar Association of California, once had an office in this building, as did Daniel Cleveland, a lawyer who founded the city's public library. The face of this building, with the exception of the fire escapes, retains its original appearance.

On the corner, at 809 Fifth Ave., stands the two-story:

7. **Marston Building.** This Italianate Victorian-style building dates from 1881 and housed humanitarian George W. Marston's department store for 15 years. In 1885, San Diego Federal Savings' first office was here, and the Prohibition Temperance Union held its meetings here in the late 1880s. After a fire in 1903, the building was remodeled extensively.

On the west side of Fifth Avenue, at no. 840, near E Street, you'll find the:

8. F.W. Woolworth Building, built in 1910. It has housed **San Diego Hardware** since 1922. The original tin ceiling, wooden floors, and storefront windows remain, and the store deserves a quick browse. The red brick Romanesque revival:

9. Keating Building, on the northwest corner of Fifth Avenue and F Street, is a San Diego landmark dating from 1890. Mrs. Keating built it as a tribute to her late husband, George, whose name can still be seen in the top cornice. Originally heralded as one of the city's most prestigious office buildings, it featured conveniences such as steam heat and a wire-cage elevator. Note the architecturally distinctive rounded corner and windows.

☕ **TAKE A BREAK**   Housed in the Keating Building, the **Croce's** (☎ **619/233-4355**) cluster of dining and entertainment possibilities serves up generous portions of good food and drink, live jazz, national acts, and inviting ambiance. Owner Ingrid Croce has created a memorial to the life and music of her late husband, musician Jim Croce, with photos, guitars, and other memorabilia. Across the street is the perennially popular **Fio's** (☎ **619/234-3467**) Italian restaurant.

Continuing south on Fifth Avenue, cross F Street and stand in front of the:

10. Spencer-Ogden Building, on the southwest corner at 429 F St. Built in 1874, it was purchased by business partners Spencer and Ogden in 1881 and has been owned by the same families ever since. *San Diego's Historic Gaslamp Quarter: Then and Now* notes that a number of druggists leased space in the building over the years, including the notorious one "who tried to make firecrackers on the second floor [and] ended up blowing away part of the building." Other tenants included realtors, an import business, a home-furnishing business, and dentists, one of whom called himself "Painless Parker."

Directly across the street stands the:

11. William Penn Hotel, built in 1913. In the building's former life as the elegant Oxford Hotel, it touted itself as "no rooming house but an up-to-the-minute, first-class, downtown hotel"; a double room with private bath and toilet cost $1.50. It reopened in 1992 as a hotel with mostly suites—and substantially higher prices.

On the west side of the street, at 722–728 Fifth Ave., you'll find the:

12. Llewelyn Building, built in 1887 by William Llewelyn; the family shoe store was here until 1906. Over the years, it has been home to hotels of various names with unsavory reputations. Of architectural note are its arched windows, molding, and cornices.

On the southwest corner of Fifth Avenue and G Street is the:

13. Old City Hall, dating from 1874, when it was a bank. This Florentine Italianate building features 16-foot ceilings, 12-foot windows framed with brick arches, antique columns, and a wrought-iron cage elevator. Notice that the windows on each floor are different (the top two stories were added in 1887, when it became the city's public library). The entire city government filled this building in 1900, with the police department on the first floor and the council chambers on the fourth.

Continue down Fifth Avenue toward Market Street, and you'll notice the three-story:

14. **Backesto Building** (1873), which fills most of the block. Originally a one-story structure on the corner, the classical revival and Victorian-style building expanded to its present size and height over its first 15 years.

    Across the street in the middle of the block, at 631–633 Fifth Ave., is the:

15. **Yuma Building**, built in 1882 and later expanded upward two floors to feature inviting bay windows. It was one of the first brick buildings downtown.

    Across Market Street, on the east side of the street, is the former:

16. **Metropolitan Hotel**, with an arresting *trompe l'oeil* by artists Nonni McKinnoon and Kitty Anderson. The building had bay windows when it was built in 1886.

    The center of the city used to be at Fifth Avenue and Market Street, but as San Diego expanded and gradually moved north, the hub became Fifth and Broadway. When Horton Plaza was completed in 1985, the center moved a block west to Broadway and Fourth Avenue. When Fifth Avenue was the main drag, it was the scene of many a parade, and Buffalo Bill Cody and John Philip Sousa were among those who marched up it.

    Proceed to Island Avenue. On the southeast corner, the unassuming:

17. **Nanking Café Building** illustrates the Chinese influence in the area. At the turn of the century, Chinatown was nearby. The building currently houses the Royal Thai Cuisine Restaurant.

    Turn right on Island. The mural-covered building on the corner is the:

18. **Callan Hotel** (1904). The artwork, by Heidi Hardin, depicts a turn-of-the-century park scene with faces of contemporary San Diego citizens who contributed to the Gaslamp Quarter's rebirth.

    The saltbox house next to the hotel is the:

19. **William Heath Davis House.** This 140-year-old New England prefabricated lumber home was shipped to San Diego around Cape Horn in 1850 and is the oldest surviving structure from Alonzo Horton's "New Town." Horton lived here in 1867. The first floor and the small park next to it are open to the public; the Gaslamp Quarter Association and Gaslamp Quarter Historical Foundation have their headquarters on the second floor. Saturday-morning walking tours of the Gaslamp Quarter leave from here.

    At the southwest corner of Island and Fourth avenues you'll see the bay windows of a building that's sure to steal your heart, the:

20. **Horton Grand Hotel.** It is two 1886 hotels that were moved here—very gently—from other sites, then renovated and connected by an atrium; the original Horton Grand is to your left, the Brooklyn Hotel to your right. The life-size papier-mâché horse (Sunshine), in the lobby near the reception area, stood in front of the Brooklyn Hotel when it was a saddlery shop. The reception desk is a recycled pew from a choir loft, and old post-office boxes now hold guests' keys. By the concierge desk, to your right, is an old photo of the original and much less elegant Horton Grand Hotel. In its small museum hangs a portrait of Ida Bailey, a local madam whose establishment, the Canary Cottage, once stood on this spot. Artist Pamela Russ had been asked to retouch the somewhat austere face of her subject, but Russ's husband murdered her before she could get around to it.

    Around the corner from the Horton Grand, at 429–431 Third Ave., stands the:

21. **former home of Ah Quinn**, the first Chinese resident of San Diego, who arrived in 1879 at the age of 27 and became known as the "Mayor of Chinatown" (an area bounded by Island Avenue, J Street, and Third and Fourth avenues. Ah Quinn helped hundreds of Chinese immigrants find work on the railroad and

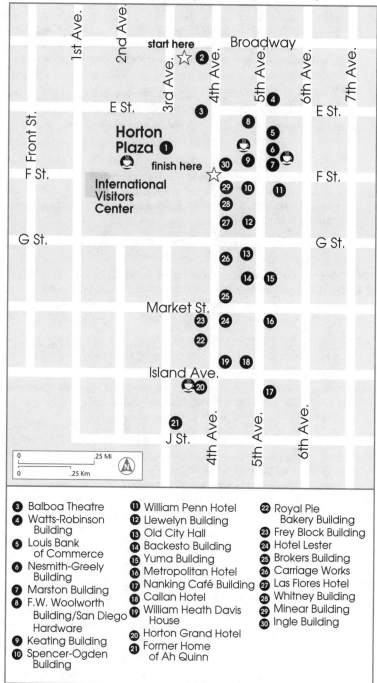

1st Ave.
2nd Ave.

start here

Broadway

3rd Ave.
4th Ave.
5th Ave.
6th Ave.
7th Ave.

E St.

Front St.

Horton Plaza ①

finish here

F St.

International Visitors Center

G St.

Market St.

Island Ave.

J St.

4th Ave.
5th Ave.
6th Ave.

0 ———— .25 Mi
0 ———— .25 Km

- ❸ Balboa Theatre
- ❹ Watts-Robinson Building
- ❺ Louis Bank of Commerce
- ❻ Nesmith-Greely Building
- ❼ Marston Building
- ❽ F.W. Woolworth Building/San Diego Hardware
- ❾ Keating Building
- ❿ Spencer-Ogden Building
- ⓫ William Penn Hotel
- ⓬ Llewelyn Building
- ⓭ Old City Hall
- ⓮ Backesto Building
- ⓯ Yuma Building
- ⓰ Metropolitan Hotel
- ⓱ Nanking Café Building
- ⓲ Callan Hotel
- ⓳ William Heath Davis House
- ⓴ Horton Grand Hotel
- ㉑ Former Home of Ah Quinn
- ㉒ Royal Pie Bakery Building
- ㉓ Frey Block Building
- ㉔ Hotel Lester
- ㉕ Brokers Building
- ㉖ Carriage Works
- ㉗ Las Flores Hotel
- ㉘ Whitney Building
- ㉙ Minear Building
- ㉚ Ingle Building

owned a successful general merchandise store on Fifth Avenue. He was a respected father (of 12 children), leader, and spokesperson for the city's Chinese population. When he died in 1914—he was hit by a motorcycle—his wealth included farmland, a mine, and other real estate. The modest house is not open to the public.

TAKE A BREAK   The **Palace Bar** (☎ 619/544-1886) in the Horton Grand Hotel is the perfect place to find yourself at teatime. The bar is part of the same choir-loft pew that has been turned into the reception desk.

When you leave the Horton Grand, head north on Fourth Avenue; in the middle of the block on the west side you will come to the:

22. **Royal Pie Bakery Building,** erected in 1911. This bakery, preceded by others, has been here since 1920; the second floor used to house the Anchor Hotel, run by "Madam Cora."

    At the southwest corner of Fourth Avenue and Market Street, at the:

23. **Frey Block Building** (1911), a plaque reads "Home of the Crossroads, the oldest live jazz club in San Diego."

    Across the street on the southeast corner, at 401–417 Market St., is the:

24. **Hotel Lester,** which dates from 1906. It housed a saloon, pool hall, and hotel of ill repute when this was a red-light district.

    On the northeast corner of Fourth Avenue and Market Street, at 402 Market St., stands the:

25. **Brokers Building,** constructed in 1889; it has 16-foot wood-beam ceilings and cast-iron columns.

    At the north end of this block, the:

26. **Carriage Works,** established in 1890, now houses the Cheese Shop; instead of wagons and carriages, you get sandwiches and pastries.

    Cross G Street and walk to the middle of the block.

27. **The Las Flores Hotel,** the gray building with blue-and-red trim at 725–733 Fourth Ave., was built in 1912. It is the only Gaslamp Quarter structure completely designed by architect Irving Gill, whose work can be seen throughout San Diego and in La Jolla.

    Next door, at 739–745 Fourth Ave., is the:

28. **Whitney Building,** dating from 1906, with striking arched windows on the second floor. While you're studying details, take a look at the trim on the top of the:

29. **Minear Building** (1910), at the end of the block, on the southeast corner of Fourth Avenue and F Street.

    Across the street is the:

30. **Ingle Building,** which dates from 1907. The mural on the F Street side of the building depicts a group of men making a toast inside the original Golden Lion Tavern, which served 'em up from 1907 to 1932. Original stained-glass windows front Fourth Avenue. Inside, the restaurant's stained-glass ceiling was taken from the Elks Club in Stockton, California, and much of the floor is original.

WINDING DOWN   Walk to **Café Lulu,** 419 F St. (☎ 619/238-0114), near Fourth Avenue, for casual coffeehouse fare; or try **Horton Plaza,** where you can choose from many kinds of cuisine, from California to Chinese, along with good old American fast food.

Walking Tour 2
The Embarcadero

Start: The Maritime Museum, Harbor Drive and Ash Street.
Finish: The Convention Center, Harbor Drive and Fifth Avenue.
Time: 1½ hours, not including museum and shopping stops.
Best Times: Weekday mornings.
Worst Times: Weekends, especially in the afternoon, when the Maritime Museum and Seaport Village are crowded; also when cruise ships are in port (days vary).

San Diego's colorful Embarcadero, or waterfront, cradles a bevy of seagoing vessels—frigates, ferries, paddle-wheelers, yachts, cruise ships, and even a merchant vessel. You'll also find equally colorful Seaport Village, a shopping and dining center with a nautical theme.

Start at the:

1. Maritime Museum, Harbor Drive at Ash Street (see listing in chapter 7). Making up part of the floating museum is the magnificent *Star of India,* the world's oldest merchant ship still afloat, built in 1863 as the *Euterpe.* The ship, whose billowing sails are a familiar sight along Harbor Drive, once carried cargo to India and immigrants to New Zealand, and it braved the Arctic ice in Alaska to work in the salmon industry. Another component of the Maritime Museum is the ferry *Berkeley,* built in 1898 to operate between San Francisco and Oakland. In service through 1958, it carried survivors to safety 24 hours a day for 4 days after the 1906 San Francisco earthquake. The *Medea,* the third and smallest display in the floating museum, is a steam yacht. One ticket gets you onto all three boats.

From this vantage point, you get a fine view of the:

2. County Administration Center, built in 1936 with funds from the Works Progress Administration and dedicated in 1938 by President Franklin D. Roosevelt. The 23-foot-high granite sculpture in front, *Guardian of Water,* was completed by Donal Hord in 1939. It represents a pioneer woman shouldering a water jug. The building is even more impressive from the other side because of the carefully tended gardens; it's well worth the effort and extra few minutes to walk around to Pacific Highway for a look. On weekdays the building is open from 8am to 5pm; there are rest rooms and a cafeteria inside.

☕ **TAKE A BREAK** The cafeteria on the fourth floor of the **County Administration Center** has lovely harbor views; it's open weekdays until 3:35pm. If you can't pass up the chance to have some seafood, return to the waterfront to **Anthony's Fishette** (☎ 619/232-5105), the simplest entity in the Anthony's group of seafood houses, which serves fish-and-chips, shrimp, and other snacks alfresco. Next door is **Anthony's Star of the Sea Room** (☎ 619/232-7408), one of the city's finest seafood restaurants, where reservations and jackets for men are a must; it's open for dinner only.

Continue south along the Embarcadero. The large carnival-colored building on your right is the:

3. San Diego Cruise Ship Terminal, on the B Street Pier. It has a large nautical clock at the entrance. Totally renovated in 1985, the flag-decorated terminal's interior is light and airy. Inside, you'll also find a snack bar and gift shop. Farther along is the location where:

4. **Harbor cruises** depart from sunup to sundown on tours of San Diego's harbor; ticket booths are right on the water.

A little farther south, near the Broadway Pier, the:

5. **Coronado Ferry** makes frequent trips between San Diego and Coronado. See "Getting Around: By Ferry" in chapter 4 for more information. Buy tickets from the Harbor Excursion booth.

To your left as you look up Broadway, you'll see the two gold mission-style towers of the:

6. **Santa Fe Railroad Station,** built in 1915. It's only 1½ blocks away, so walk up and look inside at the vaulted ceiling, wooden benches, and walls covered in striking green and gold tiles.

Continuing south on Harbor Drive, you'll stroll through a small tree- and bench-lined:

7. **Waterfront park.**

South of that, at Pier 11, is the:

8. **U.S. Air Carrier Memorial,** a compact black granite obelisk that honors the nation's carriers and crews. Erected in 1993, it stands on the site of the old navy fleet landing, where thousands of servicemen boarded ships over the years.

Continue along the walkway to:

9. **Tuna Harbor,** where the commercial fishing boats congregate. San Diego's tuna fleet, with about 100 boats, is one of the world's largest (and perhaps smelliest).

TAKE A BREAK   The red building to your right houses the **Fish Market** (☎ 619/232-FISH), a market and casual restaurant, and its elegant upstairs counterpart, **Top of the Market** (☎ 619/234-4TOP). You can be assured that a meal here is fresh off the boat. Both serve lunch and dinner, and the Fish Market has a children's menu and an oyster and sushi bar. It's acceptable to drop in just for a drink and to savor the view, which is mighty. Prices are moderate to expensive. If you prefer something quick and cheap, save yourself a walk and stop in at casual **Anthony's Fishette** (☎ 619/232-5105). A cousin of the one you passed earlier, it's just outside Seaport Village. For dessert or coffee, go inside Seaport Village to **Upstart Crow** (☎ 619/232-4855), a bookstore and coffeehouse, and sip cappuccino in the company of your favorite authors.

Keep walking south, where you can meander along the winding pathways of:

10. **Seaport Village,** with its myriad shops and restaurants. The Broadway Flying Horses Carousel is pure nostalgia. Charles Looff, of Coney Island, carved the animals out of poplar in 1890. The merry-go-round was originally installed at Coney Island and later moved to Salisbury, Massachusetts. Seaport Village bought it in the 1970s and spent more than 2 years restoring it to its original splendor—the horses even have real horsehair tails. If you decide to take a twirl, pick your mount from the 40 horses, three goats, and three St. Bernard dogs. This carousel comes complete with the elusive brass ring.

As you stroll farther, you will no doubt notice the official symbol of Seaport Village. The 45-foot-high detailed replica of the famous turn-of-the-century Mukilteo Lighthouse of Everett, Washington, towers above the other buildings.

From Seaport Village, continue your waterfront walk south to the:

11. **San Diego Marriott Marina,** adjacent to Embarcadero Marina Park, which is well used by San Diegans for strolling and jogging—and provides a terrific view of the Coronado Bridge. A concession at the marina office rents boats by the

Walking Tour: The Embarcadero

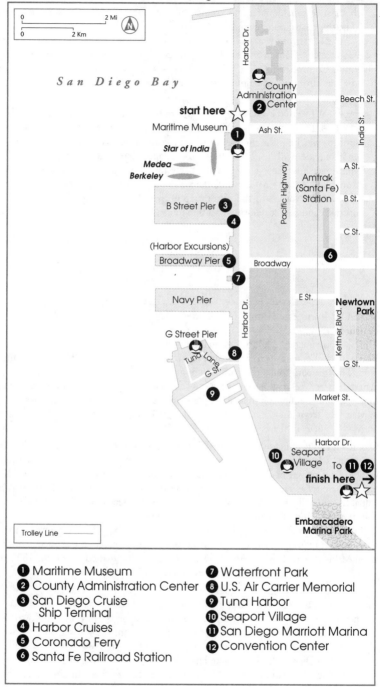

San Diego Bay

Harbor Dr.

County Administration Center

Beech St.

India St.

start here ☆

Maritime Museum ①

Ash St.

Star of India

Medea

Berkeley

A St.

Amtrak (Santa Fe) Station

Pacific Highway

B Street Pier ③

B St.

④

C St.

(Harbor Excursions)

Broadway Pier ⑤

Broadway

⑥

⑦

Navy Pier

E St.

Newtown Park

Harbor Dr.

Kettner Blvd.

G Street Pier

⑧

G St.

Tuna Lane St.

G St.

⑨

Market St.

Harbor Dr.

⑩ Seaport Village

To ⑪ ⑫

finish here →
☆

Embarcadero Marina Park

Trolley Line ————

① Maritime Museum
② County Administration Center
③ San Diego Cruise Ship Terminal
④ Harbor Cruises
⑤ Coronado Ferry
⑥ Santa Fe Railroad Station

⑦ Waterfront Park
⑧ U.S. Air Carrier Memorial
⑨ Tuna Harbor
⑩ Seaport Village
⑪ San Diego Marriott Marina
⑫ Convention Center

0 ___ 2 Mi
0 ___ 2 Km

163

hour at reasonable rates and arranges diving, water-skiing, and fishing outings. The impressive hotel resembles an ocean liner.

The waterfront walkway continues to the:

12. **Convention Center,** another striking piece of architecture on the city's water front. Completed in late 1989, it also has a seafaring theme, and its presence on the waterfront has contributed to the revitalization of downtown San Diego.

WINDING DOWN The Marriott's waterfront bar, the **Yacht Club** (☎ **619/234-1500**), looks out onto the marina and the bay beyond. It's a choice spot for watching the sunset. (You might want to plan your walking tour so the end coincides with it.) You can get drinks, appetizers, and light fare here, and if you linger into the evening, there's likely to be live music and dancing. Across from the Convention Center, at the water's edge, is the **Chart House** (☎ **619/ 435-0155**). Housed in the historic 1899 San Diego Rowing Club, it's a more upscale candidate for a drink or a bite to eat.

Walking Tour 3
Old Town

Start: Old Town State Historic Park headquarters.
Finish: Heritage Park.
Time: Approximately 2 hours, not including shopping or dining.
Best Times: Weekends (except the first one in May) and any day before 2pm or after 3pm. The free park tour runs from 2 to 3pm.
Worst Times: Weekdays, when numerous school groups are touring (although it's fun to watch on-site education in action). On Cinco de Mayo weekend, the first weekend in May, Old Town is a madhouse. The holiday celebrates Mexico's defeat of the French on May 5, 1862, in the Battle of Puebla.

Old Town is the Williamsburg of the West. When you visit, you go back to a time of one-room schoolhouses and village greens, when many of the people who lived, worked, and played here spoke Spanish. Even today, life moves more slowly in this part of the city, where the buildings are old or built to look that way. The stillness is palpable, especially at night, when you can stroll the streets and look up at the stars. You don't have to look hard or very far to see yesterday.

Begin at the park headquarters, at the eastern end of the park—not a park in the sense of having grass and trees, but a historic district. It preserves the essence of the small Mexican and fledgling American communities that existed here from 1821 to 1872. The center of Old Town is a six-block area with no vehicular traffic.

The headquarters are in the:

1. **Robinson-Rose House,** built in 1853 as a family home; it has also served as a newspaper and railroad office. Here you will see a large model of Old Town the way it looked in 1872, the year a large fire broke out (or was set). It destroyed much of the town and initiated the population exodus to New Town, now down-town San Diego. Old Town State Historic Park contains seven original buildings, including the Robinson-Rose House, and replicas of other buildings that once stood here.

From here, turn left and stroll into the colorful world of Mexican California called:

2. **Bazaar del Mundo,** 2754 Calhoun St., where international shops and restaurants spill into a flower-filled courtyard. Designer Diane Powers created the unique setting from the dilapidated Casa de Pico motel, constructed in 1936. On Saturday and Sunday afternoons, Mexican dancers perform free at the bazaar. While you're here, be sure to visit the **Guatemala Shop,** the **Design Center,** and **Libros** bookstore.

TAKE A BREAK   You can't leave San Diego without sampling the Mexican food in Bazaar del Mundo. Try **Rancho El Nopal** (☎ **619/295-0584**), **Casa de Pico** (☎ **619/296-3267**), or, a block away, **Casa de Bandini** (☎ **619/ 297-8211**). You can also enjoy Italian food at **Lino's** (☎ **619/299-7124**). All offer indoor and outdoor dining and a lively ambiance. Historic Casa de Bandini, completed in 1829, was the home of Peruvian-born Juan Bandini, who became a Mexican citizen; in 1869, the building, with a second story added, became the Cosmopolitan Hotel. Within the park, restaurants are open from 10am to 9pm and stores from 10am to 8pm (9pm in Bazaar del Mundo).

From Bazaar del Mundo, stroll into the grassy plaza, where you'll see a:

3. **large rock monument,** which commemorates the first U.S. flag flown in Southern California (on July 29, 1846). In the plaza's center stands a flagpole that resembles a ship's mast. There's a reason: The original flag hung from the mast of an abandoned ship.

Straight ahead, at the plaza's western edge, is:

4. **La Casa de Estudillo.** An original adobe building dating from 1827, the U-shaped house has covered walkways and an open central patio. The patio covering is made of corraza cane, the seeds for which were brought by Father Serra in 1769. The walls are 3 to 5 feet thick, holding up the heavy beams and tiles, and they work as terrific insulators against summer heat. In those days, the thicker the walls, the wealthier the family. The furnishings in the "upper-class" house are representative of the 19th century (don't overlook the beautiful four-poster beds); the original furniture came from the East Coast and from as far away as Asia. The Estudillo family, which then numbered 12, lived in the house until 1887; today family members still live in San Diego.

After you exit La Casa de Estudillo, turn left. In front of you is the reconstruction of the three-story:

5. **Colorado House,** built in 1851 and destroyed by fire in 1872—as were most buildings on this side of the park. Today it's the home of the **Wells Fargo Historical Museum,** but the original housed San Diego's first two-story hotel. The museum features an original Wells Fargo stagecoach, numerous displays of the overland-express business, and a video show. Next door to the Wells Fargo museum, and kitty-corner to La Casa de Estudillo, is the small, red-brick **San Diego Court House and City Hall.** (A reconstruction of the three-story Franklin House is planned to the right of the Colorado House.)

From here, continue along the pedestrian walkway one short block, turn right, and walk another short block to a reddish-brown building on your right. This is the one-room:

6. **Mason Street School,** an original building dating from 1865. It was commissioned by Joshua Bean, uncle to the notorious "hanging judge" Roy Bean; Joshua Bean was also San Diego's first mayor and California's first governor. If you look inside, you'll notice that the boards that make up the walls don't match; they were leftovers from the construction of San Diego homes. Mary Chase Walker, the first teacher, ventured here from the East when she was 38 years old. She enjoyed the larger salary but hated the fleas, mosquitoes, and truancy; after a year, she resigned to marry the president of the school board.

When you leave the schoolhouse, retrace your steps to the walkway (which is the extension of San Diego Avenue) and turn right. On your left, you will see two buildings with brown shingle roofs. The first, the:

7. **Pedrorena House** (no. 2616), is an original Old Town house built in 1869, with stained glass over the doorway. The owner, Miguel Pedrorena, also owned the house next door, which became the:

8. **San Diego Union Building.** The newspaper was first published in 1868. This house arrived in Old Town after being prefabricated in Maine in 1851 and shipped around the Horn. Inside you'll see the original hand press used to print the paper, which merged with the *San Diego Tribune* in 1992. The offices are now in Mission Valley, about 3 miles from here.

At the end of the pedestrian part of San Diego Avenue stands a railing; beyond it is Twiggs Street, dividing the historic park from the rest of Old Town, which is more commercial. In this part of town, you'll find interesting shops and galleries and outstanding restaurants.

At the corner of Twiggs Street and San Diego Avenue stands the Spanish mission–style:

9. **Immaculate Conception Catholic Church.** The cornerstone was laid in 1868, but with the movement of the community to New Town in 1872, it lost its parishioners and was not dedicated until 1919. Today the church serves about 300 families in the Old Town area. (Visitors sometimes see the little church and on a whim decide to get married here, but arrangements have to be made 9 months in advance.)

Halfway up the hill from the church, on the opposite side of Twiggs Street, is the:

10. **Theatre in Old Town,** 4040 Twiggs St., where there's usually a comedy or musical in production. This is also an Old Town Trolley stop.

Return to San Diego Avenue and continue along it one block to Harney Street. On your left is the restored:

11. **Whaley House,** the first two-story brick structure in Southern California, built from 1855 to 1857. The house is said to be haunted by the ghost of a man who was executed (by hanging) out back. It's beautifully furnished with period pieces and features the life mask of Abraham Lincoln, the spinet piano used in the film *Gone With the Wind,* and the concert piano that accompanied Swedish soprano Jenny Lind on her final U.S. concert tour in 1852. The house's north room served as the county courthouse for a few years, and the courtroom looks now as it did then.

From the Whaley House, walk uphill 1½ blocks along Harney Street to a Victorian jewel called:

12. **Heritage Park.** The seven buildings on this grassy knoll were moved here from other parts of the city and are now used in a variety of ways. Among them are a winsome bed-and-breakfast inn (in the Queen Anne shingle-style Christian House, built in 1889), a doll shop, an antique store, and offices.

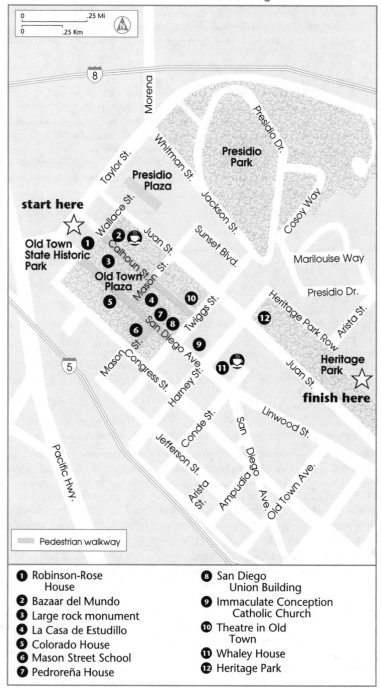

0 ___ .25 Mi
0 ___ .25 Km

Morena

Presidio Park

Presidio Dr.

Cosoy Way

Taylor St.

Whitman St.

Presidio Plaza

Jackson St.

Sunset Blvd.

Marilouise Way

start here

Wallace St.

Juan St.

Presidio Dr.

Old Town State Historic Park ❶

❷ 🔶

Calhoun St.

Mason St.

Heritage Park Row

Arista St.

❸

Old Town Plaza

❺

❹

⓲

⓰

Twiggs St.

❼

❽

Congress St.

❻

San Diego Ave.

❾

Heritage Park

⓫ 🔶

Juan St.

finish here

Mason St.

Harney St.

Conde St.

Linwood St.

Pacific Hwy.

Jefferson St.

Arista St.

Ampudia St.

San Diego Ave.

Old Town Ave.

▨ Pedestrian walkway

❶ Robinson-Rose House
❷ Bazaar del Mundo
❸ Large rock monument
❹ La Casa de Estudillo
❺ Colorado House
❻ Mason Street School
❼ Pedroreña House
❽ San Diego Union Building
❾ Immaculate Conception Catholic Church
⓰ Theatre in Old Town
⓫ Whaley House
⓲ Heritage Park

Toward the bottom of the hill is the classic revival Temple Beth Israel, dating from 1889. On Sunday, local art is often exhibited in the park. If you've brought picnic supplies, enjoy them under the sheltering coral tree at the top of the hill.

☕ **WINDING DOWN**   At the end of your walk, wend your way back down Harney Street, turn left at San Diego Avenue, and take a left just beyond the Whaley House. The brick walkway will lead you to **Garden House Coffee & Tea,** 2480 San Diego Ave. (☎ **619/220-0723**), a coffee shop in a turn-of-the-century house. It's so small that you have to take your fresh brew and sip it on the front porch or in the yard under the gnarled old pepper trees. This is a quiet, secluded spot where you can catch your breath and enjoy the scenery.

Walking Tour 4
Balboa Park

Start: Cabrillo Bridge, entry at Laurel Street and Sixth Avenue.
Finish: San Diego Zoo.
Time: 2 hours, not including museum or zoo stops. If you get tired, hop on the free park tram.
Best Times: Anytime. If you want to get especially good photographs, come in the afternoon, when the sun lends a glow to the already photogenic buildings. Most museums are open until 4:30pm. The zoo closes at 5pm in the summer, 4pm other times of the year.
Worst Times: Some say weekends, when more people (especially families) visit the park. But there is a festive spirit then—particularly on Sunday afternoons, when there is a free organ concert at the outdoor Spreckels Organ Pavilion at 2pm.

Balboa Park is the second-oldest city park in the United States, after New York's Central Park. Much of its striking architecture was the product of the Panama–California Exposition in 1915–16 and the California Pacific International Exposition in 1935–36. The structures now house outstanding museums and contribute to the park's uniqueness and beauty. The park, previously called "City Park," was renamed in 1910 when Mrs. Harriet Phillips won a name contest. "Balboa Park" honors the Spanish explorer who, in 1513, was the first European to see the Pacific Ocean.

   Take bus no. 1 or 3 along Fifth Avenue or bus no. 25 along Sixth Avenue to Laurel Street, which leads into Balboa Park through its most dramatic entrance, the:

1. **Cabrillo Bridge,** with its striking views of downtown San Diego and scenic, sycamore-lined Highway 163. Built in 1915 for the Panama–California Exposition and patterned after a bridge in Ronda, Spain, the dramatic cantilever-style bridge has seven pseudo-arches. As you cross the bridge, to your left you'll see the yellow cars of the zoo's Skyfari and, directly ahead, the distinctive California Tower of the Museum of Man. The delightful sounds of the 100-bell Symphonic Carillon can be heard every quarter-hour. Sitting atop this San Diego landmark is a weather vane shaped like the ship in which Cabrillo sailed to California in 1542. The city skyline lies to your right.

Impression

This is the most beautiful highway I've ever seen.
> —John F. Kennedy (speaking about Highway 163,
> which winds through Balboa Park), 1963

Once you've crossed the bridge, go through the:

2. **arch** (the two figures represent the Atlantic and Pacific oceans) and into the park, a treasure of nature and culture. For now, just view the museums from the outside (you can read more about them in chapter 7). You have entered the park's major thoroughfare, El Prado, and to your left is the:

3. **Museum of Man,** an anthropological museum focusing on the peoples of North and South America. Architect Bertram Goodhue designed this structure, originally known as the California Building, in 1915. Goodhue, considered the world's foremost authority on Spanish-colonial architecture, was the master architect for the 1915–16 exposition.

Just beyond and up the steps to the left is the nationally acclaimed:

4. **Old Globe Theatre,** part of the Simon Edison Centre for the Performing Arts. The Globe, as the locals refer to it, was built for the 1935 exposition. The replica of Shakespeare's Old Globe Theatre was meant to be demolished after the exposition but survived. In 1978, an arsonist destroyed the theater, which was rebuilt into what you see today. It's California's oldest professional theater. If you have the opportunity to go inside, you can see the bronze bust of Shakespeare that miraculously survived the fire with minor damage.

Beside the theater is the:

5. **Sculpture Garden of the Museum of Art.**

Across the street, to your right as you stroll along the Prado, is the:

6. **Alcazar Garden,** designed in 1935 by Richard Requa. He patterned it after the gardens surrounding the Alcazar Castle in Seville, Spain. The garden is formally laid out and trimmed with low clipped hedges; in the center walkway are two star-shaped yellow-and-blue tile fountains.

Exit to your left at the opposite end of the garden, and you'll be back on El Prado. Proceed to the corner; on your right is the:

7. **House of Charm,** the site of the San Diego Art Institute Gallery and the Mingei International Museum of World Folk Art. The gallery is a non-profit space that primarily exhibits works of local artists; the museum offers changing exhibitions that celebrate human creativity expressed in textiles, costumes, jewelry, toys, pottery, paintings, and sculpture.

To your left is the imposing:

8. **Museum of Art,** a must for anyone who fancies fine art. The latticework building you see beyond it is the:

9. **Botanical Building,** where colorful flowers and plants are shaded within.

Directly in front of you are the newly renovated House of Hospitality and the park's:

10. **Visitor Center,** where you can pick up maps and a discount ticket to some of the museums.

Turn right toward the statue of the mounted:

11. **El Cid Campeador,** created by Anna Hyatt Huntington and dedicated in 1930. This sculpture of the 11th-century Spanish hero was made from a mold of the

original statue in the court of the Hispanic Society of America in New York. A third one is in Seville, Spain.

Walk downhill to the ornate:

12. **Spreckels Organ Pavilion,** donated to San Diego by brothers John D. and Adolph B. Spreckels. Famed contralto Ernestine Schumann-Heink sang at the December 31, 1914, dedication; a brass plaque honors her charity and patriotism. Free, lively recitals featuring the largest outdoor organ in the world (its vast structure contains 4,428 pipes) are given Sunday at 2pm.

Exit to your right, cross the two-lane road, and follow the sidewalk down the hill. The pathway leading into the ravine to your right will take you to the:

13. **Palm Arboretum,** which requires some climbing. It's secluded, and may not always be as safe as the main roads, but you can get a good sense of its beauty by venturing only a short distance along the path. As you walk down the hill, you'll see the Hall of Nations on your left, and beside it, the:

14. **United Nations Building,** which houses the United Nations International Gift Shop, a favorite for its diverse merchandise, much of it handmade around the world. You'll recognize the shop by the U.S. and U.N. flags out front. Check the bulletin board, or ask inside, for the park's calendar of events. If you need to rest, there's a pleasant spot with a few benches opposite the gift shop.

You will notice a cluster of small houses with red-tile roofs. They are the:

15. **House of Pacific Relations International Cottages,** which promote ethnic and cultural awareness and are open to the public on Sunday afternoons year-round. From March through October, there are lawn programs with folk dancing. Take a quick peek into some of the cottages, then continue on the road to the bottom of the hill to see more of the park's museums, notably the:

16. **San Diego Automotive Museum,** to your right. It's filled with exquisite and exotic cars, and the cylindrical:

17. **Aerospace Museum,** straight ahead. The museums in this part of the park operate in structures built for the 1935 exposition.

It is not necessary to walk all the way to the bottom of the hill, unless you plan to tour one or two of the museums now. Instead, cross the road and go back up the hill past a parking lot and the Organ Pavilion. Take a shortcut through the pavilion, exit directly opposite the stage, and follow the sidewalk to your right, leading back to El Prado. Almost immediately, you come to the:

18. **Japanese Friendship Garden,** an 11½-acre canyon in the first stage of development. Its information center is inside a teahouse with shoji screens, and the small garden beside it inspires meditation.

 TAKE A BREAK   Now is your chance to have a bite to eat, sip a cool drink, and review the tourist literature you picked up at the Visitor Center. The **Terrace on the Prado** (☎ **619/236-1935**) in the House of Hospitality, which serves sandwiches and snacks, is open daily.

Back on El Prado, which is strictly a pedestrian mall from this point, set your sights on the fountain at the end of the street and head toward it. On weekends you'll probably pass street musicians, artists, and clowns. One of their favorite haunts is in front of the Botanical Building; it takes only a few minutes to wander through and is a delightful detour. Stroll down the middle of the street to get the full benefit of the lovely buildings on either side. On your right, in the:

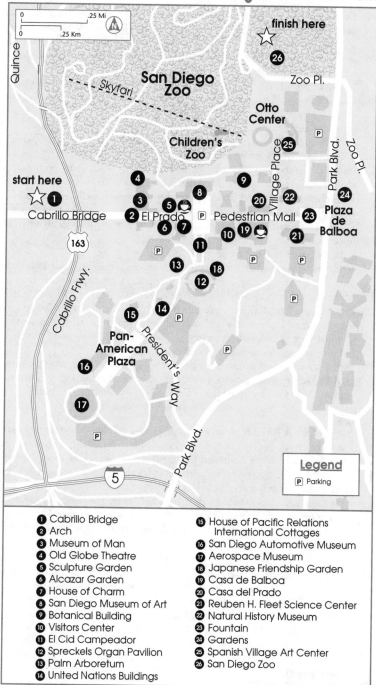

Walking Tour: Balboa Park

0 | .25 Mi
0 | .25 Km

San Diego Zoo

Skyfari

Children's Zoo

Otto Center

finish here
26

Zoo Pl.

start here
1

Cabrillo Bridge

El Prado

Pedestrian Mall

Plaza de Balboa

Village Place

Park Blvd.

Zoo Pl.

25

22

24

23

21

20

19

10

11

8

5

7

6

2

3

4

9

163

Cabrillo Fwy.

13

18

12

15

14

President's Way

Pan-American Plaza

16

17

Park Blvd.

5

Legend
P Parking

1 Cabrillo Bridge
2 Arch
3 Museum of Man
4 Old Globe Theatre
5 Sculpture Garden
6 Alcazar Garden
7 House of Charm
8 San Diego Museum of Art
9 Botanical Building
10 Visitors Center
11 El Cid Campeador
12 Spreckels Organ Pavilion
13 Palm Arboretum
14 United Nations Buildings
15 House of Pacific Relations International Cottages
16 San Diego Automotive Museum
17 Aerospace Museum
18 Japanese Friendship Garden
19 Casa de Balboa
20 Casa del Prado
21 Reuben H. Fleet Science Center
22 Natural History Museum
23 Fountain
24 Gardens
25 Spanish Village Art Center
26 San Diego Zoo

19. Casa de Balboa Building, you'll find the Hall of Champions Sports Museum, the Museum of Photographic Arts, the Model Railroad Museum, and the Museum of San Diego History, with engaging exhibits that interpret past events in the city and relate them to the present. Be sure to view the realistic-looking female figures atop the Casa de Balboa.

On the other side of El Prado, on your left, note the ornate work on the:

20. Casa del Prado. While it doesn't house a museum, it's one of the best—and most ornate—of the El Prado buildings, featuring almost rococo Spanish-Moorish ornamentation.

At the end of El Prado are two museums particularly popular with children, the:

21. Reuben H. Fleet Science Center, to your right. To the left is the:

22. Natural History Museum, where kids are likely to be climbing on the whale statue outside. Look for the sundial that is inscribed "Presented by Joseph Jessop; December 1908; I stand amid ye sommere flowers To tell ye passage of ye houres." This sundial, which is accurate to the second, was originally presented to the San Diego Public Library, and moved here in the mid-1950s when the library moved.

In the center of the Plaza de Balboa is a high-spouting:

23. fountain. This seemingly ordinary installation, built in 1972, holds 25,000 gallons of water and spouts 50 to 60 feet into the air. The unique feature is on top of the Natural History Museum, where a wind regulator is located. As the wind increases, the fountain's water pressure is lowered so that the water doesn't spray over the edges. The fountain fascinates children, who giggle when it sprays them and marvel at the rainbows it creates.

From here, cross the road to visit the nearly secret:

24. gardens, tucked away on the other side of the highway: to your left, a garden for cacti and other plants at home in an arid landscape; to your right, formal rose gardens. After you've enjoyed the flowers and plants, return to El Prado.

TAKE A BREAK   In the Casa de Balboa Building, there's a tiny **snack bar** with seating. A block from El Prado on Village Place (the street is on your left as you stand on El Prado and face the fountain) is another **snack bar** with picnic tables. You can get almost anything: sodas, iced tea, lemonade, milkshakes, pizza, burritos, sandwiches, nachos, chili, and hot dogs. In this lovely spot, towering eucalyptus trees flank the Casa del Prado Theatre. The voluptuous Moreton Bay Fig tree, which is fenced off across the street, was planted in 1915 for the exposition; now it's more than 62 feet tall, with a canopy 100 feet in diameter.

Across Village Place from the snack bar is the sleepy:

25. Spanish Village Art Center, where artists are at work daily from 11am to 4pm. They create jewelry, paintings, and sculptures in tile-roofed studios around a courtyard. There are rest rooms here, too.

Exit at the back of the Spanish Village Art Center and take the paved, palm-lined sidewalk to the left. Then turn right onto the palm-lined path that will take you to the world-famous:

Impression

Wouldn't it be splendid if San Diego had a zoo!
—Dr. Harry Wegeforth, San Diego Zoo founder, 1916

25. San Diego Zoo. You can also retrace your steps and visit some of the tempting museums you just passed, saving the zoo for another day. From here, you can walk out to Park Boulevard through the zoo parking lot to the bus stop (a brown-shingled kiosk), on your right. The no. 7 bus will take you back to downtown San Diego.

On the right, you'll pass the **San Diego Miniature Railroad** (☎ **619/239-4748**). The Miniature Train Company of Rensselaer, Indiana, made the 1:5-scale, 16-inch-gauge train, which has been a fixture here since 1948. The railroad is open every day that public schools are closed. The half-mile ride through "San Diego's back country" takes about 4 minutes. Just before you reach Park Boulevard, you will see the **Balboa Park Carousel** (☎ **619/460-9000**). The historic carousel was made in North Tonawanda, New York, in 1910. It temporarily stood in Luna Park, in Los Angeles, and Tent City, on Coronado. The carousel and its menagerie of European hand-carved animals (all original, except two pairs of miniature horses) permanently settled in Balboa Park in 1922.

9

Shopping

Whether you're looking for a souvenir, a gift, or a quick replacement for an item inadvertently left at home, you'll find no shortage of stores in San Diego. This is, after all, Southern California, where looking good is a high priority and shopping is a way of life.

1 The Shopping Scene

All-American San Diego has embraced the suburban shopping mall with vigor. At several massive complexes in Mission Valley, many residents do the bulk of their shopping; every possible need is represented. The city has even adapted the mall concept, with typically California examples like whimsical Horton Plaza and historic Old Town Plaza.

Local neighborhoods, on the other hand, offer specialty shopping that meets the needs—and mirrors the personality—of that part of town. For example, trendy Hillcrest is the place to go for cutting-edge boutiques, while conservative La Jolla offers many upscale traditional shops, especially jewelers. And don't forget that Mexico is only half an hour away; *tiendas* (stores) in Tijuana, Rosarito Beach, and Ensenada stock colorful crafts perfectly suited to the California lifestyle. San Diegans head across the border *en masse* each weekend in search of bargains.

Shops tend to stay open late, particularly in malls like Horton Plaza and Fashion Valley, tourist destinations like Bazaar del Mundo and Seaport Village, and areas like the Gaslamp Quarter and Hillcrest that see a lot of evening foot traffic. Places like these keep the welcome mat out until 9pm on weeknights and 6pm on Saturdays and Sundays. Individual stores elsewhere generally close by 5 or 6pm.

Sales tax in San Diego is 7.75%, and savvy out-of-state shoppers have larger items shipped directly home at the point of purchase, avoiding the tax.

2 Downtown & the Gaslamp Quarter

Space is at a premium in the constantly improving Gaslamp Quarter, and rents are rising. While a few intrepid shops—mostly women's boutiques and vintage clothing shops—are scattered among the area's multitudinous eateries, shopping is primarily concentrated in the destination malls listed below.

Downtown San Diego Shopping

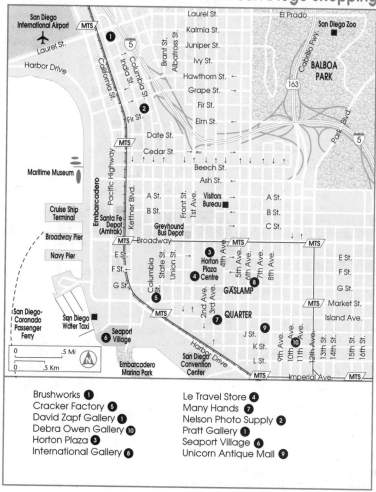

Brushworks 1
Cracker Factory 5
David Zapf Gallery 1
Debra Owen Gallery 10
Horton Plaza 3
International Gallery 8

Le Travel Store 4
Many Hands 7
Nelson Photo Supply 2
Pratt Gallery 1
Seaport Village 6
Unicorn Antique Mall 9

Horton Plaza. 324 Horton Plaza. ☎ **619/238-1596.** www.hortonplaza.com. Bus: 2, 7, 9, 29, 34, or 35. Trolley: City Center.

The Disneyland of shopping malls, Horton Plaza is in the heart of San Diego; in fact, it is the heart of the revitalized city center, bounded by Broadway, First and Fourth avenues, and G Street. Covering 7½ city blocks, the multilevel shopping center has 140 specialty shops, including art galleries, clothing and shoe stores, several fun shops for kids, and bookstores. There's a 14-screen cinema, three major department stores, and a variety of restaurants and short-order eateries. It's almost as much an attraction as Sea World or the San Diego Zoo, transcending its genre with a conglomeration of rambling paths, bridges, towers, piazzas, sculptures, fountains, and live greenery. Performers provide background entertainment throughout the year. Supposedly inspired by European shopping streets and districts like Athens' Plaka and London's Portobello Road, Horton Plaza opened in 1985 to rave reviews and has steadily grown in popularity.

Parking is free with validation for the first 3 hours (4 hours at the movie theater and the Lyceum Theatre), $1 per half-hour thereafter. The parking levels are confusing, and temporarily losing your car is part of the Horton Plaza experience. Open Monday through Friday from 10am to 9pm, Saturday 10am to 6pm, Sunday 11am to 6pm, with extended summer and holiday hours.

Seaport Village. 849 W. Harbor Dr. (at Kettner Blvd.). ☎ **619/235-4014,** or 619/235-4013 for events information. Bus: 7. Trolley: Seaport Village.

This 14-acre ersatz village snuggled alongside San Diego Bay was built to resemble a small Cape Cod community, but the 75 shops are very much the Southern California cutesy variety. Favorites include the **Tile Shop;** the **Seasick Giraffe** for resort wear; and the **Upstart Crow bookshop and coffeehouse,** with the Crow's Nest children's bookstore inside. Be sure to see the 1890 carousel imported from Coney Island, New York. Open September to May, daily from 10am to 9pm; June to August, daily 10am to 10pm.

3 Hillcrest/Uptown

Compact Hillcrest is an ideal shopping destination. You can browse the unique and often wacky shops, and check out the area's vintage-clothing stores, memorabilia shops, chain stores, bakeries, and cafes. Start at the neighborhood's hub, the intersection of University and Fifth avenues. Street parking is available; most meters run 2 hours and devour quarters at a rate of one every 15 minutes, so be armed with plenty of change. You can also park in a lot—rates vary, but you'll come out ahead if you're planning to stroll for several hours.

If you're looking for postcards or provocative gifts, step into wacky **Babette Schwartz,** 421 University Ave. (☎ **619/220-7048**), a pop-culture emporium named for a local drag queen. You'll find books, clothing, and accessories that follow current kitsch trends. A couple of doors away, **Cathedral,** 435 University Ave. (☎ **619/296-4046**), is dark and heady, filled with candles of all scents and shapes, plus unusual holders.

Around the corner, **Circa a.d.,** 3867 Fourth Ave. (☎ **619/293-3328**), is a floral design shop with splendid gift items; at holiday time it has the most extravagant Christmas ornaments in the area. Head gear from straw hats to knit caps to classy fedoras fills the **Village Hat Shop,** 3821 Fourth Ave. (☎ **619/683-5533;** www.villagehatshop.com), whose best feature may be its minimuseum of stylishly displayed vintage hats.

Lovers of rare and used books will want to poke around the used bookstores on Fifth Avenue between University and Robinson avenues. This block is also home to **Off the Record,** 3865 Fifth Ave. (☎ **619/298-4755**), a new and used music store known for an alternative bent and the city's best vinyl selection. For a comprehensive choice of brand-new CDs and tapes, you're better off at **Blockbuster Music,** 3965 Fifth Ave. (☎ **619/683-3293**), where you can preview any disc before committing to the purchase.

San Diego's self-proclaimed **Antique Row** is north of Balboa Park, along Park Boulevard (beginning at University Avenue in Hillcrest) and Adams Avenue (extending to around 40th Street in Normal Heights). Antique and collectible stores, vintage-clothing boutiques, coffeehouses and pubs, funky restaurants, and dusty used book and record stores line this L-shaped district, providing many hours of happy browsing and treasure hunting. For more information and an area brochure with a map, contact the **Adams Avenue Business Association** (☎ 619/282-7329; www.GoThere.com/AdamsAve).

Lovers of vintage clothing—both female and male—won't want to miss **Wear It Again Sam,** 3922 Park Blvd., at University Avenue (☎ 619/299-0185). It's a classy step back in time, with only the most pristine examples of styles from the '20s to the '50s. It has occupied this off-the-beaten-path corner of Hillcrest for 15-plus years, and I'm always surprised by how reasonably priced it is.

Hillcrest/Uptown Shopping

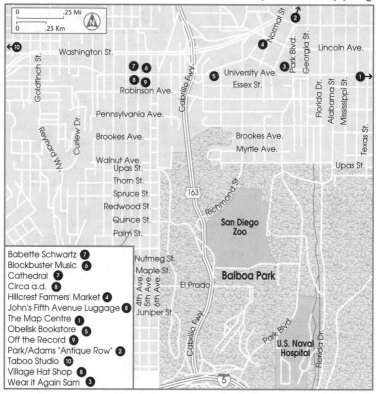

Babette Schwartz ⑦
Blockbuster Music ⑥
Cathedral ⑦
Circa a.d. ⑧
Hillcrest Farmers' Market ④
John's Fifth Avenue Luggage ⑧
The Map Centre ①
Obelisk Bookstore ⑤
Off the Record ⑨
Park/Adams "Antique Row" ②
Taboo Studio ⑩
Village Hat Shop ⑧
Wear it Again Sam ③

4 Old Town & Mission Valley

Old Town Historic Park is a restoration of some of San Diego's historic sites and adobe structures, a number of which now house shops that cater to tourists. Many have a "general store" theme, and carry gourmet treats and inexpensive Mexican crafts alongside the obligatory T-shirts, baseball caps, snow domes, and other souvenirs. A reconstruction of San Diego's first tobacco shop carries cigars and smoking paraphernalia; more shops are concentrated in colorful Bazaar del Mundo (see below).

Mission Valley is ground zero of San Diego's suburban mall explosion. There are several sprawling shopping centers here, all discussed in detail below (see "Malls").

Bazaar del Mundo. 2754 Calhoun St., Old Town State Historic Park. ☎ **619/296-3161.** Bus: 4 or 5/105.

Take a stroll down Mexico way and points south through the arched passageways of this colorful corner of Old Town. Always festive, its central courtyard vibrates with folkloric music, mariachis, and a splashing fountain. Shops feature one-of-a-kind folk art, home furnishings, clothing, and textiles from Mexico and South America. You'll also find a top-notch bookstore, **Libros,** with a large kids' selection. Don't miss the **Design Center** and the **Guatemala Store.** You won't find any bargains here—it's clearly tourist central—but there isn't a more colorful place to browse in San Diego. Open daily from 10am to 9pm.

5 Mission Bay & the Beaches

The beach communities offer laid-back shopping in typical California fashion, with plenty of surf shops, recreational gear, casual garb, and youth-oriented music stores.

If you're in need of a new bikini, the best selection is at **Pilar's,** 3745 Mission Blvd., Pacific Beach (☎ 619/488-3056), where choices range from chic designer suits to hot trends like suits inspired by surf- and skate-wear. There's a smaller selection of one-piece suits, too. It's open daily.

Some of the area's best **antiquing** can be found in Ocean Beach, along a single block of **Newport Avenue,** the town's main drag. The selection is high quality enough to make it interesting, without pricey, centuries-old European antiques. Most of the stores are mall-style, featuring multiple dealers under one roof. Highlights include **Newport Avenue Antiques,** 4836 Newport Ave. (☎ 619/224-1994), which offers the most diversity. Its wares range from Native American crafts to Victorian furniture and delicate accessories, from Mighty Mouse collectibles to carved Asian furniture. **O.B. Emporium,** 4847 Newport Ave. (☎ 619/523-1262), has a more elegant setting and glass display cases filled with superb collectible pottery and china. Names like Rockwood, McCoy, and Royal Copenhagen abound, and there's a fine selection of quality majolica and Japanese tea sets. The **Newport Ave. Antique Center,** 4864 Newport Ave. (☎ 619/222-8686), is the largest store, and has a small espresso bar. One corner is a haven for collectors of 1940s and '50s kitchenware (Fire King, Bauer, melamine); there's also a fine selection of vintage linens. Most antique stores in Ocean Beach are open daily from 10am to 6pm.

6 La Jolla

It's clear from the look of La Jolla's village that shopping is a major pastime in this upscale community. Women's clothing boutiques tend to be conservative and costly, like those lining Girard and Prospect streets (**Ann Taylor, Armani Exchange, Polo Ralph Lauren, Talbots,** and **Sigi's Boutique**).

Recommended stores include **Island Hoppers,** 7844 Girard Ave. (☎ 858/459-6055), for colorful Hawaiian-print clothing from makers like Tommy Bahama; the venerable **Ascot Shop,** 7750 Girard Ave. (☎ 858/454-4222), for conservative men's apparel and accessories; **La Jolla Shoe Gallery,** 7852 Girard Ave. (☎ 858/551-9985), for an outstanding selection of Clark's, Birkenstock, Mephisto, Josef Siebel, and other shoes built for walking; and the surprisingly affordable **Clothes Minded,** 7880 Girard Ave. (☎ 858/454-3700), a ladies' casual boutique where everything is just $15.

Even if you're not in the market for furnishings and accessories, La Jolla's many home-decor boutiques make for great window shopping, as do its ubiquitous jewelers: Swiss watches, tennis bracelets, precious gems, and pearl necklaces sparkle in windows along every street.

No visit to La Jolla is complete without seeing **John Cole's Bookshop,** a local icon discussed below under "Books."

Another unique shopping experience awaits at the **La Jolla Cave and Shell Shop,** 1325 Coast Blvd., just off Prospect Street (☎ 858/454-6080). This cliff-top treasure chest sells dozens of varieties of individual loose shells. It also carries jewelry, wind chimes, decorative hangings, nightlights, and sculptures crafted from common varieties like tiny cowrie shells. But the main attraction is **Sunny Jim Cave,** reached by a steep and narrow staircase through the rock; it lets out on a wood-plank observation deck from which you can gaze out at the sea. It's a cool treat, particularly on a hot summer day, and costs only $1.50 per person (75¢ for kids). Hold the handrail and your little ones' hands tightly.

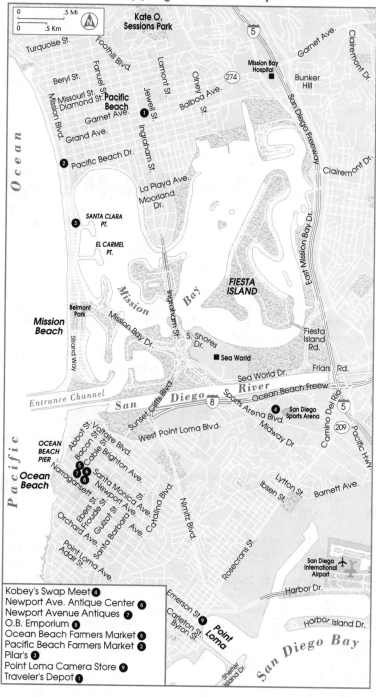

0 .5 Mi
0 .5 Km

Kate O.
Sessions Park

Turquoise St.

Foothill Blvd

Fanuel St.

Lamont St.

Jewell St.

Olney St.

Balboa St.

Garnet Ave.

Clairemont Dr.

274

Mission Bay
Hospital

Bunker
Hill

Beryl St.

Missouri St.

Diamond St.

Pacific Beach ❶

Mission Blvd.

Garnet Ave.

Grand Ave.

Ingraham St.

❷ Pacific Beach Dr.

San Diego Freeway

Clairemont Dr.

O c e a n

La Playa Ave.

Moorland
Dr.

❸ SANTA CLARA
PT.

EL CARMEL
PT.

Mission Bay

FIESTA
ISLAND

East Mission Bay Dr.

Belmont
Park

**Mission
Beach**

Mission Bay Dr.

Ingraham St.

S. Shores
Dr.

Fiesta
Island
Rd.

Strand Way

Sea World ■

Friars Rd.

Sea World Dr.

Entrance Channel

San Diego River

8

Sports Arena Blvd.

Ocean Beach Freew

❹ San Diego
Sports Arena

Camino Del Rio

5

209

Pacific Hwy.

OCEAN
BEACH
PIER

Abbot St.

Voltaire Blvd.

Bacon St.

Cable St.

Brighton Ave.

❺ ❻
❼ ❻
❽

Sunset Cliffs Blvd.

West Point Loma Blvd.

Midway Dr

**Ocean
Beach**

Narragansett

Santa Monica Ave.

Newport Ave.

Ebers St.

Froude St.

Guizot St.

Santa Barbara Ave.

Catalina Blvd.

Nimitz Blvd.

Lytton St.

Ibsen St.

Barnett Ave.

P a c i f i c

Orchard Ave.

Point Loma Ave.

Adair St.

Rosecrans St.

San Diego
International
Airport ✈

Harbor Dr.

Emerson St.

Carleton St.

Byron St.

❾ **Point
Loma**

Harbor Island Dr.

Shelter Island Dr.

San Diego Bay

Kobey's Swap Meet ❹
Newport Ave. Antique Center ❻
Newport Avenue Antiques ❼
O.B. Emporium ❽
Ocean Beach Farmers Market ❺
Pacific Beach Farmers Market ❷
Pilar's ❸
Point Loma Camera Store ❾
Traveler's Depot ❶

179

Trader Joe's. 8657 Villa La Jolla Dr. (in La Jolla Village Center). ☎ **858/546-8629.**

This Southern California institution is equal parts gourmet shop, bargain mart, and health-food emporium. Most of the specialty food items are packaged under the house label, offering exceptional deals on items like pâté, imported cheeses, dried fruits and nuts, and delicious packaged baked goods. The chain also features great deals on wine, imported beers, and high-quality liquors—many locals wouldn't consider shopping anywhere else. "TJ's" is a smart stop if you're assembling a picnic, stocking up on snack foods, or filling an in-room fridge. Open daily from 9am to 9pm.

Trader Joe's can also be found in **Hillcrest/Uptown,** at 1090 University Ave. (☎ 619/296-3122), and Pacific Beach, at 1211 Garnet Ave. (☎ 619/272-7235).

7 Coronado

This rather insular, conservative navy community doesn't have a great many shopping opportunities; the best of the lot lines Orange Avenue at the western end of the island. You'll find some scattered housewares and home-decor boutiques, several small women's boutiques, and the gift shops at Coronado's major resorts.

Also check out **Kensington Coffee Company** (see chapter 6) for coffee-related paraphernalia. Coronado also has an excellent independent bookshop, **Bay Books,** 1029 Orange Ave. (☎ 619/435-0700). It carries a nice selection in many categories, plus volumes of local historical interest, and books on tape available for rent. **La Provençale,** 1122 Orange Ave. (☎ 619/437-8881) is a little shop stocked with textiles, pottery, and gourmet items from the French countryside.

The Ferry Landing Marketplace. 1201 First St. (at B Ave.), Coronado. ☎ **619/435-8895.** Fax 619/522-6150. Take I-5 to Coronado Bay Bridge, to B Ave., and turn right. Bus: 901. Ferry: From Broadway Pier.

The entrance is impressive—turreted red rooftops with jaunty blue flags that draw closer as the ferry pulls in. As you stroll up the pier, you'll find yourself in the midst of shops filled with gifts, imported and designer fashions, jewelry, and crafts. You can get a quick bite to eat or have a leisurely dinner with a view, wander along landscaped walkways, or laze on a beach or grassy bank. Open daily from 10am to 9pm.

8 Elsewhere in San Diego County

If you're looking for San Diego's best outlet mall, head to Carlsbad, about 40 minutes north (for more information on Carlsbad, see chapter 11, "Side Trips from San Diego"). The **Carlsbad Company Stores,** 5620 Paseo del Norte (☎ 760/804-9000), include the usual outlets and upscale retailers like Barneys New York, Donna Karan, and Polo Ralph Lauren. The mall has several unique specialty shops, like **Thousand Mile Outdoor Wear** (☎ 760/804-1764), which sells outerwear manufactured from recycled products, and makes the swimsuits worn by Southern California lifeguards. To get there, take the Palomar Airport Road exit off I-5.

Garden fanciers will find North County the best hunting grounds for bulbs, seeds, and starter cuttings. **North County nurseries** are known throughout the state for rare and hard-to-find plants, notably begonias, orchids, bromeliads, succulents, ranunculus, and unusual herbs. For more information on the area's largest growers, **Carlsbad Ranch** and **Weidners' Gardens,** turn to chapter 11.

One off-the-beaten-path treasure in Carlsbad is **Charles B. Ledgerwood Seeds,** 3862 Carlsbad Blvd., between Redwood and Tamarack (☎ 760/729-3282). Open

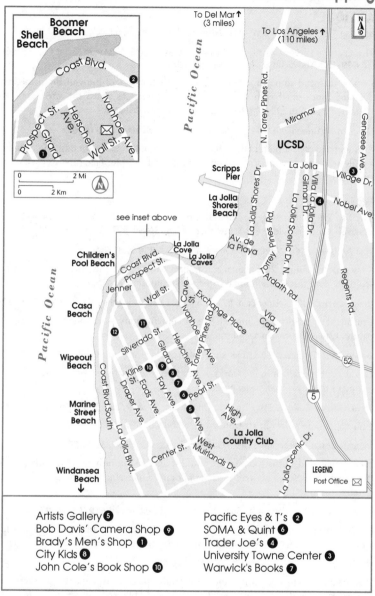

To Del Mar ↑
(3 miles)

To Los Angeles ↑
(110 miles)

Boomer Beach

Shell Beach

Coast Blvd.

Prospect St.
Girard
Herschel Ave.
Ivanhoe Ave.
Wall St.

Pacific Ocean

UCSD

Scripps Pier

La Jolla Shores Beach

La Jolla Cove
La Jolla Caves

Children's Pool Beach

Coast Blvd.
Prospect St.
Jenner
Wall St.

see inset above

Casa Beach

Pacific Ocean

Wipeout Beach

Marine Street Beach

Windansea Beach
↓

Silverado St.
Kline St.
Eads Ave.
Draper Ave.
Girard
Fay Ave.
Herschel Ave.
Torrey Pines Ave.
Cave St.
Ivanhoe Ave.
Exchange Place
Pearl St.
High Ave.
West Muirlands Dr.
Center St.
La Jolla Blvd.
Coast Blvd. South

La Jolla Country Club

La Jolla Scenic Dr.

52

5

Regents Rd.

Genesee Ave.

Village Dr.

Nobel Ave.

Villa La Jolla Dr.
Gilman Dr.
La Jolla Scenic Dr. N.
Torrey Pines Rd.
Ardath Rd.
Via Capri
Av. de la Playa
N. Torrey Pines Rd.
Miramar

La Jolla

LEGEND
Post Office ✉

0   2 Mi
0   2 Km

Artists Gallery **5**
Bob Davis' Camera Shop **9**
Brady's Men's Shop **1**
City Kids **8**
John Cole's Book Shop **10**

Pacific Eyes & T's **2**
SOMA & Quint **6**
Trader Joe's **4**
University Towne Center **3**
Warwick's Books **7**

Monday through Saturday, the 65-year-old shop has a mind-boggling selection that includes heirloom vegetables and rare herbs.

9 Shopping A to Z

Large stores and shops in malls tend to stay open until about 9pm weekdays, 6pm weekends. Smaller businesses usually close at 5 or 6pm or may keep odd hours. When in doubt, call ahead.

ANTIQUES
See also "Hillcrest/Uptown" and "Mission Bay & the Beaches," above.

The Cracker Factory Antiques Shopping Center. 448 W. Market St. (at Columbia St.). ☎ **619/233-1669.** Bus: 7. Trolley: Seaport Village.

Prepare to spend some time here, exploring three floors of individually owned and operated shops filled with antiques and collectibles. It's across the street from the Hyatt Regency San Diego, a block north of Seaport Village.

Unicorn Antique Mall. 704 J St. (at Seventh Ave.). ☎ **619/232-1696.**

Antiques and collectibles fill three floors of this 30,000-square-foot building. You'll see a wide selection of American oak and European furniture. Free off-street parking is available.

ART
The San Diego area stages numerous arts-and-crafts fairs, such as the **La Jolla Arts Festival,** which is held every September (☎ **858/454-5718**).

The Artists Gallery. 7420 Girard Ave., La Jolla. ☎ **858/459-5844.**

This gallery features 20 regional artists in a variety of media, including paintings, sculpture, and three-dimensional paper wall sculptures.

Brushworks. 2400 Kettner Blvd. #212 (south of Laurel St.), Little Italy. ☎ **619/232-7329.**

Brushworks presents changing exhibits of contemporary work, often of a whimsical nature. Call ahead for an appointment.

David Zapf Gallery. 2400 Kettner Blvd. (south of Laurel St.), Little Italy. ☎ **619/232-5004.**

David Zapf specializes in the works of San Diego–area artists. Contact the gallery for a copy of the *Arts Down Town* guide.

Debra Owen Gallery. 354 11th Ave., Downtown. ☎ **619/231-3030.** Fax 619/237-1808.

This gallery specializes in art from Mexico and California.

International Gallery. 643 G St., Gaslamp Quarter. ☎ **619/235-8255.**

Here you'll find authentic African and Melanesian primitive art, including ritual masks and sculpture, as well as contemporary American crafts in ceramics, glass, jewelry, and wood.

Many Hands. 302 Island Ave., Suite 101, Gaslamp Quarter. ☎ **619/557-8303.**

This cooperative gallery, in existence since 1972, has 35 members who engage in a variety of crafts, including toys, jewelry, posters, pottery, baskets, and wearable art.

Pratt Gallery. 2400 Kettner Blvd. ☎ **619/236-0211.**

Pratt displays original paintings, including landscapes and cityscapes by Southern California artists. It's located between Downtown and Hillcrest/Uptown.

SOMA and Quint. 7661 Girard Ave., La Jolla. SOMA ☎ **858/551-5821;** Quint ☎ **858/454-3409.**

These galleries, in the space once occupied by I. Magnin, specialize in contemporary art.

Taboo Studio. 1615½ W. Lewis St., Mission Hills. ☎ **619/692-0099.**

This impressive shop exhibits and sells the work of jewelry designers from throughout the United States. It's made of silver, gold, and inlaid stones, in one-of-a-kind pieces, limited editions, or custom work. The gallery represents 65 artists.

BOOKS

Barnes & Noble Booksellers. 7610 Hazard Center Dr., Mission Valley. ☎ **619/220-0175.** Daily 9am–11pm.

The San Diego branch of this book discounter sits among Mission Valley's mega-malls. Besides a wide selection of paperback and hardcover titles, it offers a comprehensive periodical rack.

Borders Books & Music. 1072 Camino del Rio N., Mission Valley. ☎ **619/295-2201.** Mon–Thurs 9am–11pm, Fri–Sat 9am–midnight, Sun 9am–10pm.

This full-service book and CD store in Mission Valley's main shopping region offers discounts on many titles. Borders also stocks a stylish line of greeting cards and encourages browsing; there's an adjoining coffee lounge.

John Cole's Book Shop. 780 Prospect St., La Jolla. ☎ **858/454-4766.** Fax 858/454-8377. Mon–Sat 9:30am–5:30pm.

Cole's, a favorite of many locals, is in a turn-of-the-century wisteria-covered cottage, the former guest house of philanthropist Ellen Browning Scripps. John and Barbara Cole founded the shop in 1946 and moved it into the cottage 20 years later. Barbara and her children continue to run it today. Visitors will find cookbooks in the old kitchen, paperbacks in a former classroom, and CDs and harmonicas in Zach's music corner. The children's section bulges with a diverse selection, and there are plenty of books about La Jolla and San Diego. Sitting and reading in the patio garden is acceptable, and even encouraged.

Obelisk Bookstore. 1029 University Ave., Hillcrest. ☎ **619/297-4171.** Fax 619/297-5803. Mon–Sat 10am–11pm, Sun noon–8pm.

This bookstore, which caters to gay men and lesbians, is where Greg Louganis signed copies of his book *Breaking the Surface.*

Traveler's Depot. 1655 Garnet Ave., Pacific Beach. ☎ **619/483-1421.** Fax 619/483-2743. Mon–Fri 10am–6pm (until 8pm in summer), Sat 10am–5pm, Sun noon–5pm.

This bookstore offers an extensive selection of travel books and maps, plus a great array of travel gear and accessories, with discounts on backpacks and luggage. The well-traveled owners, Ward and Lisl Hampton, are happy to give advice about restaurants in a given city while pointing you to the right shelf for the appropriate book or map.

Warwick's Books. 7812 Girard Ave., La Jolla. ☎ **858/454-0347.** Mon–Sat 9am–6pm, Sun 11am–5pm.

This popular family-run bookstore is a browser's delight, with more than 40,000 titles, a large travel section, gifts, cards, and stationery. The well-read Warwick family has been in the book and stationery business for almost 100 years, and the current owners are the third generation involved with the store.

DEPARTMENT STORES

Macy's. Horton Plaza. ☎ **619/231-4747.** Fax 619/645-3295. Mon–Fri 10am–9pm, Sat 10am–8pm, Sun 11am–7pm. Bus: 2, 7, 9, 29, 34, or 35.

Know Your Guacamole: Avocado Trivia

1. What is the avocado's nickname?
2. In which U.S. city are the most avocados eaten?
3. What is the best way to ripen an avocado?

For answers, turn the page.

There are several branches of this comprehensive store, which carries clothing for women, men, and children, as well as housewares, electronics, and luggage. Macy's also has stores in Fashion Valley (clothing only), Mission Valley (housewares only), University Towne Center, and North County Fair.

✪ **Nordstrom.** Horton Plaza. ☎ **619/239-1700.** Mon–Fri 10am–9:30pm, Sat 10am–7pm, Sun 11am–6pm. Bus: 2, 7, 9, 29, 34, or 35.

An all-time San Diego favorite, Nordstrom is best known for its outstanding customer service and fine selection of shoes. It features a variety of stylish fashions and accessories for women, men, and children. Tailoring is done on the premises. There's a full-service restaurant on the top floor, where coffee and tea cost only 25¢. Nordstrom also has stores in Fashion Valley, University Towne Center, and North County Fair.

FARMERS' MARKETS

San Diegans love their open-air markets. Throughout the county there are no fewer than two dozen regularly scheduled street fests stocked with the freshest fruits and vegetables from Southern California farms, augmented by crafts, fresh-cooked ethnic foods, flower stands, and other surprises. San Diego County produces over $1 billion worth of fruits, flowers, and other crops each year. Avocados, known locally as "green gold," are the most profitable crop and have been grown here for more than 100 years. Citrus fruit follows close behind, and flowers are the area's third most important crop; ranunculus bulbs from here are sent all over the world, as are the famous Ecke poinsettias.

Here's a schedule of farmers' markets in the area:

In **Hillcrest,** the market runs Sundays from 9am to noon at the corner of Normal Street and Lincoln Avenue, several blocks north of Balboa Park. The atmosphere is festive, and exotic culinary delights reflect the eclectic neighborhood. For more information, call the **Hillcrest Association** (☎ **619/299-3330**).

In **Ocean Beach,** there's a fun-filled market Wednesday evenings between 4 and 8pm (until 7pm in fall and winter) in the 4900 block of Newport Avenue. In addition to fresh-cut flowers, produce, and exotic fruits and foods laid out for sampling, the market features llama rides and other entertainment. For more information, call the **Ocean Beach Business Improvement District** (☎ **619/224-4906**).

Head to **Pacific Beach** on Saturday from 8am to noon, when Mission Boulevard between Reed Avenue and Pacific Beach Drive is transformed into a bustling marketplace.

In **Coronado,** every Tuesday afternoon the Ferry Landing Marketplace (corner of First and B streets) hosts a produce and crafts market from 2:30 to 6pm.

FLEA MARKETS

Kobey's Swap Meet. Sports Arena Parking Lot (west end), 3500 Sports Arena Blvd. ☎ **619/226-0650** for information. Admission Thurs–Fri 50¢, Sat–Sun $1; children under 12 free. Take I-8 to Sports Arena Blvd. turnoff or I-5 to Rosecrans St. and turn right on Sports Arena Blvd.

Know Your Guacamole: Avocado Trivia

1. Alligator pear.
2. Los Angeles.
3. Place it in an ordinary paper bag and store at room temperature. (To accelerate the process, include an apple in the bag.)

Since 1980, this gigantic open-air market has been a bargain-hunter's dream-come-true. Approximately 3,000 vendors fill row after row with new and used clothing, jewelry, electronics, hardware, appliances, furniture, collectibles, crafts, antiques, auto accessories, toys, and books. There's produce, too, along with food stalls and rest rooms. Open Thursday through Sunday from 7am to 3pm.

Insider's Tip: Skip weekdays. Saturday and Sunday are when the good stuff is out—and it goes quickly, so arrive early.

MALLS

See "Downtown & the Gaslamp Quarter" for details on **Horton Plaza.** See "Elsewhere in San Diego County," above, for information on the **Carlsbad Company Stores** factory outlet mall.

Fashion Valley Center. 352 Fashion Valley Rd. ☎ **619/297-3381.** Mon–Fri 10am–9pm, Sat 10am–6pm, Sun 11am–6pm. Hwy. 163 to Friars Rd. W. Bus: 6, 16, 25, 43, or 81.

The Mission Valley–Hotel Circle area, northeast of downtown along I-8, contains San Diego's major shopping centers. Fashion Valley is the most attractive and most upscale, with anchor stores like **Neiman Marcus, Nordstrom** (which keeps longer hours), **Saks Fifth Avenue,** and **Macy's,** plus 140 specialty shops and a quadriplex movie theater. Particularly interesting specialty shops include **Williams Sonoma, Smith & Hawken,** and **Bang & Olufsen.**

Mission Valley Center. 1640 Camino del Rio N. ☎ **619/296-6375.** Mon–Fri 10am–9pm, Sat 10am–6pm, Sun 11am–6pm. I-8 to Mission Center Rd. Bus: 6, 16, 25, 43, or 81.

This old-fashioned outdoor mall predates sleek Fashion Valley, and has found a niche with budget-minded stores like **Loehmann's, Nordstrom Rack, Michael's** (arts and crafts), and **Montgomery Ward.** There's a 20-screen movie theater and about 150 other stores and places to eat.

San Diego Factory Outlet Center. 4498 Camino de la Plaza, San Ysidro. ☎ **619/690-2999.** Mon–Fri 10am–8pm, Sat 10am–7pm, Sun 10am–6pm. I-5 or I-805 south to Camino de la Plaza exit (last exit in U.S.). Turn right and continue 1 block; center is on right. Trolley: Southbound to last stop (San Ysidro). Walk back (north) 1 block and turn left on Camino de la Plaza; it's a ½-mile walk or a short taxi ride.

This strip of 35 factory outlets saves you money because you buy directly from the manufacturers. Some familiar names include **Mikasa, Levi's, Calvin Klein, Guess?, Maidenform, Van Heusen, Bass, Nike, Carter's, Osh Kosh B'Gosh, Ray-Ban,** and **Jockey.**

University Towne Center (UTC). 4545 La Jolla Village Dr. ☎ **858/546-8858.** Mon–Fri 10am–9pm, Sat 10am–7pm, Sun 11am–6pm. I-5 to La Jolla Village Dr. and go east, or I-805 to La Jolla Village Dr. and go west. Bus: 50 express, 34, or 34A.

This outdoor shopping complex has a landscaped plaza and 160 stores, including some big ones like **Nordstrom, Sears,** and **Macy's.** It is also home to a year-round ice-skating rink, the popular Hops Bistro and Brewery, and a six-screen cinema.

TRAVEL ACCESSORIES

Along with the stores listed below, try **Eddie Bauer** in Horton Plaza (☎ **619/233-0814**) or **Traveler's Depot** (see "Books," above) for travel gear.

John's Fifth Avenue Luggage. 3833 Fourth Ave. ☎ **619/298-0993** or 619/298-0995. Mon–Fri 9am–5:30pm, Sat 9am–4pm.

This San Diego institution carries just about everything you can imagine in the way of luggage, travel accessories, business cases, pens, and gifts. The on-premises luggage-repair center is an authorized airline repair facility. There is also a store in Fashion Valley.

Le Travel Store. 745 Fourth Ave. (between F and G sts.). ☎ **619/544-0005.** Fax 619/544-0312. www.letravelstore.com. Mon–Sat 10am–10pm, Sun 11am–7pm. Bus: 2, 7, 9, 29, 34, or 35. Trolley: Gaslamp.

In business since 1976, Le Travel Store has a good selection of soft-sided luggage, travel books, language tapes, maps, and lots of travel accessories. The cafe serves beverages and snacks. The long hours and central location make this spot extra handy.

The Map Centre. 2611 University Ave. (3 blocks east of Texas St.). ☎ **619/291-3830.** Fax 619/291-3840. E-mail: GBROWN9922@aol.com. Tues–Fri 10am–5:30pm, Sat 10am–5pm.

This shop may be tiny, but it has the whole world covered—in maps, that is. If you plan to spend some serious time in San Diego, buy the *Thomas Guide;* it's $16.95, but indispensible. The Map Centre is easily recognizable by its bright yellow awning.

San Diego After Dark

San Diego's rich and varied cultural scene includes classical and contemporary plays at more than a dozen theaters throughout the year;
performances by the San Diego Opera; and rock and pop concerts.
Among the numerous movie houses and multiscreen complexes are
several that feature foreign and avant-garde films. Not all of the city
streets pulsate with nightlife, but there are growing areas of late-night
activity.

Half-price tickets to theater, music, and dance events are available at
the **Times Arts Tix** booth, in Horton Plaza Park, at Broadway and
Third Avenue. Park in the Horton Plaza parking garage and have your
parking validated, or pause at the curb nearby. The kiosk is open
Tuesday through Thursday from 11am to 6pm, Friday and Saturday
from 10am to 6pm. Half-price tickets are available only the day of the
show except for Sunday performances, for which half-price tickets are
sold on Saturday. Only cash is accepted. For a daily listing of half-price
offerings, call ☎ **619/497-5000.** Full-price advance tickets are also
sold; the kiosk doubles as a Ticketmaster outlet, selling tickets to concerts throughout California.

For a rundown of the latest performances, gallery openings, and
other events, check the listings in "Night and Day," the Thursday
entertainment section of the *San Diego Union-Tribune* (www.union-
trib.com), or the *Reader* (www.sdreader.com), San Diego's free alternative newspaper, published weekly on Thursday. For what's happening
at the gay clubs, get the weekly *San Diego Gay and Lesbian Times.*
What's Playing? is a performing arts guide produced every 2 months by
the **San Diego Performing Arts League.** You can pick one up at the
Times Art Tix booth or write to 701 B St., Suite 225, San Diego, CA
92101-8101 (☎ **619/238-0700;** www.sandiego-online.com/sdpal).

1 The Performing Arts

These listings focus on the best-known of San Diego's many talented
theater companies. Don't hesitate to try a less prominent venue if the
show appeals to you. Also, keep in mind that the **California Center
for Performing Arts** in Escondido has its own productions (see
chapter 11), as does the **East County Performing Arts Center,** 210
E. Main St., El Cajon (☎ **800/696-1929** or 619/588-0206).

The **San Diego Repertory Theatre** mounts plays and musicals at
the Lyceum Theatre, 79 Broadway Circle, in Horton Plaza (☎ **619/
544-1000;** www.SanDiegoRep.com). The theaters—the 550-seat

Lyceum Stage and the 250-seat Lyceum Space—present dance and musical programs, as well as other events. Situated at the entrance to Horton Plaza, the two-level subterranean theaters are tucked behind a tile obelisk. Ticket prices are $21 to $32.

Founded in 1948, the **San Diego Junior Theatre,** at Balboa Park's Casa del Prado Theatre (☎ 619/239-8355; fax 619/239-5048; www.juniortheatre.com), is one of the country's oldest continuously producing children's theaters. It provides training and performance opportunities for children and young adults. Students make up the cast and technical crew of six main-stage shows each year.

In Coronado, **Lamb's Players Theatre,** 1142 Orange Ave. (☎ 619/437-0600; www.lambsplayers.org), is a professional repertory company whose season runs from February through December. Shows take place in the 340-seat theater in Coronado's historic Spreckels Building, where no seat is more than seven rows from the stage. Tickets cost $18 to $34. Highlights in 1999 included *My Fair Lady* and the Dorothy L. Sayers mystery *Busman's Honeymoon.*

MAJOR THEATER COMPANIES
La Jolla Playhouse. 2910 La Jolla Village Dr. (at Torrey Pines Rd.). ☎ 858/550-1010. Fax 858/550-1025. www.lajollaplayhouse.com. Tickets $19–$49. Bus: 30, 34, or 34A.

Winner of the 1993 Tony Award for outstanding American regional theater, the playhouse stages six productions each year. Its 500-seat Mandell Weiss Theater and 400-seat Mandell Weiss Forum are on the University of California, San Diego campus. Performances are held May through November. Playhouse audiences cheered *The Who's Tommy* and Matthew Broderick in *How to Succeed in Business Without Really Trying* before they went on to Broadway. Other recent highlights were the first West Coast production of the Tony Award–winning musical *Rent,* and the American premiere of the musical *Jane Eyre.*

Gregory Peck, Dorothy McGuire, and Mel Ferrer founded the original La Jolla Playhouse in 1947; it closed in 1964. This stellar reincarnation emerged in 1983. The box office is open Monday from 11am to 6pm, Tuesday through Sunday 10am to 8pm. For each show, one Saturday matinee is a "pay what you can" performance. Reduced-price "public rush" tickets are available 10 minutes before curtain, subject to availability.

Old Globe Theatre. Balboa Park. ☎ 619/239-2255, or 619/23-GLOBE (24-hr. hot line). Fax 619/231-5879. www.oldglobe.org. Tickets $23–$39. Senior and student discounts. Bus: 7 or 25. Free parking.

This Tony Award–winning theater sits near the entrance to Balboa Park, just behind the Museum of Man. It has produced world premieres of such Broadway hits as *Into the Woods,* plus the revival of *Damn Yankees,* and has booked such notable performers as Marsha Mason, Cliff Robertson, Jon Voight, and Christopher Walken. The 581-seat Old Globe, fashioned after Shakespeare's, is part of the Simon Edison Centre for the Performing Arts. The complex, which includes the 245-seat Cassius Carter Centre Stage and the 620-seat open-air Lowell Davies Festival Theatre, mounts a dozen plays a year on the three stages between January and October. Tours are offered Saturday and Sunday at 11am and cost $3 for adults, $1 for students, seniors, and military. The box office is open Tuesday through Sunday from noon to 8:30pm.

OPERA
San Diego Opera, Civic Theatre. 202 C St. ☎ 619/570-1100 (box office) or 619/232-7636. Fax 619/231-6915. www.sdopera.com. Tickets $31 to $112. Standing room, student and senior discounts available. Bus: 2, 7, 9, 29, 34, or 35. Trolley: Civic Center.

Founded in 1964, the company showcases internationally renowned performers in operas and occasional special recitals. The season runs January through May. The 1999 season included Verdi's *Falstaff* and *A Masked Ball, Così fan tutte* by Mozart, Humperdinck's *Hansel and Gretel,* the English-language *Of Mice and Men,* and the anthological *Great Richard Wagner Concert.*

The box office is outside Golden Hall, adjacent to the Civic Theatre. It's open Monday through Friday from 10am to 5:30pm; hours vary on weekends on the day of performance. Performances are Tuesday, Wednesday, and Saturday at 7pm, Friday at 8pm, and Sunday at 2pm.

DANCE

San Diego–based dance companies include the **California Ballet** (☎ 619/ 560-5676), a traditional ballet company, plus other minor companies. San Diego's **International Dance Festival,** held annually in January, spotlights the city's ethnic dance groups and emerging artists. Most performances are at the **Lyceum Theatre,** 2 Broadway Circle, in Horton Plaza (☎ 619/235-8025 or 619/231-3586), and there are free performances in public areas. Dance companies generally perform in San Diego from September through June. For specific information or a monthly calendar of events, call the **San Diego Area Dance Alliance Calendar** (☎ 619/ 239-9255).

2 The Club & Music Scene

ROCK, POP, FOLK, JAZZ, & BLUES

Belly Up Tavern. 143 S. Cedros Ave., Solana Beach. ☎ 760/481-9022. www.bellyup.com.

This club in Solana Beach, a 20-minute drive from downtown, has played host to critically acclaimed and international artists of all genres. The eclectic mix ranges from John Mayall to Ladysmith Black Mombazo to Golden Smog to Lucinda Williams. A funky setting in recycled Quonset huts underscores the venue's uniqueness. Look into advance tickets, if possible.

The Casbah. 2501 Kettner Blvd., near the airport. ☎ 619/232-4355. www.casbahmusic. com. Ticket prices vary.

Although it's kind of a dive, the Casbah has a rep for booking breakthrough alternative and rock bands. Past headliners have included Alanis Morissette, Jon Spencer Blues Explosion, and Royal Crown Revue, plus local acts Rocket from the Crypt, the Rugburns, and many more. Look into advance tickets, if possible.

Croce's Nightclubs. 802 Fifth Ave. (at F St.). ☎ 619/233-4355. www.croces.com. Cover $5–$10.

You'll hear traditional jazz every night in Croce's Jazz Bar, and rhythm and blues at Croce's Top Hat. Both adjoin the Croce's restaurants in the heart of the Gaslamp Quarter (see chapter 6, "Dining"). The clubs are named for the late Jim Croce and owned by his widow, Ingrid. Their son, A. J., an accomplished musician, often performs. The cover charge is waived if you eat at one of the restaurants.

A Note on Smoking

In January 1998, California enacted controversial legislation that banned smoking in all restaurants and bars. While opponents immediately began lobbying to repeal the law, it's a good idea to check before you light up in clubs, lounges, or other nightspots.

4th & B. 345 B St., downtown. ☎ **619/231-4343.**

It's impossible to peg this venue, except to say that it's comfortable and bookings are always of quality. Past performers include artists as various as Bryan Adams, Joan Baez, B.B. King, and local-girl-made-good Jewel, and regular appearances by the San Diego Chamber Orchestra. Look into advance tickets, if possible.

SOMA Live. 5305 Metro St., Mission Bay. ☎ **619/296-SOMA.**

This concert venue in a warehouse-like building has booked Courtney Love, Social Distortion, Faith No More, and Fugazi, plus many other cutting-edge alternative bands. Because it's one of San Diego's few all-ages serious venues, expect the audience to include people 15 to 50. Look into advance tickets, if possible.

LARGER LIVE VENUES

San Diego has become a popular destination for many major recording artists. In fact, there is a concert just about every week. The *Reader* is the best source of concert information; check the Web site (www.sdreader.com) for an advance look. Tickets typically go on sale at least 6 weeks before the event. Depending on the popularity of a particular artist or group, last-minute seats are often available through the box office or **Ticketmaster** (☎ 619/220-8497). You can also go through an agency like **Advance Tickets** (☎ 619/581-1080) and pay a higher price for prime tickets at the last minute.

Main concert venues include the **San Diego Sports Arena** (☎ 619/225-9813; www.sandiegoarena.com), on Point Loma, west of Old Town. The 15,000- to 18,000-seat indoor venue doesn't have the best acoustics, but a majority of concerts are held here because of the seating capacity and availability of paid parking. **Qualcomm Stadium** (☎ 619/641-3131), in Mission Valley, is a 71,000-seat outdoor stadium. It has acceptable acoustics and is used only for concerts by major bands like the Who and the Rolling Stones. **SDSU Open Air Amphitheater** (☎ 619/594-6947), on the San Diego State campus, northeast of downtown along I-8, is a 4,000-seat outdoor amphitheater. It has great acoustics—if you can't get a ticket, you can stand outside and hear the entire show. **Embarcadero Marina Park,** on San Diego Bay adjacent to downtown, is a 4,400-seat outdoor setting with great acoustics.

Humphrey's, 2241 Shelter Island Dr. (☎ 619/523-1010; www.humphreysconcerts.com), is a 900-seat outdoor venue on the water. It has great acoustics, and its seasonal line-up covers the spectrum of entertainment—rock and jazz to comedy, blues, folk and international music. Concerts are held from mid-May through October only. Parking is $5.

COMEDY CLUBS

The Comedy Store. 916 Pearl St., La Jolla. ☎ **858/454-9176.** Cover $6–$10.

This southern branch of L.A.'s venerable Sunset Strip institution can be relied upon for lots of laughs. Amateur night is Monday. Shows start Sunday and Thursday at 8:30pm, Tuesday and Wednesday at 8, and Friday and Saturday at 8 and 10:30pm.

Tidbits. 3838 Fifth Ave., Hillcrest. ☎ **619/543-0300.**

A huge cabaret with outstanding drag revues, Tidbits is a class act equally patronized by Hillcrest gays and adventuresome straights. It's campy and hilarious, as is the karaoke action that often takes over between shows. Performances begin around 8 to 10pm.

DANCE CLUBS & DISCOS

The following clubs impose cover charges that vary with the night of the week and the entertainment.

Olé Madrid. 751 Fifth Ave., Gaslamp Quarter. ☎ **619/557-0146.**

Loud and energetic, this dance club features a changing line-up of celebrated DJs spinning house, funk, techno, and hip-hop. The adjoining restaurant has terrific *tapas* and sangria.

Sevilla. 555 Fourth Ave., Gaslamp Quarter. ☎ **619/233-5979.**

Most nights of the week you can salsa and meringue to Brazilian dance music; sometimes the club features Spanish-language rock. Sevilla also has a *tapas* bar.

Supper Club A-Go-Go. 322 Fifth Ave., Gaslamp Quarter. ☎ **619/235-4646.**

Postmodern swingers head to this stylish club for the 1940s ambiance; you can dance up a sweat, or just sip a martini and watch the pros.

CRUISES WITH ENTERTAINMENT

Hornblower Cruises. 1066 N. Harbor Dr. (at Broadway Pier). ☎ **619/234-8687.** Tickets Sun–Fri $49, Sat $55 adults and children. Price does not include alcoholic beverages. Bus: 2. Trolley: Embarcadero.

Aboard the 151-foot antique-style yacht *Lord Hornblower,* you'll be entertained—and encouraged to dance—by a DJ playing a variety of CDs, cassettes, and records. The three-course meal is standard-issue banquet style, but the scenery is marvelous. Boarding is at 6:30pm, and the cruise runs from 7 to 9:30pm.

San Diego Harbor Excursion. 1050 N. Harbor Dr. (at Broadway Pier). ☎ **619/234-4111.** Fax 619/522-6150. Tickets $59 adults, $30 children 3–12. Adult price includes alcoholic beverages. Bus: 2. Trolley: Embarcadero.

This company offers dinner on board the 150-foot, three-deck *Spirit of San Diego,* with two main courses, dessert, and cocktails. A DJ plays dance music during the 2½-hour cruise. Sometimes there's also a country-western band or even a karaoke singalong. Boarding is at 7pm, the cruise from 7:30 to 10pm. Cruises run Thursday through Monday only.

3 The Bar & Coffeehouse Scene

BARS & COCKTAIL LOUNGES

The Bitter End. 770 Fifth Ave., Gaslamp Quarter. ☎ **619/338-9300.**

With three floors, the Bitter End manages to be sophisticated martini bar, after-hours dance club, and relaxing cocktail lounge all in one.

Cannibal Bar. In the Catamaran Hotel, 3999 Mission Blvd. ☎ **619/539-8650.**

With a tropical theme to match the adjoining hotel, this large, lively club features Polynesian cocktails, music videos, and live bands on occasion.

Club 66. 901 Fifth Ave., Gaslamp Quarter. ☎ **619/234-4166.**

Holding court underneath popular Dakota's restaurant and the Gaslamp Plaza Suites hotel above that, this dance bar sports a Route 66 theme complete with filling-station memorabilia. Relax with a drink, or dance to disco and Top 40.

Mr. A's Restaurant. 2550 Fifth Ave. (at Laurel St.). ☎ **619/239-1377.**

Perched atop an uptown high-rise, this anachronistic Continental restaurant excels at genteel cocktails with a view. Skip the genteel dining room, which appeals to an older, conservative clientele. The bar is much more comfortable, looking out on a panorama of Balboa Park, the harbor, and planes landing at Lindbergh Field.

Pitcher This: San Diego's Microbreweries

A microbrewery revolution? Not exactly, but San Diego suds have come a long way in the last few years. It started in 1989 when Karl Strauss, a Bavarian brewmaster with 44 years of experience working for Pabst in Milwaukee, came to town. He opened Old Columbia Brewery, the first local brewery in more than 50 years. He named his brews after local attractions—Gaslamp Gold Ale, Red Trolley Ale, Black's Beach Extra Dark, Star of India Pale Ale—but used recipes from the Old World. They adhere to the Bavarian Purity Laws of 1516.

Karl's crew continues to make 23 beers a year, on a rotational basis, with eight available at any time. Want to try them all and still be able to walk? At any of the Karl Strauss breweries around town, you can order a Taster Series—4 ounces of eight brews. Free brewery tours are conducted Saturday and Sunday at 1 and 2pm at the downtown branch (see below). An in-depth tour, which includes a comparative tasting of Karl Strauss beers with America's best-selling beers, is available both days at 3pm. The cost of $20 per person includes a T-shirt, appetizers, and Karl's Taster Series, plus a pilsner of your choice. **Karl Strauss Brewery & Grill, Downtown** (formerly Old Columbia), 1157 Columbia St. (☎ 619/234-BREW), serves American fare along with beer (see listing in chapter 6). Happy hours run from 4 to 6pm Monday through Friday, and 10pm to 1am Thursday through Saturday. Other Karl Strauss locations include **Karl Strauss Brewery & Grill, La Jolla,** 1044 Wall St. (☎ 858/551-BREW), and **Karl Strauss Brewery Gardens,** 9675 Scranton Rd., Sorrento Mesa (☎ 619/587-BREW).

In contrast to the polished atmosphere of the Karl Strauss breweries, the **La Jolla Brewing Company,** 7536 Fay Ave. (☎ 858/456-BREW), feels like a neighbor-hood pub. The wood floor is appropriately worn, and you can play pool and darts in the back room. The brewmaster is John Atwater, a graduate of La Jolla High, class of 1976. During his years at UC Santa Barbara (where he earned a Ph.D. in biochemistry), John home-brewed in 5-gallon bottles. He makes his handcrafted beers from his own recipes and names them after local spots: Windansea Wheat (American-style wheat beer), Sea Lane Amber (similar to California steam beer), Red Roost Ale (red ale), and Pump House Porter (dark, slightly sweet ale balanced with a bitter finish). There's a decent bar menu, and happy hour is 4 to 7pm Monday through Friday. If you're trying to decide between the two La Jolla brew pubs, La Jolla Brewing Company has better beer, Karl Strauss Brewery & Grill better food.

The San Diego area, once strictly a white-wine-or-Perrier kind of place, now has many brew pubs. Others you may want to try include **Hops Bistro and Brewery,** 4353 La Jolla Village Dr., in University Towne Center (☎ 858/587-6677), and **San Diego Brewing Co.,** 10450 Friars Rd., at Mission Gorge (☎ 619/284-BREW).

Ould Sod. 3373 Adams Ave., Normal Heights. ☎ **619/284-6594.**

Irish through and through, this little gem sits in a quiet neighborhood of antique shops northeast of Hillcrest. Occasionally, the tavern hosts low-key folk or world-music performances.

Pacific Shores. 4927 Newport Ave., Ocean Beach. ☎ **619/223-7549.**

Straight from the 1940s, this undersea-themed neighborhood hangout with a vintage seashell bar has rock-bottom prices and an unpretentious air.

If you're looking to send e-mail or surf the Web, it's easy to do. In Hillcrest, the popular coffee house and study hall **Euphoria,** 1045 University Ave. (☎ 619/295-1769; www.1999.com/euphoria) has two Internet terminals. Resembling video games, they take dollar bills ($1 = 10 minutes). It's open daily from 6am to 1 or 2am.

In La Jolla's Golden Triangle, next to Von's supermarket, you'll find **Espresso Net,** 7770 Regents Rd., at Arriba Street (☎ 858/453-5896; www.espressonet.com). It's a comfy, welcoming hangout with tempting desserts. The state-of-the-art computer terminals have ergonomic keyboards; online time is $6 an hour, or $1.50 for 15 minutes. It's open weekdays 7am to 10pm, weekends 8am to 10pm.

Near the Gaslamp Quarter, **Internet Coffee,** 800 Broadway, at 8th Avenue (☎ 619/702-2233), has an institutional feel and isn't much on atmosphere. Still, the clunky computer stations will do the job. Open daily from 11am to midnight.

Palace Bar. In the Horton Grand Hotel, 311 Island Ave., downtown. ☎ 619/544-1886.

A class act inside the frilly Victorian Horton Grand, this cocktail lounge is close to the Gaslamp Quarter action, but nowhere near as frenetic.

Top O' The Cove. 1216 Prospect Ave., La Jolla. ☎ 858/454-7779.

At this intimate piano bar in one of La Jolla's most scenic restaurants, the vibe is mellow and relaxing. On nice evenings, the music—mainly standards and show tunes—is piped into the outdoor patio.

Turf Supper Club. 1116 25th Ave., Golden Hills. ☎ 619/234-6363.

Hidden in one of San Diego's old, obscure, and newly hip neighborhoods (about 10 minutes east of downtown), this retro steakhouse's gimmick is "grill your own" dinners. The decor and piano bar are pure '50s, and wildly popular with the cocktail crowd.

COFFEEHOUSES WITH PERFORMANCES

Twiggs Tea and Coffee Co. 4590 Park Blvd. (south of Adams Ave.), University Heights. ☎ 619/296-0616.

Tucked away in a peaceful neighborhood, this popular coffeehouse has adjoining room for poetry readings. It often books performances by artists like Cindy Lee Berryhill.

Java Joe's. 4994 Newport Ave., Ocean Beach. ☎ 619/523-0356.

A popular hangout for OB locals, this friendly coffeehouse has entertainment most nights—from acoustic folk acts to open mike to occasional poetry readings.

4 The Gay & Lesbian Nightlife Scene

Also check out **Tidbits** cabaret (see "Comedy," above).

Bourbon Street. 4612 Park Blvd., University Heights. ☎ 619/291-0173.

With an elegant piano bar and outdoor patio meant to evoke jazzy New Orleans, this relaxing spot draws mainly smartly dressed, dignified men.

Club Bombay. 3175 India St. (at Spruce St.). ☎ 619/296-6789.

Mellower than the Flame, this casual lesbian gathering place north of Little Italy has a small dance floor, occasional live entertainment, and popular Sunday barbecues.

The Brass Rail. 3796 Fifth Ave., Hillcrest. ☎ **619/298-2233.**

San Diego's oldest (since the '60s) gay bar, this Hillcrest institution is loud and proud, with energetic dancing every night, go-go boys, bright lights, and a come-as-you-are attitude.

Club Montage. 2028 Hancock St. ☎ **619/294-9590.** Fax 619/294-9592. www. clubmontage.com.

This state-of-the-art dance club has all the bells and whistles: laser-and-light show, 12-screen video bar, pool tables, and arcade games.

The Flame. 3780 Park Blvd. ☎ **619/295-4163.** Cover Sun–Fri $2, Sat $3. Bus: 7 or 7B.

The city's top lesbian hangout has a large dance floor and two bars. It's packed on Saturdays. A mixed crowd attends Friday's drag show, and gender reversal takes place for Tuesday's "Boys Night Out."

Kickers. 308 University Ave. (at Third Ave.), Hillcrest. ☎ **619/491-0400.**

This country-western dance hall next to Hamburger Mary's restaurant attracts an equally male-female crowd for two-stepping and line-dancing. There are free lessons on weekdays.

Rich's. 1051 University Ave. (between 10th and 11th aves.). ☎ **619/295-2195,** or 619/497-4588 for upcoming events.

High-energy and popular with the see-and-be-seen set, Rich's has nightly revues, plenty of dancing to house music, and a small video bar. Thursday is Club Hedonism, with compelling tribal rhythms.

5 More Entertainment

MOVIES

Many multiscreen complexes around the city show first-run films. More avant-garde and artistic current releases play at **Hillcrest Cinema,** 3965 Fifth Ave., Hillcrest, which offers 3 hours' free parking (☎ **619/299-2100**); the **Ken Cinema,** 4061 Adams Ave., Kensington near Hillcrest (☎ **619/283-5909**); and the **Cove,** 7730 Girard Ave., La Jolla (☎ **858/459-5404**). The irrepressible *Rocky Horror Picture Show* is resurrected every Friday and Saturday at midnight at the Ken. The **OMNIMAX** theater at the Reuben H. Fleet Science Center (☎ **619/238-1233**), in Balboa Park, features movies and three-dimensional laser shows projected onto the 76-foot tilted dome screen.

CASINOS

Native American tribes operate three **casinos** in east county. **Barona Casino** is at 1000 Barona Rd., Lakeside (☎ **888/7-BARONA** or 619/443-2300). Take I-8 east to Calif. 67 north. At Willow Road, turn right and continue to Wildcat Canyon Road; turn left, and continue 5½ miles to the Barona Reservation. Allow 40 minutes from downtown. **Sycuan Gaming Center** is in El Cajon, at 5469 Dehesa Rd. (☎ **800/2-SYCUAN** or 619/445-6002). Follow I-8 east for 10 miles to the El Cajon Blvd. exit. Take El Cajon to Washington Avenue, turning right and continuing on Washington as it turns into Dehesa Road; signs will direct you to the casino, about 7 miles from the freeway. Allow 25 minutes from downtown. **Viejas Casino and Turf Club** is at 5000 Willows Rd., in Alpine (☎ **619/445-5400**).

To get there, take I-8 east 25 miles to Willows Rd. exit; turn left to casino. Allow 35 to 40 minutes from downtown. All three offer Las Vegas–style casino gambling, off-track betting, and bingo.

To bet on the ponies, go to the **Del Mar** Race Track during the local racing season (July through September). At any time of the year, you can bet on races being run far and wide at **Del Mar Satellite Wagering,** at the Del Mar Fairgrounds (☎ **858/755-1167**). To place a wager on **greyhound racing** or **jai alai,** you have to cross the international border to Tijuana. It's a 40-minute ride by car or trolley from San Diego; from the border you'll need a cab to get to the racetrack or jai alai palace (see "Tijuana: Going South of the Border," in chapter 11). Bookmaker offices, where you can place a bet on just about any sport, are located throughout Tijuana.

6 Only in San Diego

San Diego's top three attractions—the San Diego Zoo, Wild Animal Park, and Sea World—keep extended summer hours. Sea World caps its **Summer Nights** off at 9pm with a free **fireworks** display. You can catch them from Sea World or anywhere around Mission Bay.

Free concerts are offered on Sunday at 2pm year-round at the Spreckels Organ Pavilion in Balboa Park. In the summer, concerts are also held on Monday nights from 8 to 9:30pm as part of **Twilight in the Park** (☎ **619/235-1105**). **Starlight Theater** presents Broadway musicals in the Starlight Bowl in Balboa Park in July and August (☎ **619/544-STAR** [7827]). This venue is in the flight path to Lindbergh Field, and when planes pass overhead, singers stop in midnote and wait for the roar to cease. The **Festival Stage** (☎ **619/239-2255**) in Balboa Park is a popular outdoor summer the-ater venue.

Another Balboa Park event, **Christmas on the Prado,** has been a San Diego tradi-tion since 1977. The weekend of evening events is held the first Friday and Saturday in December. The park's museums and walkways are decked out in holiday finery, and the museums are free and open late, from 5 to 9pm. There is entertainment galore, from bell choruses to Renaissance and baroque music to barbershop quartets. Crafts (including unusual Christmas ornaments), ethnic nibbles, hot cider, and sweets are for sale. A Christmas tree and nativity scene are displayed at the Spreckels Organ Pavilion.

Unique movie venues include **Movies Before the Mast** (☎ **619/234-9153**), aboard the *Star of India* at the Maritime Museum. Movies of the nautical genre (such as *Black Beard the Pirate, Captain Blood,* and *Hook*) are shown on a special "screensail" from April through October. At the **Sunset Cinema Film Festival** (☎ **858/454-7373**) in August, you can view classic and current films free of charge from a blanket or chair on the beach. Films are projected onto screens mounted on floating barges from San Diego to Imperial Beach. The Plunge (☎ **619/488-3110**), an indoor swim-ming pool in Mission Beach, shows **Dive-In Movies.** Viewers float on rafts in 91° water and watch water-related movies projected onto the wall. *Jaws* is a perennial favorite.

7 Late-Night Bites

See chapter 6, "Dining," for complete listings on the following restaurants. We haven't included other parts of the city because, frankly, late-night meals aren't a big part of San Diego life outside downtown and the immediate area. In La Jolla, your best bet might be the **Hard Rock Cafe,** open till midnight on Friday and Saturday only.

DOWNTOWN   The kitchen at **Croce's** stays open till midnight all week. You can order inexpensive appetizers from the eclectic menu, or opt for a full meal. The stylish coffeehouse **Cafe Lulu,** a block from Horton Plaza, stays open till 2am Sunday through Thursday and 4am Friday and Saturday. It serves health-conscious, vegetarian light meals, and bread from Bread & Cie. Or go for traditional British pub food at the **Princess Pub & Grille** in Little Italy. You can get Cornish pasties, steak-and-kidney pie, or fish-and-chips till 1am nightly.

HILLCREST/UPTOWN   These three places stay open until midnight on Friday and Saturday. The relentlessly '50s-themed **Corvette Diner** serves up terrific coffee-shop–style food—and a page-long menu of fountain favorites. Or satisfy your sweet tooth with a sublime creation from **Extraordinary Desserts.** For coffee drinks and light fare, stop into **Newbreak Coffee Co.**

Side Trips from San Diego

If you have time for a day trip, popular destinations include the beaches and inland towns of **"North County"** (as locals call the northern part of San Diego County), as well as our south-of-the-border neighbor, Tijuana. You could also relax at a spa or resort (see the box later in this chapter). All are no more than an hour away.

If you have time for a longer trip, you can explore some distinct areas, all within an hour or two of the city. They include the wine country of **Temecula,** due north of San Diego; **Disneyland,** a little farther north; the gold-mining town of **Julian,** now known for its apple pies, to the northeast; and the vast **Anza–Borrego Desert,** east of Julian. South of San Diego, just across the border, lies **Baja California** and a taste of Mexico. Whichever direction you choose, you're in for a treat.

The following excursions are arranged geographically going north from San Diego, up to Disneyland, and then heading southeast toward Julian and south to Mexico.

1 North County Beach Towns: Spots to Surf & Sun

Picturesque beach towns dot the coast of San Diego County from Del Mar to Oceanside. They make great day-trip destinations for sun worshipers and surfers.

GETTING THERE

It's a snap: **Del Mar** is only 18 miles north of downtown San Diego, **Carlsbad** about 33, and **Oceanside** approximately 36. If you're driving, follow I-5 north; Del Mar, Solana Beach, Cardiff by the Sea, Encinitas, Leucadia, Carlsbad, and Oceanside have freeway exits. The farthest point, Oceanside, will take about 45 minutes. The other choice by car is to wander up the coast road, known along the way as Camino del Mar, Pacific Coast Highway, Old Highway 101, and County Highway S21.

The Coaster commuter train provides service to Carlsbad, Encinitas, Solana Beach, and Oceanside, and Amtrak stops in Solana Beach—just a few minutes north of Del Mar—and Oceanside. Check with Amtrak (☎ **800/USA-RAIL;** www.amtrak.com) or call ☎ **619/ 685-4900** for transit information. United Airlines and American Airlines fly into Palomar Airport in Carlsbad. The San Diego North

County Convention and Visitors Bureau, 720 N. Broadway, Escondido, CA 92025 (☎ 800/848-3336 or 760/745-4741; www.sandiegonorth.com) is also a good information source.

DEL MAR

Less than 20 miles up the coast lies Del Mar, a small community with just over 5,000 inhabitants in a 2-square-mile municipality. The town has adamantly maintained its independence, eschewing incorporation into the city of San Diego. Sometimes known as "the people's republic of Del Mar," this community was one of the first in the nation to ban smoking. Come summer, the town explodes as visitors flock in for the Thoroughbred horse-racing season and the county's Del Mar Fair (see "Calendar of Events," in chapter 2).

The history and popularity of Del Mar are inextricably linked to the **Del Mar Racetrack & Fairgrounds,** 2260 Jimmy Durante Blvd. (☎ 858/753-5555; www.delmarfair.com), which still glows with the aura of Hollywood celebrity. In 1933, crooner and actor Bing Crosby owned 44 acres in Del Mar, and added a stud barn for his Thoroughbreds; he quickly turned the operation into the Del Mar Turf Club, enlisting the help of Pat O'Brien and other celebrity friends (like Jimmy Durante, whose eponymous street borders the racetrack grounds). Soon, Hollywood stars like Lucille Ball, Desi Arnaz, Harry James, Betty Grable, and Bob Hope were constantly seen around Del Mar, and the town experienced a resurgence in popularity. During World War II, racing was suspended. The club housed paratroopers in the horse stalls as well as marines taking amphibious training on the beach; aircraft assembly lines were even set up in the grandstand and clubhouse. Crosby sold his interest and moved out of the area just after the war, but the racetrack's—and the town's—image was set. You'll still hear the song Bing wrote and recorded to commemorate the track's opening day—"Where the Surf Meets the Turf"—played each season before the first race.

ESSENTIALS

For more information about Del Mar, contact or visit the **Greater Del Mar Chamber of Commerce Visitor Information Center,** 1104 Camino del Mar #1, Del Mar, CA 92014 (☎ 858/755-4844), which also distributes a detailed folding map of the area. Open hours vary according to volunteer staffing, but usually approximate weekday business hours. Call for a seasonal weekend schedule. There's also a city-run Internet site (www.delmar.ca.us).

FUN ON & OFF THE BEACH

Del Mar City Beach is a wide, well-patrolled beach popular for sunbathing, swimming, and body surfing. Take 15th Street west to Seagrove Park, where college kids

Important Area Code Changes

Dial **619** to call most of San Diego, except for La Jolla, Del Mar, Rancho Sante Fe, and Rancho Bernardo, which received the new area code **858** during 1999. Use **760** to reach the remainder of San Diego County, including Encinitas, Carlsbad, Oceanside, Escondido, Ramona, Julian, and Anza–Borrego. Toward the end of 2000, the 619 area code will split further, with Coronado and the southern portion of San Diego County getting a new area code—**935.** Don't worry, though, this change doesn't go into effect until December 8, 2000, and the rest of the city of San Diego will remain in the 619 area code.

can always be found playing volleyball and other lawn games while older folks snooze in the shade. There are **free concerts** in the park during July and August; for information, contact the City of Del Mar (☎ 858/755-9313). The earlier you go to the beach, the more likely it is that you'll snag a parking space in metered lots or on the street. Del Mar's beach is extra popular between June and September, during the Del Mar Fair and thoroughbred racing season. The sand stretches north to the mouth of the San Dieguito Lagoon. There are rest rooms and showers near the park.

Every evening near dusk, brightly colored hot-air balloons punctuate the skies above Del Mar; they're easily enjoyed from the racetrack area (and by traffic-jammed drivers on I-5). If you find a balloon ride intriguing, this is the place to do it, because flights are, on average, $25 to $35 cheaper than at other California ballooning sites. **Skysurfer Balloon Company,** 1221 Camino del Mar (☎ **800/660-6809** or 858/481-6800), has been soaring here since 1976. It offers daily 1-hour sunset flights into the San Dieguito Valley. The balloons carry 6 to 12 passengers. The weekday rate is $135 per person, weekend and holiday rates $145 per person. During December, Skysurfer runs a Christmas special, selling advance-purchase rides for only $100. They're good between January and Thanksgiving, anytime but holidays and holiday weekends.

WHERE TO STAY

Del Mar Motel on the Beach. 1702 Coast Blvd. (at 17th St.), Del Mar, CA 92014. ☎ **800/223-8449** for reservations, or 858/755-1534. 45 units (some with shower only). A/C TV TEL. $130–$180 double. Extra person $5. Off-season discounts available. AE, CB, DC, DISC, JCB, MC, V. Take I-5 to Via de la Valle exit. Go west, then south on Hwy. 101 (Pacific Coast Hwy.); veer west onto Coast Blvd.

The only property in Del Mar right on the beach, this simply furnished little white-stucco motel has been here since 1946. Upstairs rooms have one king-size bed; downstairs units have two double beds. All rooms have a refrigerator, coffeemaker, and fan. Half are reserved for non-smokers, and only ocean-view rooms have bathtubs. This is a good choice for beach lovers, because you can walk along the shore for miles, and the popular seaside restaurants Poseidon and Jake's are right next door. The motel has a barbecue and picnic table for guests' use.

L'Auberge Del Mar Resort and Spa. 1540 Camino del Mar (at 15th St.), P.O. Box 2889, Del Mar, CA 92014. ☎ **800/553-1336** or 858/259-1515. Fax 858/755-4940. 128 units. A/C MINIBAR TV TEL. $189–$389 double; from $650 suite. Spa and sports packages available. AE, DC, MC, V. Valet or self-parking $8. Take I-5 to Del Mar Heights Rd. west, then turn right onto Camino del Mar Rd.

Though it tries to capitalize on Del Mar's 1940s allure as a Hollywood hot spot, L'Auberge is modern all the way. True, it sits on the site of the historic Hotel Del Mar (1909–69) and features a replica of the original's brick fireplace, but that's where the resemblance ends. As its pretentious French name (which simply means *the inn*) suggests, an exclusive European aura permeates the property, from the four-star restaurant to the full-service spa downstairs. Rooms are formally decked out in antique reproductions and teensy French country prints. All feature marble baths, balconies, in-room coffee service, and three telephones; many have fireplaces and ceiling fans. There are tennis courts, two swimming pools, and a whirlpool. The hotel is across the street from Del Mar's main shopping and dining scene, and a short jog from the sand. The hotel courtesy van serves the Solana Beach Amtrak station.

Les Artistes. 944 Camino del Mar, Del Mar, CA 92014. ☎ **858/755-4646.** 20 units. TV TEL. Standard rooms $50–$85, designer rooms $95–$145. Rates include continental breakfast. DISC, MC, V. Free parking. Pets accepted; $50 cash deposit plus $10 cleaning fee.

What do you get when you take a 1940s motel, put it in the hands of a Thai architect with a penchant for prominent painters, and wait while she transforms each room, one at a time? The answer is an intriguingly funky hotel, just a few blocks from downtown Del Mar, that's an art primer with European and Asian touches.

Although none of the rooms have an ocean view, and an ugly strip of land sits awkwardly between the hotel and busy Camino del Mar, there are still so many charming touches—like a lily and koi pond, Oriental chimes, and climbing bougainvillea—that you feel only privacy. At last count, eight rooms had been redone, leaving about a dozen tastefully decorated but standard units. Artists spotlighted include Diego Rivera and (next door) Frida Kahlo—both give you the feeling of stepping into a warm Mexican painting. The Monet room has an almost distractingly abstract swirl of color; and Furo's room is so authentic that a stone-lined stream runs inside the threshold. Other subjects include Georgia O'Keeffe, Erté, Remington, and Gauguin. Though the inn is not for everyone, you really must see it to believe it. Downstairs rooms in the two-story structure have tiny private garden decks.

Wave Crest. 1400 Ocean Ave., Del Mar, CA 92014. ☎ **858/755-0100.** 31 units. TV TEL. Mid-June to mid-Sept $205–$230 studio, $240–$270 1-bedroom, $330 2-bedroom. Off-season discounts available; weekly rates available year-round. MC, V. Take I-5 to Del Mar Heights Rd. west, turn right onto Camino del Mar, and drive to 15th St. Turn left and drive to Ocean Ave., and turn left.

On a bluff overlooking the Pacific, these gray-shingled bungalow condominiums are beautifully maintained and wonderfully private. This place is perfect for a honeymoon or romantic getaway. The studios and suites surround a landscaped courtyard; each has a queen-size bed, sofa bed, artwork by local artists, VCR, stereo, full bath, and fully equipped kitchen with dishwasher. The studios sleep one or two people; the one-bedroom accommodates up to four. It's a 5-minute walk to the beach, and shopping and dining spots are a few blocks away. There is an extra fee for maid service. Amenities include a common lounge with a fireplace, TV, and newspapers; pool and Jacuzzi overlooking the ocean; irons, ironing boards, and laundry facilities.

WHERE TO DINE

Head to the upper level of the centrally located Del Mar Plaza, at Camino del Mar and 15th Street. You'll find **Il Fornaio Cucina Italiana** (☎ 858/755-8876), for excellent Italian cuisine; **Epazote** (☎ 858/259-9966), for Mexican, Tex-Mex, and Southwestern fare; and **Pacifica Del Mar** (☎ 858/792-0476), which serves outstanding seafood. Kids like **Johnny Rockets** (☎ 858/755-1954), an old-fashioned diner on the lower level. On the beach, **Jake's Del Mar,** 1660 Coast Blvd. (☎ 858/755-2002), and **Poseidon Restaurant on the Beach,** 1670 Coast Blvd. (☎ 858/755-9345), are both good for California cuisine and sunset views. If you want to eat at either of these popular spots, reserve early. The racetrack crowd congregates at **Bully's Restaurant,** 1404 Camino del Mar (☎ 858/755-1660), for burgers, prime rib, and crab legs. And if you're looking for fresh seafood—and lots of it—head to the Del Mar branch of San Diego's popular **Fish Market,** 640 Via de la Valle (☎ 858/755-2277), near the racetrack.

CARLSBAD & ENCINITAS

Fifteen miles north of Del Mar and around 30 miles from downtown San Diego (a 45-minute drive), the pretty communities of Carlsbad and Encinitas provide many reasons to linger on the California coast. They have good swimming and surfing beaches; a mile-long, two-tiered beach walk that is accessible for travelers with disabilities; three lagoons perfect for walks or bird watching; small-town atmosphere; an

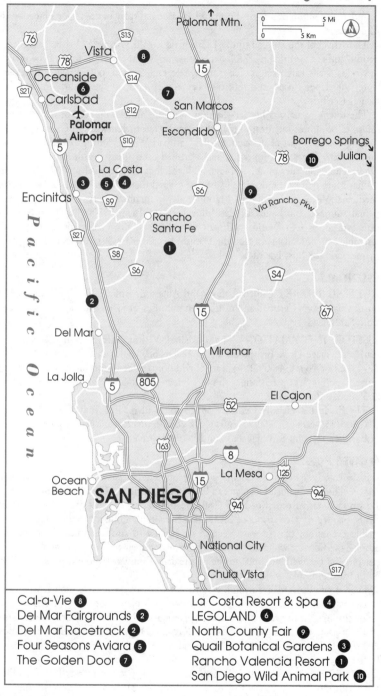

Palomar Mtn.

0   5 Mi
0   5 Km

76

S13

Vista

78

Oceanside

8

S27

Carlsbad

6

Palomar
Airport

15

S14

7

San Marcos

S12

Escondido

S10

La Costa

3   5   4

Borrego Springs

78

10

Julian

Encinitas

S9

S6

9

Via Rancho Pkw

Pacific

S21

Rancho
Santa Fe

1

S8

S6

S4

2

15

67

Del Mar

Ocean

La Jolla

5   805

Miramar

52

El Cajon

163

8

La Mesa

125

15

94

SAN DIEGO

Ocean
Beach

94

National City

Chula Vista

S17

Cal-a-Vie 8	La Costa Resort & Spa 4
Del Mar Fairgrounds 2	LEGOLAND 6
Del Mar Racetrack 2	North County Fair 9
Four Seasons Aviara 5	Quail Botanical Gardens 3
The Golden Door 7	Rancho Valencia Resort 1
	San Diego Wild Animal Park 10

abundance of antique and gift shops; and a seasonal display of the region's most beautiful flowers.

The arrival of the railroad in the 1880s heralded the arrival of Carlsbad as a destination, and the historic (ca. 1887) depot still stands in the heart of town. Having seen service as Wells Fargo stagecoach station, telegraph station, post office, and general store, the depot closed in 1960; it's been reincarnated as the Visitor Information Center (see below).

The town's name was Frazier's Station until the mineral content of its water was found to be almost identical to that of a popular resort, Karlsbad, in Czechoslovakia. During the early part of the century, the Carlsbad Mineral Springs Hotel capitalized on the water's curative properties, and Carlsbad drew many health-minded visitors. One memorable sales pitch, employing all the hyperbole typical of that era, asked, "What more powerful inducements can be offered than Mineral Wells of Wonderful Medicinal Virtues; Magnificent Marine and Mountain Scenery; a Climate of Perpetual Summer; and Balmy Breezes from the Calm Pacific?" The European connection evoked an Old World sentiment in town, and many parts of Carlsbad still resemble a quaint village. In fact, the Danish toy-maker LEGO just opened a gigantic theme park; see "Just For Kids," below.

ESSENTIALS

GETTING THERE   United Airlines and American Airlines fly into Palomar Airport, which serves Carlsbad and nearby communities. See above for driving directions from San Diego.

VISITOR INFORMATION   The **Carlsbad Visitor Information Center,** 400 Carlsbad Village Drive (in the old Santa Fe Depot), Carlsbad, CA 92008 (☎ **800/ 227-5722** or 760/434-6093), has lots of additional information on flower fields and nursery touring. It's open Monday through Friday 9am to 5pm, Saturday 10am to 4pm, and Sunday 10am to 3pm.

The **Encinitas Visitors Center,** 138 Encinitas Blvd., Encinitas, CA 92024-3799 (☎ **800/953-6041** or 760/753-6041, fax 760/753-6720), is open Monday through Friday 9am to 5pm, Saturday and Sunday 10am to 2pm.

FLOWER POWER

Carlsbad and its neighbor Encinitas make up a noted commercial flower-growing region. The most colorful display can be seen each spring at **Carlsbad Ranch,** east of I-5 on Palomar Airport Road (☎ **760/431-0352**). Its 45 acres of solid ranunculus fields, planted in wide stripes of contrasting hues, bloom into a breathtaking rainbow visible even from the freeway. Visitors are invited to stroll between the rows and admire the flowers, which are primarily grown for their bulbs. Admission is $1 per person, and the fields are open to the public daily from 9am to dusk. Flowers, bulbs, and garden gifts are for sale.

Even if you don't visit during the spring bloom—or during December, when the nurseries are alive with holiday poinsettias—there's plenty for the avid gardener to enjoy throughout the year. North County is such a destination for horticultural pursuits, in fact, there's a **North County Nursery Hoppers Association,** P.O. Box 231208, Encinitas, CA 92023-1208. Send a SASE and receive a comprehensive leaflet describing all the area growers and nurseries, including a map. Second to Carlsbad Ranch in popularity is **Weidners' Gardens,** 695 Normandy Rd., Encinitas (☎ **760/436-2194**). Its field of tuberous begonias blooms June through August, fuchsias and impatiens are colorful between March and September, and the holiday season (November 1 through December 22) brings an explosion of poinsettias and the opportunity to "dig your own" pansies.

Those of us with thumbs of a slightly more somber shade than vibrant green would be satisfied with an afternoon at **Quail Botanical Gardens,** 230 Quail Gardens Rd., off Encinitas Boulevard east of I-5, Encinitas (☎ **760/436-3036;** www.qbgardens.com). Boasting the country's largest bamboo collection, plus 30 acres of California natives, exotic tropicals, palms, cacti, and other unusual collections, this serene compound is crisscrossed with scenic walkways, trails, and benches. Guided tours are given Saturdays at 10am, and there's a gift shop and nursery. The gardens are open daily from 9am to 5pm, the gift shop and nursery daily from 10am to 4pm. Admission is $3 for adults, $1.50 children 5 to 12, free for children under 5. The gardens are free to everyone on the first Tuesday of the month.

MORE FUN THINGS TO SEE & DO

Carlsbad is a great place for **antiquing.** Whether you're a serious shopper or seriously window-shopping, park the car and stroll the three blocks of **State Street** between Oak and Beech streets. There are about 18 shops in this part of town, where diagonal street parking and welcoming merchants lend a village atmosphere. Wares range from estate jewelry to country quilts, from inlaid sideboards to Depression glass. You never know what you'll find, but—at least for me—there's always something. A good place to start is the large **Aanteek Aavenue Mall,** 2832 State St. (☎ **760/434-8742**), where there isn't a loser among the several dozen dealers. A couple have exceptional vintage linen, one a collection of Jadite glass, and there's even a selection of furniture restoration and maintenance products near the register. They're open (as are most area shops) Monday through Friday from 11am to 5pm, Saturday 10am to 5pm, Sunday noon to 5pm.

Carlsbad has two beaches, each with pros and cons. **Carlsbad State Beach** parallels downtown and is a great place to stroll along a wide concrete walkway. It attracts outdoors types for walking, jogging, and in-line skating, even at night (thanks to good lighting). Although the sandy strand is narrow, the beach is popular with bodysurfers, boogie boarders, and fishermen—surfers tend to stay away. Enter on Ocean Boulevard at Tamarack Avenue; there's a $4 fee per vehicle.

Four miles south of town is **South Carlsbad State Beach,** almost 3 miles of cobblestone-strewn sand. A state-run campground at the north end is immensely popular year-round, and area surfers favor the southern portion. Like many of the beaches along the county's shores, Carlsbad suffers from a high incidence of tar on the beach—you're likely to find packages of "Tar-Off" in your hotel room—but that doesn't seem to discourage many beach-goers. There's a $4 per vehicle fee at the beach entrance, along Carlsbad Boulevard at Poinsettia Lane.

In **Encinitas,** everyone flocks to **Moonlight Beach,** the city's long-suffering sandy playground. After overcoming a nasty sewage problem caused by a nearby treatment plant (don't ask), and receiving a much-needed replacement of eroded sand, Moonlight is back to its old, laid-back self. It offers plenty of facilities, including free parking, volleyball nets, rest rooms, showers, picnic tables and fire grates, and the company of fellow sunbathers. The beach entrance is at the end of B Street (at Encinitas Boulevard).

Also in Encinitas is the appropriately serene **Swami's Beach.** It's named for the adjacent Self Realization Fellowship, whose lotus-shaped towers are emulated in the pointed wooden stairway leading to the sand from First Street. This lovely little beach is surfer central in the winter. It adjoins little-known **Boneyard Beach,** directly to the north. Here, low-tide coves provide shelter for romantics and nudists; this isolated stretch can be reached only from Swami's Beach. There's a free parking lot at Swami's, plus rest rooms and a picnic area.

Remember the hair-raising aerial escapades in *The Great Waldo Pepper?* You can enjoy everything but wing-walking on a vintage **biplane** from **Air Combat & Biplane Adventures** (☎ 800/SKY-LOOP or 760/438-7680; www.barnstorming.com). One aircraft even has an open cockpit. Flights leave from Palomar Airport in Carlsbad, taking up to two passengers per plane on scenic flights down the coast. Prices start at $108 for biplane rides, $68 for Piper Cub rides. Air Combat flights are $249 per person for a 1-hour "dogfight" with another biplane "opponent"—expect 360° loops to be part of your combat strategy!

Bargain-hunter's tip: Discount cards are available at most hotel and visitor center activities displays, or ask when you call.

If you're ready to try **kayaking,** but a little instruction is in order, call Dan Carey's **Carlsbad Paddle Sports,** 2780 Carlsbad Blvd. (☎ 888/434-8686). In addition to selling kayaks, paddling accessories, and gear, Dan conducts weekend kayak classes in Oceanside Harbor (introductory course) and at the beach in Carlsbad (surf kayaking). The 2-hour classes cost $40, including equipment. Straight rentals are available for $12 to $15 per hour.

LEGOLAND!

The ultimate monument to the world's most famous plastic building blocks opened in Carlsbad in March 1999. **LEGOLAND** (☎ 760/438-5346; www.legolandca. com) is the third such theme park; the branches in Denmark and Britain have proven enormously successful. Attractions include "hands-on" interactive displays; a life-size menagerie of tigers, giraffes, and other animals; scale models of international landmarks (the Eiffel Tower, Sydney Opera House, and so on)—all constructed of real LEGO bricks! "MiniLand" is a 1:20 scale representation of American achievement, from a New England Pilgrim village to Mount Rushmore. There's a gravity coaster ride (don't worry, they used steel) through a LEGO castle, and a DUPLO building area to keep smaller children occupied. LEGOLAND is open daily from 10am till dusk. Admission is $32 for adults, $25 for seniors and children 3 to 16, free for children under 3. From I-5, take the Canon exit east, which leads to the entrance.

WHERE TO STAY

Beach Terrace Inn. 2775 Ocean St., Carlsbad, CA 92003. ☎ **800/433-5415** outside Calif., 800/622-3224 in Calif., or 760/729-5951. Fax 760/729-1078. www.beachterraceinn.com. 49 units. A/C TV TEL. Summer $119–$229 double; from $149 suite. Off-season $109–$189 double; from $129 suite. Extra person $15. Rates include continental breakfast. AE, CB, DC, DISC, ER, JCB, MC, V. Parking available on street.

At Carlsbad's only beachside hostelry (others are across the road or a little farther away), the rooms and the outdoor pool and whirlpool all have ocean views. This downtown Best Western property also has a helpful staff. Rooms, although not elegant, are extra large, and some have balconies, fireplaces, and kitchenettes. Suites have separate living rooms and bedrooms. VCRs and films are available at the front desk. This is a good place for families. You can walk everywhere from here.

Four Seasons Resort Aviara. 7100 Four Seasons Point, Carlsbad, CA 92009. ☎ **800/332-3442** or 760/603-6800. Fax 760/603-6801. 331 units. A/C MINIBAR TEL TV. $355–$465 double; from $575 suite. Golf, spa, and attraction packages available. AE, CB, DISC, JCB, MC, V. Valet parking $14. From I-5, take Poinsettia Lane east to Aviara Pkwy. S.

Newly arrived and giving La Costa a run for its money, this ultra-deluxe resort is the new kid with something to prove. This is the elite chain's first ocean-view golf and tennis resort in the continental United States. The resort, which opened in August 1997, offers every luxury; when not wielding club or racquet, guests can lie by the pool serenaded by Peruvian pipes. The ambiance at this latest Four Seasons is one of both privilege and comfort; rooms are decorated with Laura Ashley–esque fabrics and nature prints, and the entire resort is in vaguely Spanish-Colonial revival style.

Dining: Vivace restaurant offers a Tuscan experience down to the Murano glass on the stone fireplace and potted olive trees on the terrace. The kitchen's oak-fueled oven imparts a distinctive smoky flavor to most dishes.

Amenities: The hotel's Arnold Palmer–designed golf course, 10 years in the making, preceded it and has steadily built a stellar reputation of its own. The name Aviara is a nod to the adjacent Batiquitos Lagoon, where egrets, herons, and cranes are among the more than 130 bird species nesting in the protected coastal wetlands. In fact, the golf course was carefully designed to keep the wetlands intact. Tennis courts, full-service spa, José Eber hair salon, pool.

La Costa Resort and Spa. Costa del Mar Rd., Carlsbad, CA 92009. ☎ **800/854-5000** or 760/438-9111. Fax 760/931-7585. www.lacosta.com. 479 units. A/C MINIBAR TV TEL. $300–$470 double; from $500 suite. Golf, spa, and tennis packages available. AE, CB, DC, DISC, JCB, MC, V. Valet parking $16 overnight; self-parking $8.

La Costa sprawls over 450 landscaped acres. Attractive accommodations offer all the bells and whistles you'd expect at this price level. Travel partners can do their own things during the day (golf, tennis, or the spa) and rendezvous for dinner. While this large resort boasts many facilities, it isn't looking as fresh as it once did, particularly since the Four Seasons Aviara moved in down the road.

Dining: Five restaurants.

Amenities: La Costa boasts two championship 18-hole golf courses (home of the annual Mercedes Championships), and a 21-court racquet club (home of the WTA Toshiba Tennis Classic) with 2 grass, 4 clay, and 15 composite courts. The resident tennis pro is Pancho Segura, who has coached Jimmy Connors and Andre Agassi. There's an extensive spa with a multitude of treatments.

Pelican Cove Inn. 320 Walnut Ave., Carlsbad, CA 92008. ☎ **888/PEL-COVE** or 760/434-5995. www.pelican-cove.com/pelican. 8 units. TV. $90–$180 double. Rates include full breakfast. Extra person $15. Midweek and seasonal discounts available. AE, MC, V. Free parking. From downtown Carlsbad, follow Carlsbad Blvd. south to Walnut Ave.; turn left and drive 2½ blocks.

Located 2 blocks from the beach, this Cape Cod–style hideaway combines romance with luxury. Hosts Kris and Nancy Nayudu see to your every need, from furnishing guest rooms with soft feather beds and down comforters to providing beach chairs and towels or preparing a picnic basket (with 24 hours' notice). Each room features a fireplace and private entrance; some have private spa tubs. The airy, spacious La Jolla room is loveliest, with bay windows and a cupola ceiling. Breakfast can be enjoyed in the garden if weather permits. Courtesy transportation from the Oceanside train station is available.

Tamarack Beach Resort. 3200 Carlsbad Blvd., Carlsbad, CA 92008. ☎ **800/334-2199** or 760/729-3500. Fax 760/434-5942. www.tamarackresort.com. 77 units. A/C TV TEL. $130–$195 double; $220–$330 suite. Children under 12 stay free in parents' room. Weekly rates available. AE, MC, V. Free underground parking.

This resort property's rooms, in the village across the street from the beach, are restfully decorated. They have wicker furniture, small refrigerators, coffee-making facilities, and VCRs (movies are complimentary). The fully equipped suites have stereos, full kitchens, washers, and dryers. The pretty Tamarack has a pleasant lobby, a heated pool in a sunny courtyard setting, two Jacuzzis, exercise facilities, valet services, and barbecue grills. Dini's by the Sea is a good restaurant that is popular with locals.

WHERE TO DINE

The architectural centerpiece of Carlsbad is **Neiman's,** 2978 Carlsbad Blvd. (☎ 760/ 729-4131), a restored Victorian mansion complete with turrets, cupolas, and waving flags. Inside, there's a casual cafe and bar where LeRoy Neiman lithographs hang on the walls. The menu includes rack of lamb, chicken Dijon, and smoked chicken with cheese quesadillas. There are also burgers, pastas, and salads. Sunday brunch is a tremendous buffet of breakfast and lunch items.

If your favorite part of a diner breakfast is the spuds, head to the **Potato Shack,** 120 W. I St., Encinitas (☎ 760/436-1282), where a cartoon russet in sneakers adorns the side of the building. The food isn't fancy, is sometimes greasy, but is good and filling and tasty. This is also a great place to eavesdrop on locals shooting the breeze. It serves breakfast and lunch only.

OCEANSIDE

The northernmost community in San Diego County (actually, it's a city of 150,000), Oceanside is 36 miles from San Diego. It claims almost 4 miles of beaches and has one of the West Coast's longest over-the-water wooden piers, where a tram does nothing but transport people from the street to the end of the 1,954-foot structure and back for 25¢ each way. The '50s-style diner at the end of the pier, **Ruby's,** is a great place for a quick and inexpensive lunch over the ocean. The wide, sandy beach, pier, and well-tended recreational area with playground equipment and an outdoor amphitheater are within easy walking distance of the train station.

ESSENTIALS

For an information packet about Oceanside and its attractions, send a check for $3 to the **Oceanside Visitor & Tourism Center,** 928 North Coast Hwy., Oceanside, CA 92054 (☎ **800/350-7873** or 760/721-1101; fax 760/722-8336; www.oceanside chamber.com).

EXPLORING OCEANSIDE

One of the nicest things to do in Oceanside is to stroll around the city's upscale **harbor.** Bustling with pleasure craft, it's lined with condominiums and boasts a Cape Cod–themed shopping village. A launch ramp, visitor boat slips, and charter fishing are here. The **Harbor Days Festival** in mid-September typically attracts 100,000 visitors for a crafts fair, entertainment, and food booths.

The area's biggest attraction is **Mission San Luis Rey** (☎ 760/757-3651), a few miles inland. Founded in 1798, it is the largest of California's 21 missions. There is a small charge to tour the mission, its impressive church, exhibits, grounds, and cemetery. You might recognize it as the backdrop for one of the Zorro movies.

For a wide selection of rental watercraft, head to **Boat Rentals of America** (☎ 760/ 722-0028), on Harbor Drive South. It rents everything from kayaks, Waverunners, and electric boats for relaxed harbor touring, to 14- and 22-foot sailboats, fishing skiffs, and Runabout cruisers. Even if you have no experience, there's plenty of room for exploration in the harbor. Sample rates: single kayak, $10 per hour; 15-foot fishing skiff, $60 half day, $90 full day; Waverunner, $75 per hour. Substantial winter discounts are available; Boat Rentals keeps seasonal hours, so call for specific information.

Behind the harbor lurks the U.S. Marine Corps's **Camp Pendleton,** one of few clues that Oceanside is primarily a military town—the city hides that fact better than most.

Its other main identification is with surfers and surf lore, and there's no better place to learn all about it than the **California Surf Museum,** 223 North Coast Hwy. (☎ **760/ 721-6876**). At the (hopefully) final headquarters of this peripatetic institution— founded in 1985, the museum was first housed at a restaurant in Encinitas, then temporary digs in Pacific Beach and Oceanside, before moving to its current location—both surf devotees and the curious onlooker will delight in the museum's unbelievably extensive collection. Boards and other relics chronicle the development of the sport. Many belonged to surfers whose names are revered by local surfers, including Hawaiian Duke Kahanamoku and local daredevil Bob Simmons. Vintage photographs, beach attire, '60s beach graffiti, and "surf" music all lovingly bring the sport to life—there's even a photo display of the real-life Gidget. A gift shop offers unique items, including memorabilia of famous surfers and surf flicks, plus novelty items like a surf-lingo dictionary. The museum is open Thursday through Monday from noon to 4pm; admission is free, but donations are requested.

The **Oceanside Beach** starts just outside Oceanside Harbor, where routine harbor dredging makes for a substantial amount of fluffy, clean white sand. It runs almost 4 miles south to the Carlsbad border. Along the way you can enjoy the **Strand,** a grassy park that stretches along the beach between 5th Street and Wisconsin Avenue. Benches with scenic vistas abound, and the Strand also borders on the Oceanside Pier, which in turn is usually flanked by legions of bobbing surfers. Parking is at metered street spaces or in lots, which can fill up on nice summer days. Harbor Beach, which is separated from the rest by the San Luis River, charges $5 admission per vehicle. Farther south, there is no regulated admission, and after Witherby Street or so, parking is free (but in demand) along residential streets. Around the pier are rest rooms, showers, picnic areas, and volleyball nets.

Oceanside's world-famous surfing spots attract numerous competitions, including the Longboard Surf Contest and World Bodysurfing Championships, both in August.

Gamblers—and fans of the swingin' Rat Pack movies—can be found at Oceanside's unique gaming house, **Ocean's Eleven Casino,** 121 Brooks St. (☎ **760/439-6988;** www.oceans11.com). The inside is more contemporary banquet hall than vintage Vegas, but Ocean's Eleven does its best to evoke Sin City. It has murals of Frank Sinatra, Sammy Davis, Jr., Dean Martin, Joey Bishop, and Peter Lawford at the height of their hijinks, and retro-style Continental fare (veal Oscar, surf and turf) served up in the Rat Pack Lounge. There's nightly entertainment in the lounge, and, of course, games: blackjack, poker (Hold-Em, 7-Card Stud, Omaha Hi-Lo, Pot Limit), Pai Gow, and Pan. It's open 24 hours a day, 7 days a week.

WHERE TO STAY & DINE

The inexpensive to moderate **Marina Inn,** 2008 Harbor Dr. N., Oceanside, CA 92054 (☎ **800/252-2033** or 760/722-1561; fax 760/439-9758), has comfortable rooms and suites that offer harbor and ocean views.

Several restaurants, including the **Chart House** (☎ **760/722-1345**), offer harborside dining.

2 North County Inland: From Rancho Santa Fe to Palomar Mountain

The coastal and inland sections of North County are as different as night and day. Beaches and laid-back villages where work seems to be the curse of the surfing class characterize the coast. Inland you'll find beautiful barren hills, citrus groves, and conservative communities where agriculture plays an important role.

Rancho Santa Fe is about 27 miles north of downtown San Diego; from there the Del Dios Highway (S6) leads to Escondido, almost 32 miles from the city. Nearly 70 miles away is Palomar Mountain in the Cleveland National Forest, which spills over the border into Riverside County. The **San Diego North County Convention and Visitors Bureau**, 720 N. Broadway, Escondido, CA 92025 (☎ **800/848-3336** or 760/745-4741; www.sandiegonorth.com), can answer your questions.

RANCHO SANTA FE

Exclusive Rancho Santa Fe was once the property of the Santa Fe Railroad, and the eucalyptus trees the railroad grew create a stately atmosphere. After just a few minutes in town, it becomes apparent that Rancho Santa Fe is a playground for the *über*-wealthy, but not in the usual, pretentious sense. Proving the adage that true breeding makes everyone feel at ease, and that it's gauche to flaunt your money, this upscale slice of North County is a friendly town that's enjoyed by everyone. Primarily residential Rancho Santa Fe has two large resort hotels that blend into the eucalyptus groves surrounding the town. The **Rancho Valencia Resort** is a premier destination and choice of the First Family; the more modestly priced **Inn at Rancho Santa Fe** is closer to town (see "Where to Stay," below). Shopping and dining—both quite limited—in Rancho Santa Fe revolve around a couple of understated blocks known locally as "the Village," whose curbs are usually filled with late-model Mercedes, Lexuses, and Land Rovers.

ESSENTIALS

GETTING THERE   From San Diego, take I-5 north to Lomas Santa Fe (County Highway S8) east; it turns into Linea del Cielo and leads directly into the center of Rancho Santa Fe. If you continue through town on Paseo Delicias, you'll pick up the Del Dios Highway (County Highway S6), the scenic route to Escondido and the **Wild Animal Park**. This road affords views of Lake Hodges, as well as glimpses of expansive estates, some of the most expensive in the country.

SPECIAL EVENTS   If you're looking for Fourth of July festivities with a small-town yet sophisticated flavor, come for the annual **Independence Day Parade.** Residents come out in droves as a marching band, equestrians, and the local fire engines wind through the tiny town center. Anyone with a vintage, classic, or just luxury car gets into the act—you might see vintage Packards, restored Model Ts, classic roadsters, or just shiny new Land Rovers strutting their stuff. Festivities continue with a barbecue and concert in the park. For more information, call ☎ **800/848-3336** or 760/745-4741.

WHERE TO STAY

The Inn at Rancho Santa Fe. 5951 Linea del Cielo (P.O. Box 869), Rancho Santa Fe, CA 92067. ☎ **800/654-2928** or 858/756-1131. Fax 858/759-1604. 89 units. TV TEL. $110–$210 double; from $275 suite. AE, CB, DC, DISC, MC, V. Free parking. From I-5, take the Lomas Santa Fe exit, following signs to Rancho Santa Fe. The Inn is on the right just before town. Pets accepted.

Indulge your inner gentry with a surprisingly affordable stay here, where casual surroundings belie the international clientele. Like the town itself, the Inn is the epitome of genteel, proving that those born to money needn't flaunt it, or pay unnecessarily exorbitant rates. Early-California–style cottages are nestled throughout the resort's 20 acres; the decor is English country–flavored and sturdy, and many rooms have fireplaces, kitchenettes, and secluded patios. A fascinating collection of antique, hand-carved model sailing ships is on display in the lobby. Beautifully landscaped grounds contain towering eucalyptus, colorful flowers, and expansive rolling lawns (a favorite, I'm told, among the canine guests welcomed at the inn). Nifty extras include guest membership at Rancho Santa Fe Golf Club and use of the Inn's private Del Mar beach cottage, complete with showers and elevated deck.

Rancho Valencia Resort. 5921 Valencia Circle (Box 9126), Rancho Santa Fe, CA 92067. ☎ **800/548-3664** or 858/756-1123. Fax 858/756-0165. www.ranchovalencia.com. 43 units. A/C MINIBAR TV TEL. $410–$600 suite. Spa, tennis, golf, and romance packages available. AE, DC, MC, V. Free valet and self-parking. Take I-5 to Via de la Valle and go east to El Camino Real (Mary's Tack Shop is on the corner). Go south to San Dieguito Rd., turn east, and follow signs to resort. Pets accepted; $75 per night.

If you are in need of pampering and relaxation or a romantic getaway, read on. A member of Relais et Châteaux and Preferred Hotels, this sun-baked Spanish- and Mediterranean-style resort sits on 40 acres overlooking the San Dieguito Valley and the rolling hills of Rancho Santa Fe. Imagine having your own casita with cathedral ceilings, wood-burning fireplace, ceiling fans, oversize tiled bath, walk-in closet, and private terrace. Spa treatments and massages can even be given in the casita. Fresh-squeezed juice and a newspaper are left outside your door in the morning, and coffee-making equipment is available. Those who venture outside discover grounds filled with 2,000 citrus trees, bougainvillea, and air sweetened by flowers and birdsong.

Dining/Diversions: The resort's dining room serves Mediterranean-California cuisine, with a cellist or guitarist on Friday and Saturday nights; there's dancing under the stars on Thursday nights in July and August. Tea and cocktails are served in La Sala, from which there is a great view of the hot-air balloons at sunset.

Amenities: There are two pools, three Jacuzzis, and a fitness room. The athletically inclined can take advantage of the 18 tennis courts and tennis clinics with a 4:1 student-teacher ratio. Check out the championship croquet lawn or play a round of golf nearby. Bikes for adults and kids are available at no extra charge, and there are plenty of hiking trails.

WHERE TO DINE

Delicias. 6109 Paseo Delicias, Rancho Santa Fe. ☎ **858/756-8000.** Reservations recommended on weekends. Main courses $9–$16 at lunch, $15–$29 at dinner. AE, DC, MC, V. Tues–Sun noon–2pm and 6–10pm; extended summer hours. CALIFORNIA.

Decorated in a mix of antiques and wicker, accented by flowers, woven tapestries, and floor-to-ceiling French doors, this comfortable restaurant is equally appropriate for a casual meal or special occasion. Service is attentive and personable, and the food is delicious. Intriguing—but not overly complex—flavor blends are the hallmark of a menu that ranges from the zesty Pacific Rim to the sunny Mediterranean, interpreted with a subtle French accent. Chinese duckling is slow-roasted with ginger and soy, then served with a spicy mushroom sauce; coriander-crusted salmon is sautéed with miso and ponzu, accented by papaya salsa; and rack of lamb is bathed in tamarind-plum sauce and served with cucumber-mango-mint relish. At meals like these it's not easy to leave room for dessert; but, take my word for it, you'll kick yourself if you don't. Giant umbrellas shade a streetside outdoor patio—Delicias is also a great (and affordable) lunch choice.

ESCONDIDO

Best known as the home of the Wild Animal Park (described in chapter 7), Escondido is also the site of the **California Center for the Performing Arts,** an attractive 12-acre campus that includes two theaters, an art museum, a conference center, and a cafe.

Select Spas

It's not too surprising that two premier spa retreats—the **Golden Door** and **Cal-a-Vie**—are discreetly tucked away in the hills of North County. After all, this is Southern California, where looking good is an art form and year-round outdoor rest and relaxation are possible. It seems only natural that those yearning to get into shape would find their way here. And they do, from all over the world.

Spa-goers receive unparalleled pampering, but they also work their buns off—or at least into shape. At the **Golden Door,** 39 guests follow their own schedule; everyone is encouraged to begin the day with an early-morning hike, followed by exercise classes, healthy meals, "mocktail" parties, and—the best part—massages. You'll feel renewed by the diet, the physical exertion, and the spa's peaceful atmosphere. "Everyone leaves here happy," we were told; about three-quarters of the guests return.

Women are the primary clientele; the spa sets aside only 4 weeks for men and designates 2 weeks as "co-ed." And paradise isn't cheap: The all-inclusive rate is $4,500 a week during the winter, $4,000 during the summer. But aren't you worth it? A 3:1 staff ratio means someone is always available to do your bidding. (Rooms are cleaned every 2 hours.) For more information, write to P.O. Box 463077, Escondido, CA 92046-3077 (☎ **800/424-0777** or 760/744-5777; fax 760/744-5007).

Cal-a-Vie caters to 24 guests a week. One or two weeks a month are set aside for women only. Like the Golden Door, the spa emphasizes enacting lifestyle changes and de-stressing, but Cal-a-Vie focuses more on European spa treatments—real sybaritic stuff—and less on the spiritual side. This spot is popular with celebrities, such as Anjelica Huston, Julia Roberts, and Kathleen Turner. Oprah found Rosie here! If you can handle 16 spa treatments a week (including outdoor massages on private decks) in absolutely gorgeous surroundings, write to 2249 Somerset Rd., Vista, CA 92084 (☎ **760/945-2055;** fax 760/630-0074). This pampering costs $4,350 a week, less during the summer.

If the Golden Door and Cal-a-Vie are out of your price range, you might consider **Rancho La Puerta,** in Tecate, Mexico, just over the border from San Diego County. It's under the same ownership as the Golden Door, but because it's less expensive, its local moniker is "The Back Door." It's not as exclusive, but offers similar programs. To request a brochure, call ☎ **800/443-7565** or 011-52-665/4-1155 (www.rancholapuerta.com).

Several resorts in the San Diego area also offer extensive spa facilities: **L'Auberge Del Mar Resort and Spa** and **La Costa Resort and Spa** (both described above), and the **Marriott Coronado Bay Resort** (described in chapter 5).

It's worth the 45-minute to 1-hour drive to Escondido (along I-15 north to the Escondido exits) just to see the appealing postmodern architecture of this facility, which opened in 1994. (To find out what's playing and for ticket information, call ☎ **760/738-4100.**)

This city of 125,000 is in the heart of a major agricultural area, so it's not surprising that the farmers' market on Tuesday afternoons is one of the county's best. In total, North County is home to 36 golf courses (some are described in chapter 7). Orfila Vineyards is near the Wild Animal Park; for details, refer to "For Wine Lovers" in chapter 7. Grand Avenue, old Escondido's downtown main drag, is experiencing a pleasant renewal. Classy antique stores and new restaurants, like 150 Grand Cafe (see below), are filling historic storefronts.

WHERE TO STAY & DINE

The **Welk Resort Center,** 8860 Lawrence Welk Dr. (☎ **800/932-9355**), is a moderate-to-expensive lodging near downtown Escondido. It offers golf, tennis, and live theatrical entertainment.

150 Grand Cafe. 150 West Grand Ave. ☎ **760/738-6868.** Reservations recommended, especially for weekend nights. Main courses $7.50–$20. AE, DC, MC, V. Mon–Fri 11:30am–9pm, Sat 5–9:30pm. MODERN MULTIETHNIC.

English expatriates Cyril and Vicki Lucas run this delightful cafe on a charming stretch of historic Grand Avenue. Although Escondido is not usually associated with fine dining, this restaurant's reputation stretches to San Diego; it's definitely worth a detour. The bright, attractive decor feels like a cross between a conservatory and a library. Lunchtime favorites include grilled poblano chile (with Havarti cheese, roasted-tomato vinaigrette, tomatillos, cilantro, and red and blue tortilla strips) and flash-grilled tuna salad (Hawaiian ahi, orange basmati, mixed greens, rice noodles, and sesame-ginger vinaigrette). Dinners include grilled filet mignon, forest-mushroom pasta, sautéed salmon, and roast game hen. There's indoor and outdoor seating.

PALOMAR MOUNTAIN

Palomar Observatory (☎ **760/742-2119**) and its mammoth telescope have kept a silent vigil over the heavens since 1949. From San Diego, take I-15 north to Highway 76 east, and turn left onto County Highway S6. Even if you don't want to inch your way to the top, drive the 3 miles to the lookout or just beyond it to the campground, grocery store, restaurant, and post office. Palomar Observatory's impressive dome is 135 feet high and 137 feet in diameter. The telescope has a single 200-inch mirror and weighs 530 tons. Now completely computerized, it has an approximate light range of more than 1 billion light years.

Start your visit in the museum, which is open daily from 9am to 4pm (except December 24 and 25) and has a continuously running informative video that makes a walk up the hill to the observatory more meaningful. Palomar is primarily a research facility, and you'll only be able to look at (not through) the mammoth telescope. The museum and the observatory both have rest rooms. Try to visit the observatory in the morning; late in the day, you'll have the sun in your eyes as you back down the mountain. The observatory closes at 4pm.

For a downhill thrill, take the **Palomar Plunge** on a 21-speed mountain bike. From the top of Palomar Mountain to its base, you'll experience a 5,000-foot vertical drop stretched out over 16 miles. **Gravity Activated Sports,** P.O. Box 683, Pauma Valley, CA 92061 (☎ **800/985-4427** or 760/742-2294; fax 760/742-2293; www.gasports.com), supplies the mountain bike, helmet, gloves, lunch, souvenir photo, and T-shirt. This experience costs $80.

3 Temecula: Touring the Wineries

60 miles N of San Diego; 60 miles NW of Julian; 90 miles SE of Los Angeles

Located over the line in Riverside County, Temecula is known for its wineries and the excellent vintages they produce. The town's very name (pronounced ta-*meck*-you-la) provides the first clue to this valley's success in the volatile wine-making business/art. It translates as "where the sun shines through the mist" (from a Native

American language), which identifies two of the three climatological factors neces- sary for viticulture. The third is Rainbow Gap, an opening to the south through the Agua Tibia Mountains, which allows cool afternoon sea breezes to enter the 1,500- foot elevation. It's also one of the few California towns that still goes by its Native American names—Cholame, Lompoc, and Pismo (Beach) are three others. Helen Hunt Jackson used the region as the setting for her 1884 novel *Ramona.*

Temecula has a couple of claims to fame. Granite from its quarries (most of which closed down in 1915, when reinforced concrete became popular) constitutes most of San Francisco's street curbs. The last person sentenced to death by hanging in Cali- fornia was Temecula's blacksmith, John McNeil, who killed his wife in 1936.

Temecula is not as well known for its wines as Napa or Sonoma, because those wine-producing regions have been at it for 100 years longer. Franciscan missionaries planted the first grapevines here in the early 1800s, but the land ended up being used primarily for raising cattle. The 87,000-acre Vail Ranch operated from 1904 until being sold in 1964. Grapevines began to take root in the receptive soil again in 1968, and the first Temecula wines were produced in 1971.

ESSENTIALS

GETTING THERE   Drive north from San Diego on I-15 for 50 miles; when the Temecula Valley comes into view, it'll take your breath away. To reach the vineyards, head east on Rancho California Road.

VISITOR INFORMATION   The **Temecula Valley Chamber of Commerce,** 27450 Ynez Road, Suite 104, Temecula, CA 92591 (☎ **909/676-5090;** fax 909/ 694-0201; www.temecula.org), in a brand-new office complex, is a little hard to find. If you can, call and have the staff mail you the *Visitors Guide,* or stop by Monday to Friday between 9am and 5pm.

For detailed information on Temecula wine touring, call the **Temecula Valley Vint- ners Association** (☎ **800/801-WINE** or 909/699-3626) and request the *Wine Country* pamphlet, a comprehensive guide with winery locations, hours, and a brief description of each.

TOURING THE WINERIES

You can almost hear the murmur, audible from the twisted, grape-laden vines, "If you build a winery, they will come." With apologies to *Field of Dreams,* there was only a nanosecond's lag time between successful vintages coming out of California's south- ernmost appellation (the official government recognition of a wine-producing region) and the full-blown marketing of this area for wine touring. There has been a develop- ment explosion in Temecula during the last decade or so, with new housing develop- ments and the expanding wine-grape industry competing for space. Back in 1968, one vintner recalls, "If you heard a car come down Rancho California Road, you'd go to the window to see who could possibly be lost way out here." Well, Rancho California is now clogged with traffic during rush hour and on pretty weekends—most of the area's 16 wineries are strung along this major thoroughfare—and vintners are way too busy to listen for anything unusual.

Harvest time is usually mid-August through September, and visitors are welcome year-round to tour, taste, and stock up. Most wineries in the area are closed January 1, Easter, Thanksgiving Day, and December 25.

If bicycling is your thing, **Gravity Activated Sports,** P.O. Box 683, Pauma Valley, CA 92061 (☎ **800/985-4427** or 760/742-2294; fax 760/742-2293; www.gas- ports.com), offers a wine-country tour that includes a 10-mile ride around the area followed by a bus tour around the wineries for tasting. The tour costs $90 per person.

Temecula

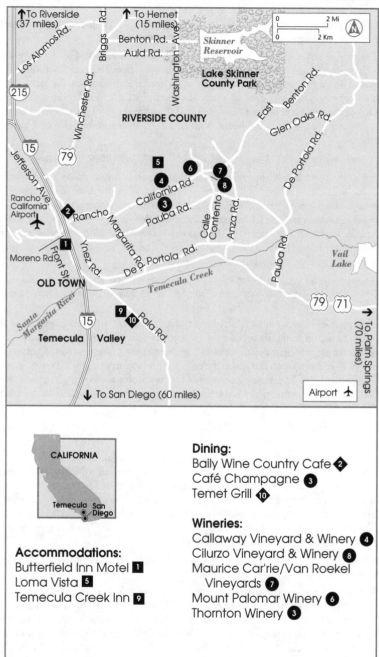

Dining:
Baily Wine Country Cafe ◆ 2
Café Champagne ● 3
Temet Grill ⑩

Wineries:
Callaway Vineyard & Winery ④
Cilurzo Vineyard & Winery ⑧
Maurice Car'rie/Van Roekel
   Vineyards ⑦
Mount Palomar Winery ⑥
Thornton Winery ● 3

Accommodations:
Butterfield Inn Motel ■ 1
Loma Vista ◆ 5
Temecula Creek Inn ◆ 9

Callaway Vineyard & Winery. 32720 Rancho California Rd. ☎ **800/472-2377** or 909/ 676-4001. www.callawaywine.com. Daily 10:30am–5pm.

The first winery established in the region is also the best known; Callaway's moderately priced Chardonnays and other whites show up frequently on California wine lists. This winery offers in-depth tours of its facilities throughout the day—every hour between 11am and 4pm on weekends, and thrice daily Monday through Friday. One of the best parts of the tours is the tasting room; the tasting fee of $4 also buys a souvenir glass. The casual bistro, Vineyard Terrace, overlooks fields of Callaway vines.

Thornton Winery. 32575 Rancho California Rd. ☎ **909/699-0099.** Daily 11am–5pm.

Across the street from Callaway stands another old-timer, which makes a good choice if you only visit one winery. Thornton provides an all-in-one taste of the Temecula wine country. It has a striking setting, fragrant herb garden, extensive gift shop, award-winning restaurant (Cafe Champagne, discussed below under "Where to Dine"), and Sunday afternoon jazz concerts. Thornton specializes in sparkling wine, a *methode champenoise* released under the Culbertson label, and also offers free hourly tours on weekends. Tastings are $6 and include a souvenir glass.

Mount Palomar Winery. 33820 Rancho California Rd. ☎ **909/676-5047.** Oct–Mar daily 10am–5pm, Apr–Sept daily 10am–6pm. Tours Sat–Sun 11:30am, 1:30 and 3:30pm; Mon–Fri 1:30 and 3:30pm.

They're doing things a little differently at Mount Palomar, and you might see unfamiliar names on some labels. Take the informative tour to learn about the process of hand-crafting Mediterranean varietals like Sangiovese, Cortese, and Rhone-style blends of French grapes; this is also the only Temecula winery producing cream sherry. The tasting fee of $3 gets you a pouring of five wines plus a souvenir glass; the tour is free. An army of picnic tables is scattered throughout the property, and on weekends there's a full-service deli.

Cilurzo Vineyard & Winery. 41220 Calle Contento (off Rancho California Rd.). ☎ **909/ 676-5250.** Daily 10am–5pm.

Celebrity photos on the wall hint that the proprietor has an alternative persona. In fact, vintner Vince Cilurzo is equally known for his work as a Hollywood lighting director (*Jeopardy!* is most prominent among his credits) as for the petite sirah he claims can be served with anything "from tomato sauce to curry." Tasting is often a friendly affair, sitting around with Vince or his wife, Audrey, pouring their latest vintage; the $1 tasting fee is refunded with any purchase. Bring lunch if you'd like to picnic overlooking the small lake on the property.

Maurice Car'rie Winery/Van Roekel Vineyards. 34225 Rancho California Rd. ☎ **909/ 676-1711.** Daily 10am–5pm.

Perhaps the most welcoming tasting room is the *nouvelle* yellow farmhouse of Maurice Car'rie. Started by Dutch Minnesotan Budd Van Roekel in 1984, and named for his wife, Maurice, the vineyard produces 14 varietals, the most popular of which is Cabernet. Farther up the road (at 34567 Rancho California Rd.) is the couple's latest venture, Van Roekel Vineyards (☎ **909/699-6961**), which opened in 1994. The souvenir-minded will love Van Roekel's gift shop, filled with logo items and wine-related gifts. Each winery also has a gourmet deli for composing a picnic to enjoy in Maurice Car'rie's rose-filled front garden and patio. There is no fee for tasting at either winery.

HISTORIC OLD TOWN TEMECULA

An eccentric counterpoint to this area's vineyards, gated housing developments, and shopping centers is the old part of the city of Temecula, preserved as it was in the 1890s—Western storefronts and all. It lies 4 miles west of the vineyards off Rancho California Road, stretches along six short blocks, and has a reputation as an antique-hunter's haven.

The best way to explore Old Town is on foot—it's quite easy to see it all in an afternoon. Park anywhere you can find a space. Be forewarned that Temecula has become a traffic-clogged town, and you will hear the drone of cars almost everywhere, even on the golf course.

Beginning in the 1850s, Temecula was a Butterfield Overland Stage stop for pioneers and tradesmen; traffic only increased once the railroad arrived in 1882, and downtown's appearance has remained virtually unchanged since the 1890s. Western souvenir shops, restaurants, and particularly collectibles stores have kept the area alive, with antique hounds and tourists tromping along the wooden sidewalks of Front Street.

The city is renovating and expanding Old Town. Good ideas include old-fashioned street lampposts and more boardwalk-style sidewalks; not-so-good ideas are large parking lots intended to lure would-be developers to the area. For many visitors, the Old Town area's rough edges add to whatever frontier realism and appeal remain, although customers of the dozens of contemporary businesses are generally oblivious to most buildings' origins. Take time to read the bronze plaques on storefronts that intrigue you, and pick up a copy of the *Old Town Temecula Walking Tour Map.* The brief leaflet, with a business index and historic building guide, is free and available at some local shops and restaurants.

At Front Street and Moreno Road is **Sam Hicks Park,** site of the *They Passed This Way* monument ("they" being famous visitors over the years, including mountain man Jedediah Smith, explorer Kit Carson, and *Ramona* author Helen Hunt Jackson). The clapboard St. Catherine's Church (ca. 1922) moved to this site to house the **Temecula Valley Museum** (☎ **909/676-0021**). The museum has Native American artifacts from the Shoshone, who named the town over 1,000 years ago. There's a collection of household and farm items from the 19th to mid-20th century, a diorama of Temecula as it appeared around 1914, and memorabilia of Temecula's favorite son, mystery novelist Erle Stanley Gardner. It's open Wednesday to Sunday 11am to 4pm; admission is free but donations are appreciated.

HISTORIC BUILDINGS   Other buildings of historical interest include the **First National Bank,** at Front and Main streets. Built in 1914, it managed to remain open during the Great Depression, gaining it the nickname "the pawn shop." It closed in 1941. The main floor now houses an eatery cleverly named the **Bank of Mexican Food.** On Main Street west of Front is the **Welty Hotel/Temecula Hotel** building; originally built in 1882 with the arrival of the railroad, it burned and was rebuilt in 1891. Restored to its turn-of-the-century decor in 1960, it was then a hotel but is now a private home. The same family was responsible for the **Welty Building** three doors down at the corner of Main and Front streets. It was built as a store and saloon, and later housed a gymnasium that played host to prizefighter Jack Dempsey. Today, an antique store and deli occupy the building. The 1891 **Temecula Mercantile** building, 42049 Main St., was the lifeblood of local ranchers well into the 1950s. Today it houses—you guessed it—an antique store. At **Morgan's Antiques** (☎ **909/ 676-2722**), the upstairs gallery holds special-interest collectibles.

ANTIQUE STORES   More antique stores worth seeking out are **Temecula Trading Post,** 42081 Main St. (☎ **909/676-5759**), which boasts that it's the town's "finest antique mall." **The Loft,** 28480 Front St. (☎ **909/676-5179**), has been open for over 25 years. It specializes in clocks—grandfather, wall, cuckoo, mantle—and other timepieces. If your eye is drawn to all that glitters and shimmers, step into **Nana's Antiques,** 28677 Front St. (☎ **909/699-3839**). While I wouldn't want to dust the place, I simply love browsing Nana's Victorian-era glass and crystal, looking at anachronistically elegant tableware (knife rests, condiment caddies, pickle jars, and such) that might have jumped from a meticulously set Edith Wharton banquet table.

OUTDOOR PURSUITS IN TEMECULA

Besides wine tasting, area activities include hot-air balloon rides over the vineyards, an unforgettable sight. One company, which has been around for about 20 years, is **Sunrise Balloons** (☎ **800/548-9912**). Proprietor Dan Glick also offers horse-drawn carriage rides through the vineyards.

For an outing in more than 7,000 acres of unspoiled terrain, take I-15 north to Clinton Keith Road and drive west for about 5 miles. The **Santa Rosa Plateau Ecological Reserve,** 22115 Tenaja Rd., Murrieta (☎ **909/677-6951** or 909/699-1856), is owned and maintained by the Nature Conservancy. Walking trails, coyotes, hawks, migrating birds, and maybe even an eagle or two await you.

GOLF   You can't get more countrified than at the **Temecula Creek Inn** (see below), whose 27-hole, 10,014-yard championship golf course features rolling hills and fairways lined with 100-year-old live oaks; wild pheasants and bobcats put in occasional appearances. Lessons and golf packages are available. Greens fees for 18 holes are $55 Monday through Thursday, $65 on Friday, and $85 on Saturday and Sunday, including a cart.

WHERE TO STAY

Butterfield Inn Motel. 28718 Front St., Temecula, CA 92390. ☎ **909/676-4833.** Fax 909/676-2019. 39 units. A/C TV TEL. $55–$65 double weekends; $42–$51 double weekdays. Extra person $5. AE, DISC, MC, V. Take I-15 north to Rancho California Rd., then go west to Front St.

Within walking distance of Old Town Temecula shops, the motel (not really an inn) has an Old West facade, a small, unheated outdoor pool, and a Jacuzzi. There's complimentary coffee in the lobby in the morning. It's your basic motel—conveniently situated and bargain priced—but far enough from luxury that you can almost imagine the old Butterfield stagecoach pulling up here any moment.

Loma Vista. 33350 La Serena Way, Temecula, CA 92591. ☎ **909/676-7047.** Fax 909/676-0077. 6 units. A/C. $100–$150 double. Rates include full champagne breakfast and evening wine and cheese. MC, V. Take I-15 to Rancho California Rd. east; inn is on left just beyond Callaway Vineyard.

This tiled-roof, mission-style contemporary house was built in 1988 as a bed-and-breakfast inn. Perfectly named, it sits on a hill (*loma* in Spanish) overlooking the best vista around. From the living room, you can see the Callaway Vineyard and the Santa Ana Mountains; most of Temecula's wineries lie along the same main road. All guest rooms are named for wines; four have private wisteria-covered balconies.

Besides complimentary fruit and a decanter of sherry in each room, wine and cheese are served by the fire at 6pm. A spa bubbles on the back patio; the front patio, a great place to while away the hours, has a fire pit. The property is a real oasis, with 85 rose bushes, ranunculuses, daisies, Australian tea bushes, and 325 grapefruit trees. The new owners, Walt and Sheila Kurczynski, took over in 1998. Old Town Temecula is 5 miles away.

✪ **Temecula Creek Inn.** 44501 Rainbow Canyon Rd., Temecula, CA 92592. ☎ **800/ 962-7335** or 909/694-1000. Fax 909/676-3422. 80 units. A/C MINIBAR TV TEL. Sun–Thurs $126 double; from $150 junior suite. Fri–Sat $165 double; $195 junior suite. Golf and wine- country packages available. AE, DC, DISC, MC, V. From San Diego, take I-15 north to exit 79 (Indio); turn right off the exit ramp. At Pala Rd., turn right, go over a little bridge, then take an immediate right onto Rainbow Canyon Rd. Entrance to inn is ½ mile away.

This small resort is more a country lodge than an inn. Its inviting lobby is replete with adobe walls, Native American artifacts, and a fireplace. Rooms in the five two-story buildings have restful views and custom-designed Native American–inspired furnish- ings. They come with down pillows, hair dryers, coffee and tea supplies (including beans and a grinder), and in-room safe. Junior suites are oversize corner rooms with sitting areas, two balconies, and floor-to-ceiling windows. The TV is cleverly hidden away under a piece of sculpture.

Magnolia trees line the walkway from the lobby to the outstanding restaurant, the Temet Grill (see "Where to Dine," below). There is live music nightly in the lounge adjoining the restaurant. Food and cocktail service is available poolside. Features include an outdoor pool, barbecue under live oaks, 27 holes of golf (see above), dri- ving range, volleyball, croquet, two tennis courts, and a golf and tennis pro shop. Guests have laundry and dry-cleaning service, and cribs are available.

WHERE TO DINE

Baily Wine Country Cafe. In the Albertson's shopping center, 27644 Ynez Rd. (at Rancho California Rd.). ☎ **909/676-9567.** www.baily.com. Reservations recommended, especially on weekends. Main courses $8–$11 at lunch, $13–$22 at dinner. AE, CB, DC, MC, V. Mon–Fri 11am–2:30pm; Mon–Thurs 5–9pm, Fri 5–9:30pm; Sat 11am–9:30pm, Sunday 11am–9pm. CALIFORNIA/CONTINENTAL.

Baily's has the largest selection of Temecula Valley wines anywhere, including those from the Baily family's winery on Rancho California Road. To show them off to best advantage, the chef concocts some mouth-watering dishes, which change every few months. At lunch, consider the penne with roasted garlic, fresh vegetables, and tomato sauce made chunky with Italian sausage; Southwestern-style grilled cheese sandwich with cilantro (a regional prizewinner); or grilled chicken piccata salad with mixed greens and lemon-caper vinaigrette. Dinner favorites include Southwestern pork ten- derloin with garlic mashed potatoes; salmon Wellington with cucumber-and-papaya relish and fresh vegetables; and chicken ravioli in basil pesto. Finish with Carol Baily's white-chocolate cheesecake, a top choice with local diners.

If you're in luck, your visit will coincide with one of the celebrated "Dinners in the Wine Cellar." The fixed-price, set-menu meal at the Temecula Crest Winery is hosted by members of the Baily family, who choose wines to accompany each course. Picnics can be provided to go with 24 hours' notice.

✪ **Cafe Champagne.** Thornton Winery, 32575 Rancho California Rd. ☎ **909/699-0088.** Reservations recommended. Main courses $10–$21 at lunch, $13–$21 at dinner. AE, DC, MC, V. Daily 11am–9pm. CALIFORNIA.

The toast of the Temecula wine country, this bistro and cafe features tasty dishes cre- ated to be served with nine Thornton champagnes. The wine list also features other Temecula and California labels. The lunch and dinner menus, California cuisine at its best, feature appetizers like warm brie en croûte with honey-walnut sauce, crab-and- shrimp strudel, and smoked salmon carpaccio. Among the entrees are angel-hair pasta primavera, angel-hair seafood pasta, mesquite-grilled tuna, and baked pecan chicken.

The list of mesquite-grilled entrees expands at dinner, and at lunch tempting lighter fare includes hearty salads and sandwiches filled with mesquite-grilled hamburger, steak, or chicken. The setting, overlooking the vineyard, is sublime. It's a small place, so do reserve ahead. If you want really good food, you're going to like it here.

Temet Grill. In the Temecula Creek Inn, 44501 Rainbow Canyon Rd. ☎ **909/676-5631.** Reservations recommended. Main courses $16.50–$21. AE, CB, DC, DISC, MC, V. Daily 6am–10pm. CALIFORNIA/FRENCH.

The Temet Grill's dramatic windows overlook woods, golf courses, and the eponymous creek. The service is outstanding, and the menu changes seasonally, always including mainstays like brandied lobster bisque, pepper New York steak, and prime rib *au jus*. The kitchen uses fine quality ingredients, so if the menu includes swordfish grilled in browned butter and roasted garlic, or roasted salmon with a thyme crust and red-wine reduction, expect them to be good. As befits the surrounding region, the wine list emphasizes California and Pacific Northwest vintages, with a few French champagnes for celebrations.

TEMECULA AFTER DARK

For a fun evening out in Old Town Temecula at any time of year, indulge in country-western dancing at the **Midnight Roundup,** 28721 Front St., opposite the Butterfield Inn (☎ **909/694-5686**). Probably one of California's biggest saloons and dance halls, the place takes up 4,000 square feet, incorporating areas for two-steppers, swing dancers, and line dancers. There's room for eight pool tables; tables and chairs; and two impressive bars, one 110 feet long and the other 60 feet long. It's open Tuesday through Sunday from 6pm until the crowd goes home, with dance lessons given on Tuesday and Thursday nights. Live bands are on hand from 8:30pm until 2am Thursday through Saturday nights, when there is a $5 cover; otherwise, there's a DJ. Devotees range in age from the minimum of 21 to 80-plus, most decked out in Western garb; weekends are crowded. The entrance is at the back of the building.

4 Disneyland & Other Anaheim Area Attractions

160 miles N of San Diego

The sleepy Orange County town of Anaheim grew up around Disneyland, the West's most famous theme park. Now, even beyond the "Happiest Place on Earth," the city and its neighboring communities are kid-central. Otherwise unspectacular, sprawling suburbs have become a playground of family-oriented hotels, restaurants, and unabashedly tourist-oriented attractions. Among the nearby draws are Knott's Berry Farm, another family-oriented theme park, in Buena Park. At the other end of the scale is the Richard Nixon Library and Birthplace, a surprisingly compelling presidential library and museum, just 7 miles northeast of Disneyland in Yorba Linda.

ESSENTIALS

GETTING THERE   From downtown San Diego, take I-5 north to the Harbor Blvd. exit and turn left. The main entrance is one-quarter mile ahead on the right. The drive from downtown San Diego takes approximately 90 minutes.

Ten **Amtrak** (☎ **800/USA-RAIL**) trains go to Anaheim daily from San Diego. The one-way fare is $17, and the trip takes about 2 hours. Amtrak also offers 1-day and 5-day excursion packages. For an additional $45, the 1-day package includes round-trip shuttle service from the train station to Disneyland, and admission fees. For an extra $75, you can extend your stay with the 5-day package, which includes admission for 5 days and shuttle service to and from the train station.

VISITOR INFORMATION   **The Anaheim/Orange County Visitor and Convention Bureau,** 800 W. Katella Ave., P.O. Box 4270, Anaheim, CA 92803 (☎ 714/ 999-8999), can fill you in on area activities and shopping shuttles. It's across the street from Disneyland inside the Convention Center, next to the dramatic cantilevered arena. It's open Monday to Friday from 8:30am to 5:30pm. **The Buena Park Convention and Visitors Office,** 6280 Manchester Blvd., Suite 103 (☎ **800/541-3953** or 714/562-3560), provides specialized information on the area, including Knott's Berry Farm.

DISNEYLAND

Disney originated the mega–theme park. Opened in 1955, Disneyland remains unsurpassed. Despite constant threats from pretenders to the crown, Disneyland and Walt Disney World (outside Orlando, Florida) remain the kings of theme parks. At no other park is fantasy elevated to an art form. Nowhere else is as fresh and fantastic everytime you walk through the gates, whether you're 6 or 60—and no matter how many times you've done it before.

The park stays on the cutting edge by continually updating and expanding, while maintaining the hallmarks that make it the world's top amusement park (a term coined by Walt Disney). The most recent additions include 1995's **Indiana Jones Adventure,** a high-tech thrill that's not to be missed, no matter how long the wait. The beloved Main Street Electrical Parade's 24-year run ended in 1996; in its place, a changing series of nighttime parades features larger-than-life fiber-optic and video light displays. At press time the parade showcased characters and themes from *Mulan.* In 1998, Tomorrowland blasted off with a bunch of new attractions to replace dated and closed features; expect long lines for the super-high-speed outer space **Rocket Rods.**

And keep your eyes open as Disney prepares to round the century mark—work has already begun on **California Adventure,** a new, separate sister park and great big hotel and resort adjacent to Disneyland that will make its debut in 2001. Until then, related construction obstructions are likely to add time and frustration to your park experience, so be prepared.

ADMISSION, HOURS & INFORMATION   Admission to the park, including unlimited rides and all festivities and entertainment, is $39 for adults and children over 11, $37 for seniors 60 and over, $29 for children 3 to 11, free for children under 3. Parking is $6. Two- and three-day passes are available; in addition, some area accommodations offer lodging packages that include admission for 1 or more days.

Disneyland is open every day, but hours vary. Call (☎ 714/781-4565 or 213/ 626-8605, ext. 4565) for information that applies to the time of your visit. The park usually is open from 9 or 10am to 6 or 7pm on weekdays, fall through spring; and from 8 or 9am to midnight or 1am on weekends, holidays, and during winter, spring, or summer vacation periods.

If you've never been to Disneyland and would like a copy of the *Souvenir Guide* to orient yourself before you go, write to Disneyland Guest Relations, P.O. Box 3232, Anaheim, CA 92803. Or pick up a copy of *The Unofficial Guide to Disneyland* (Macmillan Travel) at your local bookstore.

DISNEY TIPS   Disneyland is busiest from mid-June to mid-September and on weekends and school holidays year-round. Peak hours are from noon to 5pm; visit the most popular rides before and after these hours, and you'll cut your waiting times substantially. If you plan to arrive during a busy time, buy your tickets in advance and get a jump on the crowds at the ticket counters. Advance tickets may be purchased through Disneyland's Web site (www.disneyland.com), at Disney stores in the United States, or by calling the ticket mail order line (☎ **714/781-4043**).

Disneyland

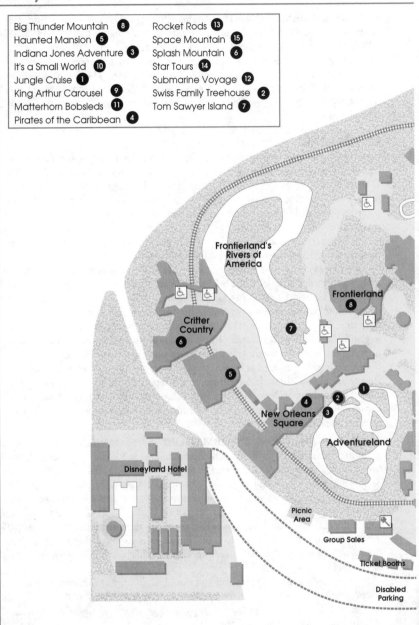

Big Thunder Mountain 8
Haunted Mansion 5
Indiana Jones Adventure 3
It's a Small World 10
Jungle Cruise 1
King Arthur Carousel 9
Matterhorn Bobsleds 11
Pirates of the Caribbean 4

Rocket Rods 13
Space Mountain 15
Splash Mountain 6
Star Tours 14
Submarine Voyage 12
Swiss Family Treehouse 2
Tom Sawyer Island 7

Frontierland's Rivers of America

Frontierland
8

Critter Country
6

7

5

New Orleans Square

4 2 1
3

Adventureland

Disneyland Hotel

Picnic Area

Group Sales

Ticket Booths

Disabled Parking

220

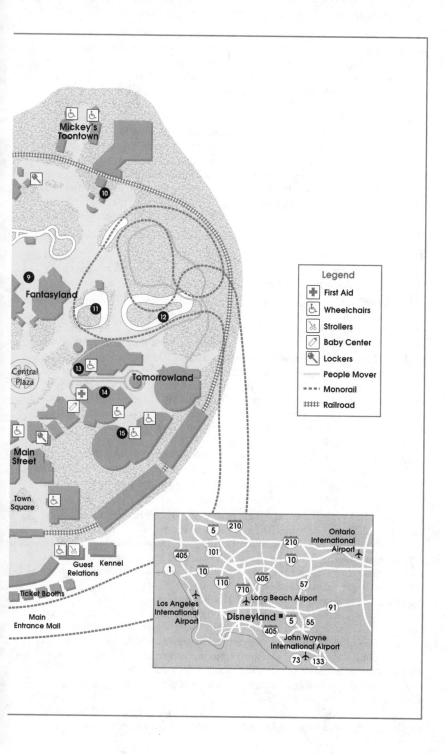

Many visitors tackle Disneyland systematically, beginning at the entrance and working their way clockwise around the park. But a better plan of attack is to arrive early and run to the most popular rides—Rocket Rods, the Indiana Jones Adventure, Star Tours, Space Mountain, Big Thunder Mountain Railroad, Splash Mountain, the Haunted Mansion, and Pirates of the Caribbean. Lines for these rides can last an hour or more in the middle of the day.

If you're going to spend the night in Anaheim, you might want to consider staying at the **Disneyland Hotel.** Hotel guests get to enter the park early almost every day and enjoy the major rides before the lines form. The amount of time varies from day to day, but usually you can enter 1½ hours early. Call ahead to check the schedule.

Attendance falls dramatically during the winter, so the park offers discounted (about 25% off) admission to Southern California residents, who may buy up to six tickets per ZIP code verification. If you'll be visiting the park with someone who lives here, be sure to take advantage.

TOURING THE PARK

The Disneyland complex is divided into several theme "lands," each of which has a number of rides and attractions that are, more or less, related to that land's theme.

MAIN STREET U.S.A.   At the park's entrance, Main Street U.S.A. is a cinematic version of turn-of-the-century small-town America. The whitewashed Rockwellian fantasy is lined with gift shops, candy stores, a soda fountain, and a silent theater that continuously runs early Mickey Mouse films. Here you'll find the practical things you might need, such as stroller rentals and storage lockers.

Because there are no rides, it's best to tour Main Street during the middle of the afternoon, when lines for rides are longest, and in the evening, when you can rest your feet in the theater that features "Great Moments with Mr. Lincoln," a patriotic (and audio-animatronic) look at America's 16th president. There's always something happening on Main Street; stop in at the information booth to the left of the main entrance for a schedule of the day's events.

You might start your day by circumnavigating the park by train. An authentic 19th-century steam engine pulls open-air cars around the park's perimeter. Board at the Main Street Depot and take a complete turn around the park, or disembark at any one of the lands.

ADVENTURELAND   Inspired by the most exotic regions of Asia, Africa, India, and the South Pacific, Adventureland is home to several popular rides. This is where you'll find the **Swiss Family Treehouse.** On the **Jungle Cruise,** passengers board a large authentic-looking Mississippi River paddleboat and float along an Amazon-like river. En route, audio-animatronic wild animals and hostile natives threaten the boat, while a tour guide entertains with running patter.

A spear's throw away is the **Enchanted Tiki Room,** one of the most sedate attractions in Adventureland. Inside, you can sit down and watch a 20-minute musical comedy featuring electronically animated tropical birds, flowers, and "tiki gods."

The **Indiana Jones Adventure** is Adventureland's newest ride. Based on the Steven Spielberg films, this ride takes adventurers into the Temple of the Forbidden Eye, in joltingly realistic all-terrain vehicles. Riders follow Indy and experience the perils of bubbling lava pits, whizzing arrows, fire-breathing serpents, collapsing bridges, and the familiar cinematic tumbling boulder (an effect that's very realistic in the front seats!). Disney "Imagineers" reached new heights with the design of this ride's line, which—take my word for it—has so much detail throughout its twisting path that 30 minutes or more simply flies by.

Disney Dossier

Believe it or not, the "Happiest Place on Earth" keeps more than a few skeletons—as well as some just plain interesting facts—in its closet. Did you know?:

- Disneyland was carved out of orange groves, and the original plans called for carefully chosen individual trees to be left standing and included in the park's landscaping. On groundbreaking day, July 21, 1954, each tree in the orchard was marked with a ribbon—red to be cut and green to be spared. But the bulldozer operator went through and mowed down every tree indiscriminately—no one had foreseen his color-blindness.

- Disneyland designers used forced perspective in the construction of many of the park's structures, giving the illusion of height and dramatic proportions while keeping the park a manageable size. The buildings on **Main Street U.S.A.,** for example, are 90% scale on the first floor, 80% on the second, and so forth. The stones on **Sleeping Beauty Castle** are carved in diminishing scale from the bottom to the top, giving it the illusion of towering height.

- The faces of the **Pirates of the Caribbean** were modeled after some early staff members of Walt Disney Imagineering. They also lent their names to the second-floor "businesses" along Main Street U.S.A.

- Walt Disney maintained two apartments inside Disneyland. His private apartment above the **Town Square Fire Station** has been kept just as it was when he lived there.

- The elaborately carved horses on Fantasyland's **King Arthur Carousel** are 100 to 120 years old; Walt Disney found them lying neglected in storage at Coney Island in New York, and brought them home to be carefully cleaned and restored.

- **It's a Small World** was touted at its opening as "mingling the waters of the oceans and seas around the world with Small World's Seven Seaways." This was more than a publicity hoax—records from that time show such charges as $21.86 for a shipment of seawater from the Caribbean.

- Disneyland's peaceful atmosphere was disturbed during the summer of 1970 by a group of radical Vietnam protesters who invaded the park. They seized **Tom Sawyer Island** and raised the Viet Cong flag over the fort before being expelled by riot specialists.

- **Indiana Jones: Temple of the Forbidden Eye,** Disneyland's newest thrill ride, won't be experienced the same way by any two groups of riders. Like a sophisticated computer game, the course is programmed with so many variables in the action that there are 160,000 possible combinations of events.

- After the 24-year run of the enormously popular **Main Street Electrical Parade** ended in 1996, 700,000 of the floats' light bulbs were sold, at $10 apiece. The proceeds went to several local charities.

NEW ORLEANS SQUARE   A large, grassy green dotted with gas lamps, New Orleans Square is home to the **Haunted Mansion.** It's the most high-tech ghost house we've ever seen. The spookiness has been toned down so kids won't get nightmares, and the events inside are as funny as they are scary.

Even more fanciful is **Pirates of the Caribbean,** one of Disneyland's most popular rides. Visitors float on boats through mock underground caves, entering an enchanting world of swashbuckling, rum-running, and buried treasure. Even in the middle of the afternoon you can dine by the cool moonlight and to the sound of crickets in the Blue Bayou restaurant, the best dining choice in the land.

CRITTER COUNTRY An ode to the backwoods, Critter Country is a sort of Frontierland without those pesky settlers. Little kids like to sing along with the audio-animatronic critters in the musical **Country Bear Jamboree** show. Older kids and grown-ups head straight for **Splash Mountain,** one of the largest water flume rides in the world. Loosely based on the Disney movie *Song of the South,* the ride is lined with about 100 characters who won't stop singing "Zip-A-Dee-Doo-Dah." Be prepared to get wet, especially if someone sizable is in the front seat of your log-shaped boat.

FRONTIERLAND Inspired by 19th-century America, Frontierland is full of dense "forests" and broad "rivers" inhabited by hearty-looking (but, luckily, not hearty-smelling) "pioneers." You can take a raft to **Tom Sawyer's Island,** a do-it-yourself play area with balancing rocks, caves, and a rope bridge, and board the **Big Thunder Mountain Railroad,** a runaway roller coaster that races through a deserted 1870s gold mine. You'll also find a petting zoo and an Abe Lincoln–style log cabin here; both are great for exploring with the little ones.

On Saturdays, Sundays, and holidays, and during vacation periods, head to Frontierland's **Rivers of America** after dark to see the FANTASMIC! show. It mixes magic, music, live performers, and sensational special effects. Just as he did in *The Sorcerer's Apprentice,* Mickey Mouse appears and uses his magical powers to create giant water fountains, enormous flowers, and fantasy creatures. There's plenty of pyrotechnics, lasers, and fog, as well as a 45-foot-tall dragon that breathes fire and sets the water of the Rivers of America aflame. Cool!

MICKEY'S TOONTOWN This is a colorful, whimsical world inspired by the "Roger Rabbit" films—a wacky, gag-filled land populated by toons. There are several rides, including **Roger Rabbit's CarToonSpin,** but they take a back seat to Toontown itself—a trippy, smile-inducing world without a straight line or right angle in sight. This is a great place to talk with Mickey, Minnie, Goofy, Roger Rabbit, and the rest of your favorite toons. You can even visit their "houses." Mickey's red-shingled home and movie barn are filled with props from some of his greatest cartoons.

FANTASYLAND With a storybook theme, this is the catch-all "land" for stuff that doesn't quite fit anywhere else. Most of the rides are geared to the under-6 set, including the **King Arthur Carousel,** the **Dumbo the Flying Elephant ride,** and the **Casey Jr. Circus Train.** Some, like **Mr. Toad's Wild Ride** and **Peter Pan's Flight,** appeal to grown-ups as well. You'll also find Alice in Wonderland, Snow White's Scary Adventures, Pinocchio's Daring Journey, and more.

The most lauded attraction is **It's a Small World,** a slow-moving indoor river ride through a saccharine nightmare of all the world's children singing the song everybody loves to hate. For a different kind of thrill, try the **Matterhorn Bobsleds,** a zippy roller coaster through chilled caverns and drifting fog banks. It's one of the park's most popular rides.

TOMORROWLAND Conceived as an optimistic look at the future, Tomorrowland has always had a hard time keeping ahead of real advances. 1955's "Rocket to the Moon" became "Mission to Mars" in 1975, only to be a dated laughingstock by the early 1980s. In 1998, Disney architects unveiled a redesigned land that employs an angular, metallic look popularized by futurists like Jules Verne.

The high-speed ride **Rocket Rods** joined Tomorrowland favorites **Space Mountain,** a pitch-black indoor roller coaster that assaults your equilibrium and ears, and **Star Tours,** the original Disney–George Lucas joint venture. It's a 40-passenger StarSpeeder that encounters a space-load of misadventures on the way to the Moon of Endor, achieved with wired seats and video effects (not for the queasy). The line can last an hour or more, but it's worth the wait.

Other new attractions include "Honey, I Shrunk the Audience," which uses a variety of theatrical effects to impart the sensation that you've dwindled to thumbnail size. The interactive pavilion of near-future technology called "Innoventions" is a feature close to what old Walt originally envisioned for Tomorrowland, when he created exhibits like the "House of the Future" and "Bathroom of Tomorrow" that featured imaginative technology of the day.

KNOTT'S BERRY FARM

Cynics say that Knott's Berry Farm is for people who aren't smart enough to find Disneyland. There's no doubt that visitors should tour Disney first, but it's worth staying in a hotel nearby so you can play at Knott's during your stay.

Like Disneyland, Knott's Berry Farm is not without historical merit. Rudolph Boysen crossed a loganberry with a raspberry, calling the resulting hybrid the boysenberry. In 1933, Buena Park farmer Walter Knott planted the boysenberry and launched Knott's berry farm on 10 acres of leased land. When things got tough during the Depression, Mrs. Knott set up a roadside stand, selling pies, preserves, and homecooked chicken dinners. Within a year she was selling 90 meals a day. Lines became so long that Walter decided to create an Old West Ghost Town as a diversion for waiting customers.

The Knott family now owns the farm that surrounds the world-famous Chicken Dinner Restaurant, an eatery serving over a million fried meals a year. And Knott's Berry Farm is the nation's no. 3 (in attendance) family entertainment complex—after the two Disney parks, of course.

Locals flock to Knott's Berry Farm in the second half of October, when the entire park is revamped as "Knott's Scary Farm." The ordinary attractions are made spooky and haunted, every grassy area is transformed into a graveyard or gallows, and even the already-scary rides get special surprise extras, like costumed ghouls who grab your arm in the middle of a roller-coaster ride!

GETTING THERE   Knott's Berry Farm is at 8039 Beach Blvd. in Buena Park. It's about a 5-minute ride north on I-5 from Disneyland. From I-5 or Calif. 91, exit south onto Beach Boulevard. The park is about half a mile south of Calif. 91.

ADMISSION, HOURS & INFORMATION   Admission to the park, including unlimited access to all rides, shows, and attractions, is $35 for adults and children over 11, $25 for seniors 60 and over and children 3 to 11, free for children under 3. Admission is $15 for everyone after 4pm. Parking is $6. Like Disneyland, Knott's offers discounted admission for Southern California residents during the off-season, so if you're bringing local friends or family members along, be sure to take advantage of the bargain. Also like Disneyland, Knott's Berry Farm's hours vary from week to week, so call ahead. The park generally is open during the summer daily from 9am to midnight. The rest of the year, it opens at 10am and closes at 6 or 8pm, except Saturday, when it stays open till 10pm. Knott's is closed December 25. Special hours and prices are in effect during Knott's Scary Farm in late October. Stage shows and special activities are scheduled throughout the day. Pick up a schedule at the ticket booth.

For recorded information, call ☎ **714/220-5200.**

TOURING THE PARK

Knott's Berry Farm maintains its original Old West motif. It's divided into seven "Old Time Adventures" areas.

OLD WEST GHOST TOWN   The park's original attraction is a collection of refurbished 19th-century buildings that have been relocated from deserted Old West towns. You can pan for gold, ride an authentic stagecoach, take rickety train cars through the Calico Mine, get held up aboard the Denver and Rio Grande Calico Railroad, and hiss at the villain during a melodrama in the Birdcage Theater.

FIESTA VILLAGE   Here you'll find a south-of-the-border theme. That means festive markets, strolling mariachis, and wild rides like Montezooma's Revenge and Jaguar!, a roller coaster that includes two heart-in-the-mouth drops and a loop that turns you upside down.

THE ROARING '20s AMUSEMENT AREA   This area contains Sky Tower, a parachute jump and drop with a 20-story free-fall. Other white-knuckle rides include XK-1, an excellent flight simulator "piloted" by the riders; and Boomerang, a state-of-the-art roller coaster that turns riders upside down six times in less than a minute. Kingdom of the Dinosaurs features extremely realistic *Jurassic Park*–like creatures. It's quite a thrill, but it may scare the little kids.

WILD WATER WILDERNESS   This is a $10 million, 3½-acre attraction styled like a turn-of-the-century California wilderness park. The top ride is a white-water adventure called Bigfoot Rapids, with a long stretch of artificial rapids; it's the longest ride of its kind in the world.

CAMP SNOOPY   This will probably be the youngsters' favorite area. It's meant to re-create a wilderness camp in the picturesque High Sierra. Its 6 rustic acres are the playgrounds of Charles Schulz's beloved beagle and his pals, Charlie Brown and Lucy, who greet guests and pose for pictures. The rides here, including Beary Tales Playhouse, are tailor-made for the 6-and-under set.

THUNDER FALLS   Here you can look Mystery Lodge right in the eye. It's a truly amazing high-tech, trick-of-the-eye attraction based on the legends of local Native Americans. Don't miss this wonderful theater piece.

THE BOARDWALK   The park's newest theme area is a salute to Southern California's beach culture. The main attraction is Windjammer, a dual roller coaster originally intended to evoke the flips and glides of windsurfing, but often advertised as a twister tornado.

WHERE TO STAY IN THE DISNEYLAND AREA
EXPENSIVE

✪ **The Disneyland Hotel.** 1150 W. Cerritos Ave. (west of the Disneyland parking lot), Anaheim, CA 92802. ☎ **714/778-6600.** Fax 714/965-6597. 1,198 units. A/C MINIBAR TV TEL. $175–$270 double; from $425 suite. AE, MC, V. Parking $10.

The "Official Hotel of the Magic Kingdom," attached to Disneyland by a monorail system that runs right to the hotel, is the perfect place to stay if you're doing the park. You'll be able to return to your room anytime, whether to take a much-needed nap or to change your soaked shorts after your Splash Mountain adventure. Best of all, hotel guests get to enter the park early almost every day and enjoy the major rides before the lines form. The amount of time varies from day to day, but usually you can enter 1½ hours early. Call ahead to check the schedule.

The theme hotel is a wild attraction unto itself. The rooms aren't fancy, but they're comfortably and attractively furnished, like a good-quality business hotel, and have balconies. In-room amenities include hair dryers, movie channels (with free Disney Channel, naturally), irons, and ironing boards. Many rooms feature framed reproductions of rare Disney conceptual art. The beautifully landscaped hotel is an all-inclusive resort, offering six restaurants, five cocktail lounges, every kind of service desk imaginable, a "wharf-side" bazaar, a walk-under waterfall, and even an artificial white-sand beach. The complex includes the adjoining Pacific Hotel, which offers a Disney version of Asian tranquillity (including a fine and pricey Japanese restaurant).

When you're planning your trip, inquire about multiple-day packages that allow you to take on the park at your own pace and usually include free parking.

Dining: The best restaurant is Stromboli's, an Italian-American eatery that serves all the pasta staples. Kids love Goofy's Kitchen, where the family can enjoy breakfast and dinner with Disney characters.

Amenities: Three large heated outdoor pools, complete health club, putting green, shuffleboard and croquet courts, concierge, room service, laundry, shoeshine, nightly turn-down, baby-sitting, special children's programs, beauty salon, 20 shops and boutiques.

Sheraton Anaheim Hotel. 1015 W. Ball Rd. (at I-5), Anaheim, CA 92802. ☎ **800/325-3535** or 714/778-1700. Fax 714/535-3889. 526 units. A/C MINIBAR TV TEL. $170–$190 double; $290–$360 suite. AE, CB, DC, MC, V. Free parking and Disneyland shuttle.

This hotel rises to the festive theme-park occasion with its fanciful English Tudor architecture; it's a castle that lures business conventions, Disney-bound families, and local high school proms. The public areas are quiet and elegant—intimate gardens with fountains and koi ponds, plush lobby and lounges—which can be a pleasing touch after a frantic day at the amusement park. The rooms are modern and unusually spacious, but otherwise not distinctive. A large swimming pool sits in the center of the complex, surrounded by attractive landscaping. Don't be put off by the high rack rates; rooms commonly go for $100 to $130, even on busy summer weekends.

Dining: The Garden Court Bistro offers indoor and outdoor dining. The California Deli, open from 6am to midnight, serves standard delicatessen fare. There's also a cocktail lounge.

Amenities: Heated outdoor pool, sundeck, room service, laundry service, concierge, overnight shoeshine, nightly turn-down, gift shop.

WestCoast Anaheim Hotel. 1855 S. Harbor Blvd. (south of Katella Ave.), Anaheim, CA 92802. ☎ **800/426-0670** or 714/750-1811. Fax 714/971-2485. 500 units. A/C TV TEL. $160 double. AE, CB, DC, DISC, JCB, MC, V. Parking $8; free Disneyland shuttle.

Although this hotel, in the Anaheim Convention Center complex (across the street from Disneyland), draws primarily a business crowd, it has much to appeal to the leisure traveler. The contemporary, comfortable rooms in the 12-story tower all have balconies overlooking either Disneyland or the hotel's luxurious pool area, which includes a large heated pool, deluxe spa, attractive sundeck, and snack and cocktail-bar gazebo. The front desk can provide guests with many in-room amenities upon request (including free hair dryers, irons and ironing boards, fax machines, and refrigerators). The hotel offers laundry and valet, an activities desk, room service, and a gift shop. The Old West frontier-themed restaurant serves steak and seafood along with a few colorful game selections.

MODERATE

Anaheim Plaza Hotel. 1700 S. Harbor Blvd., Anaheim, CA 92802. ☎ **800/228-1357** or 714/772-5900. Fax 714/772-8386. 300 units. A/C TV TEL. $79–$119 double; from $175 suite. AE, DC, DISC, MC, V. Free parking and Disneyland shuttle.

You can easily cross the street to Disneyland's main gate, or take the Anaheim Plaza's free shuttle. Once you return, you'll appreciate the way this 32-year-old hotel's clever design shuts out the noisy world. In fact, the seven two-story garden buildings remind me more of 1960s Waikiki than busy Anaheim. The Olympic-size heated outdoor pool and whirlpool are unfortunately surrounded by Astroturf, but the new management recently completed a total room renovation, so there's always hope. The overhaul didn't change the light-filled modern lobby, or the friendly rates, which often drop as low as $49. There's room service from the casual cafe in the lobby, plus valet service and coin-operated laundry.

Best Western Anaheim Stardust. 1057 W. Ball Rd., Anaheim, CA 92802. ☎ **800/222-3639** or 714/774-7600. Fax 714/535-6953. 121 units. A/C TV TEL. $70–$85 double; $105 family room. Rates include full breakfast. AE, DC, DISC, MC, V. Free parking and Disneyland shuttle.

Located on the back side of Disneyland, this modest hotel will appeal to the budget-conscious traveler who isn't willing to sacrifice everything. All rooms have a refrigerator and microwave, breakfast is served in a refurbished train dining car, and you can relax by the large outdoor heated pool and spa while using the laundry room. The extra-large family rooms accommodate virtually any brood, and shuttles run regularly to the park.

Buena Park Hotel. 7675 Crescent Ave. (at Grand), Buena Park, CA 90620. ☎ **800/422-4444** or 714/995-1111. Fax 714/828-8590. www.buenaparkhotel.com. 320 units. A/C TV TEL. $129–$139 double; $199–$279 suite. AE, CB, DC, DISC, MC, V. Free parking and Disneyland shuttle.

Within easy walking distance of Knott's Berry Farm, the Buena Park Hotel also offers a free shuttle to Disneyland, 7 miles away. The pristine lobby has the look of a business-oriented hotel, and that it is. But vacationers can also benefit from the elevated level of service. Be sure to ask about Executive Club rates as well as Knott's or Disneyland package deals. The rooms in the 9-story tower were tastefully redecorated in 1999. Facilities and services include room service, a heated outdoor pool and spa, two restaurants and a 1950s–60s dance club, and a rental-car desk.

Candy Cane Inn. 1747 S. Harbor Blvd., Anaheim, CA 92802. ☎ **800/345-7057** or 714/774-5284. Fax 714/772-5462. 173 units. A/C TV TEL. $74–$129 double. Rates include expanded continental breakfast. AE, DC, DISC, MC, V. Free parking and Disneyland shuttle.

Take your standard U-shaped motel court with outdoor corridors, spruce it up with cobblestone drives and walkways, old-time street lamps, and flowering vines engulfing the balconies of attractively painted rooms, and you have the Candy Cane. The face-lift worked, making this motel near Disneyland's main gate a treat for the stylish bargain hunter. The guest rooms are decorated in bright floral motifs with comfortable furnishings, including queen beds and a separate dressing and vanity area. Breakfast is served in the courtyard, where you can also splash around in a heated pool, spa, or kids' wading pool.

Howard Johnson Hotel. 1380 S. Harbor Blvd., Anaheim, CA 92802. ☎ **800/422-4228** or 714/776-6120. Fax 714/533-3578. www.hojoanaheim.com. 320 units. A/C TV TEL. $79–$104 double. AE, CB, DC, DISC, JCB, MC, V. Free parking and Disneyland trolley.

This hotel occupies an enviable location, directly opposite Disneyland, and a cute San Francisco trolley car runs to and from the park every 30 minutes. Guest rooms were renovated in 1999. They're divided among several low-profile buildings, all with balconies opening onto a central garden with two heated pools for adults and one for children. Garden paths lead under eucalyptus and olive trees to a splashing circular fountain. During the summer you can see the nightly fireworks display at Disneyland from the upper balconies of the park-side rooms. Try to avoid the rooms in the back buildings, which get some freeway noise. Services and facilities include in-room movies, coffeemakers, room service from the attached Coco's Restaurant, gift shop, game room, laundry service, coin-laundry room, airport shuttle, and family lodging/Disney admission packages. We think it's pretty classy for a HoJo's.

Jolly Roger Inn & Suites. 640 W. Katella Ave. (west of Harbor Blvd.), Anaheim, CA 92802. ☎ **800/446-1555** or 714/772-7621. Fax 714/772-2308. 240 units. A/C TV TEL. $119–$149 double; $259–$289 suite. Midweek, off-season, and other discounts available. AE, DC, DISC, MC, V. Free parking and Disneyland shuttle.

The only thing still sporting a buccaneer theme here is the adjoining Jolly Roger Restaurant, and even that may fall by the wayside during the Jolly Roger's massive renovation. In early 2000, management expects to unveil two all-suite towers, five-story annexes to the original two-story L-shaped motel. The comfortable but blandly furnished older rooms have always been our favorites, because they're quiet and have a palm-shaded heated pool in the center courtyard. We hear they'll be converted into suites in the fall of 2000, so get a deal on the older rooms while you can. Or check out the brand-new suites—but be sure to get a discounted or package rate. Across the driveway is the swashbuckling restaurant, where dinner will set you back more than a few doubloons. The all-day coffee shop is more reasonable, and there's nightly entertainment and dancing in the lounge. Conveniently located across the street from Disneyland, the Jolly Roger also has meeting and banquet rooms, plus another outdoor pool and a spa, beauty salon, and gift shop.

INEXPENSIVE

Colony Inn. 7800 Crescent Ave. (west of Beach Blvd.), Buena Park, CA 90620. ☎ **800/98-COLONY** or 714/527-2201. Fax 714/826-3826. 130 units. A/C TV TEL. $49–$98 double or suite. AE, MC, V. Free parking.

Although it's composed of two modest U-shaped motels, the recently refurbished Colony Inn has a lot to offer. It's the closest lodging to Knott's Berry Farm's south entrance and is just 10 minutes away from Disneyland. Management cheerfully offers discount coupons for Knott's and other nearby attractions, as well as complimentary morning coffee and doughnuts. The rooms are spacious—doubles sleep up to four people, suites up to eight—and comfortably outfitted with conservatively styled furnishings. There are two pools, two wading pools, two saunas, and a coin-operated laundry on the premises.

WHERE TO DINE IN THE DISNEYLAND AREA

Inland Orange County isn't known for its restaurants, most of which are branches of reliable California or national chains you'll easily recognize.

We've listed a few intriguing options, but if you're visiting the area just for the day, you'll probably eat inside the theme parks; there are plenty of restaurants to choose from at both Disneyland and Knott's Berry Farm. At Disneyland, in the Creole-themed **Blue Bayou,** you can sit under the stars inside the Pirates of the Caribbean ride—no matter what time of day it is. At Knott's, try the fried-chicken dinners and boysenberry pies at Mrs. Knott's historic **Chicken Dinner Restaurant.**

EXPENSIVE

Chanteclair. 18912 MacArthur Blvd. (opposite John Wayne Airport), Irvine. ☎ **949/752-8001.** Reservations recommended. Main courses $9–$16 at lunch, $22–$30 at dinner. AE, CB, DC, DISC, JCB, MC, V. Mon–Fri 11:30am–2:30pm and 6–10pm, Sat 5:30–10pm. Valet parking $2. By car, take I-405 south to MacArthur Blvd. exit. COUNTRY FRENCH.

Chanteclair is expensive and a little difficult to reach, but it's worth seeking out. Designed in the style of a provincial French inn, the rambling stucco structure centers around a garden court and houses several dining and drinking areas, each with its own ambiance. The antique-furnished restaurant has five fireplaces.

At lunch you can try reasonably priced dishes that'd be dinner anywhere else: grilled scallops and prawns on tomato risotto, lamb loin in port-ginger reduction, or pan-seared calves' liver. Dinner is a worthwhile splurge that might begin with a lobster bisque with cognac, Beluga caviar, or sautéed foie gras. Main dishes include an elegant mixed grill of filet mignon, lamb, and quail; tournedo of ahi tuna and foie gras with shiitake-merlot sauces; and showy Long island duckling flamed tableside with Grand Marnier. Many patrons dress up for dinner here.

Mr. Stox. 1105 E. Katella Ave. (east of Harbor Blvd.), Anaheim. ☎ **714/634-2994.** www. MrStox.com. Reservations recommended. Main courses $14–$28. AE, CB, DC, DISC, MC, V. Mon–Fri 11:30am–2:30pm; daily 5:30–10pm. AMERICAN.

Mr. Stox serves hearty steaks and fresh seafood in an early-California manor-house setting. Specialties include roast prime rib and mesquite-broiled fish, veal, and lamb. Chef Scott Raczek particularly excels at reduction sauces and innovative herbal preparations. Sandwiches and salads are also available. The homemade breads and desserts, such as chocolate mousse cake, are unexpectedly good. Mr. Stox has an enormous and renowned wine cellar, and there's live entertainment nightly.

MODERATE

Felix Continental Cafe. 36 Plaza Sq. (at the corner of Chapman and Glassell), Orange. ☎ **714/633-5842.** Reservations recommended for dinner. Main courses $6–$14. AE, DC, MC, V. Mon–Thurs 7am–9pm, Fri 7am–10pm, Sat 8am–10pm, Sun 8am–9pm. CUBAN/SPANISH.

If you like the re-created Main Street in the Magic Kingdom, you'll love the historic 1886 town square in the city of Orange, on view from the cozy sidewalk tables outside the Felix Continental Cafe. Dining on traditional Cuban specialties (such as citrus-marinated chicken, black beans and rice, and fried plantains) and watching traffic spin around the magnificent fountain and rose bushes of the plaza evokes old Havana or Madrid rather than the cookie-cutter Orange County communities just blocks away. The food receives praise from restaurant reviewers and loyal locals alike.

Peppers Restaurant and Nightclub. 12361 Chapman Ave. (west of Harbor Blvd.), Garden Grove. ☎ **714/740-1333.** Reservations recommended on weekends. Main courses $9–$14. AE, CB, DC, DISC, MC, V. Mon–Thurs 11am–10pm, Fri–Sat 11am–11pm, Sun 10am–10pm. CALIFORNIA/MEXICAN.

This colorful restaurant just south of Disneyland looks like a partying kind of place, and it doesn't disappoint. The varied menu features mesquite-broiled dishes and fresh seafood daily. Mexican specialties include lots of variations on tacos and burritos, but the grilled meats and fish are best, especially the signature King Fajitas, with crab legs or lobster tails. There's dancing to top-40 hits nightly starting at 9pm, and on Monday nights a Mexican group plays live music. There's a free shuttle to and from six area hotels between 6pm and the nightclub closing time of 2am.

Renata's Caffè Italiano. 227 E. Chapman Ave. (at Grand), Orange. ☎ **714/771-4740.** Reservations recommended for dinner. Main courses $8–$15. AE, DISC, MC, V. Mon–Thurs 11am–9pm, Fri 11am–10pm, Sat 4–10pm. ITALIAN.

Near Felix Cafe in the historic plaza district, owner Renata Cerchiari draws a steady stream of regulars with good if not great contemporary Italian specialties. We found the charming patio dining in this small-town atmosphere a welcome change from Orange County's frantic pace (particularly if you're staying by the amusement parks). The wide selection of appetizers and pasta dishes is more authentic and reasonably priced than anywhere else, although the creamy Caesar salad wins higher marks than the disappointing cannoli.

5 Julian: Apple Pies & More

60 miles NE of San Diego; 60 miles SE of Temecula; 35 miles W of Anza–Borrego Desert State Park

A trip to Julian (pop. 1,500) is a trip back in time. The old gold-mining town, now best known for its apples, has some good eateries and a handful of cute B&Bs, but its popularity is based on the fact that it provides a chance for city-weary folks to get away from it all.

People first ventured into these fertile hills in search of gold in the late 1860s; they discovered it in 1870 near where the Julian Hotel stands today, and 18 mines sprang up like mushrooms. During all the excitement, four cousins—all former Confederate soldiers from Georgia, two with the last name Julian—founded the town of Julian. The mines produced up to an estimated $13 million worth of gold in their day.

Before you leave, try Julian's apple pies; whether the best pies come from Mom's Pies or the Julian Pie Company is always a toss-up. Sample all of them and decide for yourself.

ESSENTIALS

GETTING THERE   You can make the 90-minute trip on Highway 78 or I-8 to Highway 79. I suggest taking one route going and the other coming back. Highway 79 winds through scenic Rancho Cuyamaca State Park, while Highway 78 traverses open country and farmland.

This is a relatively slow, but inexpensive, process. You start by taking the trolley from San Diego to the El Cajon Station, then catching the Northeast Rural bus to Julian. The bus runs in the afternoon Monday through Saturday only. The one-way trip costs $2.50, including the trolley. You must have exact change (show your trolley stub and you pay only an additional $1). Try to reserve your seat at least 24 hours in advance; call ☎ 760/767-4BUS between 7am and noon and 2 and 5pm Monday through Saturday, or leave a message on the answering machine.

VISITOR INFORMATION   For a brochure on what to see and do in Julian, contact the **Julian Chamber of Commerce,** corner of Main and Washington streets, P.O. Box 413, Julian, CA 92036 (☎ 760/765-1857; www.icsol.com/west/julian), where staffers always have enthusiastic suggestions for local activities. The office is open daily 10am to 4pm.

SOME HELPFUL TIPS   Once in Julian, you'll need a car if you want to stay at a B&B outside town. However, Main Street is only 6 blocks long, and some lodgings, shops, and cafes are on it or a block away. Town maps and accommodations flyers are available from Town Hall, on Main Street at Washington Street. Public rest rooms are behind the Town Hall. There's no self-service laundry (so come prepared), but you'll find a post office, a liquor store, and a few grocery stores. Shops are often closed on Monday and Tuesday. The town has a 24-hour hot line (☎ 760/765-0707) that provides information on lodging, dining, shops, activities, upcoming events, weather, and road conditions.

SPECIAL EVENTS   Julian's popular **Arts and Crafts Show** is held every weekend between mid-September and the end of November. Local artisans display their wares; there's also plenty of cider and apple pie, plus entertainment and brilliant fall foliage.

The **Wildflower Show** is a weeklong event sponsored by the local Women's Club. Held in Julian's historic Town Hall, the event was initiated in 1926, and features displays of native plants; it takes place in early May.

One event that's better than its name is the **Julian Weed Show,** which takes place over the second half of August. Artwork and arrangements culled from the area's myriad wildflowers and indigenous plants (OK, weeds) are displayed and sold during the festival.

If you arrive on the **Fourth of July,** count on participating in a community barbecue and seeing a quilt exhibition and parade.

It's also fun to visit in **December,** when activities include caroling and a living nativity pageant, and the town takes on a winter-wonderland appearance. Over the first 2 weekends in December, the members of the Julian Bed and Breakfast Guild hold open houses with complimentary refreshments.

The Chamber of Commerce has further details on these and other local events.

TOURING THE TOWN

If you've never heard of Julian, then you're in for a treat. While Wal-Mart (no offense) and McDonald's (no offense) have permeated formerly unspoiled mountain resorts like Big Bear and Mammoth, this 1880s gold-mining town has managed to retain a rustic, woodsy sense of its historic origins. Radiating the dusty aura of the Old West, Julian offers an abundance of early California history, quaint Victorian streets filled with apple pie shops and antique stores, crisp fresh air, and friendly people.

Be forewarned, however, that Julian's charming downtown can become exceedingly crowded during the fall harvest season. Consider making your trip another time to enjoy this unspoiled relic with a little privacy (rest assured, apple pies are baking around town year-round). At around 4,500 feet elevation, the autumn air is crisp and bracing, and Julian sees a dusting (and often more) of snow during the winter.

The best way to experience tiny Julian is on foot. Two or three blocks of Main Street offer plenty of diversion for an afternoon or longer, depending on how much pie you stop to eat. And don't worry, you'll grow accustomed to constant apple references very quickly here—the humble fruit has proven to be more of an economic boom than gold ever was.

After stopping in at the Chamber of Commerce in the old Town Hall—check out the vintage photos of Julian's yesteryear—cross the street to the **Julian Drug Store,** 2134 Main St. (☎ **760/765-0332**), an old-style soda fountain serving sparkling sarsaparilla and conjuring images of boys in buckskin and girls in bonnets. Built in 1886, the brick structure is on the National Historic Register—like many other well-preserved buildings in town—and is jam-packed with local memorabilia. Open hours are Monday through Thursday 9am to 6pm, Friday and Saturday 9am to 8pm, Sunday 10am to 5pm.

The **Eagle and High Peak Mines** (ca. 1870), at the end of C Street (☎ **760/765-0036**), although seeming to be a tourist trap, offer an interesting and educational look at the town's one-time economic mainstay. Tours take you underground to the 1,000-foot hard rock tunnel to see the mining and milling process; antique engines and authentic tools are on display. Tours are given between 10am and 3pm daily; admission is $7 for adults, $3 for children over 5, $1 for children under 6.

You'll certainly see one of Suzanne Porter's horse-drawn carriages clip-clopping around town. Some might think it touristy, while others will wax nostalgic for New York's Central Park, but a ride from **Country Carriages** (☎ **760/765-1471**) is a quintessential Julian experience. Even the locals get into the act, snuggling under a blanket on romantic evening rides to celebrate anniversaries and birthdays. The carriages are always booked solid on Christmas Eve. A rambling drive down country roads and through town is $20 per couple; an abbreviated spin around town costs $5 per adult, $2 per child. Call for reservations, or stop by when one of the carriages is parked in front of the drugstore.

APPLE PIES

You won't be able to resist partaking of the apple pie so beloved in these parts. I recommend the **Julian Pie Company,** 2225 Main St. (☎ **760/765-2449**), possibly the
most charming pie shop of them all. This blue-and-white cottage boasts a small front
patio with umbrella tables, a frilly indoor parlor, and a large patio deck in back where
overhanging apple trees are literally up for grabs. The shop serves original, Dutch,
apple–mountain berry, and no-sugar-added pies as well as cinnamon rolls, walnut
apple muffins, and cinnamon cookies made from pie-crust dough. Light lunches
(soups and sandwiches) are offered as well. Open daily 9am to 5pm.

Another great bakery is the aptly named **Mom's Pies,** 2119 Main St. (☎ 760/
765-2472). Its special attraction is a sidewalk plate-glass window through which you
can observe the Mom-on-duty rolling crust, filling pies, and crimping edges. The shop
routinely bakes several varieties of apple pie and will, with a day's notice, whip up
apple-rhubarb, peach-apple crumb, or any one of a number of specialties. Mom's is
open daily from 9am to 5pm.

SHOPPING

One of the simple pleasures of any weekend getaway is window- or souvenir-shopping
in unfamiliar little shops like the many lining both sides of Main Street. Keep an eye
open for the old barn housing the **Warm Hearth,** 2125 Main St. (☎ **760/765-1022**).
Country crafts, candles, and woven throws sit among the wood stoves, fireplaces, and
barbecues that make up the shop's main business.

Nearby is the **Julian Cider Mill,** 2103 Main St. (☎ **760/765-1430**), where you
can see cider presses at work from October through March. It offers free tastes of the
fresh nectar, and jugs to take home. Throughout the year, the mill also carries the area's
widest selection of food products, from apple butters and jams to berry preserves, several varieties of local honey, candies, and other goodies.

A terrific browsing store is the **Bell, Book and Candle Shoppe,** 2007 Main St.
(☎ 760/765-1377), which specializes in only one of the above—candles, candles,
and more candles. It sells pillars, tapers, hand-carved representational candles, custom
personalized candles, candlesticks, and holders—plus incense, essential oils, and a few
other gift items.

Book lovers will enjoy stopping into the **Old Julian Book House,** 2230 Main St.
(☎ 760/765-1989). Run by P. J. Phillips, a dedicated purveyor of new and anti-
quarian volumes alike, it carries a smattering of maps, sheet music, CDs, and
ephemera, too. This small shop also has a comprehensive, computerized book search
to help track down out-of-print or scarce material throughout the country. Most of
the Main Street merchants are open daily from 10am to 5pm.

There are dozens of **roadside fruit stands and orchards** in the Julian hills; during
autumn they're open all day, every day, but in the off-season some might open only on
weekends or close entirely. Most stands sell, depending on the season, apples, pears,
peaches, cider, jams, jellies, and other homemade foodstuffs. Many are along Highway
78 between Julian and Wynola (3 miles away); there are also stands along Farmers
Road, a scenic country lane leading north from downtown Julian. Happy hunting!

Ask any of the San Diegans who regularly make excursions to Julian; no trip would
be complete without a stop at **Dudley's Bakery,** Highway 78, Santa Ysabel
(☎ **800/225-3348** or 760/765-0488), for a loaf or three of bread. Loaves are stacked
high, and folks are often three deep at the counter clamoring for the 20 (!) varieties of
bread baked fresh daily. Varieties range from raisin-date-nut to jalapeño, with some
garden-variety sourdough and multigrain in between. Dudley's is a local tradition;

built in 1963, it has expanded several times to accommodate its ever-growing business. The bakery is open Wednesday to Sunday 8am to 5pm (and may close early on Sunday).

HISTORIC CEMETERIES

Finally, what's a visit to any historic hamlet without a peek at the headstones in the local cemetery? If this activity appeals to you—as it does to me—then Julian's **Pioneer Cemetery** is a must-see. Contemporary graves belie the haphazard, overgrown look of this hilly burial ground, and the eroded older tombstones tell the intriguing story of Julian's rough pioneer history and ardent patriotism. You can drive in from A Street, but I prefer climbing the steep stairway leading up from Main Street around the corner; until 1924 this ascent was the only point of entry, even for processions. As you climb, imagine carrying a coffin up these steps in the snow.

OUTDOOR PURSUITS IN & AROUND JULIAN

Within 10 miles of Julian are numerous hiking trails that traverse rolling meadows, high chaparral, and thick pine forests. The most spectacular hike is at **Volcan Mountain Preserve,** north of town along Farmers Road; the trail to the top is a moderately challenging hike of around 3½ miles round-trip, with a 1,400-foot elevation gain. From the top, hikers have a panoramic view of the desert, mountains, and sea. Free docent-led hikes are offered year-round (on Saturdays, about one per month). For a hike schedule, call ☎ 760/765-0650.

In **William Heise County Park,** off Frisius Drive outside Pine Hills, the whole family can enjoy hikes ranging from a self-guided nature trail and a cedar-scented forest trail to moderate- to-vigorous trails into the mountains. A ranger kiosk at the entrance dispenses trail maps.

Cuyamaca Rancho State Park covers 30,000 acres along Highway 79 southeast of Julian, the centerpiece of which is Cuyamaca Lake. In addition to lake recreation (for boat rental and fishing information, call ☎ 760/765-0515 or 760/447-8123), there are several sylvan picnic areas, three campgrounds, and 110 miles of hiking trails through the Cleveland National Forest. Activities at the lake include fishing for trout, bass, catfish, bluegill, and crappie, and boating. There's a general store and restaurant at the lake's edge. The fishing fee is $4.75 per day for adults, $2.50 per day for children 8 to 15, free for children under 8. A license is required. Rowboats are $12 per day, and outboard motors an additional $13. Canoes and paddleboats can be rented by the hour for $4 to $7. For a trail map and further information about park recreation, stop in at **park headquarters** on Highway 79 (☎ 760/765-0755) between 8am and 5pm Monday through Friday. An adjacent park museum is open Monday through Friday from 10am to 5pm, Saturday and Sunday 10am to 4pm.

The **Julian Bicycle Company,** 1897 Porter Lane, off Main Street (☎ 760/765-2200), is involved in the Julian Flat Tire Festival, held in mid- or late April, as well as several other biking-related events. Contact the company for specific information and dates, or drop by Wednesday through Saturday from 10am to 5pm.

For a different way to tour, try **Llama Trek,** P.O. Box 2363, Julian (☎ 800/LAMAPAK or 760/765-1890; fax 760/765-1512; www.wikiupbnb.com; e-mail: llamatrek@wikiupbnb.com). You'll lead the llama, which carries packs, for hikes to see rural neighborhoods, a historic gold mine, mountain and lake views, and apple orchards. Rates run $65 to $75 per person and include lunch. Overnight wilderness trips are available.

WHERE TO STAY

Julian is B&B country. At last count, there were almost 20 bed-and-breakfasts—and they fill up quickly for the fall apple harvest season. Many (though not all) are affiliated with the **Julian Bed & Breakfast Guild** (☎ **760/765-1555;** www.julianbnbguild.com), a terrific resource for personal assistance in locating accommodations. The 23 members include private cabins and other accommodations, but the agency specializes in B&Bs.

Three noteworthy choices are the **Artists' Loft** (☎ **760/765-0765**), a peaceful hilltop retreat with two artistically decorated rooms and a cozy cabin with a wood-burning stove; the **Julian White House** (☎ **800/WHT-HOUS** or 760/765-1764), a lovely faux-antebellum mansion 4 miles from Julian in Pine Hills, with four frilly Victorian-style guest rooms; and the romantic **Random Oaks Ranch** (☎ **800/BNB-4344** or 760/765-1094), which features two themed cottages, each with a wood-burning fireplace and outdoor Jacuzzi. To find out more about these and other member properties, call the guild between 9am and 9pm daily, or visit the Web site, which has links to the above-mentioned B&Bs.

A word of advice: Some people make their fall reservations as much as a year in advance; if you haven't booked by mid- to late August, you'll probably be shut out.

Julian Hotel. Main St. and B St., P.O. Box 1856, Julian, CA 92036. ☎ **800/734-5854** or 760/765-0201. Fax 760/765-0327. www.julianhotel.com. 15 units. $72–$125 double; $110–$175 cottage. Rates include full breakfast and afternoon tea. AE, MC, V.

Built in 1897 by freed slave Albert Robinson, this frontier-style hotel is a living monument to the area's gold boom days. Centrally located at the crossroads of downtown, the Julian Hotel isn't as secluded or plush as the many B&Bs in town, but if you seek historically accurate lodgings to complete your weekend time warp, this is the place. The 13 rooms and two cottages have been authentically restored and boast antique furnishings; the inviting private lobby is stocked with books, games, literature on local activities, and a wood-burning stove.

Orchard Hill Country Inn. 2502 Washington St., at Second St., P.O. Box 425, Julian, CA 92036-0425. ☎ **800/71-ORCHARD** or 760/765-1700. Fax 760/765-0290. www.orchardhill.com. 22 units. A/C MINIBAR TV TEL. $160–$265 double. Extra person $25. 2-night minimum stay if including Fri or Sat. Seasonal discounts and packages available. Rates include breakfast and hors d'oeuvres. AE, MC, V. From Calif. 79, turn left on Main St., then right on Washington St.

Hosts Darrell and Pat Straube offer the most upscale lodging in Julian, a two-story lodge and four Craftsman cottages on a hill overlooking the town. Ten guest rooms, a guests-only dining room, and a "great room" with a massive stone fireplace are in the lodge. Twelve suites are in cottages spread over 3 acres of grounds. All units feature contemporary, unfrilly country furnishings, TV/VCRs, and snacks. While rooms in the main lodge feel rather hotel-ish, the cottage suites are secluded and luxurious, with private porches, fireplaces, whirlpool tubs, and robes. Several hiking trails lead from the lodge into adjacent woods.

WHERE TO DINE

Also consider one of Julian's many pie shops, two of which are discussed in "Touring the Town," above.

Julian Cafe. 2112 Main St. ☎ **760/765-2712.** Menu items $2.50–$9. MC, V. Mon, Tues, Thurs 8am–7:30pm, Fri 8am–8:30pm, Sat 7am–9pm, Sun 7am–8:30pm. AMERICAN.

Tasty, filling chicken pie is the specialty here; it's available at lunch for $6.95 or as a full dinner for $8.95. Mashed potatoes come the old-fashioned way, smothered in country gravy. Other home-cooked offerings include fried chicken, liver and onions, meat loaf, and a hot vegetable plate. This is a good place to bring kids; the waitresses are friendly and service is quick, even when it's packed.

Julian Grille. 2224 Main St. (at A St.). ☎ **760/765-0173.** Reservations required Fri–Sun. Main courses $13–$21. AE, MC, V. Daily 11am–3pm; Tues–Sun 5–9pm. AMERICAN.

Set in a cozy cottage festooned with lacy draperies, flickering candles, and a warm hearth, the Grille is the nicest eatery in town. Lunch here is an anything-goes affair, ranging from soups, sandwiches, and large salads to charbroiled burgers and hearty omelets. Dinner features grilled and broiled meats, seafood, and prime rib. I'm partial to delectable appetizers like baked brie with apples and mustard sauce, Baja-style shrimp cocktail, and "Prime tickler" (chunks of prime rib served cocktail-style *au jus* with horseradish sauce). Dinners include soup or salad, hot rolls, potatoes, and vegetable.

Romano's Dodge House. 2718 B St. (just south of Main). ☎ **760/765-1003.** Reservations required for dinner Fri–Sat, recommended other nights. Main courses $8–$16. No credit cards. Wed–Mon 11am–8:30pm. ITALIAN.

Occupying a historic home just off Main Street (vintage photos illustrate the little farmhouse's past), Romano's is proudly the only restaurant in town not serving apple pie. It's a home-style Italian spot, with red-checked tablecloths and straw-clad Chianti bottles. Romano's offers individual lunch pizzas, pastas bathed in rich marinara sauce, veal parmigiana, chicken cacciatore, and the signature dish, pork Juliana (loin chops in a whisky–apple cider sauce). There's seating on a narrow shaded porch, in the wood-plank dining room, and in a little saloon in back.

JULIAN AFTER DARK

Fans of old-style dinner theater will feel right at home at **Pine Hills Dinner Theater** (☎ 760/765-1100), one of North County's more unusual entertainment options for a Friday or Saturday night. Located at the **Pine Hills Lodge,** 2960 La Posada Way (about 2 miles from Julian off Pine Hills Road), the theater has staged more than 80 productions since opening in 1980 in this rustic 1912 building. Theater is usually light and comedic—past productions include *I'm Not Rappaport* and *Last of the Red Hot Lovers*—but in contrast, dinner is a filling buffet of barbecued baby back pork ribs, baked chicken, baked beans, salads, veggies, and thick sheepherder's bread. With advance notice, the kitchen will prepare a vegetarian meal or accommodate other dietary restrictions. Dinner is at 7pm, curtain is 8pm, and the combined ticket costs $28.50 (show only is $14.50).

6 Anza–Borrego Desert State Park

90 miles NE of San Diego; 35 miles E of Julian

The sweeping 600,000-acre Anza–Borrego Desert State Park, the nation's largest contiguous state park, lies mostly within San Diego County, and getting there is as much fun as being there. From Julian, the first 20 minutes of the winding hour-long drive feel as if you're going straight downhill; in fact, it's a 7-mile-long drop called Banner Grade. A famous scene from the 1954 movie *The Long, Long Trailer* with Lucille Ball and Desi Arnaz was shot on the Banner Grade, and countless westerns have been filmed in the Anza–Borrego Desert.

The desert is home to fossils and rocks dating from 540 million years ago; human beings arrived only 10,000 years ago. The terrain ranges in elevation from 15 feet to more than 6,000 feet above sea level. It incorporates dry lake beds, sandstone canyons, granite mountains, palm groves fed by year-round springs, and more than 600 kinds of desert plants. After the spring rains, thousands of wildflowers burst into bloom, transforming the desert into a brilliant palette of pink, lavender, red, orange, and yellow. The rare bighorn sheep can often be spotted navigating rocky hillsides, and an occasional migratory bird stops off on the way to the Salton Sea. A sense of timelessness pervades this landscape; travelers tend to slow down and take a long look around.

Many people also visit the park without caring a bit for desert flora and fauna. They're here to relax and sun themselves in tiny Borrego Springs, a city surrounded by the state park but exempt from regulations limiting commercial development. It is, however, somewhat remote, and its supporters proudly proclaim that Borrego Springs is and will remain what Palm Springs used to be—a small, charming resort town, with more empty lots than built ones. Yes, there are a couple of country clubs, some chic fairway-view homes, a luxurious resort, and a regular influx of celebrity vacationers, but it's still plenty funky. One of the valley's unusual sights is scattered patches of tall, lush palm tree groves, perfectly square in shape: Borrego Springs' tree farms are a major source of landscaping trees for San Diego and surrounding counties.

When planning a trip here, keep in mind that temperatures rise to as high as 115° in summer.

ESSENTIALS

GETTING THERE   Anza–Borrego Desert State Park is about a 2-hour drive from San Diego. The fastest route is I-15 north to the Poway exit, then Highway 78 east at Ramona, continuing to Julian and on to the desert. Highway 79 to county roads S2 and S22 will also get you there. Another option is to take I-8 to Ocotillo, then Highway S2 north. Follow the Southern Overland Stage Route of 1849 (be sure to stop and notice the view at the Carrizo Badlands Overlook) to S3 east into Borrego Springs.

The **Northeast Rural** bus (☎ 760/767-4BUS) connects Julian and Borrego Springs. There is no bus service from San Diego to Borrego Springs, but you can get the Northeast Rural bus in Escondido or El Cajon (the San Diego Trolley connects with the El Cajon Station).

As we go to press, there's a rumor that flights from Palomar Airport will soon provide another form of transportation for desert-bound travelers. The phone number for the **Borrego Airport** is ☎ 760/767-7415.

GETTING AROUND   You don't need a four-wheel-drive vehicle to tour the desert, but you do need to get off the main highways and onto the jeep trails. The Anza–Borrego Desert State Park Visitor Center staff (see below) can tell you which jeep trails are in condition for two-wheel-drive vehicles. You can also call ☎ 760/767-ROAD for information on Borrego Springs road conditions. There's a $5 fee per vehicle per day for a Back Country Permit, which is required to camp or use the jeep trails in the park. You can also explore with Desert Jeep Tours (see below). The Ocotillo Wells area of the park has been set aside for off-road vehicles such as dune buggies and dirt bikes. To use the jeep trails, a vehicle has to be licensed for highway use.

Another good way to see the desert is to tour on a bicycle. Call **Carrizo Bikes** (☎ 760/767-3872) and talk with Dan Cain (a true desert rat) about bike rentals and tours in the area.

ORIENTATION & VISITOR INFORMATION   In Borrego Springs, the Mall is on Palm Canyon Drive, the main drag. Christmas Circle surrounds a grassy park at the entry to town. The **Anza–Borrego Desert State Park Visitor Center** (☎ 760/767-4205 or 760/767-4684 for recorded wildflower information in season; www.anzaborrego.statepark.org) lies just west of the town of Borrego Springs. It supplies

The Desert in Bloom

From mid-March to the beginning of April, the desert wildflowers and cacti are usually in bloom—a hands-down, all-out natural special event that's not to be missed. It's so incredible, there's a hot line to let you know exactly when the blossoms burst forth: ☎ 760/767-4684.

information, maps, and two 15-minute audiovisual presentations, one on the desert's changing faces and the other on wildflowers. The Visitor Center is open October through May daily from 9am to 5pm, June through September weekends from 10am to 5pm.

For information on lodging, dining, and activities, contact the **Borrego Springs Chamber of Commerce,** 622 Palm Canyon Dr., Borrego Springs, CA 92004 (☎ **800/ 59-5524** or 760/767-5555; www.borregosprings.com).

EXPLORING THE DESERT

Remember that when you're touring in this area, hydration is of paramount importance. Whether you're walking, cycling, or driving, always have a bottle of water at your side.

You can explore the desert's stark terrain on one of its trails or on a self-guided driving tour; the Visitor Center can supply maps. For starters, the **Borrego Palm Canyon self-guided hike** (1½ miles each way) starts at the campgrounds near the Visitor Center. It is beautiful, easy to get to, and easy to do, leading in about half an hour to a waterfall and massive fan palms. It's grand for photos early in the morning.

You can also take an organized tour of the desert with **Desert Jeep Tours** (☎ **888/BY-JEEPS** or 619/528-2241; www.desertjeeptours.com). Led by Paul Ford ("Borrego Paul"), tours go to the awesome view point at Font's Point, where you can look out on the Badlands—named by the early settlers because it was an impossible area for moving or grazing cattle. Paul tells his passengers about the history and geology of the area. Scorpion spotting is a favorite after-dark activity. Even if you aren't interested in insects, drive a little way out of town on S22 to admire the starry night sky at its best.

Note: Whether you tour with Paul Ford or on your own, don't miss the sunset view from Font's Point. Savvy travelers plan ahead and bring champagne and beach chairs for the nightly ritual.

If you have only 1 day, a good day trip from San Diego would include driving over on one route, going to the Visitor Center, hiking to Palm Canyon, having a picnic, and driving back to San Diego using another route.

GOLF & BIKING

Golfers will be content on the 18-hole, par-72 championship golf course at **Ram's Hill Country Club** (☎ **760/767-5124;** www.ramshill.com), on Yaqui Pass Road just south of La Casa del Zorro. The 6,886-yard course has seven artificial lakes, and the weekend greens fee is $105. For a thrilling 12-mile bicycle ride down Montezuma Valley Grade, try the Desert Descent offered by **Gravity Activated Sports,** P.O. Box 683, Pauma Valley, CA 92061 (☎ **800/985-4427** or 760/742-2294; fax 760/ 742-2293; www.gasports.com). See "Biking," in chapter 7.

WHERE TO STAY

Borrego Springs is small, but there are enough accommodations to suit all travel styles and budgets. One decent option is **Palm Canyon Resort,** 221 Palm Canyon Dr.

(☎ **800/242-0044** or 760/767-5341), a large complex that includes a moderately priced hotel, RV park, restaurant, and recreational facilities. Camping in the desert is a meditative experience, to be sure; but if you truly want to splurge, you can do that too.

La Casa del Zorro Desert Resort. 3845 Yaqui Pass Rd., Borrego Springs, CA 92004. ☎ **800/824-1884** or 760/767-5323. Fax 760/767-5963. www.lacasadelzorro.com. 77 units. A/C TV TEL. Jan 15–Apr 30 $115 double weekends, $95 weekdays; from $235 suite weekends, $180 weekdays; from $235 casita weekends, $175 weekdays. May 1–31 and Oct 1–Jan 15, $110 double weekends, $85 weekdays; from $165 suite weekends, $115 weekdays; from $190 casitas weekends, $135 weekdays. June 1–Sept 30 $95 double weekends, $75 weekdays; from $105 suite weekends, $80 weekdays; from $125 casita weekends, $95 weekdays. Weekday rates do not apply on holidays. Extra person $10. Tennis, jazz, holiday, and other packages available. AE, CB, DC, DISC, MC, V.

This pocket of heaven on earth was built in 1937, and the tamarind trees that were planted then have grown up around it. Accommodations are scattered around the lushly landscaped grounds; guests can choose from standard hotel rooms, suites, or one-, two-, or three-bedroom adobe casitas with tile roofs. Each casita has a mini-fridge and microwave, some have a fireplace or pool, and each bedroom has a separate bathroom. If you come to this desert oasis during the week, you'll benefit from lower room rates.

Dining/Diversions: The Presidio and Butterfield dining rooms serve breakfast, lunch, and dinner; a breakfast buffet is served poolside on Saturday and Sunday during the summer, indoors the rest of the year. The Fox Den Lounge features live entertainment and dancing. Men are required to wear a jacket and a collared shirt at dinner October through May.

Amenities: Three pools and Jacuzzis, six championship tennis courts, pro shop, nine-hole putting green. Room service (9am to 11pm), bicycle rentals, massage therapy, child care and holiday kids' camp, in-room movies, VCR and movie rentals, free transportation to golf and the airport, beauty shop. Horseshoes, Ping-Pong, volleyball, jogging trails, basketball, shuffleboard, a life-size chess set.

✪ The Palms at Indian Head. 2220 Hoberg Rd., P.O. Box 525, Borrego Springs, CA 92004. ☎ **800/519-2624** or 760/767-7788. Fax 760/767-9717. www.ramonamall.com/ thepalms.html. 10 units. A/C TV. Nov–May $105–$159 double; June–Oct $95 double. Extra person $20. Rates include breakfast. Midweek discounts available. DC, DISC, MC, V. Take S22 into Borrego Springs; at Palm Canyon Dr., S22 becomes Hoberg Rd. Continue north ½ mile.

It takes a sense of nostalgia and an active imagination for most visitors to truly appreciate Borrego Springs' only bed-and-breakfast. The once-chic resort is slowly being renovated by its fervent owners, David and Cynthia Leibert. Originally opened in 1947, then rebuilt after a fire in 1958, the art deco–style hilltop lodge was a favorite hideaway for San Diego's and Hollywood's elite. It played host to movie stars like Bing Crosby, Clark Gable, and Marilyn Monroe. The Leiberts rescued it from extreme disrepair in 1993, clearing away some dilapidated guest bungalows and uncovering original wallpaper, light fixtures, and priceless memorabilia. As soon as they'd restored several rooms in luxurious Southwestern style, they began taking in guests to help finance the ongoing restoration.

Now up to 10 rooms, the inn also boasts a restaurant, the Krazy Coyote (see "Where to Dine," below), that's a culinary breath of fresh air in town. Also completely restored is the 42-by-109-foot pool, with the original subterranean grotto bar behind viewing windows at the deep end. The inn occupies the most envied site in the valley—shaded by palms, adjacent to the state park, with a panoramic view across the entire Anza–Borrego region. A hiking trail begins just steps from the hotel. If you don't mind getting an insider's view of this work-in-progress, the Palms at Indian Head rewards you with charm, comfort, and convenience.

CAMPING

The park has two developed campgrounds. **Borrego Palm Canyon,** with 117 sites, is 2½ miles west of Borrego Springs, near the Visitor Center. Full hookups are available, and there's an easy hiking trail. **Tamarisk Grove,** at Highway 78 and county road S3, has 27 sites. The overnight rate at both is $10 to $15. Both have rest rooms with showers and a campfire program; reservations are a good idea. The park allows open camping along all trail routes. For more information, check with the Visitor Center (☎ 760/767-4205).

WHERE TO DINE

Pickings are slim in Borrego Springs. There's not much between the high-priced (but admittedly excellent) dining room at La Casa del Zorro and an earthy "steakhouse" with glaring neon beer logos and lots of chrome-redolent "hogs" parked out front. Your best bet is the surprisingly good **Krazy Coyote,** which presents trendy ingredients and gourmet preparations previously unheard of in this small town.

Bailey's Cafe. In the Mall, Borrego Springs. ☎ **760/767-3491.** Main courses $3.50–$7.95 at lunch; $5.95–$10.95 at dinner. MC, V. Sept–May daily 6am–8pm; June–Aug Thurs–Mon 6am–8pm. COFFEE SHOP.

Here's an economical little spot to grab a quick bite. Emu burgers from the local emu and ostrich farm are the specialty of the house. Buffalo burgers and Mexican dishes are also popular. Dinner choices include pork chops and chicken-fried steak. The cafe claims its apple pies are better than Julian's. Anything can be packed to go if you'd rather dine overlooking the desert.

The Coffee & Book Store. 590 Palm Canyon Dr. (in the Center). ☎ **760/767-5080.** Most items under $6. MC, V. Daily 6am–4pm. LIGHT FARE.

Rely upon this small but well-stocked shop for books, postcards, maps, and a freshly ground espresso or cup o' joe. It also has a nice selection of sandwiches, salads, muffins, and desserts, making it a reliable choice for a quick breakfast or lunch at cafe tables set amidst the book displays. You can also pack up a pretty good picnic if you're off to explore the desert.

Krazy Coyote Saloon & Grille. In the Palms at Indian Head, 2220 Hoberg Rd. ☎ **760/767-7788.** Main courses $7–$12. AE, MC, V. Open daily; call for seasonal hours. ECLECTIC MENU.

The same style and perfectionism that pervades David and Cynthia Leibert's bed-and-breakfast is evident in this casual restaurant, which overlooks the inn's swimming pool and the vast desert beyond. An eclectic menu encompasses quesadillas, club sandwiches, burgers, grilled meats and fish, and individual gourmet pizzas. The Krazy Coyote also offers breakfast (rich and hearty for an active day, or light and healthy for diet-watchers). The evening ambiance is welcoming and romantic, as the sparse lights of tiny Borrego Springs twinkle on the desert floor below.

7 Tijuana: Going South of the Border

16 miles S of San Diego

Like many large cities in developing nations, Tijuana is a mixture of new and old, rich and poor, modern and traditional. With almost 1.8 million people, it's the second-largest city on the west coast of North America; only Los Angeles is larger. The Mexico you may be expecting—charming town squares and churches, women in colorful embroidered skirts and blouses, bougainvillea spilling out of every orifice—can be found in southern Baja California and even more so in the interior, in places such as San Miguel de Allende and Guanajuato. But that's another trip, and a different guidebook.

What you'll find in Tijuana is poverty—begging in the streets is common—sanitary conditions that may make you nervous, and, surprisingly, a local populace that seems no more or less happy than their north-of-the-border counterparts.

If you're spending a few days or more in Baja, refer to "Baja California: Exploring More of Mexico," later in this chapter.

ESSENTIALS

GETTING THERE   If you plan to visit only Tijuana, I recommend leaving the car behind, because the traffic can be challenging. However, bus tours only give you several hours in Tijuana in the afternoon, so you miss evening activities. Another alternative is walking across the border; you can park in one of the safe long-term parking lots on the San Diego side for about $8 a day, or take the San Diego Trolley to the border. Once you're in Tijuana, it's easier to get around by taxi than to fight the local drivers. Cab fares from the border to downtown Tijuana run about $5.

If you plan to visit the Baja Peninsula south of Tijuana, I suggest driving. Take I-5 south to the Mexican border at San Ysidro. The drive takes about half an hour.

Many car-rental companies in San Diego now allow their cars to be driven into Baja California, at least as far as Ensenada. **Avis** (☎ **619/231-7155**) and **Courtesy** (☎ **619/497-4800**) cars may be driven as far as the 28th parallel and Guerrero Negro, which separates Baja into two states, North and South. **Bob Baker Ford** (☎ **619/297-5001**) and **Colonial Ford** (☎ **619/477-9344**) allow their cars to be driven the entire 1,000-mile stretch of the Baja Peninsula.

Keep in mind that if you drive in, you'll need Mexican auto insurance in addition to your own. You can get it in San Ysidro, just north of the border at the San Ysidro exit; from your car-rental agency in San Diego; or from a AAA office if you're a member.

Another easy way to get to Tijuana from downtown San Diego is to hop aboard the bright-red **trolley** headed for San Ysidro and get off at the last, or San Ysidro, stop (it's nicknamed the Tijuana Trolley for good reason). From there, just follow the signs to walk across the border. It's simple, quick, and inexpensive; the one-way trolley fare is $2. The last trolley to San Ysidro departs downtown around midnight; the last returning trolley from San Ysidro is at 1am. On Saturdays, the trolley runs 24 hours.

Mexicoach/Five Star Tours (☎ **619/232-5049;** fax 619/4575-3075) offers a $2 round-trip fare (children under 5 free) between the border parking lots and trolley stop and downtown Tijuana, with departures every 15 minutes. The Mexicoach stop is at the Tijuana Tourist Terminal, 1025 Av. Revolución (between calles 6 and 7).

Gray Line (☎ **619/491-0011**) offers a tour to Tijuana for $26, $36 with lunch, with a drop-off in the middle of town; you can spend a few hours or all day. **San Diego Mini Tours** (☎ **619/477-8687**) also offers a tour to Tijuana for $26.

GETTING AROUND   If you've come to Tijuana on the San Diego Trolley or if you leave a car on the U.S. side of the border, you will walk through the border crossing. The first structure you'll see on your left is a Visitor Information Center, open daily from 9am to 7pm; ask for a copy of the *Baja Visitor* magazine and the *Baja Times*. From here, you can easily walk into the center of town or take a taxi.

Taxicabs are easy to find; they queue up around most of the visitor hot spots, and drivers often solicit passengers. It's customary to agree upon the rate before stepping into the cab, whether you're going a few blocks or hiring a cab for the afternoon.

One-way rides within the city cost $4 to $8, and tipping is optional. Some cabs are "local" taxis, frequently stopping to take on or let off other passengers during your ride; they are less expensive than private cabs.

VISITOR INFORMATION   Prior to your visit, you can request information, brochures, and maps from the **Tijuana Convention & Visitors Bureau,** P.O. Box 434523, San Diego, CA 92143-4523. Another good idea is to contact **Baja California Tourism Information** (☎ **800/522-1516** in California, Arizona, or Nevada; 800/225-2786 in the rest of the U.S. and Canada; or 619/298-4105; e-mail: impamexicoinfo@worldnet. att.net). These capable folks dispense information and make bookings throughout Baja California.

Once in Tijuana, you can pick up visitor information at the **Mexican Tourism Office** (☎ **011-52-668/8-0555**), which opens daily at 9am, and the **National Chamber of Commerce** (☎ **011-52-668/5-8472**), which is open weekdays only. Both have offices at the corner of Avenida Revolución and Calle 1 (*calle* is "street" in Spanish), and are extremely helpful with maps and orientation, local events of interest, and accommodations.

The Mexican Tourism Office provides legal assistance for visitors who encounter problems while in Tijuana. The following countries have consulate offices in Tijuana: the **United States** (☎ **011-52-668/1-7400**), **Canada** (☎ **84-04-61**), and the **United Kingdom** (☎ **011-52-668/1-7323** or 6-5320).

You can also get a preview of events, restaurants, and more online at **www. tijuananet.com**.

SOME HELPFUL TIPS   The city does not take time for an afternoon siesta; you'll always find shops and restaurants open, as well as people in the streets, which are safe for walking. (Observe the same precautions you would in any large city.) Most people who deal with the traveling public speak English, often very well. To maneuver around someone on a crowded street or in a shop, say "*con permiso*" ("with permission").

CLIMATE & WEATHER   Tijuana's climate is similar to San Diego's. Don't expect sweltering heat just because you're south of the border, and remember that the Pacific waters won't be much warmer than those off San Diego. The first beaches you'll find are about 15 miles south of Tijuana.

CURRENCY   The Mexican currency is the *peso,* but you can easily visit Tijuana (or Rosarito and Ensenada, for that matter) without changing money—dollars are accepted just about everywhere. Many prices are posted in American (indicated with the abbreviation "dlls.") and Mexican "m.n." (*moneda nacional*) currencies—both use the "$" sign. Bring a supply of smaller-denomination ($1, $5, and $10) bills; although change is readily given in American dollars, many merchants are reluctant to break a $20 bill for small purchases. Visa is accepted in many places, but some places will only grudgingly take your card; don't be surprised if the clerk scrutinizes your signature and photo I.D. When using credit cards at restaurants, it's a nice gesture to leave the tip in cash. At press time, the dollar was strong, worth between 9 to 10 pesos.

TAXES & TIPPING   A sales tax of 10%, called an IVA, is added to most bills, including those in restaurants. This does not represent the tip; the bill will read "*IVA incluído,*" but you should add about 15% for the tip if the service warrants.

TELEPHONES   To call Mexico from the United States, after dialing "011" for an international line, dial "52" (the country code), then the three-digit city code (indicated in the listings in front of the slash), followed by the five-digit local number.

EXPLORING TIJUANA

One of the first major tourist attractions below the border is also one of the strangest—the **Museo de Cera** ("Wax Museum"), Calle 1 between avenidas Revolución and Madero (☎ 011-52-668/8-2478). Come to think of it, what wax museum isn't strange? But that doesn't explain the presence of Whoopi Goldberg, Laurel and Hardy, and Bill Clinton in an exhibit otherwise dominated by figures from Mexican history. If you aren't spooked by the not-so-lifelike figures of Aztec warriors, brown-robed friars, Spanish princes, and 20th-century military leaders (all posed in period dioramas), step into the Chamber of Horrors, where wax werewolves and sinister sadists lurk in the shadows. When the museum is mostly empty, which is most of the time, the dramatically lit Chamber of Horrors can be a little creepy. This side-street freak show is open daily from 10am to 8pm; admission is $1.

For many visitors, Tijuana's "main event" is bustling **Avenida Revolución,** the street whose reputation precedes it. Beginning in the 1920s, American college students, servicemen, and hedonistic tourists discovered this street as a bawdy center for illicit fun. Some of the original attraction has fallen by the wayside: Gambling was outlawed in the 1930s, back-alley cockfights are also illegal, and the same civic improvements that repaved Revolución to provide trees, benches, and wider sidewalks vanquished the girlie shows whose barkers once accosted passersby. Drinking and shopping are the main order of business these days. While youngsters from across the border knock back tequila shooters and dangle precariously at the upstairs railings of glaring neon discos, bargain hunters peruse the never-ending array of goods (and not-so-goods) for sale. You'll find the action between calles 1 and 9; the information centers (above) are at the north end, and the landmark Jai Alai Palace anchors the southern portion. To help make sense of the tchotchkes, see "Shopping in Tijuana," below.

Visitors can be easily seduced, then quickly repulsed, by tourist-trap areas like Avenida Revolución, but it's important to remember there's more to Tijuana than American tourism. Tijuana's population, currently around 1.8 million, makes it the fourth-largest city in Mexico. While many residents live in poverty-ridden shanty-towns (you can see these *colonias* spread across the low hills surrounding the city), Tijuana has a lower unemployment rate than neighboring San Diego County, thanks to the rise in *maquiladoras.* They are foreign-owned manufacturing operations that continue to proliferate under NAFTA (the North American Free Trade Agreement). High-rise office buildings testify to increased prosperity and the rise of a white-collar middle class, whose members shop at modern shopping centers away from the tourist zone. And there's tourism from elsewhere in northern Mexico; visitors are drawn by the availability of imported goods and the lure of the "big city" experience.

If you're looking to see a different side of Tijuana, the best place to start is the **Centro Cultural Tijuana,** Paseo de los Héroes, at Avenida Independencía (☎ 011-52-668/4-1111). You'll easily spot the ultramodern Tijuana Cultural Center complex, designed by irrepressible modern architect Pedro Ramírez Vásquez. Its centerpiece is a gigantic sand-colored dome that houses an OMNIMAX theater, which screens two different 45-minute films (subjects range from science to space travel). Each has one English-language show per day. Inside, the center houses the museum's permanent collection of Mexican artifacts from pre-Hispanic times through the modern political era, plus a gallery for visiting exhibits. They have included everything from the works of Diego Rivera to a disturbing, well-curated exhibit chronicling torture and human-rights violations through the ages. Music, theater, and dance performances are held in the center's concert hall and courtyard, and there's a cafe and an excellent museum bookshop. The center is open daily from 9am to 8:30pm; admission to the museum's permanent exhibits is free, there's a $2 charge for the special event gallery, and tickets for OMNIMAX films are $4 for adults and $2.50 for children.

Don't be discouraged if the Tijuana Cultural Center sounds like a field trip for schoolchildren; it's a must-see on my list, if only to drag you away from tourist kitsch and into the more sophisticated Zona Río (river area). While there, stop to admire the wide, European-style **Paseo de los Héroes.** The boulevard's intersections are marked by gigantic traffic circles (*glorietas*), at the center of which stand statuesque monuments to leaders ranging from Aztec Emperor Cuauhtémoc to Abraham Lincoln. Navigating the congested *glorietas* will require your undivided attention, so it's best to pull over to admire the monuments. In the Zona Río you'll find some classier shopping and a colorful local marketplace, plus the ultimate kid destination, **Mundo Divertido,** Paseo de los Héroes at Calle José Maria Velasco (no phone). Literally translated, it means "world of amusement," and one parent described it as the Mexican equivalent of "a Chuck E. Cheese restaurant built inside a Malibu Grand Prix." You get the idea—noisy and frenetic, it's the kind of place kids dream about. Let them choose from miniature golf, batting cages, a roller coaster, a kid-sized train, a video game parlor, and go-carts. There's a food court with tacos and hamburgers; if you're in luck, the picnic area will be festooned with streamers and piñatas for some happy tyke's birthday party. The park is open daily, from around 11am to 10pm. Admission is free, and several booths inside sell tickets for the rides.

Tijuana's most unusual attraction is **Mexitlán,** Calle 2 at Avenida Ocampo (☎ **011-52-663/8-4101**). Built on the roof of a parking structure, it's an open-air museum with 200 scaled-down replicas of Mexico's most famous buildings throughout history. The exhibit represents, in exacting detail, everything from pre-Columbian pyramids to Mexico City's opulent 19th-century cathedrals and grand plazas, from the 1968 Olympic Stadium (complete down to the Diego Rivera mosaic on one side) to a topographically correct representation of coastal landmarks. Opened in 1990 to great fanfare, the complex originally included restaurants and gift shops, but hasn't been drawing the crowds envisioned by its ambitious designers (including contemporary architect Pedro Ramírez Vásquez, whose work is amply represented). As a result, some of the exhibit is looking a little worn; still, this "Mexico-land" is awfully fun to see, especially for kids (and former kids) fascinated by miniatures. Mexitlán is open Tuesday through Sunday, and admission is $1.25 per person. Because it faces an uncertain future, including the possibility of being moved to Mexico City, I recommend you call to verify schedule information.

The fertile valleys of Northern Baja produce most of Mexico's wine, and export many high-quality vintages to Europe; they're unavailable in the United States. For an introduction to Mexican wines, stop into **Cava de Vinos L. A. Cetto** (L. A. Cetto Winery), Av. Cañon Johnson 2108, at Av. Constitución Sur (☎ **011-52-668/ 5-3031**). Shaped like a wine barrel, the building's striking facade is made from old oak aging barrels in an inspired bit of recycling. In the entrance stand a couple of wine presses (ca. 1928) that Don Angel Cetto used in the early days of production. His family still runs the winery, which opened this impressive visitor center in 1993. L. A. Cetto bottles both red and white wines, some of them award winners, including petite sirah, nebbiolo, and Cabernet Sauvignon. Most bottles cost about $5; the special reserves are a little more than $10. The company also produces tequila, brandy, and olive oil, all for sale here. Admission is $2 for tour and tastings (for those 18 and older only; those 17 or younger are admitted free with an adult but cannot taste the wines), $3 with souvenir wine glass. Open Monday through Saturday, 9:30am to 6:30pm.

Tijuana

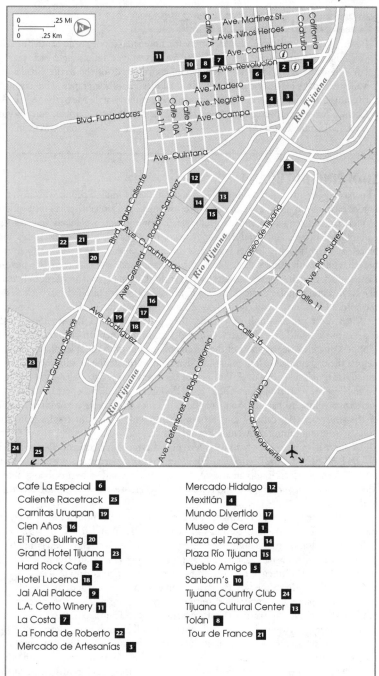

0   .25 Mi
0   .25 Km

Calle 7A
Ave. Martinez St.
Ave. Ninos Heroes
California
Coahuila
Ave. Constitucion
Ave. Revolucion
Ave. Madero
Ave. Negrete
Ave. Ocampo
Blvd. Fundadores
Calle 11A
Calle 10A
Calle 9A
Ave. Quintana
Rio Tijuana
Blvd. Agua Caliente
Ave. Rodolfo Sanchez
Ave. General Cuauhtemoc
Rio Tijuana
Paseo de Tijuana
Ave. Pino Suarez
Calle 11
Ave. Rodriguez
Ave. Gustavo Salinas
Rio Tijuana
Ave. Defensores de Baja California
Calle 16
Carretera al Aeropuerto

Cafe La Especial **6**
Caliente Racetrack **25**
Carnitas Uruapan **19**
Cien Años **16**
El Toreo Bullring **20**
Grand Hotel Tijuana **23**
Hard Rock Cafe **2**
Hotel Lucerna **18**
Jai Alai Palace **9**
L.A. Cetto Winery **11**
La Costa **7**
La Fonda de Roberto **22**
Mercado de Artesanías **3**

Mercado Hidalgo **12**
Mexitlán **4**
Mundo Divertido **17**
Museo de Cera **1**
Plaza del Zapato **14**
Plaza Río Tijuana **15**
Pueblo Amigo **5**
Sanborn's **10**
Tijuana Country Club **24**
Tijuana Cultural Center **13**
Tolán **8**
Tour de France **21**

If you enjoyed a visit to Tijuana's winery (or Ensenada's Bodegas de Santo Tomás), you might want to come back for the festive harvest celebration, held each year in late August or early September. In the endless vineyards of the fertile Guadalupe Valley, the day's events include the traditional blessing of the grapes, wine tastings, live music and dancing, riding exhibitions, and a country-style Mexican meal. **L. A. Cetto** offers a group excursion from Tijuana (about an hour's drive); San Diego's **Baja California Tours** (☎ 619/454-7166) also organizes a day-long trip from San Diego.

SHOPPING IN TIJUANA

Tijuana's biggest attraction is shopping—ask any of the 44 million people who cross the border each year to do it. They come to take advantage of reasonable prices on a variety of merchandise: terra-cotta and colorfully glazed pottery, woven blankets and serapes, embroidered dresses and sequined sombreros, onyx chess sets, beaded necklaces and bracelets, silver jewelry, leather bags and huarache sandals, "rain sticks" (bamboo branches filled with pebbles that simulate the patter of raindrops), hammered tin picture frames, thick drinking glasses, novelty swizzle sticks, Cuban cigars, and Mexican liquors like Kahlúa and tequila. You're permitted to bring $400 worth of purchases back across the border (sorry, no Cuban cigars allowed), including one liter of alcohol per person.

When most people think of Tijuana, they picture **Avenida Revolución,** which appears to exist solely for the extraction of dollars from American visitors. Dedicated shoppers quickly discover most of the curios spilling out onto the sidewalk look alike, despite the determined sellers' assurances that their wares are the best in town. Browse for comparison's sake, but duck into one of the many *pasajes,* or passageway arcades, for the best souvenir shopping. There you'll find items of a slightly better quality and merchants willing to bargain. Some of the most enjoyable *pasajes* are on the east side of the street between calles 2 and 5; they also provide a pleasant respite from the quickly irritating tumult of Avenida Revolución.

An alternative is to visit **Sanborn's,** Avenida Revolución between calles 8 and 9 (☎ 011-52-668/8-1462), a branch of the Mexico City department store long favored by American travelers. It sells an array of regional folk art and souvenirs, books about Mexico in Spanish and English, and candies and bakery treats. You can have breakfast in the sunny cafe.

One of the few places in Tijuana to find better-quality crafts from a variety of Mexican states is **Tolán,** Avenida Revolución between calles 7 and 8 (☎ 011-52-668/8-3637). In addition to the obligatory selection of standard souvenirs, you'll find blue glassware from Guadalajara, glazed pottery from Tlaquepaque, crafts from the Oaxaca countryside, and distinctive tilework from Puebla. Prices at Tolán are fixed, so you shouldn't try to bargain the way you can in some of the smaller shops and stands.

If a marketplace atmosphere and spirited bargaining are what you're looking for, head to **Mercado de Artesanías (Crafts Market),** Calle 2 and Avenida Negrete. Vendors of pottery, clayware, clothing, and other crafts fill an entire city block.

Shopping malls are as common in Tijuana as in any big American city; you shouldn't expect to find typical souvenirs, but shopping alongside residents and other intrepid visitors is often more fun than feeling like a sitting-duck tourist. One of the biggest, and most convenient, is **Plaza Río Tijuana** (on Paseo de los Héroes at Avenida Independencía). It's an outdoor plaza, anchored by several department stores, that features dozens of specialty shops and casual restaurants.

If you have a sweet tooth, seek out **Suzett** bakery, tucked in a corner behind **Comercial Mexicana,** which is kind of a Mexican Target with a full grocery store. At Suzett, grab a tray and a pair of tongs, and stroll through aisles of industrial bakery carts stacked high with fresh-baked breads, pastries, and other sweet treats. All the different shapes and patterns are irresistible; just pluck the ones you want and carry them to the register—a couple of bucks will buy enough for the whole family. *Helpful hint:* Plaza Río Tijuana has ample free parking, and is across the street from the Cultural Center, where private lots charge $5 to $8 to park.

On the other side of Paseo de los Héroes from Plaza Río Tijuana is **Plaza del Zapato,** a two-story indoor mall filled with only shoe (*zapato*) stores. Though most are made with quality leather rather than synthetics, inferior workmanship ensures they'll likely last only a season or two. But with prices as low as $30, why not indulge? Men's styles include dress and casual oxfords and loafers, while women's tend toward casual sandals or traditional pumps. In general, styles tend to mimic current European trends rather than American fashion, and there are almost no athletic shoes.

For a taste of every-day Mexico, visit **Mercado Hidalgo** (one block west at Avenida Sánchez Taboada and Avenida Independencía), a busy indoor-outdoor marketplace where vendors display fresh flowers and produce, sacks of dried beans and chiles by the kilo, and a few souvenir crafts, including some excellent piñatas. Morning is the best time to visit the market, and you'll be more comfortable paying with *pesos,* because most sellers are accustomed to a local crowd.

SPECTATOR SPORTS

If the thrill of athletic prowess and contests lure you, Tijuana is a spectator's (and bettor's) paradise.

BULLFIGHTING   While some maintain that this spectacle employs the same cruel disregard for animal rights as the now-illegal cockfights once popular in Tijuana, bullfighting does occupy a prominent place in Mexican heritage. Matadors' skill and bravery is closely linked with cultural ideals regarding *machismo,* and some of the world's best competitors perform at Tijuana's two stadiums. The season runs from May through September, with events held Sundays at 4:30pm. Ticket prices range from $17 to $35 (the premium seats are on the shaded side of the arena). Tickets are for sale at the bullring or in advance from **Five Star Tours** (☎ 619/232-5049). **El Toreo** (☎ 011-52-668/6-1510) is 2 miles east of downtown on Boulevard Agua Caliente at Avenida Diego Rivera. **Plaza de Toros Monumental,** or Bullring-by-the-Sea (☎ 011-52-668/0-1808), is 6 miles west of downtown on Highway 1-D, before the first toll station. It's perched at the edge of the ocean and the California border.

If you want to catch the bullfights but don't want to drive, **Five Star Tours** (☎ 619/232-5049), based in the San Diego train station, offers bus trips organized around attending the bullfights. It charges $14 round-trip, plus the cost of your bullfight ticket (prices vary). You can easily take a taxi to El Toreo—fares are negotiable, and around $10 one-way should be fair. You can also negotiate a fare to Bullring-by-the-Sea, but fares are unpredictable.

JAI ALAI   A lightning-paced ball game played on a slick indoor court, jai alai (pronounced *high*-ah-lye) is an ancient Basque tradition that incorporates elements of tennis, hockey, and basketball. You can't miss the **Frontón Palacio,** Avenida Revolución at Calle 7; it's a huge, box-like arena in the center of town painted with giant red letters spelling JAI ALAI. Games are held Monday through Saturday at 8pm, with matinees Monday and Friday at noon. General admission is $2, and there are betting windows inside the arena. For more information, call ☎ 619/231-1910.

GOLF Once the favorite of golfing celebrities and socialites (and a very young Arnold Palmer) staying at the now-defunct Agua Caliente Resort, the **Tijuana Country Club,** Boulevard Agua Caliente at Avenida Gustavo Salinas (☎ 011-52-668/1-7855), is near the Caliente Racetrack and behind the Grand Hotel Tijuana. It's about a 10-minute drive from downtown. The well-maintained course attracts mostly business travelers staying at nearby hotels, many of which offer golf packages (see Grand Hotel Tijuana in "Where to Stay," below). Weekend greens fees are $35, and optional cart rental is $20; if you register a foursome, the group plays for $105, not including carts. Stop by the pro shop for balls, tees, and a limited number of other accessories; the clubhouse also has two restaurants with cocktail lounges.

WHERE TO STAY

When calculating room rates, remember that hotel rates in Tijuana are subject to a 12% tax.

Grand Hotel Tijuana. Agua Caliente 4500, Tijuana; P.O. Box BC, Chula Vista, CA 92012. ☎ **800/GRANDTJ,** or 011-52-668/1-7000 in Tijuana. Fax 8/1-7016. www.grandhoteltijuana. com. 422 units. A/C TV TEL. $80–$90 double; from $150 suite. AE, DC, MC, V. Free underground parking.

You can see the unusually high (32-story) mirrored twin towers of this hotel from all over the city. Modern and sleek, it opened in 1982—the height of Tijuana's prosperity—under the name "Fiesta Americana," a name locals (and many cab drivers) still use. Popular for business travelers, visiting celebrities, and society events, the hotel has the best-maintained public and guest rooms in Tijuana, which helps make up for what it lacks in regional warmth.

Rooms have well-stocked minibars and spectacular views of the city from the top floors; other amenities include 24-hour room service, a heated outdoor pool, laundry service, and a sauna.

The lobby has dark carpeting and '80s mirrors and neon accents that feel like a Vegas hotel-casino. It gives way to several ballrooms and an airy atrium that serves elegant international cuisine at dinner and weekend brunch. Next to it is a casual Mexican restaurant; beyond there, the Vegas resemblance resumes with an indoor shopping arcade. The hotel offers a golf package for $82 per person—it includes one night's lodging with a welcome cocktail and a round of 18 holes (including cart) at the adjacent Tijuana Country Club.

Hotel Lucerna. Av. Paseo de los Héroes 10902, Zona Río, Tijuana. ☎ **800/582-3762** or 011-52-663/4-2000. 179 units. TV TEL. $85 double; $88 suite. AE, DC, MC, V.

Once the most chic hotel in Tijuana, Lucerna now has slightly worn furnishings, but the place has personality. If you enjoy Mexican-Colonial style—wrought-iron railings and chandeliers, rough-hewn wood furniture, brocade wallpaper, and traditional tiles—Lucerna is the place for you. The hotel is in the Zona Río, away from the noise and congestion of downtown, so a quiet night's sleep is easy. The five-story hotel's rooms all have balconies or patios, but are otherwise unremarkable. Sunday brunch is

---

Planning Pointer

This guide uses the term "double" when listing rates, referring to the American concept of "double occupancy." However, in Mexico a single or double room rate refers to beds: A single room has one bed, a double has two, and you pay accordingly. Keep this in mind when making your reservations.

served outdoors by the swimming pool; there's also a coffee shop that provides room service. The hotel staff is friendly and attentive, and there's a travel desk.

WHERE TO DINE
EXPENSIVE

If you're interested in haute cuisine, the buzz around Tijuana is all about **Cien Años,** Jose Maria Velazco 1407 (☎ **011-52-663/4-3039** or 4-7262). The elegant Zono Río eatery offers artfully blended Mexican flavors (tamarind, poblano chile, mango) stylishly presented. It's open daily, and serves lunch beginning at 1pm.

La Costa. Calle 7, no. 8131 (just off Av. Revolución), Zona Centro. ☎ **011-52-668/5-8494.** E-mail: fpedrin@telnor.net. Main courses $8–$20. AE, MC, V. Daily 10am–midnight. MEXICAN-STYLE SEAFOOD.

Fish gets top billing here, starting with the hearty seafood soup. There are combination platters of half a grilled lobster, stuffed shrimp, and baked shrimp; fish fillet stuffed with seafood and cheese; and several abalone dishes. La Costa is very popular with San Diegans, and the food lives up to its reputation.

Tour de France. Gobernador Ibarra 252 a.k.a. Av. 16 de Septiembre (on the old road to Ensenada between the Palacio Azteca Hotel and the La Sierra Motel). ☎ **011-52-668/1-7542.** www.sdro.com/tourfrance. Reservations recommended. Main courses $18–$21. AE, MC, V. Mon–Thurs 8am–10:30pm, Fri–Sat 8am–11:30pm. FRENCH.

Martín San Román, Tour de France's chef and co-owner, was sous chef at San Diego's famous Westgate Hotel, then went on to open the top-notch Marius restaurant in the former Le Meridien resort in Coronado. His loyal clientele has followed him from San Diego, and he has acquired new devotees in Tijuana. It's worth a trip to Tijuana just to sample Martín's pâtés or escargots; the vegetables, prepared and presented with the flair of an artist, all come fresh from local farms. Entree prices include soup and salad. You might try beef tournedos in peppercorn sauce, quail flambéed with cognac, or shrimp in pernod and garlic sauce. The wine list is extensive and international, and the atmosphere is as fine as the food.

MODERATE

Hard Rock Cafe. 520 Av. Revolución (near Calle 1), Zona Centro. ☎ **011-52-668/5-0206.** Menu items $5–$10. MC, V. Daily 11am–2am. AMERICAN/MEXICAN.

Had an overload of Mexican culture? Looking for a place with all the comforts of home? Head for the Tijuana branch of this ubiquitous watering hole, which promises nothing exotic. It serves the standard Hard Rock chain menu, which admittedly features an outstanding hamburger, in the regulation Hard Rock setting (dark, clubby, walls filled with rock 'n' roll memorabilia). While the restaurant's street presence is more subdued than that of most Hard Rock locations, you'll still be able to spot the trademark Caddy emerging from above the door. The restaurant and all its trimmings may have migrated south of the border, but prices are more in line with what you'd see in the United States—and therefore no bargain in competitive Tijuana.

INEXPENSIVE

Cafe La Especial. Av. Revolución 718 (between calles 3 and 4), Zona Centro. ☎ **011-52-668/5-6654.** Menu items $3–$12. Daily 9am–10pm. MEXICAN.

Tucked away in a shopping *pasaje* at the bottom of some stairs (turn in at the taco stand of the same name), this restaurant is a well-known shopper's refuge. It offers home-style Mexican cooking at reasonable (though not dirt-cheap) prices. The gruff, efficient waitstaff carries out platter after platter of *carne asada*, grilled marinated beef served with fresh tortillas, beans, and rice—it's La Especial's most popular item. Traditional dishes like tacos, enchiladas, and burritos round out the menu, augmented by frosty cold Mexican beers.

Carnitas Uruapan. Blvd. Díaz Ordáz 550 (across from Plaza Pacífica), La Mesa. ☎ **011-52-668/1-6181.** Menu items $2.50–$8. No credit cards. Daily 7am–3am. Follow Blvd. Agua Caliente south toward Tecate. It turns into Blvd. Diaz Ordaz, also known as Carretera Tecate and Highway 2. MEXICAN.

Carnitas, a beloved dish in Mexico, consists of marinated pork roasted on a spit till it's falling-apart tender, then served in chunks with tortillas, salsa, cilantro, guacamole, and onions. It's the main attraction at Carnitas Uruapan, where the meat is served by the kilo (or portion thereof) at long, communal wooden tables to a mostly local crowd. The original is a little hard to find, but now there's a branch in the fashionable Zona Río. A half-kilo of carnitas is plenty for two people, and costs around $12, including beans and that impressive array of condiments. It's a casual feast without compare, but vegetarians need not apply. Another location is on Paseo de los Héroes at Av. Rodríguez (no phone).

La Fonda de Roberto. In the La Sierra Motel, 2800 Blvd. Cuahutemoc Sue Oeste a.k.a. Av. 16 de Septiembre (on the old road to Ensenada). ☎ **011-52-668/6-4687.** Most dishes $5–$11. MC, V. Daily 10am–10pm. MEXICAN.

Though its location may appear out of the way, this modest restaurant's regular appearances on San Diego "Best Of" lists attest to its appeal. A short drive (or taxi ride) from downtown Tijuana, La Fonda's colorful dining room opens onto the courtyard of a kitschy 1960s motel, complete with retro kidney-shaped swimming pool. The festive atmosphere is perfect for enjoying a variety of regional Mexican dishes, including a decent chicken *mole* and generous portions of *milanesa* (beef, chicken, or pork pounded paper thin, then breaded and fried). A house specialty is *queso fundido*, deep-fried cheese with chiles and mushrooms served with a basket of freshly made corn tortillas.

TIJUANA AFTER DARK

Tijuana has several lively discos, and perhaps the most popular is **Baby Rock Discoteca,** 1482 Diego Rivera, Zona Río (☎ 011-52-663/4-2404). A cousin to Acapulco's lively Baby O, it features everything from jungle rock to hard rock. It's close to the Guadalajara Grill restaurant.

A recent addition to Tijuana's nightlife is "sports bars," cheerful watering holes that feature satellite wagering from all over the United States, as well as from Tijuana's Caliente Racetrack. The most popular bars cluster in **Pueblo Amigo,** Via Oriente and Paseo Tijuana in the Zona Río, a new center designed to resemble a colonial Mexican village. Even if you don't bet on the horses, you can soak up the atmosphere. Two of the town's hottest discos, **Rodeo de Media Noche** (☎ 011-52-668/2-4967) and **Señor Frogs** (☎ 011-52-668/2-4962), are also in Pueblo Amigo, as is **La Tablita de Tony** (☎ 011-52-668/2-8111), an Argentine restaurant. Pueblo Amigo is conveniently located less than 2 miles from the border, a short taxi ride or—during daylight hours—a pleasant walk.

8 Baja California: Exploring More of Mexico

If you have a car, you can easily venture into Baja California for a getaway of a few days. Since 1991, American car-rental companies have allowed their cars to be driven into Baja. **Avis** (☎ 619/231-7155), **Courtesy** (☎ 619/497-4800), and many other rental companies let their cars go as far south as the 28th parallel, the dividing line between the Baja North and Baja South states. **Bob Baker Ford** (☎ **619/297-5001**) and **Colonial Ford** (☎ **619/477-9344**) allow their cars to be driven the entire 1,000-mile stretch of the Baja Peninsula. Whether you drive your own car or a rented one, you'll need Mexican auto insurance in addition to your own; it's available at the border in San Ysidro or through the car-rental companies.

It takes relatively little time to cross the border in Tijuana, but be prepared for a delay of an hour or more on your return to San Diego. If you take local buses down the Baja coast, the delays come en route rather than at the border.

You can also visit Rosarito and Ensenada through a tour. **San Diego Mini Tours** (☎ **619/477-8687**) makes daily trips.

BAJA ESSENTIALS

See "Essentials," above under "Tijuana" for currency and transportation information.

VISITOR INFORMATION   The best source of information is **Baja California Tourism Information** (☎ **800/522-1516** in California, Arizona, or Nevada; 800/225-2786 in the rest of the U.S. and Canada; or ☎ **619/298-4105**). This office provides advice and makes hotel reservations throughout Baja California. You can also contact the **Secretaria de Turismo of Baja California,** P.O. Box 2448, Chula Vista, CA 91912 (☎ **011-52-668/1-9492;** fax 1-9579).

A SUGGESTED ITINERARY   Begin your trip in Tijuana with an afternoon and maybe an overnight stay that includes watching some fast-paced jai alai (see "Spectator Sports," in section 7, "Tijuana"). Then head down the coast to the seaside town of Rosarito Beach, and on to Puerto Nuevo and Ensenada, the third-largest city in Baja.

Two well-maintained roads run between Tijuana and Ensenada: the scenic, coast-hugging toll road (marked *cuota* or 1-D) and the free but slower public road (marked *libre* or 1). I strongly recommend starting out on the toll road, but use the free road along Rosarito Beach—where to exit is readily apparent—so that you can pull on and off easily to shop and look at the view.

Rosarito Beach is 18 miles from Tijuana; Ensenada is 68 miles from Tijuana, and 84 miles from San Diego.

ROSARITO BEACH

Once a tiny resort town that remained a best-kept secret despite its proximity to Tijuana, Rosarito Beach saw an explosion of development in the prosperous '80s; it's now garish and congested beyond recognition. Why does its popularity persist? Location is one reason—it's the first beach resort town south of the border, and party-minded young people aren't always too discriminating. That should give you an idea of the crowd to expect on holiday weekends and during school breaks.

Reputation is another draw: For years the **Rosarito Beach Hotel** (see "Where to Stay," below) was the preferred hideaway of celebrities and other fashionable Angelenos. Movie star Rita Hayworth and her husband Prince Aly Khan vacationed here; Paulette Goddard and Burgess Meredith were married at the resort. Although the hotel's entry still features the gallant inscription "*Por esta puerta pasan las mujeres mas hermosas del mundo*" ("Through this doorway pass the most beautiful women in the world"), today's vacationing starlets are more often found at resorts on Baja's southern tip. While the glimmer (as well as the glamour) has worn off, the Rosarito Beach Hotel is still the most interesting place in town. Nostalgia buffs will want to stop in for a look at some expert tile- and woodwork, as well as the panoramic murals throughout the lobby. Check out the colorful Aztec images in the main dining room, the magnificently tiled rest rooms, and the glassed-in bar overlooking the sparkling pool and beach. Or peek into the original owner's mansion, now home to a spa and gourmet restaurant.

Sleepy Rosarito Beach has caught Hollywood's attention for years. Most recently, the mega-hit *Titanic* was filmed here in a state-of-the-art production facility, boosting the local economy and spearheading an effort to bring more high-profile (and high-profit) productions across the border. See below for information on the *Titanic* museum.

If it's not too crowded, Rosarito is a good place to while away a few hours. Swim or take a horseback ride at the beach, then munch on fish tacos or tamales from any one of a number of family-run stands along **Boulevard Benito Juárez,** the town's main (and only) drag. You can wet your whistle at the local branch of Ensenada's enormously popular **Papas & Beer** (see below), or shop for souvenirs along the Old Ensenada Highway, south of town.

SHOPPING

The dozen or so blocks of Rosarito north of the Rosarito Beach Hotel are packed with the stores typical in Mexican border towns: **curio shops, cigar** and *licores* (liquor) stores, and *farmacias* (where drugs like Retin-A, Prozac, Rogaine, and many more are available at low cost and without a prescription).

Rosarito has also become a center for **carved furnishings,** which are plentiful downtown along Boulevard Benito Juárez, and **pottery,** which is best purchased at stands along the old highway south of town. A reliable, but more expensive, furniture shop is **Casa la Carreta,** at Km. 29.5 on the old road south of Rosarito ☎ **011-52-661/2-0502**). You can see plentiful examples of the best workmanship—chests, tables, chairs, headboards, cabinets, and cradles.

For quality **silver jewelry** from Taxco, in the Mexican state of Guerrero, follow the stream of Amex-bearing *Americanos* to **Enrico Sterling,** 890 Blvd. Benito Juárez (☎ **011-52-661/2-2418**). Enrico looks exactly like a U.S. jeweler and carries the cream of the crop—exceptionally artistic creations whose bargain prices belie their quality.

WHERE TO STAY

Rosarito Beach Hotel & Spa. Blvd. Benito Juárez, Rosarito, BC, Mexico; P.O. Box 430145, San Diego, CA 92143. ☎ **800/343-8582** or 011-52-661/2-0144. Fax 011-52-661/2-1125. www.rosaritohtl.com. 275 units. TV TEL. $59–$129 Sept–June, $89–$139 July–Aug and U.S. holidays. 2 children under 12 stay free in parents' room. Packages available. MC, V. Free parking.

Although this once-glamorous resort has held steady since its heyday, the vestiges of vacationing movie stars and 1930s elegance have been all but eclipsed by the glaring nighttime neon and party-mania that currently define Rosarito. Despite the resort's changed personality, unique features of artistic construction and lavish decoration remain, setting it apart from the rest. You'll pay more for an ocean view, and more for the newer, air-conditioned rooms in the tower (about two-thirds of the units). The older rooms in the poolside building have only ceiling fans, but they prevail in the character department, with hand-painted trim and original tile.

Dining: The mansion's dining room (now Chabert's Steakhouse), complete with crystal chandeliers, antiques, and dinnertime harpists, charges top dollar for Continental cuisine; there's also Azteca, a casual Mexican restaurant in the main building.

Amenities: In addition to the wide, family-friendly beach, the hotel has two swimming pools, racquetball and tennis courts, and a playground. The stately home of the original owners has been transformed into the full-service Casa Playa Spa, where massages and other treatments are only a smidgen less costly than at home.

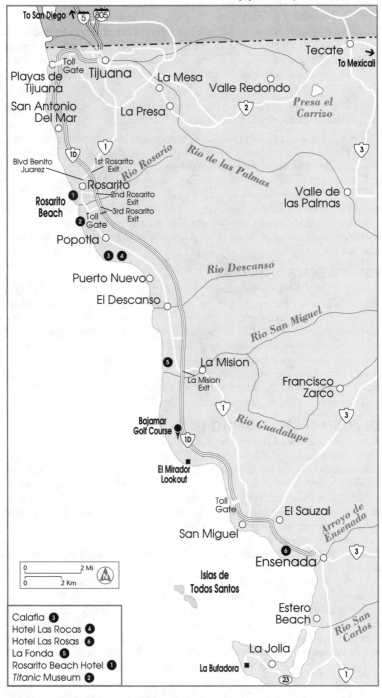

Upper Baja California

To San Diego ↑ 5 805

Tecate ○ →
To Mexicali

Playas de Tijuana

Toll Gate
Tijuana

La Mesa

Valle Redondo

2

Presa el Carrizo

San Antonio Del Mar

La Presa

3

Blvd Benito Juarez

1

1D

1st Rosarito Exit

Rio Rosario

Rio de las Palmas

Valle de las Palmas

Rosarito

2nd Rosarito Exit

Rosarito Beach 1

3rd Rosarito Exit

Toll Gate 2

Popotla ○

3 4

Rio Descanso

Puerto Nuevo ○

El Descanso

Rio San Miguel

5

La Mision

Francisco Zarco

La Mision Exit

Bajamar Golf Course ●

1

Rio Guadalupe

3

1D

El Mirador Lookout

Toll Gate

El Sauzal

Arroyo de Ensenada

San Miguel

6

3

Ensenada ○

Islas de Todos Santos

Estero Beach ○

Rio San Carlos

La Jolla

La Bufadora ■

23

1

0   2 Mi
0   2 Km

Calafia 3
Hotel Las Rocas 4
Hotel Las Rosas 6
La Fonda 5
Rosarito Beach Hotel 1
Titanic Museum 2

253

WHERE TO DINE

The elegant French restaurant **Chabert's** and the more casual **Azteca Restaurant** are in the Rosarito Beach Hotel. Outside the hotel, a branch of Puerto Nuevo's **Ortega's** on the main drag is the place for lobster. Early risers out for a stroll can munch on fresh, hot *tamales,* a traditional Mexican breakfast treat sold from sidewalk carts for about 50¢ each.

El Nido. Blvd. Juárez 67. ☎ **011-52-661/2-1430.** Main courses $5.50–$20. No credit cards. Daily 8am–midnight. MEXICAN/STEAKS.

One of the first restaurants in Rosarito, El Nido remains popular with visitors unimpressed by the flashier, neon-lit joints that court the college-age set. The setting is Western frontier, complete with candles and rusting wagon wheels; sit outside in the lush enclosed patio, or opt for the dark, cozy interior warmed by a large fireplace and grill. The mesquite fire flavors the grilled steaks and seafood that are El Nido's specialty; the menu also includes free-range (and super-fresh) quail and venison from the owner's ranch in the nearby wine country. The generous meals include hearty bean soup, American-style green salad, baked potatoes, and all the fresh tortillas and zesty salsa you can eat.

ROSARITA BEACH AFTER DARK

Because the legal drinking age in Baja is 18, the under-21 crowd from Southern California flocks across the border on Friday and Saturday nights. The most popular spot in town is **Papas & Beer,** a relaxed, come-as-you-are club on the beach, a block north of the Rosarito Beach Hotel. Even for those young in spirit only, it's great fun, with open-air tables and a bar surrounding a sand volleyball court. Several other adjacent clubs offer thunderous music, spirited dancing, and all-night-long energy. Cover charges vary depending on the season, the crowd, and the mood of the staff. The **Salon Méxican** in the Rosarito Beach Hotel attracts a slightly more mature crowd, with live music on Friday, Saturday, and Sunday nights.

EN ROUTE FROM ROSARITO TO ENSENADA

A few miles south of Rosarito proper lies the seaside production site of 1997's megablockbuster *Titanic.* An 800-foot-long replica was constructed for filming, and many local residents served as extras in the movie. Rosarito officials are eager to attract more films to the state-of-the-art facility left behind by the *Titanic* staff; in the meantime, a makeshift "museum" has sprung up on the site. The gargantuan ship was sunk and destroyed during filming, but sound stages still contain partial sets (like a first-class hallway) and numerous props, including lifeboats, furnishings, and crates from dockside scenes. Admission is a hefty $5 per person, but if you're *really* a fan . . . The *Titanic* **Museum** is open weekends from 10am to 6pm, and often also on Fridays, on holidays, and during busy seasons.

Leaving Rosarito, drive south on the toll highway or the local-access road that parallels it. It offers a look at the curious juxtaposition of ramshackle villages and luxurious vacation homes. You'll also pass a variety of restaurants and resorts—this stretch of coastline has surpassed Rosarito in drawing the discriminating visitor. Many places are so Americanized that you feel as if you never left home. My favorites are the funkier, more colorfully Mexican places, like **Calafia** restaurant, **Puerto Nuevo** lobster village, and **La Fonda** resort (see "Where to Stay" and "Where to Dine," below).

After La Fonda, be sure to get back on the toll highway, because the old road veers inland and you don't want to miss what's coming next. Development falls off somewhat for the next 15 miles, and the coastline's natural beauty picks up. You'll see green

Surfing, Northern Baja Style

Surfers from California and beyond come to the northern Baja coastline for perpetual right-breaking waves, cheap digs and eats, and an "Endless Summer" atmosphere. If you're a surfer looking to get your bearings, or a spectator wanting to get your feet wet, stop by **Inner Reef** (Km. 34½; no phone). Opened in 1998 by a friendly Southern California ex-pat named Roger, this tiny shack offers all the essentials: wax, leashes, patch kits, surfboard sales and rentals, and even expert repairs at bargain prices. Roger's there from noon every day in summer, Wednesday through Sunday in winter.

---

meadows running down to meet white-sand beaches and wild sand dunes, all skirting rocky cliffs reminiscent of the coast at Big Sur.

The ideal place to take it all in is **El Mirador** lookout, about 11 miles south of La Fonda. The drama builds as you climb the stairs and gasp at the breathtaking view. It sweeps from the deep-blue open sea past steep cliffs and down the curved coastline to Salsipuedes Point. (Ensenada lies on the other side.) If vertigo doesn't trouble you, look straight down from the railing and you'll see piles of automobiles lying where they were driven off before El Mirador was built. Whether the promontory was a popular suicide spot or merely a junkyard with an enticing twist is best left to urban legend-makers; it nevertheless reinforces your sense of a different culture—nowhere in image-conscious California would the twisted pile of metal be left on the rocks.

A few miles farther south on the toll road, you'll come to a sign for **Salsipuedes Bay** (the name means "leave if you can"). The dramatic scenery ends here, so you can take the exit if you want to turn around and head north again. If you plan to do some camping, head down the rutted road, nearly a mile long, to **Salsipuedes Campground,** set under olive trees on a cliff. Each campsite has a fire ring and costs $5 a day (day use is also $5). The campground has a natural rock tub with hot-spring water, and some basic cottages that rent for $30 a day. There is no easy access to the beach, known for its good surfing, from the campground.

Ensenada, with its shops, restaurants, and winery, is another 15 miles away.

NEARBY GOLFING

Located 20 miles north of Ensenada, **Bajamar** (☎ **800/225-2418** or 011-52-615/5-0152) is a self-contained resort with 27 spectacular holes of golf. It's the place to go if you want to feel as though you're in the United States. It was conceived as a vacation home and planned community with a country club, before the bottom dropped out of the market after '80s speculation. The main attraction is now the golf club and hotel, which play host to high-level retreats, conventions, and Asian tourists attracted by the great golf deals. With oceanfront, Scottish-style links reminiscent of the courses on the Monterey Peninsula, Bajamar lets you combine any two of its three nine-hole courses. Public greens fees for 18 holes (including mandatory cart) are $50 Sunday through Thursday, $60 Friday or Saturday. Hotel guests pay $5 less, and the lavish Hacienda las Glorias offers a bevy of golf packages (see "Where to Stay," below). There are a pro shop, putting and chipping greens, a driving range, and an elegant bar and restaurant.

WHERE TO STAY

Hacienda Las Glorias. At Bajamar Golf Resort, Highway 1-D, Km 77. Mailing address 416 W. San Ysidro Blvd., Suite #L-732, San Ysidro, CA 92173. ☎ **800/225-2418** or 011-52-615/5-0152. 81 units. TV. $65–$85 double; $120–$130 suite. Children under 12 stay free in parents' room. Golf packages available. AE, MC, V.

Situated 20 miles north of Ensenada, this hotel is tucked away in the Bajamar golf resort and community. Popular with business conventions and family gatherings, Bajamar is as Americanized as it gets, and so is this luxury hotel near the clubhouse. Signs for phases of the surrounding vacation-home development, which never really got off the ground, line the long road from the highway. Architecture buffs will note that the hotel is built like an early-Spanish mission, with an interior outdoor plaza and garden surrounded by long arcades shading guest-room doorways. Rooms and suites are very spacious and comfortable, with vaguely colonial furnishings and luxurious bathrooms.

The hotel has a heated outdoor swimming pool and spa, tennis courts, and 27 holes of golf, which are the main draw (see "Nearby Golfing," above). A variety of golf packages, including deals for couples with only one golfer, are available.

Hotel Las Rocas. Km 38.5 Free Rd. Mailing address P.O. Box 189003 HLR, Coronado, CA 92178-9003. ☎ **888/LAS-ROCAS**, 011-52-661/2-2140, or 619/234-9810 from San Diego. www.lasrocas.com. 74 units. TV TEL. $75–$95 double; $115–$250 suite. Midweek rates available Oct–Apr. Packages and senior discounts available. AE, MC, V. Take the second Rosarito exit off the toll road and drive 6 miles south, or follow the free road south from Rosarito; hotel is on the right.

This polished hotel is run by an American, for Americans, and it shows. English is spoken fluently everywhere, and there are only as many signs in Spanish as you'd expect to see in Los Angeles. Built in Mediterranean style, with gleaming white stucco, cobalt blue accents, and brightly painted tiles everywhere, Las Rocas is in a lovely setting perched above the sea. *Tip:* Try to stay in the main building, and don't rule out a suite—even the $115 junior suite is spacious and includes a romantic fireplace and kitchenette.

There's no beach below the rocky edge, but the hotel's oceanfront swimming pool and secluded whirlpool lagoons more than make up for it. The thatched-roof palapa in the poolside garden dispenses tropical drinks and snacks, and swaying palms rustle throughout the property.

Like most Baja resorts, Las Rocas is oriented toward the sea; all rooms have an oceanfront private terrace. The rooms and suites are nicely furnished in Mexican-Colonial style, and bathrooms are well equipped and beautifully tiled.

The hotel's restaurant, Cafe Carnaval, attempts to offer both Mexican cuisine and Continental fare. It doesn't really succeed at either, but does make outstanding soups—and guacamole, which you can order by the bowl for chip-dipping at the indoor or poolside bar.

La Fonda. Highway 1-D, Km 59, La Mision exit. Mailing address P.O. Box 430268, San Ysidro, CA 92143. No phone. 22 units. TV. $55 standard rooms, $75 deluxe (with fireplace and/or full kitchen). No credit cards. Write for reservations; allow 2 weeks for response.

Just as American-style Las Rocas has its staunch devotees, many are loyal to La Fonda, a place for people who truly want to get away from it all. The rustic rooms don't come with minibars, state-of-the-art TVs, or phones. What they do have is an adventuresome appeal unlike that of any other northern Baja coast resort. Relaxation and romance are the key words at this small hotel and restaurant, which opened in the '50s and hasn't changed a whole lot since. Perched cliffside above a wide, sandy beach, all of La Fonda's rooms have wide-open views of the breaking surf below. Although there are some newer motel-style rooms, there's more charm to the older apartments with fireplaces (some with kitchenettes), which are reached by narrow winding staircases much like the pathway down to the sand. The best rooms are numbers 18 to 22, closest to the sand and isolated from the main building. During particularly cold winter months, unheated La Fonda can get chilly—an important consideration. At least be sure you're in a room with a fireplace.

Bamboo and palm fronds decorate the bar next to the acclaimed casual restaurant (see "Where to Dine," below). Ensenada is a scenic 45-minute drive south, and Puerto Nuevo a mere 8 miles up the road—if you decide you need to leave this hideaway at all.

WHERE TO DINE

Three miles south of Rosarito Beach, elaborate stucco portals beckon drivers to pull over for **Calafia** (☎ **011-52-661/2-1581**), a restaurant and trailer park that isn't visible from the highway. We don't recommend the dismal accommodations, but Calafia's restaurant is worth a stop, if only to admire the impressive setting above the crashing surf. Tables sit on terraces, balconies, and ledges wedged into the rocks all the way down to the bottom, where an outdoor dance floor and wrecked Spanish galleon sit on the beach. At night, when the outdoor landings are softly lit, and the mariachis complement the sound of crashing waves, romance is definitely in the air. The menu is standard Mexican fare, with some Americanized dishes like fajitas, all prepared well and served with fresh, warm tortillas and good, strong margaritas. Calafia serves breakfast, lunch, and dinner daily.

Another excellent choice for sunset cocktails is the Moroccan-style **Hotel Cafe Americana** (☎ **011-52-661/4-0070**), about 10 minutes south of Rosarito Beach by car. Whimsical white minarets beckon travelers to the former private home, now an inn and restaurant. The bar offers a superb selection of premium tequilas, for sipping by the fire or on a dramatic oceanfront terrace.

A trip down the coast just wouldn't be complete without stopping at **Puerto Nuevo,** a tiny fishing town with nearly 30 restaurants—all serving exactly the same thing! Some 40 years ago the fishermen's wives started serving local lobsters from the kitchens of their simple shacks; many eventually built small dining rooms onto their homes or constructed restaurants. The result is a lobster lover's paradise, where a feast of lobster, beans, rice, salsa, limes, and fresh tortillas costs around $10.

Puerto Nuevo is 12 miles south of Rosarito on the Old Ensenada Highway (parallel to the toll Highway 1). Drive through the arched entryway, park, and stroll the town's three or four blocks for a restaurant that suits your fancy. Some have names and some don't; **Ortega's** is one of the originals, and has expanded to five locations in the village. There's also **La Casa de la Langosta** ("House of Lobster"), which has a branch in Rosarito Beach. Regulars prefer the smaller, family-run spots, where mismatched dinette sets and chipped plates underscore the earnest service and personally prepared dinners.

About 10 miles farther south, roughly halfway between Rosarito and Ensenada, is the **La Fonda** hotel and restaurant (see "Where to Stay," above). Plenty of San Diegans make the drive on Sunday morning for La Fonda's outstanding buffet brunch, an orgy of meats, traditional Mexican stews, *chilaquiles* (a saucy egg-and-tortilla scramble), fresh fruit, and pastries. Breakfast, lunch, and dinner are always accompanied by a basket of Baja's best flour tortillas (try rolling them with some butter and jam at breakfast). The best seating is under thatched umbrellas on La Fonda's tiled terrace overlooking the breaking surf. There's a bar, and live music keeps the joint jumping on Friday and Saturday nights (strolling mariachis entertain the rest of the time). House specialties include banana pancakes, pork chops with *salsa verde,* succulent glazed ribs, and a variety of seafood; plan to walk off your heavy meal along the sandy beach below, accessible by a stone stairway. Relaxing ambiance coupled with exceptionally good food and service make La Fonda a must-see along the coast. Sunday brunch is around $12 a person; main courses otherwise are $4 to $15. The restaurant is open daily from around 9am to 10pm; Sunday's buffet brunch runs from 10am to 3:30pm.

ENSENADA

Ensenada, 84 miles south of San Diego and 68 miles south of Tijuana, is a pretty town surrounded by sheltering mountains. It's about 40 minutes from Rosarito. This is the kind of place that loves a celebration, and at almost any time you visit, the city is festive, be it for a bicycle race or a seafood festival.

ESSENTIALS

The **Tourist and Convention Bureau booth** (☎ 011-52-617/8-2411) is at the western entrance to town, where the waterfront-hugging Boulevard Lázaro Cárdenas—also known as Boulevard Costero—curves to the right. The booth is open daily from 9am till dusk, and the staff can provide a downtown map, directions to major nearby sites, and information on special events. As in most of the commonly visited areas of Baja, one or more employees speak English fluently.

Eight blocks south you'll find the **State Secretary of Tourism,** Boulevard Lázaro Cárdenas No. 1477, Government Building (☎ 61-72-30-22; fax 61-72-30-81). It's open Monday through Friday from 9am to 7pm, Saturday 10am to 3pm, Sunday 10am to 2pm. Both offices have extended hours on U.S. holidays. Taxis park along López Mateos.

EXPLORING ENSENADA

After passing through the last toll gate, Highway 1-D curves sharply toward downtown Ensenada. Watch out for brutal metal speed bumps slowing traffic into town—they're far less forgiving on the average chassis than those in the United States!

Although Ensenada technically is a "border town," one of its appeals is its multilayered vitality—it's concerned with much more than tourism. The bustling port consumes the entire waterfront (the only beach access is north or south of town), and the economy is dominated by the Pacific fishing trade and agriculture in the fertile valleys surrounding the city.

Try not to leave Ensenada without getting a taste of its true personality; for example, stop by the indoor-outdoor **fish market** at the northernmost corner of the harbor. Each day, from early morning to midday, merchants and housewives gather to assess the day's catch—tuna, marlin, snapper, and many other varieties, plus piles of shrimp. Outside the market are several stalls—the perfect place to sample the culinary craze sweeping *Alta* (upper) California, the Baja fish taco. Strips of freshly caught fish are battered and deep-fried, then wrapped in corn tortillas and topped with shredded cabbage, cilantro, salsa, and various other condiments. They're delicious, cheap, and filling, and it's easy to see why surf bums and collegiate vacationers consider them a Baja staple.

A WINERY   Elsewhere in town, visit the **Bodegas de Santo Tomás Winery,** Avenida Miramar 666, at Calle 7 (☎ 011-52-617/8-2509; www.santotomas.com.mx). While most visitors to Mexico are quite content to quaff endless quantities of cheap *cerveza* (beer), even part-time oenophiles should pay a visit to this historic winery. The oldest in Mexico, and the largest in Baja, it uses old-fashioned methods of processing grapes grown in the lush Santo Tomás Valley, first cultivated by Dominican monks in 1791.

A 45-minute tour introduces you to low-tech processing machinery, handhammered wood casks, and cool, damp, stone aging rooms. It culminates in an invitation to sample several vintages, including an international medal–winning Cabernet and delightfully crisp sparkling blanc de blanc. The wood-paneled, church-like tasting room is adorned with paintings of mischievous altar boys being scolded by stern friars for pilfering wine or ruining precious grapes. Anyone used to the pretentious, assembly-line ambiance of trendier wine regions will relish the friendly welcome and informa-tive tour here. Tours in English are conducted daily at 11am, 1pm, and 3pm. Admis-sion is $2 (including tastings; $3 more gets you a souvenir wineglass), and wines for sale range from $3.50 to $10 a bottle. *Note:* Most of the winery's product is exported for the European market; none is available in the United States. The Web site is in Spanish.

Be sure to poke around a bit after your tour concludes, because Santo Tomás has more treasures to give up. The little modern machinery installed here freed up a cav-ernous space now used for monthly jazz concerts, and a former aging room has been transformed into **La Embottelladora Vieja** ("the old aging room") restaurant (see "Where to Dine," below). Across the street stands **La Esquina de Bodegas** ("the corner wine cellar"), former aging rooms for Santo Tomás. One of Ensenada's many pleasant cultural treats, the industrial-style building now functions as a gallery that shows local art. There's a skylit bookstore on the second level, and a small cafe (punc-tuated by giant copper distillation vats) in the rear.

POLITICAL MONUMENTS   Spend just a few hours in Ensenada, and you will begin to see evidence that helps elevate the city beyond mere "border town" status and underscore its national pride. Lending a European air to the city—not to mention a sense of poignancy when you consider Mexico's bloody and still tumultuous political history—are several larger-than-life political monuments concentrated in the down-town area.

The most visible is **Plaza Cívica** (along Boulevard Lázaro Cárdenas, also known as Costero, at Avenida Riveroll), where a wide stone platform dramatically displays 12-foot copper busts of former Mexican presidents Benito Juárez, Miguel Hidalgo, and Venustiano Carranza. A full-figure, mounted representation of Juárez is nearby, in a traffic-stopping monument along the street bearing his name (Avenida Juárez at Avenida Reforma). Contemporary hero **General Lázaro Cárdenas** is honored at the corner of avenidas Reforma and López Mateos, and a statue of **Miguel Hidalgo,** the priest revered as the "father of Mexican independence," stands tall on Avenida Juárez one block north of Avenida Ruiz.

A CULTURAL CENTER   Ensenada's primary cultural center is another must-see in my book: the **Centro Cívico, Social y Cultura** (Boulevard Lázaro Cárdenas at Avenida Club Rotario). The impressive Mediterranean building was formerly **Riviera del Pacífico,** a glamorous 1930s bayfront casino and resort frequented by Holly-wood's elite. Tiles in the lobby commemorate "Visitantes Distinguidos 1930–1940," including Marion Davies, William Randolph Hearst, Lana Turner, Myrna Loy, and Jack Dempsey. Now used by the Rotary Club as offices and for cultural and social events, the main building is open to the public. Go on, take a peek: Elegant hallways and ballrooms evoke a bygone elegance, and every wall and alcove glows with original murals depicting Mexico's colorful history. Lush formal gardens span the front of the building, and there's a small art gallery tucked away to one side. Through the lobby, facing an inner courtyard filled with the ghosts of parties past, is Bar Andaluz, which is sporadically open to the public. It's an intimate, dark-wood place where you can just imagine someone like "Papa" Hemingway holding cocktail-hour court beneath a col-orful toreador mural.

A NEARBY ATTRACTION   South of the city, 45 minutes away along the rural Punta Banda Peninsula, is one of Ensenada's major attractions: **La Bufadora,** a nat-ural sea spout in the rocks. With each incoming wave, water is forced upward through the rock, creating a geyser whose loud grunt gave the phenomenon its name (*la bufadora* means "buffalo snort"). From downtown Ensenada, take Avenida Reforma (Highway 1) south to Highway 23 west. It's a long, meandering drive through a semi-swamp-like area untouched by development; look for grazing animals, bait shops, and fishermen's shacks along the way. La Bufadora is at the end of the road. You park ($1 per car) in crude dirt lots, then walk downhill to the viewing platform, at the end of a 600-yard pathway lined with souvenir stands. In addition to running a gauntlet of determined vendors (hawking the usual wares: woven blankets and fanny packs, painted wooden masks, leather shoes and wallets, carved soapstone animals, cheap sunglasses, silver chains, and earrings), visitors can avail themselves of plentiful, inexpensive snacks, including freshly made churros, grilled corn, and tasty fish tacos. While some sightseers proclaim the display spectacular, I think you need to have a real thing for geysers to make the drive when there's so much else to see and do. Nevertheless, visitation is enormous, and there are plans to pave the dirt parking lots and build permanent restaurants and shops. If you do go, stop and sample the wares along Highway 1 south of the city before you reach the La Bufadora cutoff. I was impressed by the hard-working ladies on the side of the road selling homemade tamales with a variety of fillings, including the sweet-spicy *piña* (pineapple). They also have colorful, eye-catching rows of pickled olives, vegetables, and chile peppers in reclaimed mayonnaise and applesauce jars.

SHOPPING

Ensenada's equivalent of Avenida Revolución is crowded **Avenida López Mateos,** which runs roughly parallel to Boulevard Lázaro Cárdenas (Costero); the highest concentration of shops and restaurants is between avenidas Ruiz and Castillo. Beggars fill the street, but the sellers are less likely to bargain—I think they're used to the gullible cruise-ship buyers. Compared to Tijuana, there is more authentic Mexican **art- and craftwork** in Ensenada—pieces imported from rural states and villages, where different skills are traditionally practiced.

Though from the outside it looks dusty and unlit, **Curiosidades La Joya,** 725 Av. López Mateos (☎ **011-52-617/8-3191**), is a treasure trove of stained-glass lamps, hangings, and other hand-crafted curios. Piles of intricately designed glass lampshades lie side by side with colorful tiles and wrought-iron birdcages, the shop's other specialty. The shopkeepers are stubborn about bargaining, perhaps because they know the value of their unusual wares.

You'll see colorfully painted glazed **pottery** wherever you go in northern Baja. Quality can range from sloppy pieces quickly painted with a limited palette to intricately designed, painstakingly painted works evocative of Tuscan urns and pitchers. You'll get the best prices at the abundant roadside stands lining the old road south of Rosarito; but if you're willing to pay extra for quality, head to **Artesanias Colibri,** 855 Av. López Mateos (☎ **011-52-617/8-1312**). You can learn about the origins of this "Talavera" style—how invading Moors set up terra-cotta factories in the Spanish city of Talavera, and subsequent migration brought the art to the Mexican state of Puebla.

SPORTFISHING

Ensenada, which bills itself as "the yellowtail capital of the world," draws sportfishers eager to venture out from the beautiful *Bahía de Todos Santos* (Bay of All Saints) in search of albacore, halibut, marlin, rockfish, and sea bass.

A wooden boardwalk parallel to Boulevard Lázaro Cárdenas (Costero) near the northern entrance to town provides access to the sportfishing piers and their many charter boat operators. Open-party boats leave early, often by 7am, and charge around $35 per person, plus an additional fee (about $5) for the mandatory fishing license. Non-fishing passengers must, by law, also be licensed. Those disinclined to comparison shop can make advance arrangements with San Diego–based **Baja California Tours** (☎ 619/454-7166). In addition to daily fishing excursions, the company offers 1- to 3-night packages that include hotel, fishing, some meals, and transportation from San Diego.

WHERE TO STAY IN ENSENADA

Remember, in Mexico, a single room has one bed, and a double has two.

Estero Beach Resort. Mailing address Apdo. Postal 86, Ensenada, BC, Mexico. ☎ **011-52-617/6-6225.** 106 units. TV. $53–$300 per room; about $80 for average ocean-view cottage for 2. MC, V. From Ensenada, take Hwy. 1 south; turn right at Estero Beach sign.

About 6 miles south of downtown Ensenada, this sprawling complex of rooms, cottages, and mobile-home hook-ups is popular with families and active vacationers. The bay and protected lagoon at the edge of the lushly planted property are perfect for swimming and launching sailboards; there's also tennis, horseback riding, volleyball, and a game room with Ping-Pong and billiards. The guest rooms are a little worn, but no one expects anything fancy. The casual beachfront restaurant serves a mix of seafood and other Mexican fare mingled with hamburgers, fried chicken, and omelets. Some suites and cottages have kitchenettes, and some can easily accommodate a whole family.

Hotel Las Rosas. Highway 1, 2 miles north of Ensenada. Mailing address Apdo. Postal 316, Ensenada, BC, Mexico. ☎ **011-52-617/4-4310.** 32 units. TV. $101–$165 double. Child under 12 $16; extra adult $22. MC, V.

Modern and luxurious, this pink oceanfront hotel outside Ensenada is the favorite of many Baja aficionados. It offers all the comforts of an upscale American hotel—which doesn't leave room for much Mexican personality. The atrium lobby is awash with pale pink and sea-foam green, the color scheme throughout—including the guest rooms, which are furnished with quasi-tropical hotel furniture. No luxury is unheard of here. Many rooms have fireplaces, whirlpools, or both.

There's a cliff-top hot tub, a health club, tennis and racquetball courts, a fine restaurant, and a cocktail lounge. One of the resort's main photo ops is the spectacular outdoor swimming pool—it overlooks the Pacific and features a vanishing edge that appears to merge with the ocean beyond. If you're looking to maintain the highest comfort level possible, this would indeed be your hotel of choice.

San Nicolas Resort Hotel. Avs. López Mateos and Guadalupe, Ensenada. Mailing address P.O. Box 437060, San Ysidro, CA 92073-7060. ☎ **011-52-617/6-1901.** Fax 011-51-667/6-4930. 150 units. A/C TV TEL. $48–$88 double; from $130 suite. Extra person $10. MC, V.

Most rooms at this modern motor inn face the courtyard or have balconies overlooking an Olympic-size swimming pool. The place is surprisingly quiet, considering it's right on the main drag. The San Nicolas also boasts the city's only indoor swimming pool, and has a casual restaurant, cocktail lounge, and discothèque. There's a branch of Caliente Sports Book, where you can gamble on games and races throughout the United States.

Villa Fontana Days Inn. Av. López Mateos 1050, Ensenada, BC, Mexico. ☎ **800/4-BAJA-04** or 011-52-617/8-3434. www.villafontana.com.mx. 66 units (most with shower only). Summer $60 double; $115 suite. Rates higher on holidays. Midweek and winter discounts available. Rates include continental breakfast. AE, MC, V.

This motel is notable for its out-of-place architecture—who'd expect a peak-roofed, gabled, New England–style structure in a land dominated by red-tiled roofs? This bargain-priced motel is otherwise unremarkable; well located and run by the Days Inn chain, it does have a small outdoor pool and enclosed parking. Ask for a room at the back, away from the street noise.

WHERE TO DINE

El Charro. Av. López Mateos 475 (between Ruiz and Gastellum). ☎ **011-52-617/8-3881.** Menu items $5–$12; lobster $20. No credit cards. Daily 11am–2am. MEXICAN.

You'll recognize El Charro by its front windows: Whole chickens rotate slowly on the rotisserie in one, while a woman makes tortillas in the other. This little place has been here since 1956 and looks it, with charred walls and a ceiling made of split logs. The simple fare consists of such dishes as half a roasted chicken with fries and tortillas, and *carne asada* with soup, guacamole, and tortillas. Giant piñatas hang from the walls above the concrete floor. Kids are welcome; they'll think they're on a picnic. Wine and beer are served, and beer is cheaper than soda.

✪ **El Rey Sol.** Av. López Mateos 1000 (at Blancarte). ☎ **011-52-617/8-1733.** Reservations recommended on weekends. Main courses $9–$19. AE, MC, V. Daily 7:30am–10:30pm. FRENCH/MEXICAN.

Opened by French expatriates in 1947, the family-run El Rey Sol has long been considered Ensenada's finest restaurant. Decked out like the French flag, the red, white, and blue building is a beacon on busy López Mateos. It has wrought-iron chandeliers and heavy oak farm tables, but the menu's prices and sophistication belie the casual decor.

House specialties include seafood puff pastry; baby clams steamed in butter, white wine, and cilantro; chicken in brandy and chipotle chile cream sauce; tender grilled steaks; and home-made French desserts. Portions are generous, and always feature fresh vegetables from the nearby family farm. Every table receives a complimentary platter of appetizers at dinnertime; lunch is a hearty three-course meal.

La Embottelladora Vieja. Av. Miramar 666 (at Calle 7). ☎ **011-52-617/4-0807.** Reservations recommended on weekends. Main courses $8–$20. MC, V. Lunch and dinner; call for seasonal hours. FRENCH/MEXICAN.

If you're planning to splurge on one fine meal in Ensenada (or all of northern Baja, for that matter), this insider's find is the place. Hidden on an industrial side street, from the outside it looks more like a chapel than the elegant restaurant it is. Sophisticated foodies will feel right at home in the stylish dining room. It's a former aging room for the attached Bodegas de Santo Tomás winery, resplendent with red oak furniture (constructed from old wine casks), high brick walls, and crystal goblets and candlesticks on linen tablecloths.

It goes without saying that the wine list is exemplary, featuring bottles from Santo Tomás and other Baja vintners, and the "Baja French" menu features dishes carefully crafted to include or complement wine. Look for appetizers like abalone ceviche or cream of garlic soup, followed by grilled swordfish in cilantro sauce, filet mignon in port wine–Gorgonzola sauce, or quail with tart sauvignon blanc sauce.

ENSENADA AFTER DARK

No discussion of Ensenada would be complete without mentioning **Hussong's Cantina,** Av. Ruiz 113, near Avenida López Mateos (☎ **011-52-617/8-3210**). The bar opened in 1892, and nothing much has changed—the place still sports Wild West–style swinging saloon doors, a long bar to slide beers along, and strolling mariachis bellowing to rise above the din of revelers. There's definitely a minimalist appeal to Hussong's, which looks as if it sprang from a south-of-the-border episode of *Gunsmoke*. Beer and tequilas at astonishingly low prices are the main order of business, but good luck when you need the rest rooms, where hygiene and privacy are a low priority.

While the crowd (a pleasant mix of tourists and locals) at Hussong's can really whoop it up, you ain't seen nothing until you stop into **Papas & Beer,** Avenida Ruiz near Avenida López Mateos (☎ **011-52-617/8-4231**), across the street. A tiny entrance leads to the upstairs bar and disco, where the music is loud and the youthful crowd is definitely here to party. Happy patrons hang out of the second-story windows hollering at their friends, stopping occasionally to munch on papas (french fries) washed down with local beers. Papas & Beer has quite a reputation with the Southern California college crowd, and has opened a branch in Rosarito Beach (see above). You might notice bumper stickers from these two quintessential Baja watering holes, but they don't just give them away. In fact, each bar has not one, but several, souvenir shops along Avenida Ruiz. They carry shirts, duffel bags, sport sippers, pennants, hats, and innumerable other items decorated with the familiar logos.

Appendix: Useful Toll-Free Numbers & Web Sites

MAJOR HOTEL & MOTEL CHAINS

Best Western
☎ 800/528-1234
☎ 800/528-2222 TDD
www.bestwestern.com

Clarion Hotels
☎ 800/CLARION
☎ 800/228-3323 TDD
www.hotelchoice.com

Comfort Inns
☎ 800/228-5150
☎ 800/228-3323 TDD
www.hotelchoice.com

Courtyard by Marriott
☎ 800/321-2211
☎ 800/228-7014 TDD
www.courtyard.com

Days Inn
☎ 800/325-2525
☎ 800/325-3297 TDD
www.daysinn.com

Doubletree/Red Lion Hotels
☎ 800/222-TREE
☎ 800/528-9898 TDD
www.doubletreehotels.com

Econo Lodges
☎ 800/55-ECONO
☎ 800/228-3323 TDD
www.hotelchoice.com

Embassy Suites
☎ 800/EMBASSY
☎ 800/458-4708 TDD
www.embassy-suites.com

Fairfield Inns by Marriott
☎ 800/228-2800
☎ 800/228-7014 TDD
www.fairfieldinn.com

Hampton Inns
☎ 800/HAMPTON
☎ 800/451-HTDD TDD
www.hampton-inn.com

Hilton Hotels
☎ 800/HILTONS
☎ 800/368-1133 TDD
www.hilton.com

Holiday Inn
☎ 800/HOLIDAY
☎ 800/238-5544 TDD
www.holiday-inn.com

Howard Johnson
☎ 800/654-2000
☎ 800/654-8442 TDD
www.hojo.com

Hyatt Hotels & Resorts
☎ 800/228-9000
www.hyatt.com

ITT Sheraton
☎ 800/325-3535
☎ 800/325-1717 TDD
www.sheraton.com

La Quinta Motor Inns
☎ 800/531-5900
☎ 800/426-3101 TDD
www.laquinta.com

Marriott Hotels
☎ 800/228-9290
☎ 800/228-7014 TDD
www.marriott.com

Motel 6
☎ 800/4-MOTEL6
www.motel6.com

Omni Hotels
☎ 800/843-6664
www.omnihotels.com

Quality Inns
☎ 800/228-5151
☎ 800/228-3323 TDD
www.hotelchoice.com

Radisson Hotels
☎ 800/333-3333
www.radisson.com

Ramada Inns
☎ 800/2-RAMADA
☎ 800/228-3232 TDD
www.ramada.com

Red Carpet Inns
☎ 800/251-1962

Red Roof Inns
☎ 800/843-7663
☎ 800/843-9999 TDD
www.redroof.com

Residence Inn by Marriott
☎ 800/331-3131
☎ 800/228-7014 TDD
www.residenceinn.com

Rodeway Inns
☎ 800/228-2000
☎ 800/228-3323 TDD
www.hotelchoice.com

Super 8 Motels
☎ 800/800-8000
☎ 800/533-6634 TDD
www.super8motels.com

Travelodge
☎ 800/255-3050
www.travelodge.com

Vagabond Inns
☎ 800/522-1555
www.vagabondinns.com

CAR-RENTAL AGENCIES

Advantage
☎ 800/777-5500
www.arac.com

Alamo
☎ 800/327-9633
www.goalamo.com

Avis
☎ 800/331-1212
☎ 800/TRY-AVIS in Canada
☎ 800/331-2323 TDD
www.avis.com

Budget
☎ 800/527-0700
☎ 800/826-5510 TDD
www.budgetrentacar.com

Dollar
☎ 800/800-4000
www.dollarcar.com

Enterprise
☎ 800/325-8007

Hertz
☎ 800/654-3131
☎ 800/654-2280 TDD
www.hertz.com

Kemwel Holiday Auto (KHA)
☎ 800/678-0678
www.kemwel.com

National Car Rental
☎ 800/CAR-RENT
☎ 800/328-6323 TDD
www.nationalcar.com

Payless
☎ 800/PAYLESS
www.paylesscar.com

Rent-A-Wreck
☎ 800/535-1391
www.rent-a-wreck.com

Sears
☎ 800/527-0770

Thrifty
☎ 800/367-2277
☎ 800/358-5856 TDD
www.thrifty.com

Value
☎ 800/327-2501
www.go-value.com

AIRLINES

Aer Lingus
☎ 800/IRISH-AIR
☎ 01-705-3333 in Dublin
www.aerlingus.ie

Aeromexico
☎ 800/237-6639
www.aeromexico.com

Air Canada
☎ 800/776-3000 in the U.S.
☎ 88/247-2262 in Canada
www.aircanada.ca

Air New Zealand
☎ 800/262-1234
☎ 0800/737-000 in Auckland
www.airnz.com

Alaska Airlines/Alaska Commuter
☎ 800/426-0333
www.alaskaair.com

America West
☎ 800/235-9292
www.americawest.com

American Airlines/American Eagle
☎ 800/433-7300
☎ 800/543-1586 TDD
www.aa.com

British Airways
☎ 800/247-9297
☎ 0345/222-111 in Britain
www.british-airways.com

Canadian Airlines
☎ 800/426-7000 in the U.S.
☎ 800/665-1177 in Canada
☎ 800/465-3611 TDD in Canada
www.cdnair.ca

Continental Airlines
☎ 800/525-0280
☎ 800/343-9195 TDD
www.flycontinental.com

Delta Air Lines
☎ 800/221-1212
☎ 800/831-4488 TDD
www.delta-air.com

Hawaiian Airlines
☎ 800/367-5320 in the
Continental U.S.
☎ 800/882-8811 in Hawaii
www.hawaiianair.com

Japan Airlines
☎ 800/JAL-FONE
☎ 0354/89-1111 in Tokyo
www.japanair.com
(in the U.S. and Canada)
www.jal.co.jp (in Japan)

Midwest Express
☎ 800/452-2022
www.midwestexpress.com

Northwest Airlines/Northwest Airlink
☎ 800/225-2525
www.nwa.com

Qantas
☎ 800/227-4500
☎ 13-13-13 in Australia
www.qantas.com.au

Reno Air
☎ 800/RENO-AIR
www.renoair.com

Skywest Airlines
☎ 800/453-9417
www.skywest.com

Southwest Airlines
☎ 800/435-9792
www.iflyswa.com

Tower Air
☎ 800/34-TOWER outside
New York
☎ 718/553-8500 in New York
www.towerair.com

Trans World Airlines (TWA)
☎ 800/221-2000
www.twa.com

United Airlines/United Express
☎ 800/241-6522
www.ual.com

US Airways/US Airways Express
☎ 800/428-4322
www.usair.com

Virgin Atlantic Airways
☎ 800/862-8621
☎ 0293/747-747
www.fly.virgin.com

Frommer's Online Directory

by Bruce Gerstman and Michael Shapiro
Michael Shapiro is the author of *Internet Travel Planning*
(The Globe Pequot Press).

Frommer's Online Directory is a new feature designed to help you take advantage of the Internet to better plan your trip. Section 1 lists some general Internet resources that can make any trip easier, such as sites for booking airline tickets. It's not meant to be a comprehensive list—it's a discriminating selection of useful sites to get you started. In section 2, you'll find some top online guides specifically for the San Diego area, which cover local lodging, the top attractions, and getting around.

We've awarded stars to the best sites, which are earned, not paid for (unlike some Web-site rankings that are based on payment).

1 The Top Travel-Planning Web Sites

Among the most popular sites are online travel agencies. The top agencies, including Expedia, Preview Travel, and Travelocity, offer an array of tools that are valuable even if you don't book online. You can check flight schedules, hotel availability, car-rental prices, or even get paged if your flight is delayed.

While online agencies have come a long way over the past few years, they don't *always* yield the best price. Unlike a travel agent, for example, they're unlikely to tell you that you can save money by flying a day earlier or a day later. On the other hand, if you're looking for a bargain fare, you might find something online that an agent wouldn't take the time to dig up. Because airline commissions have been cut, a travel agent may not find it worthwhile spending half an hour trying to find you the best deal. On the Net, you can be your own agent and take all the time you want.

Online booking sites aren't the only places to book airline tickets—all major airlines have their own Web sites and often offer incentives, such as bonus frequent-flyer miles or Net-only discounts, for buying online. These incentives have helped airlines capture the majority of the online booking market.

Note: See the Appendix for toll-free numbers and Web addresses for airlines, hotel chains, and rental-car companies.

WHEN SHOULD YOU BOOK ONLINE?

Online booking is not for everyone. If you prefer to let others handle your travel arrangements, one call to an experienced travel agent

---

Factoid

Far more people look online than book online, partly due to fear of putting their credit cards through on the Net. Though secure encryption has made this fear less justified, there's no reason why you can't find a flight online and then book it by calling a toll-free number or contacting your travel agent. To be sure you're in secure mode when you book online, look for a little icon of a key (in Netscape) or a padlock (Internet Explorer) at the bottom of your Web browser.

---

should suffice. But if you want to know as much as possible about your options, the Net is a good place to start, especially for bargain hunters.

The most compelling reason to use online booking is to take advantage of last-minute specials, such as American Airlines' weekend deals or other Internet-only fares that must be purchased online. Another advantage is that you can cash in on incentives for booking online, such as rebates or bonus frequent-flyer miles.

Online booking works best for trips within North America; for international tickets, it's usually cheaper and easier to use a travel agent or consolidator.

Online booking is certainly not for those with a complex international itinerary. If you require follow-up services, such as itinerary changes, use a travel agent. Though Expedia and some other online agencies employ travel agents available by phone, these sites are geared primarily for self-service.

Please remember, though: The descriptions below were true at press time, but the pace of evolution on the Net is relentless, so you'll probably find some advancements by the time you visit these sites.

LEADING BOOKING SITES

Below are listings for the top travel-booking sites. The starred selections are the most useful and best designed sites.

Cheap Tickets. **www.cheaptickets.com**
Essentials: Discounted rates on domestic and international airline tickets and hotel rooms.

Sometimes discounters such as Cheap Tickets have exclusive deals that aren't available through more mainstream channels. Registration at Cheap Tickets requires inputting a credit card number before getting started, which is one reason many people elect to call the company's toll-free number rather than book online. One of the most frustrating things about the Cheap Tickets site is that it will offer fare quotes for a route, and later show this fare is not valid for your dates of travel (other Web sites, such as Preview), consider your dates of travel before showing what fares are available. Despite its problems, Cheap Tickets can be worth the effort because its fares can be lower than those offered by its competitors.

✪ Expedia. **expedia.com**
Essentials: Domestic and international flights, plus hotel and rental-car booking; late-breaking travel news, destination features, and commentary from travel experts; deals on cruises and vacation packages. Free registration is required for booking.

Expedia makes it easy to handle flight, hotel, and car booking on one itinerary, so it's a good place for one-stop shopping. Expedia's hotel search offers crisp, zoomable maps to pinpoint most properties; click on the camera icon to see images of the rooms and facilities. But, like many online databases, Expedia focuses on the major chains, such as Hilton and Hyatt, so don't expect to find too many one-of-a-kind boutique hotels or B&Bs here.

Once you're registered (it's only necessary to do this once from each computer you use), you can start booking with the Roundtrip Fare Finder box on the home page, which expedites the process. After selecting a flight, you can hold it until midnight the following day or purchase online. If you think you might do better through a travel agent, you'll have time to try to get a lower price. And you may do better with a travel agent because Expedia's computer reservation system does not include all airlines. Most notably absent are some leading budget carriers, such as Southwest. (*Note:* At press time, Travelocity was the only major booking service that included Southwest.)

Expedia's World Guide, offering destination information, is a glaring weakness; it takes lots of page views to get very little information. However, Expedia compensates by linking to other Microsoft Network services, such as its Sidewalk city guides, which offer entertainment and dining advice.

Preview Travel. **www.previewtravel.com**

Essentials: Domestic and international flights, plus hotel and rental car booking; Travel Newswire lists fare sales; deals on cruises and vacation packages. Free (one-time) registration is required for booking. Preview offers express booking for members, but at press time, this feature was buried below the fold on Preview's reservation page.

Preview features the most inviting interface for booking trips, though the wealth of graphics involved can make the site somewhat slow to load. Use Farefinder to quickly find the lowest current fares on flights to dozens of major cities. Carfinder offers a similar service for rental cars, but you can only search airport locations, not city pick-up sites. To see the lowest fare for your itinerary, input the dates and times for your route and see what Preview comes up with.

In recent years, Preview and other leading booking services have added features such as Best Fare Finder, so after Preview searches for the best deal on your itinerary, it will check flights that are a bit later or earlier to see if it might be cheaper to fly at a different time. While these searches have become quite sophisticated, they still occasionally overlook deals that might be uncovered by a top-notch travel agent. If you have the time, see what you can find online and then call an agent to see if you can get a better price.

With Preview's Fare Alert feature, you can set fares for up to three routes and you'll receive email notices when the fare drops below your target amount. For example, you could tell Preview to alert you when the fare from New York to San Diego drops below $300. If it does, you'll get an e-mail telling you the current fare.

Minor quibbles: When you search for a fare or hotel (at least when we went to press), Preview launches an annoying little "Please Wait" window that gets in the way of the main browser window, even when your results begin to appear. The hotel search feature is intuitive, but the images and maps aren't as crisp as those at Expedia. Also, all sorts of information that's irrelevant to travelers (such as public school locations) is listed on the maps.

Note to AOL users: You can book flights, hotels, rental cars, and cruises on AOL at keyword: Travel. The booking software is provided by Preview Travel and is similar to Preview on the Web. Use the AOL "Travelers Advantage" program to earn a 5% rebate on flights, hotel rooms, and car rentals.

Priceline.com. **www.priceline.com**

Even people who aren't familiar with too many Web sites have heard about Priceline.com, which lets you "name your price" for domestic and international airline tickets. In other words, you select a route and dates, guarantee with a credit card, and make a bid for what you're willing to pay. If one of the airlines in Priceline's database has a fare that's lower than your bid, your credit card will automatically be charged for a ticket.

Take a Look at Frommer's Site

We highly recommend Arthur Frommer's Budget Travel Online (**www.frommers. com**) as an excellent travel-planning resource. Of course, we're a little biased, but you will find indispensable travel tips, reviews, monthly vacation giveaways, and online booking.

Subscribe to Arthur Frommer's Daily Newsletter (**www.frommers.com/newsletters**) to receive the latest travel bargains and inside travel secrets in your mailbox every day. You'll read daily headlines and articles from the dean of travel himself, highlighting last-minute deals on airfares, accommodations, cruises, and package vacations. You'll also find great travel advice by checking our Tip of the Day or Hot Spot of the Month.

Search our Destinations archive (**www.frommers.com/destinations**) of more than 200 domestic and international destinations for great places to stay, tips for traveling there, and what to do while you're there. Once you've researched your trip, you might try our online reservation system (**www.frommers.com/booktravelnow**) to book your dream vacation at affordable prices.

But you can't say when you want to fly—you have to accept any flight leaving between 6am and 10pm, and you may have to make a stopover. No frequent-flyer miles are awarded, and tickets are non-refundable and can't be exchanged for another flight. So if your plans change, you're out of luck. Priceline can be good for travelers who have to take off on short notice (and who are thus unable to qualify for advance-purchase discounts). But be sure to shop around first—if you overbid, you'll be required to purchase the ticket and Priceline will pocket the difference.

Travelocity. **www.travelocity.com**
Essentials: Domestic and international flight, hotel, and rental-car booking; deals on cruises and vacation packages. Travel Headlines spotlights latest bargain airfares. Free (one-time) registration is required for booking.

Travelocity almost got it right. Its Express Booking feature enables travelers to complete the booking process more quickly than they could at Expedia or Preview, but Travelocity gums up the works with a page called "Featured Airlines." Big placards of several featured airlines compete for your attention. If you want to see the fares for *all* available airlines, click the much smaller box at the bottom of the page labeled "Book a Flight."

Some have worried that Travelocity, which is owned by American Airlines' parent company AMR, directs bookings to American. This doesn't seem to be the case—I've booked there dozens of times and have always been directed to the cheapest listed flight (for example, on Tower or ATA). But this "Featured Airlines" page seems to be Travelocity's way of trying to cash in with ads and incentives for booking certain airlines. (*Note:* It's hard to blame these booking services for trying to generate some revenue. Many airlines have slashed commissions to $10 per domestic booking for online transactions, so these virtual agencies are groping for revenue streams.) There are rewards for choosing one of the featured airlines. You'll get 1,500 bonus frequent-flyer miles if you book through United's site, for example, but the site doesn't tell you about other airlines that might be cheaper. If the United flight costs $150 more than the best deal on another airline, it's not worth spending the extra money for a relatively small number of bonus miles.

On the plus side, Travelocity has some leading-edge techie tools. Exhibit A is Fare Watcher E-mail, an "intelligent agent" that keeps you informed of the best fares offered for the city pairs (round-trips) of your choice. Whenever the fare changes by $25 or more, Fare Watcher will alert you by e-mail. Exhibit B is Flight Paging: If you own an alphanumeric pager with national access that can receive e-mail, Travelocity's paging system can alert you if your flight is delayed. Finally, though Travelocity doesn't include every budget airline, it does include Southwest, the leading U.S. budget carrier, which now flies into Long Island's Islip airport.

FINDING LODGINGS ONLINE

While the services above offer hotel booking, it can be best to use a site devoted primarily to lodging; you may find properties that aren't listed on more general online travel agencies. Some lodging sites specialize in a particular type of accommodation, such as B&Bs, which you won't find on the more mainstream booking services. Other services, such as TravelWeb, offer weekend deals on major chain properties, which cater to business travelers and have more empty rooms on weekends.

Note: See the Appendix for toll-free numbers and Web addresses for airlines, hotel chains, and rental-car companies. In chapter 5, "Accommodations," we've noted Web addresses for every hotel that has one.

All Hotels on the Web. www.all-hotels.com
Well, this site doesn't include *all* the hotels on the Web, but it does have tens of thousands of listings throughout the world. Bear in mind that each hotel listed has paid a small fee of ($25 and up) for placement, so it's not an objective list but more like a book of online brochures.

Hotel Reservations Network. www.180096hotel.com
Bargain on room rates at hotels in more than two dozen U.S. cities. The cool thing is that HRN pre-books blocks of rooms in advance, so sometimes it has rooms—at discount rates—at hotels that are "sold out." Select a city, input your dates, and you'll get a list of best prices for a selection of hotels. Descriptions include an image of the property and a locator map (to book online, click the "Book Now" button). HRN is notable for some deep discounts, even in cities where hotel rooms are expensive. The toll-free number is printed all over this site; call it if you want more options than are listed online.

InnSite. www.innsite.com
B&B listings for inns in all 50 U.S. states and dozens of countries around the globe.
Find an inn at your destination, have a look at images of the rooms, check prices and availability, and then send e-mail to the innkeeper if you have further questions. This is an extensive directory of B&Bs, but only includes listings if the proprietor submitted one. (*Note:* It's free to get an inn listed.) The descriptions are written by the innkeepers and many listings link to the inn's own Web sites, where you can find more information and images.

Places to Stay. www.placestostay.com
Mostly one-of-a-kind places in the United States and abroad that you might not find in other directories, with a focus on resorts. Again, listing is selective—this isn't a comprehensive directory, but can give you a sense of what's available at different destinations.

✪ TravelWeb. www.travelweb.com
TravelWeb lists more than 16,000 hotels worldwide, focusing on chains such as Hyatt and Hilton, and you can book almost 90% of these online. TravelWeb's Click-It Weekends, updated each Monday, offers weekend deals at many leading hotel chains. TravelWeb is the online home for Pegasus Systems, which provides transaction-processing systems for the hotel industry.

LAST-MINUTE DEALS & OTHER ONLINE BARGAINS

There's nothing airlines hate more than flying with lots of empty seats. The Net has enabled airlines to offer last-minute bargains to entice travelers to fill those seats. Most of these are announced on Tuesday or Wednesday and are valid for travel the following weekend, but some can be booked weeks or months in advance. You can sign up for weekly e-mail alerts at airlines' sites (see above) or check sites such as WebFlyer (see below) that compile lists of these bargains. To make it easier, visit a site (see below) that will round up all the deals and send them in one convenient weekly e-mail. But last-minute deals aren't the only online bargains; some of the sites below can help you find value even if you can't wait until the eleventh hour.

✪ **1travel.com. www.1travel.com**

Deals on domestic and international flights, cruises, hotels, and all-inclusive resorts such as Club Med.

1travel.com's Saving Alert compiles last-minute air deals, so you don't have to scroll through multiple e-mail alerts. A feature called "Drive a little using low-fare airlines" helps map out strategies for using alternative airports to find lower fares. And Farebeater searches a database that includes published fares, consolidator bargains, and special deals exclusive to 1travel.com. *Note:* The travel agencies listed by 1travel.com have paid for placement.

BestFares. www.bestfares.com

Budget seeker Tom Parsons lists some great bargains on airfares, hotels, rental cars, and cruises, but the site is poorly organized. News Desk is a long list of hundreds of bargains, but they're not broken down into cities or even countries, so it's not easy trying to find what you're looking for. If you have time to wade through it, you might find a good deal. Some material is available only to paid subscribers.

Go4less.com. www.go4less.com

Specializing in last-minute cruise and package deals, Go4less has some eye-popping offers, such as off-peak Caribbean cruises for under $100 per day. The site has a clean design, but the bargains aren't organized by destination. However, you avoid sifting through all this material by using the Search box and entering vacation type, destination, month, and price.

Moment's Notice. www.moments-notice.com

As the name suggests, Moment's Notice specializes in last-minute vacation and cruise deals. You can browse for free, but if you want to purchase a trip, you have to join Moment's Notice, which costs $25.

Smarter Living. www.smarterliving.com

Best known for its e-mail dispatch of weekend deals on 20 airlines, Smarter Living also keeps you posted about last-minute bargains on everything from Windjammer Cruises to flights to Iceland.

✪ **WebFlyer. www.webflyer.com**

WebFlyer is the ultimate online resource for frequent flyers and also has an excellent listing of last-minute air deals. Click on "Deal Watch" for a round-up of weekend deals on flights, hotels, and rental cars from domestic and international suppliers.

TRAVELER'S TOOLKIT

✪ **CultureFinder. www.culturefinder.com**

Up-to-date listings for plays, opera, classical music, dance, film, and other cultural events in more than 1,300 U.S. cities. Enter the dates you'll be in a city and get a list of events; you can also purchase tickets online.

Intellicast. www.intellicast.com
Weather forecasts for all 50 states and for cities around the world.

✪ **MapQuest. www.mapquest.com**
Specializing in U.S. maps, MapQuest enables you to zoom in on a destination, calculate step-by-step driving directions between any two U.S. points, and locate restaurants, hotels, and other attractions on maps.

✪ **Net Café Guide. www.netcafeguide.com**
Locate Internet cafes at hundreds of locations around the globe. Catch up on your e-mail, log on to the Web, and stay in touch with the home front, usually for just a few dollars per hour.

TheTrip: Airport Maps and Flight Status. www.thetrip.com
A business travel site where you can find out when an airborne flight is scheduled to arrive. Click on "Guides and Tools" to peruse airport maps for more than 40 domestic cities.

Visa. www.visa.com/pd/atm/
MasterCard. www.mastercard.com/atm
Find Cirrus and Plus ATMs in hundreds of cities in the United States and around the world. Both include maps for some locations and both list airport ATM locations, some with maps. Remarkably, MasterCard lists ATMs on all seven continents (there's one at Antarctica's McMurdo Station). *Tip:* You'll usually get a better exchange rate using ATMs than exchanging traveler's checks at banks.

2 Top Web Sites for San Diego
CITY GUIDES

Access San Diego. www.accessandiego.com
This non-profit site lists restaurants, hotels, transportation services, and local attractions that accommodate travelers with disabilities.

Gaslamp Quarter Online. www.gaslamp.com
Listings and basic contact information for restaurants, cafes, nightclubs, galleries, theaters, and shopping in the neighborhood. There are a few quick suggestions at the start of each section.

Go There San Diego. www.GoThere.com/sandiego.htm
Histories, descriptions, and photo tours of neighborhoods including the Gaslamp Quarter, Hillcrest, and University Heights.

Home Port of San Diego. www.homeport-sd.com/fun
A vast web directory to link to museums, theaters, dining guides, sports, and outdoor recreation.

Handy Tip

While most people learn about last-minute weekend deals from e-mail dispatches, it can be best to find out precisely when these deals become available and check airlines' Web sites yourself at this time. To find out when bargains will be announced, check the pages devoted to these deals on airlines' Web pages. Because these offerings are limited, seats can vanish within hours (sometimes even minutes), so it pays to log on as soon as they're available. An example: Southwest's specials are posted at 12:01am Tuesdays (Central time). So if you're looking for a cheap flight, stay up late and check Southwest's site at www.iflyswa.com to grab the best new deals.

Check Your E-Mail While You're on the Road

Until a few years ago, most travelers who checked their e-mail while traveling carried a laptop, but this posed some problems. Not only are laptops expensive, but they can be difficult to configure, incur expensive connection charges, and are attractive to thieves. Thankfully, Web-based free e-mail programs have made it much easier to stay in touch.

Just open an account at a freemail provider, such as Hotmail (hotmail.com) or Yahoo! Mail (mail.yahoo.com), and all you'll need to check your mail is a Web connection, easily available at Net cafes and copy shops around the world. After logging on, just point the browser to www.hotmail.com, enter your username and password and you'll have access to your mail.

Internet cafes have become ubiquitous, so for a few dollars an hour you'll be able to check your mail and send messages back to colleagues, friends, and family. If you already have a primary e-mail account, you can set it to forward mail to your freemail account while you're away. Freemail programs have become enormously popular (Hotmail claims more than 10 million members), because they enable users, even those who don't own a computer, to have an e-mail address they can check wherever they log on to the Web.

Local Guy's Guide to San Diego. bargains.k-online.com/~davemail/LGG/
Dave, the Local Guy, recommends his favorite beaches, accommodations, attractions, neighborhoods, nearby trips, and includes history and interesting personal tidbits. Consider his suggestions, but check specific addresses and contact information, as he has not updated it since December 1997.

✪ **San Diego Convention and Visitors Bureau. www.sandiego.org**
The Leisure Traveler section consists of a big directory of links for the actual sites. The bureau has organized sites for lodging, transportation, shopping, dining, arts, sports, and a section on travel to Mexico. Though they don't offer reviews, each restaurant, hotel, and point of interest includes a brief description, price range, and contact information. An event calendar and local maps will give you further ideas about where to go.

San Diego Gay and Lesbian Chamber of Commerce. www.gsdba.org
Search the business directory to find all kinds of restaurants, cafes, hotels, and other businesses that welcome gay and lesbian clients.

✪ **San Diego Insider. www.sandiegoinsider.com**
This well-rounded guide contains bar, club, and movie reviews written by editors. The dining guide includes descriptions, some very lengthy, of each restaurant. However, few offer opinionated critiques. The sports section suggests hiking and other outdoor excursions. For a day in the sun, use the beach guide.

San Diego's Restaurants and Entertainment Online. www.sdro.com
Ad-based restaurant, lodging, and nightlife listings comprise this bare-bones guide, though the photos will give you an idea of what to expect around the city.

✪ **San Diego Sidewalk. sandiego.sidewalk.com**
Since locals write details about the city and surrounding area, you can find San Diegan perspectives on restaurants, clubs, cafes, outdoor activities, special events, movies, and performing arts. Peruse their Local Guide section for highlighted spots as well as a travel guide to Baja. A shopping section includes articles explaining specialty stores. Don't miss their Visitors Guide, which aggregates all the most relevant topics for travelers. Bachelors and bachelorettes might meet through the Singles Guide.

For AOL Users

Type the keyword "San Diego" and peruse AOL's **Digital City** guide, which is geared primarily for locals. Visitors will find useful information, such as maps, weather forecasts, and Zoom San Diego's event listings. The Top 10 Eateries section reviews local restaurants rated by readers. Eat and submit your own review. Digital City is also available on the Web at **digitalcity.aol.com/sandiego**.

○ Sign On San Diego. **sandiego.citysearch.com**
The *San Diego Union Tribune* has teamed up with City Search to publish Sign On's Entertainment and Visitor Guides sections. Search for restaurant reviews by price range, location, and type of cuisine. When you're looking for something to do, find reviews and descriptions about music, movies, performing arts, museums, outdoor recreation, beaches, and sports. In the Visitor Guide, there's information on tours, transportation, attractions, and lodging, with some reviews of lodgings from editors.

Zoom San Diego Arts & Entertainment. **www.zoomsd.com**
This calendar of events lists times and locations for theater, museums, movies, music, kids' activities, and performing arts. After reading small descriptions, link out to the actual sites.

NEWSPAPERS & MAGAZINES

San Diegan. **www.sandiegan.com**
This tourist magazine highlights lodgings, restaurants, events, and places to shop. Print out coupons for some of the city's attractions.

○ San Diego Magazine Online. **www.sandiego-online.com**
In addition to local features, visitors will find ideas for outdoor excursions and venues for performing arts and music. Refer to the Metro section for guides to attractions, transportation, neighborhoods, beaches, and hotels. San Diego Sidewalk provides the business listings.

San Diego Metropolitan. **www.sandiegometro.com**
Monthly business publication posts some daily articles. Their Food, Booze & Beds section includes new spots to explore. One restaurant review is presented each month.

San Diego Union Tribune. **www.uniontrib.com**
The staff at San Diego's leading daily covers the local news, while Associated Press articles fill up the national and international stories. Check out the entertainment and travel sections provided by City Search.

DINING GUIDES

CuisineNet: San Diego. **www.menusonline.com/cities/san_diego/locmain.shtml**
Search by location, restaurant name, or cuisine for restaurant listings, some of which include reviews by readers.

○ Restaurant Guide: San Diego Sidewalk. **sandiego.sidewalk.com/restaurants**
Search this big selection of restaurants by location, price, and cuisine for honest reviews by local writers.

San Diegan Restaurant Reviews. **www.sandiegan.com/rest.html**
Reviews of the city's top restaurants, though they all seem to shower every place with praise. Anyway, you can get contact information and price ranges for restaurants.

San Diego Magazine Online Dining Guide. www.sandiego-online.com/dining
In addition to locating a restaurant by cuisine type and location, you can search
through restaurant reviews in the Dining Critiqued section.

World Guide to Vegetarianism: San Diego. www.veg.org/veg/Guide/
    USA/California/San_Diego.html
Find out where to eat healthy in the city and nearby areas. Generally uncritical reviews
accompany descriptions, addresses, and phone numbers of each establishment.

ATTRACTIONS

Balboa Park. www.sddt.com/features/balboapark
Read basic descriptions of the museums, theaters, and the zoo that make up the park.

Birch Aquarium. aqua.ucsd.edu
In addition to getting basic facts, you can navigate the clickable map of the premises
for text-only descriptions of the tide pool exhibit, aquarium, and museum showcases.

Cabrillo National Monument. www.nps.gov/cabr
Enjoy the view where the first Europeans landed in the region, watch creatures swim-
ming around in the coastal tide pools, and tour the Old Point Loma Lighthouse. The
National Park Service posts visitation hours, directions, and entrance fees.

Japanese Friendship Garden. www.niwa.org
Architecture, interior design, botanical gardening, art, and other aspects of Japanese
culture entice visitors to these grounds for a meditative day. Read about the garden's
history, take a virtual photo tour of the grounds, and get a map and contact information.

Mission Trails Regional Park. www.mtrp.org
Less than 10 miles from downtown San Diego, 5,800 acres of valleys and hilly wilderness welcome visitors to explore. Consult the site's trail guide, operation hours, driving
directions, park activities, and read about the local history and ecology.

Museum of Contemporary Art. www.mcasd.org
This interactive site offers essentials, plus descriptions and photos that go along with
each exhibit. Download a free version of QuickTime VR or LivePicture to enjoy a rich
media tour of selected exhibits. The guide for children attempts to help young folks
appreciate abstract artistic concepts.

Museum of Photographic Arts. www.mopa.org
Descriptions and examples of the permanent collection, temporary exhibitions, and
tours.

Natural History Museum. www.sdnhm.org
Bugs, birds, rocks, and fish are just a tiny sampling of what visitors learn about at this
museum dedicated to the region's ecology. The Field Guide section offers lots of facts
about the climate, terrain, and life in the area. Read about the programs for kids and
get basic info about the facility.

Old Globe Theater. oldglobe.org/home.html
Since 1935, this renovated theater has been hosting performances. Find listings and
local reviews of the dramas. Order tickets online and read about the history behind
this venue.

Reuben H. Fleet Science Center. www.rhfleet.org
Find essentials about visiting this center, which hosts astronomy exhibits for kids and
IMAX films of adventurous expeditions.

San Diego Aerospace Museum. www.aerospacemuseum.org
Aviation and space-buffs take an online tour to learn history and see photos of the museum's exhibits.

San Diego Maritime Museum. www.sdmaritime.com
Walk around the *Star of India,* claimed to be the oldest ship in the world that still sails. On the site, read about this flagship's history and find a map to get there.

San Diego Model Railroad Museum Virtual Tour. www.globalinfo.com/ noncomm/SDMRM/sdmrm.html
Though it's a limited virtual tour of photos, model-train enthusiasts can get the basics here, including an events calendar, a map to the museum, and the newsletter.

San Diego Museum of Art. www.sdmart.com
Besides logistical information, including directions, you'll find well-organized sections on the permanent collection and special exhibitions.

San Diego Museum of Man. www.museumofman.org
View the past through mummies and hieroglyphics; don't miss the photos and history text about this anthropology museum's exhibitions.

San Diego Opera. www.sdopera.com
Consult the calendar of performances, order tickets online, take a quiz to test your opera knowledge, and flip through production photos.

✪ San Diego Railroad Museum. www.sdrm.org
Choo-choo lovers: Listen to files of railroad sounds; read detailed histories; and check out photos of the trains in the museum's collection, including steam locomotives, freight cars, passenger cars, diesel locomotives, and cabooses. You can also find out about the museum's library and public train excursions.

San Diego Zoo. www.sandiegozoo.org
An animated reptile welcomes you to the site of one of the world's most renowned zoos. Organized by exhibit, the descriptions and photos preview the bears, gorillas, hippos, birds, and other living creatures you'll meet. The Zoological Society of San Diego gives details on tours, plus directions and other logistical information.

Timkin Museum of Art. gort.ucsd.edu/sj/timken
Brief descriptions of classical American, Dutch and Flemish, French, Italian, and Russian artists accompany samples of their work housed in this museum. View and purchase online the postcards and slides sold at the store, and learn about upcoming lectures and other events.

SPORTS

San Diego Golf Pages. www.golfsd.com
Tee off at one of the area's public, private, executive, or military courses. The description of each club includes address, phone number, ratings, fees, and reservation information. You'll also find guides to golfing with children, tournaments, golf stores, and places to practice.

San Diego-La Jolla Underwater Park. scilib.ucsd.edu/sio/ocean/uwpk
Divers who wish to explore beneath the waters get the rules of this ecological reserve and marine-life refuge.

San Diego Padres. www.padres.com
Beware, hardcore Padres fans: You might not leave. Check scores, schedules, ticket

prices, and directions to Qualcomm Stadium. Player bios, team history, and an online store for Padres merchandise might help get you psyched for the next game.

San Diego Sports Arena. **www.sandiegoarena.com**
View seating charts and an event calendar of upcoming games as well as concerts. Order tickets online.

SCUBA Diving in San Diego. **heff.net/scuba**
This guide to diving offers opinionated and informal descriptions of spots including La Jolla Cove, Casa Cove, South Casa Cove, and La Jolla Shores. The text, photos, and Web cams give a good idea of what to expect. Check diving conditions, a diving FAQ, and boat listings.

GETTING AROUND

QuickAID's Guide to the San Diego International Airport. **www.
quickaid.com/airports/san/mainmenu.html**
Basic, low-tech artwork decorates this airport site. The list of ground transportation options is the main part that makes it useful. Also find terminal maps, airlines that fly in, and nearby hotels.

San Diegans. **www.amtrakwest.com**
Want to hop on a train? Check out the schedule of Amtrak's *San Diegan,* which travels between San Luis Obispo and San Diego.

San Diego Metropolitan Transit System. **www.sdcommute.com/sdmts**
For buses, trolleys, and trains along the coast (Coasters), this is the place to catch timetables, maps, fares, and passes. Learn how the system accommodates seniors and travelers with disabilities.

SIDE TRIPS
DISNEYLAND

Disneyland (Official Web Site). **disney.go.com/Disneyland**
Check out the resorts, dining facilities, travel-package options, and the activities and rides in the Magic Kingdom. Download free software to view a QuickTime VR video of the waterfalls.

Disneyland Inside & Out. **ccnet.simplenet.com**
An independent guide to Disneyland posts updates of activities, rides, entertainment additions, and news. Consult tips on what to bring, best times of year to visit, directions to the park, admission, parking, and more. Though the author obviously loves Disneyland, the articles include some critical opinions and links from other news sources. The photos may bring out the kid in you.

NORTH COUNTY BEACH TOWNS

Del Mar Chamber of Commerce. **delmar.ca.us**
A brief visitors guide offers an event calendar, town history, and beach rules.

Del Mar Thoroughbred Club. **www.dmtc.com**
Bet the whole farm at this famous racetrack. Find out which horse is racing and when.

Encinitas Online. **www.encinitas.com**
The Walking Tour section's descriptions and sketches give a decent overview of this historic town. Also check out weather, local events, and businesses.

In Carlsbad. **www.in-carlsbad.com**
The strengths of this bare directory to the town are the sections on surfing and golfing. Otherwise, find contact information for shopping and dining and links to hotels.

Oceanside Chamber of Commerce. **www.oceansidechamber.com**
Oceanside's attractions and activities are described in the Visitors Information section. Find dining and lodging listings and links.

BAJA CALIFORNIA

Baja Guide: San Diego Sidewalk. **sandiego.sidewalk.com/bajaguide**
Going south of the border? Get crossing tips, a shopping guide, ideas for golf, and suggestions of things to do in Ensenada, Mexicali, Rosarito, Tecate, and Tijuana.

Baja.com. **www.baja.com**
This slick guide to the peninsula covers Ensenada, Tecate, Mexicali, San Felipe, and other locales. Read facts and articles about beaches, lodging, dining, nightlife, transportation, and outdoor recreation. Navigating the site is not simple, but you will be glad you figured it out once you find all practical travel tips.

Tijuana Net. **www.tijuana-net.com**
Ad-based listings for restaurants, accommodations, shopping, and businesses, with links to relevant sites.

Index

See also Accommodations and Restaurant indexes, below.
Page numbers in *italics* refer to maps.

General Index

FROMMER'S® COMPLETE TRAVEL GUIDES

Alaska
Amsterdam
Arizona
Atlanta
Australia
Austria
Bahamas
Barcelona, Madrid & Seville
Beijing
Belgium, Holland & Luxembourg
Bermuda
Boston
Budapest & the Best of Hungary
California
Canada
Cancún, Cozumel &
  the Yucatán
Cape Cod, Nantucket & Martha's Vineyard
Caribbean
Caribbean Cruises & Ports of Call
Caribbean Ports of Call
Carolinas & Georgia
Chicago
China
Colorado
Costa Rica
Denmark
Denver, Boulder & Colorado Springs
England
Europe
Florida
France
Germany
Greece
Greek Islands
Hawaii
Hong Kong
Honolulu, Waikiki & Oahu
Ireland
Israel
Italy
Jamaica & Barbados
Japan
Las Vegas
London
Los Angeles
Maryland & Delaware
Maui
Mexico
Miami & the Keys

Montana & Wyoming
Montréal & Québec City
Munich & the Bavarian Alps
Nashville & Memphis
Nepal
New England
New Mexico
New Orleans
New York City
Nova Scotia, New Brunswick &
  Prince Edward Island
Oregon
Paris
Philadelphia & the
  Amish Country
Portugal
Prague & the Best of the Czech Republic
Provence & the Riviera
Puerto Rico
Rome
San Antonio & Austin
San Diego
San Francisco
Santa Fe, Taos &
  Albuquerque
Scandinavia
Scotland
Seattle & Portland
Singapore & Malaysia
South Africa
Southeast Asia
South Pacific
Spain
Sweden
Switzerland
Thailand
Tokyo
Toronto
Tuscany & Umbria
USA
Utah
Vancouver & Victoria
Vermont, New Hampshire
  & Maine
Vienna & the Danube Valley
Virgin Islands
Virginia
Walt Disney World & Orlando
Washington, D.C.
Washington State

FROMMER'S® DOLLAR-A-DAY GUIDES

Australia from $50 a Day
California from $60 a Day
Caribbean from $70 a Day
England from $70 a Day
Europe from $60 a Day
Florida from $60 a Day

Hawaii from $70 a Day
Ireland from $50 a Day
Israel from $45 a Day
Italy from $70 a Day
London from $85 a Day
New York from $80 a Day

New Zealand from $50 a Day
Paris from $85 a Day
San Francisco from $60 a Day
Washington, D.C.,
  from $60 a Day

FROMMER'S® PORTABLE GUIDES

Acapulco, Ixtapa & Zihu-
  atanejo
Alaska Cruises & Ports of Call
Bahamas
Baja & Los Cabos
Berlin
California Wine Country
Charleston & Savannah
Chicago

Dublin
Hawaii: The Big Island
Las Vegas
London
Maine Coast
Maui
New Orleans
New York City
Paris

Puerto Vallarta, Manzanillo
  & Guadalajara
San Diego
San Francisco
Sydney
Tampa & St. Petersburg
Venice
Washington, D.C.

FROMMER'S® NATIONAL PARK GUIDES

Family Vacations in the
  National Parks
Grand Canyon

National Parks of the American West
Rocky Mountain

Yellowstone & Grand Teton
Yosemite & Sequoia/
  Kings Canyon
Zion & Bryce Canyon

FROMMER'S® GREAT OUTDOOR GUIDES

New England
Northern California

Southern California & Baja
Washington & Oregon

FROMMER'S® MEMORABLE WALKS

Chicago
London

New York
Paris

San Francisco
Washington D.C.

FROMMER'S® IRREVERENT GUIDES

Amsterdam
Boston
Chicago
Las Vegas

London
Los Angeles
Manhattan

New Orleans
Paris
San Francisco

Seattle & Portland
Vancouver
Walt Disney World
Washington, D.C.

FROMMER'S® BEST-LOVED DRIVING TOURS

America
Britain
California

Florida
France
Germany

Ireland
Italy
New England

Scotland
Spain
Western Europe

THE UNOFFICIAL GUIDES®

Bed & Breakfast in New England
Bed & Breakfast in the Northwest
Beyond Disney
Branson, Missouri
California with Kids
Chicago

Cruises
Disneyland
Florida with Kids
The Great Smoky & Blue Ridge Mountains
Inside Disney
Las Vegas

London
Miami & the Keys
Mini Las Vegas
Mini-Mickey
New Orleans
New York City
Paris
San Francisco

Skiing in the West
Walt Disney World
Walt Disney World for Grown-ups
Walt Disney World for Kids
Washington, D.C.

SPECIAL-INTEREST TITLES

Born to Shop: France
Born to Shop: Hong Kong
Born to Shop: Italy
Born to Shop: New York
Born to Shop: Paris
Frommer's Britain's Best Bike Rides
The Civil War Trust's Official Guide to the Civil War Discovery Trail
Frommer's Caribbean Hideaways
Frommer's Europe's Greatest Driving Tours
Frommer's Food Lover's Companion to France
Frommer's Food Lover's Companion to Italy
Frommer's Gay & Lesbian Europe
Israel Past & Present
Monks' Guide to California

Monks' Guide to New York City
The Moon
New York City with Kids
Unforgettable Weekends
Outside Magazine's Guide to Family Vacations
Places Rated Almanac
Retirement Places Rated
Road Atlas Britain
Road Atlas Europe
Washington, D.C., with Kids
Wonderful Weekends from Boston
Wonderful Weekends from New York City
Wonderful Weekends from San Francisco
Wonderful Weekends from Los Angeles

WHEREVER
YOU TRAVEL,
*H*ELP IS NEVER
FAR AWAY.

From planning your trip to providing travel assistance
along the way, American Express® Travel Service Offices
are always there to help you do more.

San Diego

American Express Travel Service
7610 Hazard Center Dr.
Suite 515
619/297-8101

Anderson Travel Group (R)
11828 Rancho Bernardo Rd.
Suite 113
619/487-7758

American Express Travel Service
258 Broadway
619/234-4455

Anderson Travel Group (R)
4223 Genesee Ave.
619/292-4100

Anderson Travel Group (R)
11952 Bernardo Plaza Dr.
619/487-7722

Travel

www.americanexpress.com/travel

**American Express Travel Service Offices
are located throughout the United States.
For the office nearest you, call 1-800-AXP-3429.**